The Pearl-Shellers of Torres Strait

The Pearl-Shellers of Torres Strait

Resource Use,
Development and Decline,
1860s–1960s

Regina Ganter

MELBOURNE UNIVERSITY PRESS
1994

First published 1994
Typeset by Syarikat Seng Teik Sdn. Bhd., Malaysia, in 11/13 Baskerville
Printed in Malaysia by
SRM Production Services Sdn. Bhd. for
Melbourne University Press, Carlton, Victoria 3053

Distribution agents
Australia: Penguin Books Australia Ltd,
487 Maroondah Highway, PO Box 257,
Ringwood, Victoria 3134
U.S.A. and Canada: International Specialized Book Services, Inc.,
5804 N.E. Hassalo Street, Portland, Oregon 97213-3644
United Kingdom, Europe and Africa:
UCL Press Limited, Gower Street, London WC1E 6BT
The name University College London (UCL) is a registered trade mark used by UCL Press Limited with the
consent of the owner.

National Library of Australia Cataloguing-in-Publication entry

Ganter, Regina.
  The pearl-shellers of Torres Strait.
  Bibliography.
  Includes index.
  ISBN 0 522 84547 9.
  1. Divers—Queensland—Torres Strait Islands—History. 2.
  Pearl button industry—Queensland—Torres Strait Islands—
  History. 3. Mother-of-pearl. I. Title.
338.372411

Contents

Illustrations

Maps

Figures

Tables

Plates

Takenaka Yasuichi ready for dress-diving
Courtesy of Ogawa Taira and Ayumi Shuppan Co., Ltd

The Japanese cemetery on Thursday Island

The Japanese Club, Thursday Island, Culture Day, 1910
Courtesy of Ogawa Taira and Ayumi Shuppan Co., Ltd

Kushimoto celebrates the departure of the first fleet of
pearl-shelling boats for the Arafura Sea
Courtesy of Ogawa Taira and Ayumi Shuppan Co., Ltd

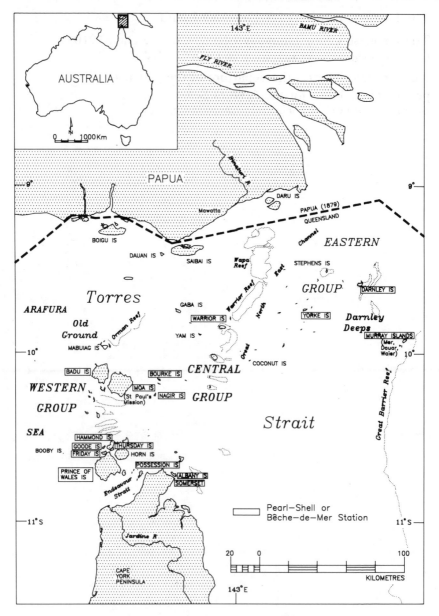

Map 1   Torres Strait—pearl-shell and bêche-de-mer stations

Nomenclature of Torres Strait Islands

Most islands of Torres Strait have both an English and an indigenous name. Increasingly, indigenous names are used for the larger populated islands. The names by which islands are referred to in the text are printed in bold type.

Indigenous name	*English name*
Aurid	—
Badu	Mulgrave Island
Boigu	Talbot Island
Buru	**Turnagain Island**
Daru	—
Dauan	Mt Cornwallis Island
Dauar	(one of the Murray Islands)
Erub	**Darnley Island**
Gaba (or Gebar, Gabba)	Two Brothers
Gialug	**Friday Island**
Iama	**Yam Island**
Keriri	**Hammond Island**
Mabuiag (or Mabuyag)	Jervis Island
Masig	**Yorke Island**
Maurura (or Mawai)	**Wednesday Island**
Mer	**Murray Island**
Moa (and It)	Banks Island
Muralug	**Prince of Wales Island**

Muri	**Adolphus Island**
Nagir (or Naghi, Nagheer, Naghir)	Mt Ernest Island
Narupai	**Horn Island**
Packe	—
Paliling	**Goode Island**
Paremar (or Poruma)	**Coconut Island**
Saibai	—
Tuined	**Possession Island**
Tutu	**Warrior Island**
Ugar	**Stephens Island**
Waiben	**Thursday Island**
Waier	(one of the Murray Islands)
Waraber	**Sue Island**
Zapker	—
Zuna	**Entrance Island**

Conversions

In 1972 metric measurements were adopted in Australia.

1 inch	2.54 centimetres
1 yard	0.91 metres
1 fathom	1.82 metres
1 mile	1.61 kilometres
1 acre	0.405 hectares
1 pound	0.45 kilograms
1 hundredweight (cwt, 112 pounds)	50.4 kilograms
1 ton (2240 pounds)	1.02 tonnes

Currency

On 14 February 1966 Australian currency changed from pounds, shillings and pence (£, s, d) to dollars and cents at the rate of £1 = $2. Twelve pence made up one shilling; twenty shillings made up one pound.

Preface

This book traces the development of Queensland's pearl-shell industry over a span of one hundred years, from the time when pearl-shell was first commercially exploited in the reef province in the 1860s to the time when the industry collapsed in the 1960s. It re-examines the factors leading to that collapse in the light of new ways of thinking about the use of limited natural resources, about how industries can best contribute to the national economy and regional prosperity, and about the history of race relations in Australia. These are, generally speaking, the three areas in which longstanding problems in the industry were recognised by its contemporaries and administrators.

Not only were the problems known, but so were their solutions. Indeed, some bold, and short-lived, attempts to impose a sustainable regime on the industry punctuate its administrative history. It was the first limited licence fishery in Queensland, and briefly had a state-controlled marketing board. One head of a state department personally tried to recruit newcomers (Europeans) overseas, and another moved his headquarters from Brisbane to Thursday Island to supervise the fishery. But the complacency of 'tradition' militated against radical departures from industrial strategies which were relics of a colonial world. This was the only industry exempted from the provisions of the White Australia Policy. For far longer than tropical agriculture, it relied on the importation of indentured workers, and clamoured for their reintroduction after World War II. An apt characterisation of the industry is the recollection by one of its former administrators that in this industry, licences with pounds, shillings and pence were used well after the introduction of decimal currency in 1966. In its treatment of workers, in its use of resources, and in its dependent position as supplier of raw material to overseas markets, the industry was fossilised. Its history of depletion vindicates the restrictive principles of current fisheries management.

The book explores why such principles could not be implemented before the industry declined. It contributes to an understanding of the evolutionary processes from which many present-day Australian industries suffer, and it is of interest for environmental management and for its history of race relations in Australia.

It is thirty-five years since the history of the pearl-shell indstry has received such detailed academic attention as this book represents. J. P. S. Bach, writing in 1956, was seconded to the Department of Commerce and Agriculture to furnish the historical background necessary to refute Japanese claims to prescriptive rights in Australian pearl-shell fishery. My study, too, was initiated by a federal agency, the Great Barrier Reef Marine Park Authority (GBRMPA). As their consultant I had the brief to produce an oral history of reef experience prior to 1960, with particular reference to early sightings of the crown-of-thorns starfish.

That this study deals only with the Queensland branch of the pearl-shell fishery is partly because the fishery intersected here with the Great Barrier Reef Province; and resource use in this area has lately received the particular attention of scientists, conservationists, and administrators. My fieldwork served the dual purpose of supporting this study and furnishing a collection of reef experiences. The pattern of industrial strategy evident in Queensland's pearl-shell fishery is repeated in the fisheries of Darwin and Broome, so that a consideration of the Australian industry as a whole would add nothing substantially new to the arguments made here. The Australian pearl-shell fishery commenced in Torres Strait in 1868, and Thursday Island remained, next to Broome, a major pearling centre, while Darwin, and for a time, Cossack, played only a minor role. Several of the industry's weaknesses are in particularly sharp focus in Queensland. Torres Strait Islanders provided a ready pool of labour, yet the Japanese were even more dominant as divers here than in the other centres. Large companies were more entrenched than in other pearling ports, and this meant that pearl-shellers were almost always divided on management issues. Of particular interest in the

Queensland fishery is a lugger scheme operated by Torres Strait Islanders.

I am much indebted to my interviewees who developed in me an enthusiasm for this study through their positive responses. In Japan I was greatly assisted by Yamaguchi Masashi as facilitator, Yamaguchi Mariko as interpreter, and Kyuhara Shuji and Watanabe Fumiya as guides in Wakayama and Ehime respectively. Pedro and Gloria Guivarra, Joyce Isua, Gloria Kabai, and Elma Yoelu looked after me in Torres Strait. Since the conclusion of my fieldwork in 1988 I have received sad news of the death of several of the informants mentioned here, and I thank those Aboriginal families whom I approached for kindly granting permission to continue to refer to their relatives by name. Reg Dodd is most particularly missed. Soon after my arrival in Australia, and for many years thereafter, he tutored me in Aboriginal affairs.

I gratefully acknowledge the funding of the GBRMPA, and the support from its research staff, especially Elaine Eager. Financial and administrative support was provided during my PhD candidature through the Institute of Applied Environmental Research, and the Division of Humanities at Griffith University. The people who contributed valuable material are too numerous to list, but I particularly thank Joan Humphries of the Burns Philp Archives, Aubrey Chandica for the meticulous execution of maps, and Noel Haysom, the now retired Director of the Queensland Fisheries Service. He, as well as Sister Mary Albertus Bain, Bill Metcalf and Elaine Eager made perceptive comments on my manuscript. I also thank the Australian Historical Association for awarding its inaugural history prize to my thesis, and Venetia Nelson, Susan Keogh and John Iremonger for helping me to turn it into a book. Lyndall Ryan, Mark Finnane, Athol Chase and Chilla Bulbeck gave welcome advice liberally, the latter two helping to refine my drafts. The greatest debt is owed to the staunch support and intellectual companionship of my principal supervisor Linda Weiss.

Introduction

At the faded margin of Australian historical consciousness are the shadows of a once vibrant industry which provided the pulse of bustling little townships on the northern extremities of the continent. Daring pearl-shell divers were perilously submerged in the unrivalled solitude of deep seas resounding only with the gargle of their breath, to harvest the precious lustre of pearl-shell. These memories, having gained romantic appeal through historical distance, bear no resemblance to the recent reports of incursions by Indonesian trochus-fishers into Australian waters, swiftly detected by navy patrols, of Indonesian trochus fishermen. During 1990 about 500 Indonesians were apprehended while poaching in Australian waters. They were jailed, charged, fined, and repatriated, their boats confiscated and burned, without offering the slightest deterrent to another fleet, of 232 trochus-fishers, detected early in 1991.

These trochus-fishers from Sulawesi continue a time-honoured tradition. Time-honoured, because the fleets from Celebes form part of a prehistoric trade link to the Australian mainland; because they continue the practice, ever popular among pearl-shellers, of ignoring the territorial boundaries of nation-states; and because it has always been a characteristic of the pearl-shell fishery in Australian waters that it was conducted by foreign nationals.

Very few of the pearl-shellers of Torres Strait, who were almost all white Australians, ever worked as divers themselves. The pearl-shellers were entrepreneurs who, individually, in partnerships, or as company managers, organised the collection of pearl-shell, trochus

1

shell and bêche-de-mer. From the 1860s to the 1960s these collection fisheries formed a single industry, administered under the same legislation. This was the first marine industry based in Northern Queensland. While oyster and fin-fishing were still part-time occupations, pearl-shelling represented a fully fledged industry with fairly concentrated ownership patterns and full-time, albeit seasonal, wage labour by the 1880s.

Pearl-shell (*Pinctada* spp.) grows below 13 metres depth in Torres Strait and in several other locations around the north Australian coast. If impurities, such as grains of sand, enter the shell, they sometimes form a pearl as a natural defence. It has been estimated that only 1 in 1000 shells found contains a natural pearl of any value. The Australian pearl-shell fishery was organised not around the harvesting of pearls, but of the shell itself, which has a nacreous internal lining, called mother-of-pearl. Trochus shell (*Trochus niloticus*) also contains mother-of-pearl. This is a conical shell which forms no pearls and which grows in shallow reef locations. Trochus shell was harvested all along the Great Barrier Reef, from Thursday Island to Mackay. Administratively, this fishery was part and parcel of the pearl-shell fishery.

The pearl-shell fishery was of the greatest importance for several areas in northern Australia, where whole townships depended on it for their existence. Mother-of-pearl was exported unprocessed, primarily for the button industry in Europe and America. In the 1880s the annual value of mother-of-pearl exports was between £50 000 and £100 000. It became an important export earner for the North next to beef, wool and gold, and even after World War II, when production was almost at a standstill, it was considered one of the most important single units of Australian marine industries. But all was not well with the industry—it never really entered the twentieth century. The introduction of plastic buttons finally spelled its demise in the 1960s. The reasons for that sudden collapse, and the structural weaknesses which heralded it, are the theme of this book.

The industry was based on colonial models of resource use, both in its interaction with human and with natural resources. These strategies are explored in detail in this book, the first half addressing the industry's workforce, and the second half resource use proper. Colonial resource-use strategies were inspired by the vision of unlimited resources in an ever-expanding world. The notion of inexhaustible oceans, for example, underpinned the principle of freedom of the high seas, which dominated international legal thought from the late eighteenth century to the 1970s. The lasting impact of the colonial world view was a commitment to expansion, development, and the subjugation of nature to human will. In the dichotomous colonial perspective on nature (nature/human will, or nature/culture), native peoples occupied the side of nature. They, too, were subjugated to the expansion of capitalism.

A retrospective analysis of resource use is vulnerable to the accusation that it is judgemental, particularly if it has recourse to a 'post-industrialist discourse' to communicate with a post-industrial readership, by using terms like 'depleted yield', 'resource-raiding', or 'sustainable development'. The concept of a 'spaceship earth', in which resources are finite, is now widely accepted. To judge *a posteriori* from the relative safety of historical distance, and from the position of a different philosophical paradigm, would be doubly anachronistic. The task is therefore not to pass judgment on whether actors behaved sensibly from either within or without the then dominant paradigm but to document and analyse the processes of development and change, and to point out the consequences of certain choices.

I am explaining the decline of a once important, lively industry, as the failure to innovate—to replace colonial practices with sustainable industrial strategies, to react to historical forces and pressures in a changing political and economic world system. The result of this inquiry is not a chronological history of pearl-shelling. The book is organised thematically in order to underline the way in which such changes affected every aspect of the fishery.

This thematic orientation sacrifices the misfortunes, the scandals, and the romance which should form the common fare of a narrative history of pearl-shelling. The ghostly apparitions at the divers' graveyard in Darnley Deeps, the shark attacks and fearful encounters with giant gropers and whales, the retrieval of dead mates, horribly disfigured, from the deep waters when the airpipe was fouled, or they 'threw their helmet'—these recollections go unmentioned. The marvellous rescue of Douglas Pitt, who was marooned on a reef for an entire night, and 'died a thousand deaths' of fear, is absent from this book, as are the engineering feats of shoestring budget navigation, where the same crankshaft made do for reverse gear and anchor chain release. Such anecdotes flowed naturally, without soliciting, into the interviews I conducted. They are the lore of pearl-shelling, but there is no place for them here. There is only scant reference to the most tragic event in the fishery, when a cyclone destroyed more than half the fleet off Cape Melville in 1899; and no mention at all of the pitiful death of Mrs Watson, the wife of a bêche-de-mer fisher, and her baby and Chinese servant, who died of thirst when escaping in an iron tank, a bêche-de-mer boiler, from the revolt of their indigenous workforce on Lizard Island.

Women in general played only a minor role in the fishery, mainly confined to the sexual companionship of the men engaged in the industry. Sometimes Aboriginal women were engaged in the collection and drying of bêche-de-mer, though official reporting invariably cast them as willing or unwilling prostitutes. The employment of Aboriginal women on vessels was prohibited by law in 1902, but had been locally disallowed since at least 1885. The surviving accounts of relationships between white or Japanese skippers and Aboriginal women are too much coloured by moral condemnation to render such interaction intelligible. The Japanese geishas in all the major pearling centres also have a more sensational than analytic appeal, although they did make an economic contribution to the Japanese participation in the industry. The exceptions to the rule of male exclusivism in the fishery are the women of Murray Island, who harvested the 'home reefs' as a traditionally female activity, and the 'diving girls' of Japan.

Apart from these, reference to women in the fishery is anecdotal, such as the highly sensationalised account by Fred Keim in 1925, a German adventurer who had a stint on a Broome lugger, and found that the most incompetent of his indentured crew was in fact a young female, the sister of his top diver from Nagasaki, concealed as a male. The explanation given for the charade was that they had arrived as 'blind passengers' from Singapore without realizing that they would not be allowed to settle in Australia. Another exception was Tina Mass, who accompanied her husband on their trochus-fishing adventure on the *Tina* after migrating from Britain in 1949. In the 1980s some women were taken on board as cooks, again in the course of adventure rather than as a vocation.

Living conditions on the luggers were poor. There were no sanitary facilities, and only the most primitive bunks for the divers and tenders, while the sleeping quarters of the crew were invaded by shell as the lugger was loaded. The annual overhaul began with a complete submersion of the lugger to rid it of cockroaches.

Although the entire 100-year span of the pearl-shell fishery in Queensland is covered here, most attention is paid to the period from 1890 to World War I. During this phase the pearl-shell industry was fully established and all its structural weaknesses were in sharp, public focus. Its production strategies were challenged by the state, and alternative methods were discussed, and discarded. Subsequent debates over the course which the industry ought to take were merely a rehearsal of the arguments raised during that period.

Mass production/mass extraction

The history of human use of the Great Barrier Reef harbours a recurrent pattern of intensive use and consequent resource exhaustion. The pearl-shell industry was the first large-scale instance of this pattern, followed by fishing, and tourism. Several other industries failed because resources declined dramatically. Queensland's postwar whaling industry at Tangalooma lasted a mere ten years, from 1952 to 1962. Turtle-canning, guano-mining and the collecting of ornamental shells were never more than a sideline before protective legislation was implemented. Sandalwooding enjoyed only brief popularity on Cape York Peninsula from 1910 to 1915. In each case, the intensification of effort hastened the destruction of the natural assets on which the industry relied. Some scientists have raised the concern that the entire reef environment may be under threat from intensive human use because as a complex ecosystem the reef is particularly sensitive to intensive intervention. This concern was raised with reference to oil-drilling, the crown-of-thorns starfish aggregations of the 1970s, and terrestrial run-off.

Ecological problems are well within the area social scientists feel called on to address; they are as much a matter of social and political organisation as of technological know-how. This is most authoritatively argued by John Passmore, and John Bennett directly links modes of production to ecological imbalances. Barry Commoner goes so far as to suggest that the 'technological fix' is against the interests of society. He argues that not economic growth *per se*, but the displacement of several low-technology production methods, has been responsible for environmental problems. Paul Ehrlich, on the other hand, holds that population explosion is the root cause of environmental pressures. Population control, again, is a question of values, ethics, and socio-economic organisation. Stephen Cotgrove stresses the importance of adequate political responses to environmental challenges.[1] The realization that a 'technological fix' cannot resolve major problems is now well accepted. Still, sociologists and political economists are not recruited on any significant scale into positions of research and advice, let alone decision-making, for environmental management.

The destruction of self-renewing resources by short-sighted overuse underlines more clearly than the usurpation of finite resources that self-defeating production strategies need reappraisal. They are the result of a basic contradiction in the use of common resources for private profit. According to Garrett Hardin, population growth requires the closing of increasing numbers of 'commons' (common land) because as rational actors, all private users of the commons must seek to maximise their own use of it so that the commons inevitably come under increasing pressure. This is what Hardin refers to as 'the tragedy of the commons'.

A major rethinking of human involvement in the Great Barrier Reef is well under way, expressed as the search for a sound scientific basis for reef management. The Great Barrier Reef Marine Park Authority, set up under federal legislation in 1975 to manage and monitor multi-purpose use of the reef, bases its management decisions largely on marine biological advice. But environmental management necessarily also entails choices which are based not on scientific criteria but on values, and on circumstance such as political structures, interest-group pressures, dominant production strategy, and continuity. The socio-economic mechanisms of depletion, and the importance for resource use of socio-political organisation expressed as attitudes, are strongly apparent in the case of the pearl-shell industry. Available scientific knowledge and advice were not seriously applied because vested interests in the industry had their horizons set low on short-term gains, displaying an attitude of resource-raiding rather than resource husbandry.

Over-use, exhaustion and volatile markets have become such familiar problems of resource industries as to appear almost inevitable. Typically, Australian resource industries aim at mass extraction to supply an overseas market with raw materials.

Mass extraction, or mass production, refers to the delivery of large quantities of standard items. The strategies of mass production are the combination of large factories, single-purpose machines, and unskilled labour.[2] To transpose this principle from manufacturing to the primary sector, as 'mass extraction', the increase in productivity is sought primarily by exploiting large tracts of land (or sea) for a single resource. The classical manifestations of this strategy are monocultural plantation farming, clear-fell logging or open-cut mining. Emphasis is on the maximisation of output rather than on the maximisation of the resource potential. This means that mass extraction poses a particular problem which differs from that of mass production in manufacturing. Success is expressed in terms of turn-over, volume and value of (in most cases) exports, without consideration of opportunity cost, which can be considerable in resource industries where the large-scale extraction of one resource is at the expense of utilising the full resource potential of the harvested area. This problem has been forcefully raised in the public arena with reference to the logging of rainforests, which destroys species of plants of largely unexplored (e.g. medicinal) potential.

Classical political economy portrays the centralisation of productive effort as a precondition for capitalist growth and vitality. Smith, Marx and Ricardo hold in common that mass production, now known as Fordism, or 'giantism'—the phenomenon of large factories and large corporations premised on economies of scale and standardised production—are the *sine qua non* of capitalist development. This is the premise which is referred to as 'industrial logic', (the 'logic of capital' in Marx). A rapidly growing body of literature, however, questions the inevitability of mass production for capitalist development. Charles Sabel and Jonathan Zeitlin point to historical alternatives where commercial prosperity, expansion and technological vitality was achieved through flexible specialisation, which means 'the flexible use of multi-purpose or universal machines and skilled labour to make an ever changing assortment of semi-customized products: a system that reverses the principles of mass production'.[3] Flexible specialisation encourages the swift adaptation to market demands by curbing or raising production, or by switching to other products. The organisational forms best suited to this strategy are small-scale and co-operative enterprises immersed in a local or regional infrastructure of pooled resources, skills and ideas.

Because political economy explains the development of mass production as the result of an 'industrial logic', the influence of the state in the emergence of mass production has received little attention.

Conversely, the centrality of the state in the persistence of alternative production methods is much better documented, because it presents a 'puzzle' in the paradigmatic order of knowledge in political economy.[4]

Closer examination of economic development in several nations reveals that the increasing dominance of mass production on the one hand and the decline of alternative, small-scale production strategies on the other is not due to a logic of industrialisation, but the result of politically based, technological choices. Linda Weiss argues that in most Western nations the small-business sector was actively subordinated as the mass production paradigm became a 'futuristic vision eclipsing its alternatives'.[5] She compares actual patterns of development and government policies to underline the point that the state takes an active role in the breakthrough to mass production. Classical political economy understands the state as a subordinate actor *vis-à-vis* economic forms. The role of the state in expediting the concentration of production under circumstances of war might be seen as an uncharacteristic insertion of the state into the economy. Weiss, however, demonstrates that at least since World War I, states have been important economic agents in their own right. Indeed, her comparative investigations reveal that 'states, not markets *per se*, have generalized the impulse to scale and concentration'. That is, the state is actively involved in shaping national configurations of industrial organisation; its relative autonomy can transform economic structures.[6]

This recent literature which deals with the mass production paradigm is macro-historical in scope. Sabel and Zeitlin found that they had to rely largely on sources and case studies which fully embrace the notion that the breakthrough to mass production was a historical necessity. As a result, the countless small conflicts in which choices towards one or the other production paradigm were made, and the particular ways in which states have intervened in this choice, are not easily accessible. As a micro-historical exercise, the present account of the pearl-shell industry is more sensitive to these obscure moments of choice, and can therefore document the ways in which the subordination of alternative production styles was the subject of collective choice, rather than a prerequisite for development, and how centrally the state was involved in this process. It supplies the kind of evidence which Sabel and Zeitlin invite, by paying particular attention to the suppression of alternative production strategies.

The problem of decline

The decline of the pearl-shell industry in the early 1960s was a major industrial crisis in far north Queensland. The standard explanation for the decline is that shell-beds were getting so depleted that shell became unprofitable to raise, and that mother-of-pearl was displaced by the introduction of plastics. In other words, resource exhaustion presumably led to a decline in the rate of profit, and competing cheaper products deprived the industry of its traditional markets. There is a weakness in this explanation supplied by participants, historians, and government reports. While it accurately describes the situation faced by producers at the time, it is not an explanation of the industry's decline in analytical terms, first because similar problems had frequently beset the industry before, and second because similar crises were faced by other industries (particularly wool-farming and coal-mining), where these obstacles did not lead to the cessation of the industries concerned. Clearly, the decline of this fishery deserves further explanation. The timing of the crisis reveals something of its proximate causes. It was reached at a time when the industry had no major advocates, and the unsustainable nature of its resource strategies was well understood. The state, which had sheltered the industry with various concessions, surrendered the industry to its own self-defeating forces. This book therefore looks at the kind of interest which the state vested in the industry at various periods.

The final decline of the industry was not simply due to the problems associated with resource exhaustion. This study identifies two other structural weaknesses of the industry: its ethnically segmented, unfree labour force, and its exposure to a volatile overseas market.[7] These became the fossilised luggage of colonial strategies. Several official reports and commissions of inquiry sought to deal with these problems, but within an ideational framework fully committed to mass production they were considered to be beyond redress—radical restructuring would have been at the expense of mass extraction.

Once we dismiss the supposed 'logic' of capitalist development and understand the trend towards mass production strategies as a set of political choices, according to Sabel and Zeitlin,

> it is necessary to shift vantage point and imagine a theoretical world in which technology can in principle develop in different ways: a world that might have turned out differently from the way it did, and therefore a world with a history of abandoned but potentially viable alternatives to what actually exists.[8]

The decline of the pearl-shell fishery was not inevitable. An industry which would have turned out differently would have used one or more of the following strategies: (1) comprehensive resource management and/or artificial cultivation to avoid depletion; (2) product diversification and domestic processing of mother-of-pearl to gain greater control of marketing; and (3) the encouragement of owner-operated fleets to raise shell as a supplement to subsistence activities. All of these strategies were available and had received some attention. Pearl-shellers, however, defended their archaic practices.

A note about oral history and other sources

Because this study grew out of my working relationship with GBRMPA, oral history forms part of the baseline from which it proceeds. As GBRMPA's consultant I conducted 101 interviews with 108 informants during four field-trips in 1986 and 1987. The fieldwork phase amounted to 93 days, spent in Japan, Torres Strait, the Aboriginal communities on the east coast of Queensland, and various coastal centres from Cooktown to Hervey Bay. The list of interviewees in the Bibliography indicates the places and dates at which interviews were conducted. The age of interviewees indicated in brackets refers to the age at the time of the interview. I have retained the practice for Japanese names to state surnames first, and the foreign-language interviews were translated simultaneously. Interviewees responded to a range of questions in a loosely structured interview, so that their accounts were not locked into a rigid question-and-answer structure but were assembled around a set of topics which permitted both the individual reminiscence of each respondent and a comparison between the experiences of interviewees. The tape-recordings have been lodged with the Australian Institute of Aboriginal and Torres Strait Islander Studies in Canberra.

Interviews have contributed an understanding of the human dimension of the industry—the motivations, limitations, and self-conception of actors, and they act as a counterpoise to official interpretations of the fishery's history rendered in departmental reports. The dominant themes of these interviews were the declining resources of the reef during the experience of informants, the cataclysmic collapse of the pearl-shell industry, and the pride with which those who were able to say so stated, 'I was a diver'. These issues raised the question why the industry, which was so important for the self-conception of its participants, suddenly declined. An agenda of inquiry into the use of resources was thus set. Moreover, several interviewees expressed their desire to re-enter the industry, so that a historical evaluation of the fishery and its failure seemed appropriate.

While much of the insight and agenda of this book is based on oral history, the scope of the inquiry owes more to the legislative framework surrounding the industry. The pearl-shell, trochus and bêche-de-mer fisheries were administered as a single industry, and this is how they are treated here, despite significant differences drawn by former participants. Also, this industry was administered on a State level, whereas many participants traversed the territorial boundaries of the States.

My interpretation of public documents has been influenced by the perspective gained from former participants. Such an admission may be seen as fuel to the debate which raged around oral history in the 1970s and 1980s, when labour historians, many of them concerned with women's history or the history of non-literate societies, offered oral history as radical historiography, as an instrument against oppression and exclusion, whereas others guarded against the subjective nature of oral history, referring particularly to the selective nature of memory.[9]

The problem of subjectivity is more apparent in, but by no means unique to, oral history. To take up, for example, the selective nature of living memory, which is indisputable, those familiar with archival research must have a keen appreciation of the serendipity involved in retrieving information from archives. One might chance on the most detailed documentation concerning, say, the Papuan Industries Limited from 1905 to 1907, but, with all due effort, be unable to obtain anything referring to this institution at any date before, or afterwards. Departmental information undergoes several processes of selection between desk, file, storage, archive, indexation and retrieval. With considerable diligence, it is often possible to re construct the principles of selection used at various points, but what the result really amounts to is a selective nature of archival sources. Published sources undergo a comparable process of selection, guided by different principles.

The verbal statement, say, of a former administrator can in no way be of less prima facie value than the hurriedly researched written account of a journalist. There can be no general principle according written sources more objective value than oral ones. Oral testimony and written records are to be treated with the same confidence, discretion, and scepticism.

The distinction between written and oral sources is, in any but the most pragmatic sense, an artificial one. With regard to the problem of access, when oral sources are recorded they are as accessible to other researchers as many written sources. A quaint publication of a local historical society in the far North, a book held in the special collection of some library, and a departmental memorandum found in an archive, are as difficult to access for subsequent researchers as tape-recorded interviews deposited in a public institution—and both may be governed by access restrictions. The class of information which may be completely inaccessible to other researchers—diaries, minutes, or photographs held by individual informants, and the personal communications or correspondence with office-holders—do not fit the distinction between verbal and written sources.

This much is agreed by all protagonists in the oral history debate, and there is no need for any 'further verbals' on my part.[10] As John Murphy observed, there is nothing novel about oral history as a method of data collection. Herodotus used oral sources; biography and autobiography are commonly based on oral testimony; and journalists routinely use oral history as a technique.

Archival, governmental, published and oral sources and concepts from a range of disciplines have been used to construct this account of the pearl-shell fishery. The reliability of these sources was judged not by generic criteria but by their particular qualities and circumstances of production; and the principle of selection was to explain, and not merely describe, the development and decline of the pearl-shell fishery. Oral history is used as a technique to gain access to data which is not otherwise available, and the particular insights which it contributes are the indigenous explanation of absconding from luggers, the social cohesion among the Japanese workforce, cemented by the recruiting practices ('letters of calling') and *oyakata*-style leadership, the role of the Torres Strait Pearl-Shellers' Association, and the degree of financial dependence on overseas shell-buyers.

Much of the information used here belongs to a 'grey area' between written and oral sources. To this 'grey area' belong the testimonials of witnesses called in several public inquiries. The transcribed proceedings of two of these inquiries have been drawn upon as life-like glimpses into the lived experience of the industry.

Another substantial part of the data comes from the annual reports of two departments. I had two excellent guides to archival documentation. One was the book about the pearl-shell industry by Mary Albertus Bain, a Dominican nun who had access to several private collections in Western Australia in the Battye Library in Perth, renowned for its oral history archives. This account was written from the perspective of the Broome fishery. The other was a history of the industry by J. P. S. Bach of the then Newcastle University College of the NSW University of Technology. Bach's account was initially a confidential report for the Commonwealth Department of Commerce and Agriculture, and was based exclusively on archival and departmental sources and news clippings. He had unrestricted access to departmental files and enjoyed a close working relationship with the relevant sections in the Commonwealth Government.[11] Wherever prudent, I have relied on such secondary sources so as not to duplicate the efforts of previous researchers. I have also availed myself of the on-line search function at the Australian Archives in Canberra, which had not been available to previous researchers in this field.

Oral history has no fixed or privileged status in this study, defined somehow by the technique itself. In Chapters 1 and 2, the perspective of Aborigines and Torres Strait Islanders tends to compete with departmental interpretations. This reflects more on the practice of race relations than on oral history as a technique. In Chapters 3 and 4, oral and written sources complement each other, contributing different kinds of knowledge. The chapters dealing with marketing and resource management (Chapters 5 and 6), are largely based on written sources with the occasional glimpse into the experience of participants. Chapter 7, describing the position of the industry since the 1960s, emanates from interviews and draws on written sources for support.

A Colonial Birthmark?
The Emergence of an Ethnically
Stratified Labour Market

From a socio-historical perspective, the most interesting aspect of the pearl-shell industry is the way in which people from 'all kind of nation'[1] worked together. The industry was an arena of race relations and Thursday Island was popularly referred to as the 'sink of the Pacific' because of the variety of nationalities employed. In 1890, the population of 526 at Thursday Island was composed of Europeans, Chinese, Torres Strait Islanders and Aborigines, South Sea Islanders, Malays, Filipinos, Japanese, Singhalese, and Indians (in that order of numerical strength), with a sprinkling of Thais, Arabs and Africans.[2]

The industry's workforce was hierarchically organised: until World War II indigenous Australians (Aborigines and Torres Strait Islanders) were employed only as unskilled labourers while imported labour filled the more responsible roles of skippers, divers and tenders. Of all the cultural groups engaged in the Great Barrier Reef industries, the Japanese always appeared the most successful, and caused the most resentment.

Following Sabel and Zeitlin's invitation to imagine the world from a different vantage point, where the outcome of historical developments is not already known, we may pose some rhetorical questions indicating what it is that requires explanation: why did indigenous labour not, as a rule, progress into skilled employment? Torres Strait Islanders and coastal Aborigines already held valuable knowledge about local conditions and were familiar with the marine environment. Having exploited pearl-shell traditionally, they held a certain responsibility for the long-term viability of the resource. They were not, as on the pastoral frontier, competitors for land, so they were not 'displaced and dispersed', although considerable diminution resulted here too. Why, indeed, did they not become a maritime yeomanry, collectively organised to produce pearl-shell and dealing directly with exporting companies? Is the marginalisation of indigenous labour sufficiently explained by racism? What other factors must be taken into account to explain it? These questions will be addressed at the end of this chapter.

South Pacific trading extends into northern Australia

The pearl-shell industry was an offshoot of the colonial trade with the South Pacific in copra, sandalwood, and other island produce, such as pearl-shell and bêche-de-mer. This parentage left a lasting imprint on the fishery's employment and production strategies, both in terms of its financial organisation—the dependence of producers on large trading companies—and in terms of its labour requirements.

The fishery began in Queensland's far North long before the northward spread of land settlement warranted an interest in the Cape York area. The integration of the far north coast and Torres Strait into colonial administration and commerce was politically motivated in order to control the shipping lanes to the French colony of New Caledonia. It was not motivated by pastoral expansion or gold-rush fever; it was not driven by land-hungry Europeans. Consequently the indigenous population was not subjected to dispersal, diminution and displacement to any degree comparable with that on the pastoral frontier. On the 'unsettled' Cape York Peninsula, and particularly in Torres Strait, indigenous labour was a valuable asset. George Dalrymple, the police magistrate at Somerset in 1874, pointed out how "vast are the yet undeveloped resources of these seas, and the density of their populations, which are capable of being converted into producers".[3] However, the emergence of a stratified wage labour force assigned to indigenous people a subsidiary role in the exploitation of the marine resources. They were considered valuable labour only because they were cheap to employ, not because of their intimate knowledge of local conditions. The approach of the pearl-shell and bêche-de-mer industry to indigenous people was guided by experience from South Sea Island trading, which also served as a role model for the organisation of fishing stations.

A huge trading deficit beset white Australia. In the penal colony, tea imports from China alone exceeded the value of all export earnings from wool, oil, hides, horns, seal skins, and timber. Tea formed part of the weekly rations of government officers and was one of the largest import items between 1825 and 1830.[4] Trade with China was very important for Australia, but the Chinese merchants had little interest in the trade goods from Australia. There was a keen demand though for sandalwood, used as incense, and bêche-de-mer, which could be obtained from the islands in the Pacific. Bêche-de-mer, also referred to as trepang, is used in Chinese *haute cuisine* and credited with aphrodisiac qualities.

Dorothy Shineberg's study of the sandalwood trade traces two shifts in South Pacific trading strategies. South Pacific trading at first relied on bartering relationships with Polynesians, whose social organisation facilitated exchange: chiefs could entrench their power through the acquisition of scarce commodities and could marshal labour to obtain the produce sought by the traders. In this bartering network, the Polynesians were trading partners with a significant influence on the terms of exchange. Traders relied on the self-paced labour of islanders and on their demand for trade goods. Sometimes trading was refused because islanders had no demand for the commodities offered and their market was saturated, or because the procurement of trading produce conflicted with traditional calendars.

This bartering relationship was expensive for traders. As they extended their field of operation further west into Melanesia, they began to establish trading stations with white resident managers, to which they imported labour from other islands. These shore stations were more economical because smaller craft were used to procure and process the sandalwood, bêche-de-mer or tortoiseshell, while the large, expensive vessels capable of voyaging to Sydney and China were only employed to fetch produce from the stations and bring supplies.[5]

With the development of shore stations in the south-west Pacific in the 1840s, a migrant wage labour force was created which was highly dependent on its employers for accommodation, provisions, and protection from local tribes. Because of the poverty of the south-west Pacific islands, these islanders were readily available for contract work in return for food and trade items. The gold-rushes of the

1850s created an intense labour shortage in Australia, and it became common to crew vessels substantially with South Sea Islanders. The practice of contracting large crews who worked in gangs of thirty to fifty on islands far from their homes set the scene for the South Sea Islander labour trade to Queensland and Fiji, pioneered by Robert Towns in the 1860s. Shineberg's account of sandalwooding suggests that the notorious 'blackbirding' trade was an extension of a time-honoured practice in Pacific trading.

South Pacific traders were essentially resource-raiders. When the supply of a tradable resource was exhausted in one area, they moved on to another. They habitually employed imported workers who held no custodianship over the resource that was exploited. Neither the workforce nor the entrepreneurs, therefore, had a vested interest in ensuring the long-term conservation of that resource. In the 1860s tradable resources, particularly sandalwood, declined in the South Pacific. Moreover, whaling was in crisis from dwindling numbers and petroleum was supplanting whale oil. Robert Towns's Sydney whaling fleet was falling into disrepair and by the late 1850s it was becoming known as 'Rotten Row'.[6] The Sydney-based Pacific trading companies diversified into other shipping ventures, such as the importation of indentured Chinese, and recruiting for Queensland and Fiji, and explored trade in a wider range of island produce such as trepang, tortoiseshell and pearl-shell. 'High on the list of itinerant enterprises was the search for pearl-shell, which offered the prospect of a quick fortune . . . and which, largely for that reason, was launched in an atmosphere of secrecy and intrigue.'[7] The traders started to prospect and set up stations in Torres Strait, at the margin of the South Pacific. Resource-raiding as a style of management was imported into the far northern industry along with the boats from 'Rotten Row'.

North Queensland's bêche-de-mer resources had been discovered by Sydney traders as a result of the accident of the *Porpoise*, captained by Matthew Flinders, on Wreck Reef, named after the incident, on 17 August 1803. While its sister vessel *Investigator* sailed to Sydney to get help, the shipwrecked sailors collected bêche-de-mer for soup, something they had just learned from the 60-ship Macassan bêche-de-mer fleet encountered on the north-east tip of Arnhem Land (which was subsequently named Malay Roads). These bêche-de-mer fishers came from Makasar (now Ujung Pandang in Sulawesi, Indonesia) in low-lying 60-foot *perahus* (prows), each with a fleet of canoes. About a thousand Macassans worked under a commodore, Nakhoda Pobassoo, who informed the Europeans that they acted on behalf of Salu, the Rajah of Boni in Celebes (now Sulawesi) and that for at least twenty years they had been coming to 'Marege' through the Arafura Sea on the changing monsoon winds. The linguistic, artistic and ceremonial Malay influences on Aborigines around the Gulf of Carpentaria suggest that the trade may have begun in a small, irregular way up to 200 years before Flinders' chance discovery. In north-eastern Arnhem Land, Groote Eylandt, and Gove Peninsula the reminders of the annual Malay visits, which continued well into this century, are tamarind trees on former Malay camp-sites, and many Malay words in local Aboriginal languages. The Macassans introduced cereal agriculture, pottery, dugout canoes with sails, and a shovel-nosed spear; and *perahus* and trepang feature in many bark and cave paintings and have in some places acquired totemic significance. The Malays occasionally employed Aborigines, and even took some to Makasar, but generally Aborigines were wary of them and sometimes attacked *perahus*.[8]

Although the shipwrecked sailors of the *Porpoise* were reportedly unsuccessful in acquiring a taste for trepang, Flinders subsequently suggested that north Queensland trepang might be profitably exploited. The first recorded commercial trepang fishery in North Queensland was the effort of James Aicken, one of the rescue party, who collected some trepang for sale in Sydney while salvaging the wreck. John MacGillivray observed some Sydney-based boats fishing trepang and tortoiseshell in Torres Strait in 1848, but it has recently been pointed out that curing on board was not introduced until the 1890s, so that it is unlikely that the trepang was obtained in Torres Strait at that time. It is more likely that it was obtained from the Great Barrier Reef, whereas tortoiseshell trading with Torres Strait Islanders had already begun in the 1840s. In 1827 10 tons of bêche-de-mer were shipped from the Cooktown area to Koepang in Timor, and in 1829 a Sydney vessel reported that it had successfully fished for trepang in the north.[9]

The exploitation of the bêche-de-mer resources of the Great Barrier Reef by Sydney traders developed haphazardly until South Pacific trading declined and interest focused on Australia's North. This meant that South Pacific trading became the model for the conduct of the industry here. Shore stations served as a base for imported labourers, who lived and worked on them on a semipermanent basis. From its inception, therefore, the pearl-shell industry in Queensland operated on a model which relied significantly on imported labour. More than any other industry, and for a longer period than the sugar industry, the pearl-shell industry relied on a transient workforce of indentured aliens. Local indigenous labour was merely a supplement to the imported workforce.

The captains who started stations in Torres Strait had available experienced crews from the south-west Pacific and were themselves experienced in setting up and managing stations. The effects of these shore stations in Torres Strait differed little from that in the south-west Pacific. With provisions from Sydney sometimes delayed, labour gangs were apt to raid local gardens, which ensued in much fighting between local Islanders and imported crews.[10] White pearl-shellers also felt that they were operating in a legal no-man's land in their interaction with indigenous people. For example, the Government Resident at Somerset, John Jardine, noticed a change in the Mabuiag Islanders, remarking that their normally confident and 'fearless demeanour . . . has given place to a cowed and sullen manner'. This was after a whole canoe full of them had been shot and drowned by one of these captains.[11]

First stations in Torres Strait

Both the first bêche-de-mer and the first pearl-shell station in Torres Strait had links with the largest Pacific trading company, that of Robert Towns. The first known bêche-de-mer station in Torres Strait was established in 1862 by Charles Edwards, on Albany Island just off the mainland at Cape York. Edwards's pioneering station was something of a coloniser's grand dream. He had been the business partner of James Paddon, another one of the foremost Pacific Island traders, who had died the previous year. When Queensland became an independent colony in 1859, Paddon had contemplated removing his island trading stations to Torres Strait and proposed to remove the whole population of Uvea to Queensland for that purpose. Such was the hold of trading companies over some islands.[12]

In the same year, 1862, the Queensland and imperial governments established a joint northern outpost, at first also on Albany Island.[13] In 1865 Edwards moved his bêche-de-mer station outside the ambit of government presence, to Darnley Island. Until 1879, when Queensland's jurisdiction was extended to cover the whole of Torres Strait, the bêche-de-mer industry tended to be conducted largely outside its supervision, on Stephens, Yorke and Darnley islands. By 1871 several vessels used Darnley Island as shelter and had establishments there, and the island was referred to as the centre of the bêche-de-mer industry in Torres Strait. The indigenous population on Darnley had dwindled from an estimated four or five hundred to 120–130 people.[14]

Only six years after the start of trepanging in Torres Strait, a new industry began, with the raising of pearl-shell. In 1863 William Banner established a bêche-de-mer station on Warrior Island, again operated on the model of Pacific trading. This island was home to forty-three families, and Banner employed seventy South Sea Islanders, mainly from Mare and the Sandwich Islands, as well as some Yorke Islanders. The impact of culture contact on the Warrior Islanders was swift, expedited by intermarriage with the station workforce. Within two years Warrior Islanders had parted with most of their ornaments, and corrugated iron had replaced their traditional drums. Eventually the location of their pearl-beds was revealed to one of the Tongans employed on the station (Joseph John, sometimes referred to as Tongatapu Joe who had married a local woman). This patch was exhausted in just over a year.

One source ascribes to Banner's arrival on Warrior 'the express purpose of spending a season exploiting the pearl beds of the Torres Strait' and points out that the *Julia Percy* on which he arrived from Sydney was armed with a cannon.[15] An eyewitness account by Henry Chester in 1870 makes no reference, however, to such an intention:

> During Capt. Banner's absence in Sydney in the beginning of the year the station was left in charge of one the Kanakas, a man about 60 years of age, who has served in all manner of vessels including H.M.S. 'Leopard' at the siege of Sebastopol. The Toot men showed him the part of the reef from whence they obtained the pearl oyster, and on Captain Banner's return at the end of April he found six tons of shell had been collected. Thenceforward the Beche de Mer fishery was given up and their attention turned to the more cleanly and lucrative trade.[16]

From Chester's account it appears as if the discovery of pearl-shell was by chance. But it was already known that some Torres Strait Islanders, such as those of Warrior Island, wore crescents of pearl-shell which was a highly prized commodity in the Pacific trade.[17] It is very likely that Banner chose the island, which had so far been avoided, as his shore station with a view to locating the pearl-beds which were the source of the traditional ornaments. But as pearl-shells grow on the leeward side of reefs, the bêche-de-mer crews, working on sandy bottoms, were unlikely to have come across them in their routine diving. It required local knowledge to find the actual pearl-shell beds. Neither the assumption of an 'express purpose' nor the impression of chance discovery, therefore, are an apt description of the beginning of pearl-shelling in Torres Strait. The arrival of these captains was clearly part of a policy shift by the main Sydney-based South Pacific trading companies.[18] They arrived with considerable experience, and with an open eye for opportunity.

Nor were the bêche-de-mer stations at the time as independent of each other as most historical accounts portray. Edwards had been a sandalwooder in the New Hebrides.[19] Since 1852 he had managed sandalwood stations for James Paddon at Tana and Eromanga (where John MacGillivray had worked for him as a sandalwooder for a short time); by 1859 he was a full partner in Paddon's New Caledonian ventures. The schooner *Bluebell*, which he used to set up the Albany Island station, was registered in Paddon's name. By 1870 he operated the *Kate Kearney*, which belonged to Robert Towns, and collaborated on Darnley Island with Captain Fraser, whose brig *Melanie* was also part of the Towns fleet. Banner, who arrived on Paddon's *Julia Percy*, took over the *Bluebell* from Edwards. After Banner's discovery of pearl-shell on Warrior Reef, Edwards soon joined the search for new beds. Whether Edwards and Banner were in co-operation or competition as share-trading captains, they both worked on behalf of the same trading empire. Their financial patrons, Towns and Paddon, had been in keen competition, with Towns several times following in the footsteps of the enterprising Paddon, and adopting the shore station system pioneered by Paddon, but by 1864 Paddon was 'in treaty with Towns'.[20] In November 1870 five boats were engaged in pearl-shelling (*Pakeha*, *Bluebell*, *Kate Kearney*, *Melanie* and *Fanny*), four of which can be directly linked to the estates of either Towns or Paddon.[21] (See Appendix I.)

Pacific trading as a role model for ownership structure

Pacific trading supplied the model for the employment and remuneration practices in the industry as well as for its financial organisation. In 1856 Towns began to act as buyer, exporter and financier to share-trading captains engaged in the collection of sandalwood, bêche-de-mer and tortoiseshell in the south-west Pacific. He remarked that 'trading among the Islands will only pay the Man in his own small craft'.[22] These share-trading captains were provided with boats and equipment to operate their own vessels on scattered stations. While the vessels were being paid off, the financing company claimed a half-share in the proceeds as well as interest on the loan.

Most of the bêche-de-mer and pearl-shell captains active in Torres Strait in the 1860s and 1870s had such share-trading agreements with financing companies in Sydney such as Towns, Burns (later Burns Philp & Co.), John Bell, or James Merriman. These share-trading connections are difficult to discover. As share-trading captains were able to pay off their debts, the ownership of vessels and stations in Torres Strait diversified. Still, the industry as a whole remained financially dependent on companies active in South Pacific trading. As Figure 1 (p. 244) demonstrates, the links are strongest between the earliest stations.

In 1870 only Banner and Edwards were operating, both using vessels belonging to Towns and Paddon. Banner died in 1872, Paddon in 1861, and the name of Edwards does not appear after 1870. He had been active in South Pacific trading since at least 1856, and it must be presumed that he was of a similar age to Banner and Paddon. The younger Towns continued to be involved in pearl-shelling through share-trading with his vessels *Kate Kearney* (Capt. Wells), *Australasian Packet* (Capt. Hovell), and *William and Mary* (Capt. Parkyns) until at least 1875. Banner's station was continued by Merriman of Sydney.

By 1875, the date of the next detailed report about the fishery, the names had changed, but not the practices. James Merriman and John Bell, both of Sydney, dominated the fishery, and both companies were strongly involved in blackbirding, as was the German company to whom they sold their shell, Godeffroy, which was Bismarck's Pacific trading protégé.[23] The captain of Godeffroy's lugger in Torres Strait, E. Redlich, was the brother of the Consul-General in Hamburg. Local government officials had also joined the fishery (see below pp. 31ff.). There were seventeen luggers on six island stations, belonging to Merriman (Warrior and Mabuiag), John Bell (Mabuiag), Frank Jardine (Nagir), Charles Beddome (Nagir), and Edward Brown (Somerset). Redlich and three other pearl-shelling captains were not established on any particular island. Brown and Beddome were closely associated with Jardine, so that in fact only three separate island station fisheries were operating in 1875.

Thereafter the fishery proliferated, yet it was not an uncoordinated rush into a new industry. Table 1 gives an indication of the exponential growth of the fishery during its first decade, and also shows that after 1877 the trend was for the number of companies concerned with pearl-shelling to decrease, and for their size to increase. Figure 1 (p. 244) shows the Torres Strait Islands which are known to have been used as pearl-shell or bêche-de-mer stations between 1862 (the year when the first known bêche-de-mer station was established) and 1885 (the year when Thursday Island was opened for residential leases to attract pearl-shellers in from the islands), that is, during the 'island station' phase of the industry.

These fishing stations formed a network of co-operation and ownership at the centre of which were four large Sydney companies. Since reference to links between them in the primary sources is incidental, this is unlikely to be a complete network. It is all the more significant, then, that almost all known island stations are linked into this network. For those who are familiar with the fishery's history, the most surprising linkage was that between Towns and Frank Jardine, since Jardine has generally been described as a genuinely independent pearl-sheller. According to T. G. Chapman, who was pearl-shelling from Friday Island, Towns had a share-trading agreement with Jardine. Chapman's letter also alleges that Jardine pursued a policy of displacing Melbourne-owned vessels from the fishery.[24]

TABLE 1   GROWTH OF STATION OWNERSHIP (1870–80)

Year	Boats	Owners	Average boats per owner	Boats not assigned to network (App. I)
1870	5 luggers	2	?	0
1875	17 luggers 40 boats	5	8	0
1877	109	16	6.8	18%
1879 May	104	14	7.4	20%
1879 Sept.	88	11	8.0	19%
1880	99	11	9	6%

At least 80 per cent of boats in the fishery at any time during the island station phase can be assigned to the network of ownership described in Appendix I. In 1877, 109 vessels were registered in the name of sixteen companies, all except two from Sydney. Only five of these, representing 17 boats, could not be allocated to the network of partnership in Figure 1.[25] In May 1879, 104 vessels were registered in the name of fourteen companies. Again only four of these, representing 15 vessels, are not part of the network.[26] In September 1879 there were eleven companies, owning 88 boats; again, all except two were from Sydney, and again, the same four owners, representing 12 boats, have not been assigned to the network.[27]

Share-trading continued to be a characteristic of the industry, although it is more difficult to trace in detail after 1877, because official reporting of the fishery shifted from a listing of names to quantitative information on exports, labour and revenue. A further large Sydney trader, Henry Burns, also moved into pearl-shelling soon after Towns and Paddon. His sandalwood boats *Pearl* and *Dart* became famous pearling luggers, the *Dart* being used until it was destroyed by the army in World War II. Burns Philp's initial involvement at Thursday Island was the procurement of Malayan labourers from Singapore, which they began the year after their incorporation in 1883. In 1886 they started a subsidised monthly service between Thursday Island and Port Moresby, made possible by the good offices of John Douglas, then Special Commissioner for British New Guinea. Douglas hoped that Burns Philp would establish trading stations along the route to encourage copra, bêche-de-mer and pearl-shell trading. The line proved uneconomical and was discontinued in 1888. By this time Burns Philp had a substantial interest in the pearl-shell industry. They owned several luggers directly or through share-trading agreements, bought the shell, and supplied the industry with merchandise. In 1895 they had a financial interest in thirty-four boats and recruited labour for the industry in New Guinea, through their trading post at Daru. Burns Philp became the largest pearl-shelling company at Thursday Island, owning a slipway, large premises on the foreshore, and a jetty built in 1892 at public expense of £40 000. In 1901 the company established its London office and was now able to market pearl-shell directly. In the same year it intensified its involvement in the fishery, adopting the floating-station system. Joseph Mitchell was appointed as manager of the Thursday Island branch, where he remained until 1912 as a strong advocate of pearl-shelling within the firm. He later became one of the company's directors (1929–66). In 1913 Burns Philp's Wyben fleet (named after the indigenous name for Thursday Island—*Waiben*) became a subsidiary company capitalised at £14 400. Wyben's incorporation constituted a partial withdrawal of Burns Philp from the industry, a withdrawal which Burns had already suggested in 1908. Wyben gradually withdrew from the industry after World War II.[28]

Another pearling company active from the 1890s to World War II was also involved in South Pacific trading. In 1908, eight boats were registered by J. B. Carpenter & Sons, and a further eight by Walter R. Carpenter. W. R. Carpenter managed Burns Philp's Esperance branch, and then joined his father's pearling business at Thursday Island in 1897. He returned to Burns Philp a few years later. Another Carpenter brother, J. A. Carpenter, was also an employee in Burns Philp's Pacific ventures. W. R. Carpenter formed his own company in Fiji in 1913, which became a rival of Burns Philp's copra-trading activities in the 1920s and 1930s. Meanwhile J. B. Carpenter & Sons acted as agents for Lever Brothers in the copra trade at Thursday Island. Lever Brothers remained in the background of the industry. They participated financially in Papuan Industries Limited which encouraged indigenous involvement in copra and pearl-shell activities, and they were also involved, much later, in the development of synthetic pearl-shell substitutes.

Aplin, Brown and Crawshay, Burns Philp's main competitors in coastal trade, were also active in pearl-shelling. Their manager at Thursday Island was Fred Morey, who later took over the business, which became part of Bowden Pearling Company after World War II. Carpenter, BP, Morey and Bowden are well within the living memory of the industry, but their common south-pacific trading lineage is hardly remembered.

Burns Philp remained the main exporter of pearl-shell through their London office until the world pearl-shell market shifted to New York during World War I. The Gerdau Company then became the dominant pearl-shell buyer at Thursday Island, similarly financing pearl-shellers. The level of financial dependence in the twentieth century was quite comparable to that of the share-trading captains (see Chapter 6). Gerdau, too, fits the groove of colonial traders, since the company dealt exclusively in colonial merchandise such as pepper, sugar, coffee and pearl-shell.

The role of South Sea Islanders in Torres Strait

As island stations were being set up in Queensland's north, crews from the south-west Pacific were imported to work on them. The

Melanie was recruiting in the south-west Pacific throughout the 1870s to import labour for the pearl-shell and bêche-de-mer stations in Torres Strait. 'Literally thousands' of Melanesians were imported to Torres Strait for work in the pearl-shell industry.[29] It was part of the recruiting policy of the trading companies to import labour rather than employ resident Islanders; even in Torres Strait, Islanders from neighbouring islands were often employed on the stations in preference to those who already lived there. Crews were paid in 'trade', receiving the equivalent of 10s a month and rations consisting of sharps (inferior flour), cornmeal, molasses, tea and sugar, and sometimes beef.

With the aid of pearl-shellers, the London Missionary Society (LMS) established its first missions in Torres Strait in 1871. Their arrival, too, was the result of developments in the Pacific area. The LMS was having difficulties with the Catholic Church and the French government in the Loyalty Islands, and decided to expand into New Guinea. To create strategic 'stepping stones' for the Christian advance, some Pacific Island missionary teachers and their wives were deposited on Murray and Dauan Islands. These Polynesian missionary teachers were largely unsupervised by the missionaries, who concentrated their efforts on the Papuan mainland. They had a free rein to interpret the 'civilising influence' which they were to emit, a role in which they were somewhat overzealous. From Mabuiag Island, complaints were heard about the raids on women made by South Sea Islanders, and at Murray Island the missionaries established an 'arbitrary and despotic rule', where even trivial offences such as quarrelling or passing jokes about the missionaries were punished with severe floggings: 'The chief is a helpless poor fellow, completely under the thumb of the missionary teacher, who is supported by a staff of idle loafing South Sea Islanders located around the mission station'.[30] After complaints about such an autocratic rule on Murray Island, the South Sea Islanders were removed and resettled on Darnley.

The missionary teachers also formed business alliances with pearl-shellers and were able to withhold or supply local labour to pearl-shell or bêche-de-mer stations. Some of them became partners in pearl-shell and bêche-de-mer fishing ventures employing indigenous people on the islands outside the ambit of the Queensland government. Chester reported:

These islands have hitherto afforded a refuge for discharged South Sea Islanders and others, who prefer living on the natives or the missionary teachers to working for their livelihood. They usually contrive to procure a boat, and induce the natives to work for them; but I am unable to state how they are paid, or whether they are paid at all, for their labour.[31]

Industry and policy

The government's concern over the treatment of indigenous people gave rise to a complex body of protective legislation which formalised a ranked hierarchy of ethnic groups. In order to understand why different ethnic groups assumed their particular position in the industry, it is first necessary to sketch out some aspects of the industry which influenced government decision-making.

The politics of 'miscegenation'

Both missionary activity and the marine industry at first relied on the importation of Pacific Islanders, so that on some islands the European culture contact was mediated by Pacific influences. The strong presence of South Sea Islanders in Torres Strait transformed the lives of local indigenous people and eventually helped to heighten the difference between them and mainland Aborigines. South Sea Islanders were considered, and considered themselves to be, superior to Australian indigenes. Because of missionary and trading activities in the Pacific, they had a whole generation of direct experience with the European cash economy ahead of the Australian indigenous people—they 'knew the value of money', that is, they were already socialised into a European work ethic. In Torres Strait, they formed a power elite dominating the indigenous people.

Several South Sea Islanders who arrived in Torres Strait as pearl-shell industry workers settled permanently in Torres Strait. At Darnley Island in 1908 an estimated 200 out of 230 residents were South Sea Islanders and their descendants. Some became political leaders, such as the Nona family on Badu Island.

Not only South Sea Islanders settled in Torres Strait and 'went native'. White bêche-de-mer captains, too, formed local dynasties by procreation, employing their sons and in-laws in the industry. Edward Mosby ('Yankee Ned'), a whaler from Boston, arrived in Torres Strait in 1871 as a seaman and became the partner in a pearl-shell venture in 1873. He settled on Yorke Island in partnership with Jack Walker, to run a bêche-de-mer station for which they leased half the island. Douglas Pitt from Jamaica also arrived in 1871 and started a bêche-de-mer station on Murray Island with partners Doyle and Bruce. (J. S. Bruce arrived on Murray Island in 1886 and was appointed government teacher by Douglas in 1892.) Jardine referred to the recent 'undesirable addition of two West Indian blacks' who had settled on Murray Island and had 'already become a terror to the natives of the smaller islands' by taking women and forcing them to work on the station.[32] By marrying into the local communities such newcomers immersed themselves into relationships of reciprocal obligations and could command a labour force for their stations. Today's Torres Strait Islanders frequently refer to their recent genealogy: 'On Stephen Island we had Morrison, Pearson, and Kennell, a Scotchman, and Mosby. They were pearl-seekers and pearl-traders who stayed on the islands and lived with the people, and we are the seeds come up'.[33]

The sexual politics of the bêche-de-mer captains and missionary teachers turned to the advantage of Torres Strait Islanders when it came to defending themselves against paternalistic rule by the Queensland government. They were recognised as an ethnic identity separate from mainland Aborigines.

Labour requirements

A differentiated view of ethnic groups was well within the interest of the station managers, because the industry developed differentiated labour requirements. As early as 1871, an experimental diving apparatus was introduced into the Torres Strait fishery, which permitted diving to depths of 15 fathoms (27.4 m). By 1874 several luggers had been fitted with pumps in order to gain access to more shell as the shallower beds accessible to swimming-divers became depleted, and in 1877 63 out of 109 vessels at Thursday Island were equipped for dress-diving.[34]

The introduction of dress-diving created a new type of hierarchy on the luggers. The entire workday was organised around the single diver who was also the captain of the lugger. A stand-by diver, or second diver, was second in command. Next in line was the tender, then the cook and deckhands. While the diver was precariously submerged, his life depended on the vigilance of the tender, and their relationship needed to be one of trust. It became the practice, therefore, to recruit divers and tenders from the same ethnic background for each lugger. This arrangement gave rise to various arguments concerning the relative utility of different ethnic groups.

Dress-diving required fewer divers, but since productivity depended largely on the divers, these had to be better trained and more highly motivated than swimming-divers. The industry could no longer avail itself of a numerous, unskilled and casual workforce; it now needed a skilled and reliable workforce of divers supported by unskilled crew. This led to a hierarchy of employment according to the degree of skill required. This shift in labour needs did not present itself as a radical departure, though, because indigeneous swimming-divers continued to be employed both for pearl-shell and bêche-de-mer gathering on shallow grounds.

At first the new diving technique raised the level of production enough to provide high wages. White divers were employed and some of the station managers themselves donned the diving dress. Pacific Islanders, Maoris, and four or five Norfolk Islanders were also employed as divers. They were paid by the 100 shell and claimed any pearls found as an additional incentive.

> White divers only worked until they could buy their own boats, or some went away to buy farms. They were mostly Scandinavians and other foreigners, and there were some good chaps from New South Wales. They had nothing when they started. I also taught some miners from Cloncurry and Croydon to dive . . . I got men who were hard up, and could not get away from here, and they did very well, as a rule.[35]

As shell in the easily accessible locations became scarcer it became more difficult and therefore less profitable to gather it. Asian divers were introduced from the Philippines and Dutch East Indies ('Manillamen' and 'Malays'). Filipinos were considered very suitable, but the Philippines had their own pearl-shell industry, and recruiting was not always satisfactory. Coloured divers and tenders were under indenture agreements. Paid at lower rates than whites, they were much cheaper to employ. One pearl-sheller employed white tenders at a regular wage of £4 a month, so that they had a guaranteed income, whereas coloured tenders, mainly Malays, received £3 10s a ton. John Bleakley estimated that white divers made no less than £100 and up to £250 a year, whereas a Manilla diver might not make £20.[36] Elsewhere the annual income of a white diver was estimated to have been as high as £400 or £500 a year plus windfall profits from pearls.

After 1876 a few Japanese were recruited from Singapore and Hong Kong, and when pearl-shellers started to recruit directly in Japan in the 1880s, Japanese became the preferred labour force and began to become increasingly dominant, not only numerically but hierarchically, appropriating the more responsible roles on the luggers as tenders and divers. The preponderance of Japanese from the 1890s meant also that the great variety of nationalities initially employed in the pearl-shell industry, which gave Thursday Island the reputation as the 'sink of the Pacific', gave way to a more clearly ethnically stratified labour force, consisting mainly of Japanese, Torres Strait Islanders, and Aborigines.[37]

It is quite misleading to say, as Gaynor Evans does in a study of race relations at Thursday Island, that representatives of every ethnic group 'were employed in the fisheries as divers, men-in-charge and boats' crews, without any distinction', and plainly false to assume that employment on boats 'presented the complete antithesis of occupational stratification along racial lines'.[38] From the 1890s, labour relations ossified into the three ethnic groups dealt with in this book. Until World War II, these groups remained clearly stratified into occupational niches within the industry, and this stratification was popularly recognised and institutionally sanctioned.

South Sea Islanders occupied an intermediate position between Japanese and Torres Strait Islanders. Papuans were used as a supplement to Aboriginal labour, sharing their occupational niche with Aborigines; and Malayans were introduced intermittently to break the hold of Japanese on the diving positions. These practices did not amount to a breakdown in the pattern of ethnic stratification: they underpinned it. One of the Burns Philp managers expressed this policy quite candidly:

> it would be very bad policy to man all boats by Japs as we then have no foil to play against them: by all means keep two or three crack Manilla men even if they do not pay us as well as the Jap hirers. It was only by putting a Manilla-man into the *Cissy* and threatening to do likewise with other boats that I induced the Japs to accept my improved hiring agreement of January, 1897.[39]

In 1886 there were about thirty-four white divers in Torres Strait (the fleet consisted of about 200 boats). After a boom in 1891–92, pearl-shell prices fell sharply and the white divers drifted out of the industry. In 1897, only seven were left of a total of 272 divers licensed in that year. The reasons given for their departure were the dangers of diving, their intemperance, discontent with the arduous and monotonous work, the declining profitability of diving because of scarcity of shell, and the competition from cheaper alien labour.

The departure of white divers from the industry, and their eventual replacement with indentured Japanese, marks a step in the shift to mass production. Island stations, based on the personal authority of station managers over a pool of unskilled non-white labour, were replaced by fleets with a more clearly defined hierarchy of functional differentiation. This functional differentiation coincided with ethnic boundaries. The introduction of Asian dress-divers meant that the indigenous workers already employed did not progress to positions of responsibility in the industry, and until after World War II Aborigines, Torres Strait Islanders, and New Guineans were recruited only for swimming-diving and rarely as dress-divers.

Pearl-shellers' access to government

In the sparsely settled far North, the distinction between government officers and businesspeople was obscured. Many offices at Thursday Island were only fractional appointments with minor emoluments (the first postmaster received £24 a year). Often local pearl-shellers were entrusted with such offices as shipping master or pearl-shell inspector, or officers stationed at Thursday Island developed a personal interest in pearl-shelling. Legal and industrial disputes were also settled by the pearl-shellers. According to a report in 1897, it was 'next to impossible to find on Thursday Island justices who are not more or less directly interested in pearl-shelling'.[40]

Between 1868 and 1885, the northern outpost (which was shifted from Albany Island to Somerset to Thursday Island) had three police magistrates (Government Residents) of any permanency, all of whom took up pearl-shelling. Henry Chester, while waiting for a passage south after leaving his position as police magistrate (1869–70), tried his luck at trading for pearl-shell and bêche-de-mer with Badu Islanders and employed fifteen Prince of Wales Islanders to dive for pearl-shell. Frank Jardine, the police magistrate at Somerset (1868–69, 1870–73), began in 1872 to use government vessels for private pearl-shelling until his practice came to the notice of the Colonial Secretary. He resigned before the matter was pursued, and continued his station first on Nagir Island and then at Somerset. He also continued to serve as justice of the peace.[41] Charles E. Beddome, who had two brief appointments (police magistrate at Somerset 1873–74, Government Resident at Thursday Island, 1877) ran five boats on Jardine's lease at Nagir Island in 1875.

Several of Jardine's official staff, who had been employed for pearl-shelling, became pearl-shellers in their own right. E. L. Brown was employed by Jardine while drawing entitlements as sergeant of water police (£104), government storekeeper (£20) coxwain (£20) and policeman (£208) until 1873. In 1875 a lugger was registered in his name at Somerset, probably still in association with Jardine. In 1877 he signed a pearl-shellers' petition, and in the following year was appointed as postmaster. He later became a Torres Strait pilot and a storekeeper on Thursday Island. Captain C. Pennefather, who in-spected Torres Strait as lieutenant-commander on the government schooner *Pearl*, enforcing compliance with protective legislation, had up to four apparatus boats registered in his name (one of them the *Crinoline*), and Pennefather also signed a petition with other pearl-shellers in 1877 requesting concessions for the industry. Captain Wilkie, another of Jardine's staff since 1873, became a Torres Strait pilot in 1877, and was subsequently appointed as shipping master. He was still pearl-shelling in 1882. Edward Hamon, the pearl-shell inspector, also had a pearl-shelling station on Darnley Island.

It is not surprising, therefore, that the advice received by the Queensland government from its officials at Thursday Island nor-mally closely mirrored the demands of the pearl-shellers. In 1885 John Douglas, the former Premier of Queensland, who had been instrumental in establishing the northern outpost, became Govern-ment Resident at Thursday Island. He stayed in office until 1904 and exerted considerable influence over policy decisions affecting the industry. He was not directly involved in pearl-shelling, but was a strong champion of the industry's views, since the outpost depended solely on the fishery. He actively encouraged the pearl-shellers of the island stations to settle on Thursday Island, which now became the headquarters of the industry:

> Within a few years many pearling companies gravitated in from the various island bases. Names synonymous with T.I. history began to ap-pear—Jim Clark (the Pearl King), Reg Hockings (Wanetta Co.), Tommy Farquhar from New Zealand, W. R. Carpenter, Paddy Doyle, Fred Morey, Jack Cowling, E. J. Hennessey, Cleveland and Vigden.[42]

Douglas advocated a system of local government to administer the pearl-shell and bêche-de-mer fishery, which would formalise the political muscle of pearl-shellers:

> I have always thought it desirable to have some form of self-government amongst the shellers themselves—that they should arrange matters in the form of regulations, after due deliberation amongst themselves, in the same way that the divisional boards do . . . The shellers might easily form amongst themselves an advising committee, and their recommendation would go a long way towards the adopting of them . . . I do not see why they should not be able to frame by-laws with power to enforce them. It is conceivable that a system applicable on land might be applied to an industry afloat.

The franchise would be restricted to pearl-shellers holding boat licences: 'I hardly think the fact that a man is employed would entitle him. I should imagine, if any attempt was made to apply the principle, the licensees would be the constituency'.[43] The scheme did not have the support of pearl-shellers, who were divided between shore-station owners and floating-station owners, but pearl-shellers continued to be the dominant force in local politics. The last mayor of Thursday Island, Jack Dunwoodie, was manager for Bowden's pearling company.

The large companies were vast commercial empires in themselves, with direct access to government, such as Aplin Brown & Crawshay and Burns Philp, the two giants of coastal trade. Aplin and Brown became members of Queensland's legislative assembly, and Robert Philp, who entered State politics in 1886, became Premier (1899–1903). He fiercely defended the industry's continued access to cheap indentured labour.

The role of policy in labour market segmentation

It was largely due to the excesses and abuses in the marine industry that increasingly paternalistic protective legislation was passed in Queensland. From extracts of official reports it will be seen that the government's management of various ethnic groups was guided by the Darwinian doctrine of a unilinear map of social evolution. Social Darwinism refers to the hierarchical ranking of races on the basis of aggregate biological differences. Relative superiority was measured in terms of proximity to Western civilisation on a range of biological and social indicators. These indicators were, most importantly, sedentarism and agriculturalism but also characteristics such as single-deity religion, the wearing of clothes, monogamous marriage and warlike conflict resolution. The degree of protection required was measured against the position of an ethnic group on this 'race ladder'.

Different sets of rules governing different ethnic groups magnified cultural differences as criteria of employability. Moreover, by placing a check on the recruitment and employment of labour, protective policies restricted the liberty not only of employers but of employees as well. And since it embedded Social Darwinist principles, legislation was most stringent in regard to those who occupied the lowest rungs on this evolutionary ladder in the European consciousness. Aborigines were left little incentive to participate in the industry. Not surprisingly, they were found to be generally unreliable and often unwilling workers. Racist notions became a self-fulfilling prophecy, and race relations became empirically indistinguishable from class relations.[44]

I argue that indigenous involvement in the fishery was shaped by the dialectical process of accommodation on the part of Aboriginal people, and the role of public policy in the allocation of ethnic groups into separate niches of a segmented labour market. This perspective owes much to the recent literature which is conscious of the active construction of a unified concept of Aboriginality (through cultural, scholarly and political conventions) and to critiques of the 'fatal impact' historiography of culture contact that has tended to portray indigenous people as the passive victims of colonisation. A more differentiated approach acknowledges that the pattern of contact varied across geographical regions (rainforests, coastal areas) and between industries (gold-mining, pastoralism), and produced various strategies of accommodation.[45]

Marking differences: the case of South Sea Islanders

The first ethnic group to become the subject of specific protective legislation were South Sea Islanders. As a result of humanist protests in Britain against abuses in the labour trade, the British imperial government passed the Pacific Islanders Protection Act 1872 (Kidnapping Act). At the same time Queensland's jurisdiction was extended to cover all islands within 60 miles from Cape York, to permit the colonial government to regulate the pearl-shell industry. Those Islanders north of 10th degree latitude (see Map 1, p. x) were considered natives under the Kidnapping Act ('not under the influence of any civilized power').[46]

The pearl-shell and bêche-de-mer fishery was strongly involved in the labour trade. In response to the labour shortage slave markets developed as close to home as the Aru Islands of New Guinea. An inspection by Captain Moresby in 1871 revealed that on one boat South Sea Islanders had been working for six years, just for clothing and tobacco, and only nine out of twenty were on the ship's articles: 'imported native divers were detained there [on Torres Strait fishing stations] beyond their stipulated period of service, and so ill-fed as to be driven to make raids on the supplies of the native inhabitants'.[47]

The 1872 Kidnapping Act drew the first significant legislative distinction between Pacific Islanders and Queensland indigenes. The Kidnapping Act only required that recruiting vessels be specially licensed and that a bond be entered for the licence in order to prevent 'the decoying of Pacific Islanders without their consent'. It did not specify the form of that consent. The legislation was vague and did not put an end to abuses, and inspectors found it difficult to pin charges. But several convictions were made and some vessels impounded. Steve Mullins suggests that as a result employers became somewhat wary of employing South Sea Islanders and had more recourse to local labour. That may be so, but the Act initially made no provision to employ South Sea Islanders at sea except as crew of the vessel, so that pearl-shellers were effectively barred from recruiting South Sea Islanders as well as most Torres Strait Islanders. In 1875 the Act was amended to permit such employment.

In 1879 Queensland's border was extended over the whole of Torres Strait, so that the fishery, including the bêche-de-mer stations on the eastern islands, could be regulated. Thomas de Hoghton conducted a tour of inspection of the fishery in 1879 on the *Beagle*. He gave a favourable review of the industry, suggesting that apart from the South Sea Islanders dominating the eastern islands, the industry did not require supervision. Regarding the labour trade, he argued that 'green hands' were not found as desirable in the industry as experienced seamen. Most were engaged in Sydney and were already experienced in seafaring. It is useful to remember that Thursday Island officials, who supplied such information, were themselves engaged in the fishery at this time. Mullins points out that at Thursday Island more concern was expressed about the indolence of South Sea Islanders than about their oppression. They organised their first labour strike in 1872, and in 1877 Chester reported that there was 'still a tendency on the part of the South Sea Islanders to combine to refuse duty'.[48] Pearl-shellers used this 'high state of civilization' of South Sea Islanders as a bargaining tool to lobby against restrictive legislation. They sought to reserve pools of cheap labour by emphasising distinctions between ethnic groups. A blunt statement, made by a departmental commission in 1897, reveals the place which South Sea Islanders occupied on the conceptual map of race hierarchies:

> It is not considered desirable to perpetuate the differentiation between Polynesians employed in pearl-shelling and other nationalities besides 'native labourers'. Polynesians have hitherto formed the intermediate class between the two extremes of intelligent aliens and dense-headed Binghis.[49]

This view allowed for upward mobility for South Sea Islanders, so that they could be used to displace Asians at a time when Japanese were becoming a well-organised labour force with wage-bargaining power, while at the same time creating a niche for Aborigines to take up the lowest positions in the industry.

Queensland's *Pacific Islanders Protection Act 1880* paid much greater attention to detail than the Kidnapping Act and offered more protection by specifying what medical attention, provisions, and space were to be provided on the transporting vessels. However, it again specifically excluded Pacific Island labourers imported for the pearl-shell and bêche-de-mer fisheries. South Sea Islanders in the fishery were therefore not subject to restrictive regulation. Pearl-shellers had successfully defended the fishery from the first legislative infringements.

A further piece of legislation (the Pearl-Shell and Bêche-de-Mer Fisheries Bill) was about to be introduced. It was not aimed primarily at the protection of labour but at authorising the Queensland government to regulate the industry and get some revenue from it through licensing of boats and divers. For this purpose it required that all labour be signed on in Queensland under written agreements. Again, pearl-shellers insisted on a distinction between ethnic groups. They argued that it was unnecessary to protect the interests of South Sea Islanders by signing them on in Queensland because the class of Polynesian labourers so employed in the Fisheries are mostly seamen who have served in the trade for many years, and who being in a high state of civilization are thoroughly acquainted with, and accustomed to, and satisfied with the conditions of their service . . . Moreover, the services rendered by them [are] in most cases . . . of a skilled and peculiar nature, for which they are specially adapted.[50]

This kind of argument—the identification of skills attributed to racial groups—characterised employment strategies in the industry.

The distinction between Torres Strait Islanders and mainland Aborigines

The position of Torres Strait Islanders on the scale of races was the subject of much consideration. Torres Strait Islanders were of Melanesian origin and experienced a significant cultural and social infiltration from the Pacific Islands as a result of both missionary penetration and the activities of the pearl-shell industry. In particular the villagers of the eastern Torres Strait islands, that is those from Murray, Darnley, Stephens and also Warrior islands, had earned a certain respect from the colonisers as a result of a series of attacks on European ships.[51] In 1791 the *Pandora* was attacked by Warrior and Erub islanders, and in 1792 the *Providence* and *Assistance* under Captains Bligh and Flinders were attacked at Warrior Island. In 1793 two British whalers, *Chesterfield* and *Shah Hormuzeer*, were attacked at Darnley Island. Darnley islanders told the missionary Steve McFarlane that a shore party of sailors were polluting their only water supply with soap and dirty clothes. Six offenders were killed and two escaped to Timor, but in reprisal Captains Alt and Bampton organised the destruction of 135 huts and 16 large canoes (15–21 m long) and sugar-cane plantations. Henry Chester wrote in 1870 that Warrior Island was avoided by bêche-de-mer vessels 'on account of the ferocity of its inhabitants', until trepang became so scarce that the initial scruples were overcome in 1868.

On several of the Torres Strait islands, particularly the volcanic islands, gardens were maintained and as a result of their recognisably sedentary and agricultural lifestyle, combined with a warrior-like reputation, Torres Strait Islanders took a higher place than their Aboriginal and Papuan neighbours on the 'evolutionary scale':

These people are strongly differentiated from our own mainland aborigines on the one hand and from the Papuans of New Guinea on the other, and, while in some respects approximating to some islanders of the South Seas, they still retain a marked ethnic individuality of their own . . . As contrasted with our mainland aborigines they present a type of humanity advanced several stages in mental evolution beyond that reached by their continental cousins, as is evidenced by their habit of living in houses in settled communities, of cultivating the soil, and by their skill in agriculture, in the construction and navigation of canoes, and by the use of bow and arrow . . . It is not necessary to say more to show the difference between the two races and to make clear the fact that different methods of management are requisite in dealing with them.[52]

Torres Strait culture was more comprehensible to Europeans than that of Aborigines, and therefore more highly respected. Beginning with the earliest accounts, the difference between mainland Aborigines and Torres Strait Islanders had been expressed in terms of relative superiority:

In their intellectual qualities and dispositions [the Aborigines] were still further removed from the islanders, and much below those of Murray and Darnley Islands. Houseless and homeless, without gardens, or any kind of cultivation, destitute of the cocoa-nut, the bamboo, the plaintain, and the yam, as of almost all useful vegetables, they pass their lives either in the search for food, or in listless indolence.[53]

Australian Aborigines together with Papuans were assigned the lowest position on this evolutionary scale, distinctly below Torres Strait Islanders, some of whom had gardens and villages. Torres Strait Islanders were more akin to Melanesians who 'could be taught to settle down and cultivate the soil'. Under the influence of missionary and trading contacts, Torres Strait Islanders moved closer towards the latter group in terms of their 'evolutionary ranking', but other factors intervened in the translation of this 'rise' from Darwinist ideology into employment practice.

Labour market segmentation closely mirrored this hierarchical classification of races. Aborigines were employed mostly for bêche-de-mer fishing and curing, that is as swimming-divers and on shore stations. They earned 10s–12s a month, and were engaged for twelve months. Torres Strait Islanders were employed as deckhands and swimming-divers on pearling luggers and paid at a higher rate than Aborigines and Papua New Guineans. A 1926 regulation under the Aborigines Protection Act stipulated a higher minimum wage for Torres Strait Islanders than for Aborigines employed in the pearl-shell and bêche-de-mer industry: Torres Strait Islanders were to receive a minimum of £3 15s a month with food, Aborigines £2 5s a month with food, tobacco and specified clothing, and for Sunday work, Torres Strait Islanders were to receive 7s 6d and mainland Aborigines 5s.[54]

For several years, the largest pearling company, Burns Philp, relied entirely on Papua New Guineans as crew, with Japanese as divers, tenders and cooks. Because they were far away from home, they were less likely than Aborigines and Torres Strait Islanders to abscond, so that they were considered more reliable. Torres Strait Islanders, moreover, had 'an inflated idea of their own value' since they had their own luggers.[55] Papuans were under separate protection regulations, and an 1889 ordinance limited their recruitment. They came from the coastal areas of Mawatta in the Western Division, between the Binaturi and Bamu Rivers. It cost 2s to sign them on and 2s to take them outside the Possession. They were engaged and paid off in Daru by the shipping inspector and were paid £1 a month plus clothing and tobacco. They, too, did not enter into the career structure. Pearl-shellers testified that 'New Guinea natives don't have the heart to be good divers'.[56] Even after twenty years of participation it was asserted that 'their sorcery beliefs agitate against them being good divers, if one man was knocked out, they would all knock off'.[57] Such summary statements about different ethnic groups were often enough repeated to become unchallengeable.

Formalising differences: protective legislation

The *Pearl-Shell and Bêche-de-Mer Fisheries Act 1881* required that both Polynesians and indigenous labourers were employed under written agreements, but in 1884 regulations for Australian indigenous people were tightened. The *Native Labourers' Protection Act 1884* was passed exclusively for the purpose of protecting indigenes of Australia and New Guinea employed in the marine industries. It required native labourers to be signed on and paid off before the shipping master, and to be returned home after a maximum term of twelve months. Torres Strait Islanders, Aborigines and Papuans were now clearly more restricted in their employment than South Sea Islanders. Aborigines particularly resented being taken far away from home, to Thursday Island or Cooktown, to be signed on and off according to the new legislation.

Thirteen years later the Queensland government passed the *Aborigines Protection and Prevention of the Sale of Opium Act 1897*. It officially represented the assumption of state responsibility for a 'dying race'. The Act was concerned with the prohibition of opium and alcohol. It also provided for the setting up of indigenous reserves and the creation of districts supervised by Protectors of Aborigines. It required permits to be obtained from the Protector to allow the employment of Aborigines, and practically declared Aborigines of Queensland wards of the state.

The timing of the 1897 Act owed much to Archibald Meston, who had prepared a report as Special Commissioner, suggesting three radical measures: the abolition of the Native Police, the prohibition of employing indigenous people in the bêche-de-mer industry, and the segregation of all non-employed Aborigines in large central reserves. Upon the submission of Meston's controversial report, the Commissioner of Police, W. Parry-Okeden, made a hasty tour of the North and relied largely on the advice of local government officers to recommend a mediation of Meston's proposals.[58] Both reports made extensive reference to abuses of indigenous labour in the pearl-shell and particularly in the bêche-de-mer industry.

It was intended to place further restrictions on the employment of indigenes in the fishing industry, but the officials concerned with the pearl-shell industry quickly moved to protect the pearl-shellers' access to labour by emphasising the distinction between mainland Aborigines and Torres Strait Islanders. When the Act was introduced, it did not make specific reference to indigenous employment in the fishing industries—a further victory for the pearl-shellers. The Colonial Secretary justified this lacuna with reference to a pending inquiry into the industry. This inquiry, headed by John Hamilton, was extremely well disposed towards the northern entrepreneurs (see pp. 172ff.) and argued that 'Murray Islanders and the natives of other Straits islands need no inclusion among the "native labourers" specially safeguarded by law. They are quite as intelligent as Polynesians, and fully understand the nature of a shipping agreement'.[59]

In Western Australia the employment of women on pearl-shell and bêche-de-mer vessels was prohibited under the Pearl-Shell Fisheries Act of 1871. In Queensland this prohibition had not yet been enshrined in law, but Douglas had implemented local restrictions against signing on women and children. He had also limited work agreements to six months and accepted only those agreements which had been 'passed' by the officer in charge of police, or, in the case of recruits from Mapoon, by missionary Hey. Exploiting the lacuna left by the new Protection Act, pearl-shellers succeeded in having these restrictions declared *ultra vires* in 1897.

When Walter Roth was appointed as Northern Protector of Aborigines, he fully confirmed the earlier reports by Meston and Parry-Okeden about malpractices in the fishery. A 1901 amendment to the Protection Act was passed with a view to better protection of indigenous people in the pearl-shell industry. It stipulated a minimum monthly wage of 10s for Aborigines employed on a vessel and 5s for those employed elsewhere. It prohibited the employment of women and children on boats, and Aborigines were no longer allowed to leave the territorial waters of Queensland, so that they were not allowed to be taken on bêche-de-mer cruises to the outer Barrier Reef. It also required a written permission from the Protector to visit Aboriginal camps, in order to check Japanese recruiting at unsupervised camps along the coast. These Protection Acts placed considerable limitations on Aboriginal participation in the marine industry. They were no longer at liberty to negotiate the terms of their employment.

Torres Strait Islanders were exempted from the Protection Act. Their exemption was due largely to the influence of John Douglas, the Government Resident at Thursday Island (1885–1904). Douglas insisted on the superior qualities of Torres Strait Islanders, and Chief Protector Roth endorsed this view: Torres Strait Islanders were 'of a somewhat superior race to mainland natives, and better able to look after themselves'.[60]

Only after the death of Douglas in 1904 were Torres Strait Islanders gradually drawn under the Act, but a distinction between Torres Strait Islanders and Aborigines was maintained by departmental policy. When the local Protector began to take charge of the earnings of Torres Strait Islanders, the department acquired a direct interest in maintaining a minimum wage rate, particularly since indigenous labour was much sought after. In 1904 a minimum wage was set at 2s 6d a week for Torres Strait Islanders, and in 1907 this minimum wage had reached 11s (12s for experienced hands). It was not until 1914 that a State-wide graduated minimum wage was introduced for all indigenous people. In 1919 the minimum wage for Torres Strait Islanders in the marine industry was from £3 to £4 10s a month, whereas wages for Aborigines started at £1 10s.

The differences between Torres Strait Islanders and Aborigines were indeed significant—but so were differences between mainland groups. In this instance, however, it suited the industry to draw a distinction clearly. The difference between mainland Aborigines and Torres Strait Islanders became magnified by different management policies, and was finally embedded in law in 1939.[61] When introducing two separate bills for the administration of Aborigines and Torres Strait Islanders, the Minister for Health and Home Affairs addressed the crucial difference between them—Torres Strait Islanders had not been displaced from their land:

> We propose to deal with the Torres Strait islanders under an entirely separate Act because they have proved that they are capable of doing a great deal for themselves and do not need the strict control that is exercised over the mainland aboriginals . . . I have been requested by the islanders to have them taken from the jurisdiction of the protectors under the Aboriginals Protection and Restriction of the Sale of Opium Act, as they object to being regarded as aboriginals. There are social grades even there, the islander regarding himself as being superior to the mainland aboriginal. The question whether our mainland aboriginal would not have done as well as the islander if he had been given the same opportunity is a matter of opinion, but the islander has had greater advantages than the mainland aboriginal, inasmuch as his territory has been preserved to him. All of those islands are reserves upon which no white man can trespass without the permission of the protector of aboriginals, and, consequently, the islander has had his garden and fishing left to him, while the mainlander has had his natural means of living taken from him.[62]

With the introduction of the 1897 Protection Act, and the exemption of Torres Strait Islanders from its provisions, clear distinctions were now drawn between South Sea Islanders, Torres Strait Islanders, and mainland Aborigines. Their employment was governed by different sets of restrictions.

Aborigines in the pearl-shell industry

It is difficult to assess the number of Aborigines employed in the pearl-shell and bêche-de-mer industry. Estimates at various times either did not distinguish between them and Torres Strait Islanders, or referred to all work permits issued irrespective of type of employment, or referred only to the bêche-de-mer industry; and only those legally signed on appeared in the returns. For instance, in 1898, Chief Protector Roth estimated that 300 Aborigines were employed all told, but the Government Resident's report indicated that 300 were signed on to articles at Thursday Island alone, just for the bêche-de-mer industry, so that the figure would be much greater when those on pearl-shell boats, those signed on in Cooktown, and those casually employed, were taken into account. In 1902 about 580 Aborigines were signed on for the industry in Cooktown and Thursday Island. For 1908, 141 Aborigines were signed on officially in the bêche-de-mer industry at Cooktown and Thursday Island, and in 1915, 537 Aborigines were in the bêche-de-mer and trochus industry.[63] In 1916, 699 Aborigines were engaged by the Thursday Island fleets. The indications are that from 1902 to 1916 at least, more than 500 mainland Aborigines officially participated in the fishery. There was, at any rate, considerable pressure on the coastal Aborigines on Cape York to participate.

Some Aboriginal groups (like those at Albatross Bay) responded to the onslaught of the industry by habitually hiding women and children at the approach of strangers, while others were more receptive to the commodities that could be obtained from intercourse with whites and hired out young members of the group to bêche-de-mer captains, to be engaged or for prostitution. Meston observed that the Mapoon residents were polygamous and it has been suggested that old male Aborigines welcomed the chance to send their younger competitors away on a lugger.[64]

Aborigines were mostly engaged in the bêche-de-mer fishery, a low-technology, labour-intensive activity. Bêche-de-mer was gathered from reefs by swimming-diving or 'dry picking' (reef-wading at low tide), and the fish had to be gutted and smoke-cured the same day. This was done on islands on the reef, where itinerant trepang camps were set up. The bêche-de-mer fishery was more decentralised than pearl-shelling, and more difficult to supervise. Aborigines were also recruited for trochus-collecting, which became part of the pearl-shelling industry after 1912.

There are ample descriptions of outrages in the early government reports from Thursday Island and Cooktown. Women and even 6-year-old children were set to work. Teenagers were preferred because they were more manageable and in some instances a minor slave traffic developed.[65] In 1884 about half of the 500 men and boys employed in the bêche-de-mer fishery on Murray, Darnley and Yorke islands were mainland Aborigines, many of them had been

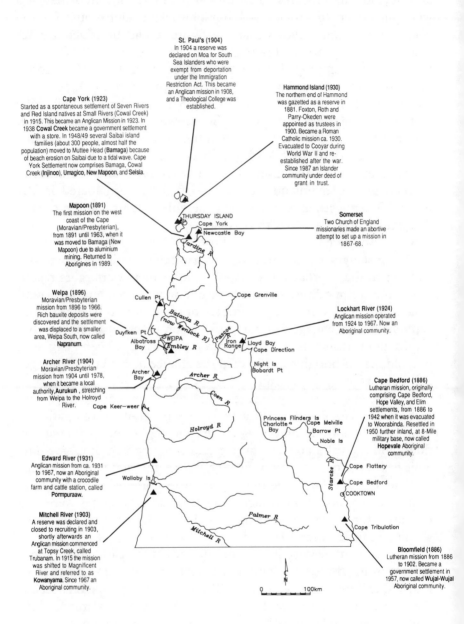

St. Paul's (1904)
In 1904 a reserve was declared on Moa for South Sea Islanders who were exempt from deportation under the Immigration Restriction Act. This became an Anglican mission in 1908, and a Theological College was established.

Hammond Island (1930)
The northern end of Hammond was gazetted as a reserve in 1881. Foxton, Roth and Parry-Okeden were appointed as trustees in 1900. Became a Roman Catholic mission ca. 1930. Evacuated to Cooyar during World War II and re-established after the war. Since 1987 an Islander community under deed of grant in trust.

Cape York (1923)
Started as a spontaneous settlement of Seven Rivers and Red Island natives at Small Rivers (Cowal Creek) in 1915. This became an Anglican Mission in 1923. In 1938 **Cowal Creek** became a government settlement with a store. In 1948/49 several Saibai island families (about 300 people, almost half the population) moved to Muttee Head (**Bamaga**) because of beach erosion on Saibai due to a tidal wave. Cape York Settlement now comprises Bamaga, Cowal Creek (**Injinoo**), Umagico, New Mapoon, and Seisia.

Mapoon (1891)
The first mission on the west coast of the Cape (Moravian/Presbyterian), from 1891 until 1963, when it was moved to Bamaga (New Mapoon) due to aluminium mining. Returned to Aborigines in 1989.

Somerset
Two Church of England missionaries made an abortive attempt to set up a mission in 1867-68.

Weipa (1896)
Moravian/Presbyterian mission from 1896 to 1966. Rich bauxite deposits were discovered and the settlement was displaced to a smaller area, Weipa South, now called **Napranum.**

Lockhart River (1924)
Anglican mission operated from 1924 to 1967. Now an Aboriginal community.

Archer River (1904)
Moravian/Presbyterian mission from 1904 until 1978, when it became a local authority, **Aurukun** , stretching from Weipa to the Holroyd River.

Cape Bedford (1886)
Lutheran mission, originally comprising Cape Bedford, Hope Valley, and Elim settlements, from 1886 to 1942 when it was evacuated to Woorabinda. Resettled in 1950 further inland, at 8-Mile military base, now called **Hopevale** Aboriginal community.

Edward River (1931)
Anglican mission from ca. 1931 to 1967, now an Aboriginal community with a crocodile farm and cattle station, called **Pormpuraaw.**

Mitchell River (1903)
A reserve was declared and closed to recruiting in 1903, shortly afterwards an Anglican mission commenced at Topsy Creek, called Trubanam. In 1915 the mission was shifted to Magnificent River and referred to as **Kowanyama.** Since 1967 an Aboriginal community.

Bloomfield (1886)
Lutheran mission from 1886 to 1902. Became a government settlement in 1957, now called **Wujal-Wujal** Aboriginal community.

Map 2   Cape York Peninsula—Aboriginal missions and reserves

kidnapped.[66] Professional recruiters earned up to £4 a head,[67] and Aborigines were often marooned on distant islands, to perish or to sign on again.

The Commissioner of Police gave the following impression of recruiting in 1897: bêche-de-mer captains recruited from Aboriginal camps by distributing flour, tobacco, sugar, tea, calico or alcohol to the elders of a camp. (Most of these commodities were addictive substances, so that further demand was practically guaranteed. Europeans had few qualms about sharing their addictions with indigenous people by disbursing addictive substances as a matter of protective policy: the daily rations prescribed by the *Pacific Islanders Protection Act 1880* included sugar, tea, and tobacco as the minimal necessities of life.) Women and men were then boarded and deposited at some island, while the ship returned to Thursday Island with only a few males to be properly signed on. These had to be signed off again and paid at Thursday Island. All of the recruits were then taken further into the Great Barrier Reef, the Eastern Fields or the Great North-East Channel where a headquarters with a smokehouse was established. The men were sent by dinghy to a sandbank while the women were employed on the station and used as entertainment by the captain, his mate and the cook. Being stranded on an island or sandbank, Aborigines often made desperate attempts to return to their homes after working for a while. Many employers were killed in such escape attempts (between 25 and 30 non-Aborigines were killed by Aborigines in the 1870s, and from 39 to 45 during the 1880s[68]), and many more Aborigines perished because they were unable to command the ship after such mutiny.

Although the reports of the 1890s of the treatment of Aborigines in the marine industry had helped to bring about a shift in policy towards Aborigines, there were no effective enforcement mechanisms until 1901 when the Protectors gained powers to deal with such abuses. Still, some bêche-de-mer stations simply 'escaped the Protector's vigilance' by shifting from shore camps to islands off the coast.

The Aborigines on the Cape were not yet organised on missions and reserves. In the 1870s and 1880s the Queensland government had called on the churches to 'educate the young and protect the old' Aborigines, without committing funds to their efforts, and had generally confined its efforts to declaring 'reserves' (which meant that the land could not be leased and recruiting could be nominally prohibited) and setting up ration depots in the settled areas. The establishment of missions depended on individual initiatives such as that of two missionaries at Somerset in 1867–68.[69] The evangelising efforts became more organised under the umbrella of churches in the mid-1880s. The German Lutherans were expanding into New Guinea and set up three missions in Queensland, one at Bowen and two on the Cape in 1886. Cape Bedford (Hope Valley) and Bloomfield were the first missions on the Cape. The Moravian-Presbyterian church soon followed with an advance along the west coast of the Cape, where Mapoon was established in 1892, Weipa in 1896, and Aurukun in 1904. (See Map 2.)

Missions were notoriously short of funds.[70] They were on poor soil, and government grants of up to £250 a year paid only for rice and flour at Mapoon, whereas Cape Bedford and Bloomfield received no government assistance for several years. The missionaries' attitude towards wage labour on boats was ambivalent. On the one hand, any cash income for the mission was a welcome, and sometimes necessary, contribution; on the other hand, abuses at sea were difficult to check. Yet again, it was thought preferable that recruiting took place where it could be supervised.

During two weeks while the Northern Protector was visiting Mapoon, eleven boats had called on the mission for recruiting. Any earnings were channelled into the upkeep of the mission. For each £3 earned by a resident, he was allowed to draw on the store for 10s and keep 5s as pocket money. The remainder was banked to the credit of the Mapoon Natives' store account. Upon their return, recruits received a standard issue of tobacco, flour, clothes, handkerchief and a tomahawk.

> Having put his wages into the common fund, each boy, as a matter of right, can also draw from the store anything he wants in reason—e.g. fishhooks, lines, turtle-rope, knives, tools, nails, buckets, further supply of clothing and tobacco, and, when he marries, the galvanized iron to roof his house. At Christmas time the store supplies every visitor (including, of course, those from Albatross Bay [Weipa]), with a suit of clothes. Each boy thus learns that he is labouring not only for himself, but for the common good.[71]

By 1900 all Aborigines on the east coast of Cape York were familiar with the industry and recruiters gradually moved further down the west coast of the Cape. The Seven Rivers Aborigines on the west coast north of Mapoon were 'completely dependent on prostitution and had already discarded their hunting weapons'.[72] But those to the south of Mapoon were 'still freed from the abuse and contamination in the way of slavery, disease, alcohol, and opium, and other sources of annihilation consequent on the visits of the recruiters and the hardships endured in employment on the boats'.[73]

In 1901 Reverend Hey at Mapoon prohibited recruiting from the mission.[74] He observed that two-thirds of the young boys who had spent a season on the luggers died within six months of their return. The exposure on the boats, sleeping in wet clothes, led to consumption. The missionaries at Mapoon and Weipa became outspoken opponents of recruiting, and the Northern Protector prohibited recruiting in the area between the two missions. A few years later the protected area was again extended, so that the Mapoon reserve stretched along 240 kilometres of coastline (from 32 kilometres north of Mapoon to the Archer river), but only at the missions themselves could supervision be exercised. Hey had the idea that some income could be generated from gathering black-lip pearl-shell on the beaches,[75] and intended to obtain a cutter for that purpose, but the demand for labour from the pearl-shell industry was heavy, and recruiters and employers complained about the missionaries who sought to 'deprive them of labour'. In response to this pressure, Roth permitted recruiting as far as Albatross Bay (now Weipa) which had become the main recruiting area despite the earlier prohibition. He described the Aborigines between Albatross Bay to south of the Archer River (now Aurukun) as 'myalls' or wild blacks, who were not used to contact with whites and were 'recruited by stratagem' (kidnap and decoy).[76]

Aboriginal labour was a local resource, and as for natural resources, the raiders had to resort to territorial expansion for a continued supply. Aboriginal populations were diminished in number through consumption and other introduced diseases, and Roth referred to the need for opening further areas to recruiting because others had 'become more and more worked out'.[77] The advance into new recruitment areas was led by the bêche-de-mer collectors, who paid lower wages than pearl-shellers (they could not afford to pay more than 10s a month when Aborigines in pearl-shelling were receiving no less than £1 a month). Each time a new area was entered for recruiting, the culture clash was repeated. As a result of this 'frontline' role, the bêche-de-mer industry became 'paralysed' because of the frequent violent attacks on employers in the early

1890s. In 1893 alone, thirteen non-Aborigines were killed in such attacks.[78]

On the east coast, the government facilitated recruiting as much as possible in order to regulate it. A boat-owner could apply for crew at Thursday Island to be made available by the reserve superintendents. For Aborigines, this procedure was not an unmixed blessing. One recruit described it as a case of 'policemen come along and hunt you out; send you out to work'.[79] The Sydney *Daily Herald* made reference to Aborigines being herded up like cattle by police and sent in chain gangs to the pearl-shell fleets.[80]

For many years, pearl-shellers and Protectors clamoured for the establishment of a recruiting station on the east coast. The industry required a convenient access to labour which was legally sanctioned, and the Protectors sought to regulate wages and conditions and to collect the wages owing to Aborigines. There were already four missions on Cape York Peninsula, but much recruiting took place at Aboriginal bush camps off the reserves.[81] The legal requirements were that permission was obtained at Thursday Island or Cooktown to recruit a specified number of Aborigines, who then had to be brought to the courthouse to be legally signed on to the ship's articles. They were signed off again at the expiry of their contract, when they were paid off before the Protector of Aborigines.

When Richard Howard presented his first annual report as Chief Protector of Aborigines in 1906, he suggested that such a recruitment depot would 'once and for all solve the vexed question of native labour on boats engaged in the fishing industries' and end recruiting at Aboriginal camps, which was conducted 'in the most undesirable, pernicious and demoralising manner'.[82] Lloyd Bay was considered an ideal site for a labour depot because it was halfway between Cooktown and Thursday Island, where most east-coast recruiting was taking place. This idea was frequently repeated in annual reports. Lloyd Bay was a popular recruiting spot, and in 1910, when sandalwooding enjoyed a sudden renaissance,[83] 300 Lloyd Bay Aborigines were engaged and three boats were in charge of Aborigines. In 1912 it was reported that 'practically the whole of the labour supply of the North point of the Peninsula and the Torres Strait islands is absorbed by the pearling and beche-de-mer industry'.[84] By 1913, about 350 Aborigines lived permanently at Lloyd Bay, and a Mr Giblett employed twenty-five Aborigines in gathering bêche-de-mer and sandalwood at Lloyd Island.[85]

In 1915 the Chief Protector permitted recruitment between the Archer and Mitchell Rivers on the east coast (whose population had earlier been described as 'myalls') because the demand for Aboriginal labour from the pearl-shell industry was so great. In 1916, forty-two Aborigines from Kendall River (now Aurukun) were engaged for the first time. With the opening up of new recruiting areas, the problems of early contact experience were repeated. Whereas among the experienced recruits desertions had become less frequent, more than half of the Kendall River recruits absconded and were recaptured several times. Five drowned in an attempt to swim from Entrance Island to the mainland. The Chief Protector referred to 'numerous complaints' about alien recruiters (mostly Japanese skippers) who employed Aborigines illegally, abused women, and supplied alcohol to camps.

> If any social progress is to be made by the aboriginal, he will have to be zealously protected from the type of alien usually met with in fishing fleets . . . I would again urge the early establishment of a government recruiting depot to superintend this recruiting and the disbursement of the wages earned, an institution which, if conducted on business lines, should be practically self-maintained.[86]

In 1924, the Church of England jumped into the breach and Lockhart River Mission was finally opened.[87]

Since the departure of Walter Roth as Chief Protector in 1906, the department's policy had changed. His successor Richard Howard felt that 'hitherto in the care of the aborigines much spoonfeeding has been practised', which had encouraged pauperism rather than helped to remove it. Now the prejudice of missionaries against marine work had to be overcome, and all mission residents were encouraged to work outside the missions.[88] Gradually several missions and reserves entered the fishery on their own boats, along similar lines, but on a smaller scale than the lugger scheme which operated in Torres Strait. By 1935 the reserves acted as pools of labour for the industry:

> The labour requirements of the Thursday Island Pearlshellers' Association and private employers were met by the Protector of Aboriginals, Thursday Island, making available such labour as they indicated could be employed on their vessels. The balance, comprising Torres Strait Islanders and coastal natives in the Somerset district, were employed in the Torres Strait Islanders' community vessels . . . An effort is made by the Protector of Aboriginals, Thursday Island, to train natives from the west coast of the peninsula for work in the marine industry.[89]

The aim of training selected mainland Aborigines on the community vessels in Torres Strait was to extend the scheme to the mainland. This was achieved only in 1955, when Father Warby at Lockhart River formed an Aboriginal trochus co-operative with two boats rented and one purchased from the Bishop of Carpentaria.

The Aboriginal perspective

It was almost proverbial that the bêche-de-mer industry attracted 'the lowest class of whites',[90] who used subterfuge, corruption and force to recruit. By associating closely with Aborigines—'an inferior race'—white and Japanese bêche-de-mer captains themselves became 'tainted'. No doubt Aborigines were often exploited, harassed and deceived. But, as Athol Chase observes, any long-standing relationship like that formed between many captains and Aboriginal camps must have been substantially founded on accommodation and acceptance with a degree of mutual benefit. William Saville-Kent commented on the attraction of Aborigines to swimming-diving:

> As previously related, the aborigines from the Queensland mainland are extensively employed in this fishery, undoubtedly one of the few industries in which Australian native labour can be turned to profitable account. The native as a rule does not take kindly to agriculture or to any manual work of a persistent character. To fishing and hunting, however, he is 'to the manner born', and there is not an employment that could be more to his liking than his attachment, accompanied by his wife and piccaninnies, to a liberally-found Bêche-de-mer camp, with comfortable quarters, plenty of 'tucker' and work which is to him almost his natural recreation. The attachment of the aborigines to fishing pursuits is practically demonstrated by the persistence with which the same families, or individuals, will year after year seek re-engagement at the hands of honest employers.[91]

Camp Aborigines developed relationships with particular captains and lit fires to guide the approaching luggers during the recruiting season. One Lockhart River resident gave this account of his recruitment:

> My father took me down to Cape Sidmouth where my mother's country is, because he heard a Japanese lugger was there. We went down and we signed up for crew. My father looked after me on the boat and that Japanese skipper taught me about boatwork. The skipper made a camp at Cape Sidmouth, gave people a lot of flour, tobacco and other things. He was like a friend to that mob. If another skipper came to get a crew, he would say: 'Go away! This is my mob here, I look after them.' That was a long time ago, before that first war.[92]

The normal mode of recruiting from Aboriginal camps involved the distribution of commodities to Aboriginal elders. This ritual exchange, understood as gifts or bribes by Europeans, was more important for camp Aborigines than the wages received at Thursday Island upon discharge. The commodities became a valuable contribution to their economy, and they offered labour in return. Athol Chase and Chris Anderson observe that the elders of a tribe exerted their influence over the younger males to work for the captains with whom they entertained such exchange relationships.[93]

Absconding continued to be a familiar feature of Aboriginal employment on luggers. Because they frequently absconded, sometimes by violent resistance, they gained a reputation as treacherous, unreliable workers, a further justification for their poor wages. One resident of Palm Island had a particular reputation (among Palm Islanders) for absconding from luggers. He used lugger work as the only means to leave the reserve and visit his homeland for a brief spell before the police would again pick him up and return him to Palm Island.[94] Noel Loos refers to this strategy as 'exploiting the exploiters'. Among the more experienced recruits there were those who beat a habitual refugee trail during the 1890s:

> absconders recruited on the west coast of Cape York Peninsula at the Batavia River, ran off with boats and stores on the opposite east coast at Cape Grenville, and made their way back, via the Ducie River, to the Batavia River. There, when they felt so inclined, they would enlist on another boat.[95]

The *Torres Strait Pilot* referred to the 'hallelujah band at the Batavia River' who waited for a 'free cruise to this port and out again to some island, from whence they can elope with a good supply of stores'.[96]

Some recruits devised their own defensive mechanisms against an essentially exploitative condition, but these do not fully account for the practice of absconding. From the Aboriginal viewpoint, working on the lugger was not a contractual relationship which placed recruits under an obligation to work for a specified period. After a period of absence, the recruits started to feel 'ready to go home', and therefore often absconded. If they waited to be discharged formally at Thursday Island or Cooktown, their wages, when brought back to the camp as commodities, were also subject to claims on the basis of kinship obligations.

One recruit from Wujal-Wujal explained absconding as an expression of labour discontent, the routine exercise of workers' discretion: 'My father worked for a Japanese skipper. Some were good, some bad. He had a good skipper. If you had a bad skipper you came back'.[97] Roth had observed that absconding was frequently the result if the skipper for whom they worked was not the one who had recruited them.

One South Sea Islander who absconded together with a group of Lockhart men retrospectively ascribed it to the lure of female company, but Aborigines themselves do not explain it in those terms— the Aboriginal recruits were mostly very young adolescents.[98] Maltreatment, homesickness, and the search for adventure are the reasons frequently given. Jimmie Doctor from Lockhart worked on Farquhar's *Quita* collecting bêche-de-mer and trochus shell under Georgie Kosaka before he absconded.

> I'm sorry to say I left the *Quita* outside Palm Island. We got a dinghy. We were tired of swimming and wanted to go cane-cutting. He was a good skipper but rough, we worked very hard, even in strong winds . . . Three of us ran away, John Mattie and Ned Punda from Lockhart . . . We got to Innisfail and worked on a fishing boat. We sold the dinghy to a farmer to get some money for clothes. They caught us at the wharf in Innisfail, put us in a cell for a week. Then to Cairns, where we stayed overnight, then to TI. We spent two months in jail: no smoke—no work. We had a court case first, Mr Pryor was the government then [the Protector at Thursday Island], not Killoran. Farquhar got the dinghy back.[99]

Homesickness could become a powerful force. One former crew member from Lockhart, Sandy Yiela, rendered a repertoire of island-style songs expressing the sadness of leaving home, sailing past Noble Island—the most distant familiar point of reference— with the outline of family members vanishing from sight. He also described the heartache of an 18-year-old sailing past his home without stopping after a season's work, in order to be signed off at Thursday Island before being allowed to return. He was working on Captain Kono's *Mildred* fishing bêche-de-mer as far south as Townsville for three months. Because it is so descriptive it is rendered here verbatim, unlike the other statements which have been anglicised in transcription.

> Alright, we going to leave now, skipper say, leave today. Morning. About 8 o'clock. Out. Come this way [north], come ready for Christmas. Right up—aah, Cairns. Stay there one night, next day start the same: [indicates

coastline with gestures] come, come, Cooktown, spend there one night—
one night up, morning leave Cairns. Come on, come on, Cape Melville,
go round, right around, Flinders Island, come, come, come, come, come,
long way home right outside, come, until—passed it. Right through coming, right through, right through coming, passed it! Skipper say 'We go
right through to TI. Alright? Happy Christmas then. Don't worry, TI
straightaway first.' Not allowed to get a little bit of finished [rest]. [He]
want to get to TI, you know. We ready for come home, see. We come
in the one boat, right on outside. Back to TI, we finish then, sign off,
we sign there, courthouse, O'Leary.[100]

If a recruit died or absconded, his wages were paid into the
Aborigines Protection Account held by the Protector at Thursday
Island, rather than to his family. (This was intended to protect
Aborigines from ill-treatment and to make sure that they would be
duly returned to their reserve.) All wages due were paid to the local
Protector who banked the money and paid out small amounts if he
approved of the purpose for which it was required and the place
where it would be spent. Protector Costin at Thursday Island felt it
his duty to see that their wages were spent in European-owned shops.
Indigenous workers showed considerable reluctance to have their
wages banked since they were likely to encounter some difficulty in
drawing on their accounts. Their passbooks showed only how much
of their wages they had drawn, not how much credit they had.[101]
One pearl-sheller described how his Aboriginal crew were paid off
at the shipping office:

> They never got a farthing of their money . . . It was put into the bank,
> and, I suppose, it is in the bank yet, because the boys will never call for
> the money . . . I had to promise [them] that, if they came with me, they
> would receive their wages . . . When a boy wants his money he goes to
> the sergeant of police, and very likely the sergeant will give him his boot
> and turn him out. The sergeant has no way of knowing whether the boy
> applying for the money is the boy who has an account in the bank. The
> boys never have the same name half-a-dozen times, and they have no
> book or anything else to show that they have money in the bank.[102]

From Costin's explanation of how he paid out the money it is
apparent that he was concerned to get a receipt to cover himself,
but not that the account-holders had any kind of receipt to prove
their credit: 'To draw on the money they have deposited, I keep on
hand £10 . . . if a native applies for any of his money, I can give it
to him straight away, and get a witnessed receipt from him'.[103]
Aborigines themselves gave these accounts of the procedure: 'We

were discharged with O'Leary at the courthouse in TI . . . We got only a little bit of pocket-money when we signed off, the rest stayed in the bank . . . I brought back rations from TI: flour, rice, sugar, tea—everything'.[104] They knew that their wages were very low, but were not dissatisfied with their earnings, because they could meet their needs with what they received: 'When we got discharged after one year we got big amounts of money . . . We got our money into the passbook and we could ask for £10 or £5, or some of them got less'.[105]

If their families were on missions, a portion of their wages was subtracted for their family's upkeep during their absence. Some Hopevale mission residents only ever worked for the mission boat: 'But we didn't get paid for it. We worked for the whole mission. [The money went towards] McIvor, Cape Bedford and the school. They put the money in the bank, and the mission ordered provisions'.[106]

To be confined to working for the mission was often seen as a lack of opportunity:

As soon as I left school [in 1928] I worked on the mission boat . . . We worked all the reefs that you can see from the plane, Lizard Island, Bloom-field—200 or 300 TI luggers worked there, too . . . Our TI skipper knew all the reefs and how to go about things, the mission employed him. There were no wages those days, not even on TI boats, it all went through DAIA . . . Everybody had to work for their living, not charities like today and governments—it makes the whole society lazy . . . No-one from here [Hopevale] worked on TI luggers . . . We only worked for the mission. Only lately we are allowed to work anywhere. We were segregated. Only during the war did the DAIA break that habit. We didn't know much about the outside world until we went to Woorabinda.[107]

Many Aborigines did not aspire to a career in the marine industry, and attached no privileged status to this work over other types of employment, because of the harsh life at sea. They spent a season on a boat, or worked on a mill or station as opportunity arose. Some, however, did attach a more personal significance to it, and working on a lugger became part of their identity. Sandy Yiela continued his account:

After next year, we still go. We can't work on dry land, you know, we go out in port all the time, everytime in the lugger. Diving, you know. I never learn horse. I learn boat. I don't learn station. I never been learned it. I been learned in a boat till today. 'Cause we diver, you know. Special, you know, some of the boys this local work in a horse-wa, station, but I never learned it, I always learn boat. Same [as the other] old people. Doctor, Michael, me, some older ones, they died now. I always boat. Work on the boat, Japanee. Every year. I not ride horse—[if I tried to] ride horse [it would be] chucking me down on the ground there. (Laughs.) Yeah, I never learned horse, cart-wheel, I never learned bullock, no, nothing, always in the boat. I understand the boat, sea life, how the boat run, the sea, you know, sea, when the sea swell [technical description follows].

Aboriginal interaction with Japanese

Unlike New Guineans and Torres Strait Islanders, who preferred to be engaged in pearl-shelling rather than trepanging, Aborigines did not prefer one type of work over the other. They placed more importance on the captain for whom they worked.[108] Most captains were Japanese, and Aborigines apparently preferred to deal with Japanese: 'When a Japanese is recruiting boys in the north, a European has little or no show of getting any boys'.[109]

Pearl-shellers observed that indigenous crew preferred to make their purchases in Asian-owned shops, and feared that all would abscond if the Japanese captains were replaced by whites.[110] They liked to argue that this was because Japanese distributed alcohol among them, which was prohibited. But the Chief Protector of Aborigines, Walter Roth, found that 'the alien employers, taking them all through, have a greater regard for the care and welfare of the aboriginals than the whites'.[111] When asked about disciplinary action on board, a Japanese diver from Ehime described the relationship between Japanese and Aborigines:

> We treated them like one of the family. Everyone had their own work to do, we didn't have to communicate very much. I was the only one who made any mistakes, anyway, because I was the cook. There was no corporal punishment, only verbal abuse, if something went really wrong. The people on the boat were like one family.[112]

Aborigines and Japanese refer to each other as 'honest', a term that expresses mutual respect. The sailing skills of Japanese skippers have assumed legendary proportions, and Japanese are usually described as 'too smart' for the rest, able to outwit the government and the pearl-shellers. Several names of Japanese captains are still remembered by Aborigines and validated by Japanese. Captain Kono, a bêche-de-mer captain, has almost mythical status. Kono Tesaburo from Ehime is well known among the Japanese divers. He fished illegally in New Caledonian waters, avoiding the regular patrols, and for the Australian indigenous crew, who were not permitted outside Australian borders, a trip with Captain Kono was both adventurous and slightly traumatic. One account of such an excursion was rendered to me in lowered voices, intimating that there were girls for money, and detailing the adventure provided by rough seas and huge waves. Reference was often made to 'Japanee time', to indicate the period when Japanese captains used to come to recruit.[113]

This Aboriginal–Asian camaraderie was specifically addressed by Athol Chase, who described it as a relationship of mutual dependence. The Japanese did not come as colonists competing with Aborigines for land. Like Aborigines, Japanese were subject to racist hostility and political and economic handicaps, and therefore valued a peaceful relationship. According to their own testimony, Aborigines preferred to work with Japanese because they were not 'flash', that is, they were willing to eat and sleep with Aborigines and their word could be trusted, unlike Europeans who were 'cunning' or 'cheeky'. Chase points out that Japanese respected Aboriginal knowledge of the sea, the weather, and bush foods. He analyses the Aboriginal motivation for participating in the industry:

> From the Aboriginal viewpoint, Japanese luggers and shore stations provided . . . the chance to embark on great odysseys to distant places, seeing all manner of strange places and people in a world whose horizons had been considerably expanded . . . Out of this new and exciting rite of passage grew a feeling of self-reliance which cut across the more localised dependencies upon kin and totem.[114]

Aborigines learned the lingua franca which has been called 'Sandalwood English' or colloquially 'beach-la-mar', and adopted Island-style songs and Japanese cooking. Chase says that by participating in the industry, 'cultural as well as geographical horizons had been enlarged'.[115] Sandy Yiela made the same point:

> Swimming and diving keeps you fresh all the time. Japanese gave good tucker. We ate all sorts of Japanese tucker sometimes, but we helped out with turtle, dugong, and mackerel. They look after the boys properly. They used to always ring Jack Dunwoodie at TI for pocket-money. [The fleet manager had to authorise advances to be paid to crew during port visits.] Sometimes people from Lockhart and from the Islands made friends. I've been to Darnley, Murray, Yorke, Yam, Mabuiag, Dauan, Badu, Moa, when I was young. I used to dance with them . . . Islanders and mainlanders used to always fight before. But now a lot intermarried.

Aborigines had good reason to enter into an exchange relationship with lugger captains. But as wards of the state they had little incentive to embark on a career in the industry. Whether they lived on reserves or on camps, the pearl-shell industry did not mean a short period of hard work in order to improve the condition of their families or to achieve social mobility as it did for their Japanese captains. Their wages were fixed by regulation, and handled by the Protector, so that their work afforded them little discretionary spending. The benefits which accrued to them were adventure and enlargement of their social and cultural horizons, and the supply of Western commodities, and did not depend on the type of work they performed. At some camps, elders may have been able to use their influence over younger males to accommodate wage labour into traditional social structures for a while. The supply of otherwise unobtainable commodities was welcomed, and the lure of adventure and the chance of becoming worldly-wise was attractive to young men. But unlike Torres Strait Islanders, Aborigines did not aspire to become tenders and divers as a matter of prestige. Subject to paternalistic legislation and petty regulations, reserve residents were powerless to improve their condition. Sometimes it seemed to them that they were starting to uplift themselves, by working together on a project, such as clearing land for a garden, building houses, or learning trades. It seemed that if they could just put in that extra effort and complete the task at hand, a better life would emerge: a future would be created. Today those elders who were once inspired by the zeal of their missionaries are at a loss to explain the aimlessness of reserve life. Aboriginal elders look back on their lugger time with pride, but without a sense of achievement.

Locked into manual employment at low wages and with a tight departmental control over their earnings, Aborigines had little incentive to perform well in the industry, or to aspire to promotion to more responsible roles. They could not improve their lifestyles on missions by personal exertion. For camp Aborigines outside reserves and missions, the irregular, seasonal employment required some kind of accommodation with traditional lifestyles and economies. This meant that traditional values and expectations were placed on the activity which were largely unintelligible to employers and Protectors. The recruitment practices of Japanese skippers (themselves employees) responded in a sense to those values and expectations:

they distributed alcohol and other commodities to camp elders and made extended visits, involving sexual intercourse, to camps with which they had long-standing relations. Although it is true that these recruiting methods were detrimental to Aborigines (venereal disease was rampant throughout Cape York)—and were prohibited—Aborigines valued the opportunity to gain access to commodities and to expand their cultural horizons through contact with other ethnic groups on the luggers.

The state was ambivalent in its attitude to Aboriginal employment in the pearl-shell industry. On the one hand, there was a deep distrust of the 'alien employers' (Japanese captains) and transgressions of rules such as 'miscegenation', unauthorised recruiting, or supply of alcohol were considered very serious. On the other hand, the state was reluctant to deny the industry access to cheap labour. The option taken was increased control and regulation of Aboriginal employment. Aborigines became wards of the state, and the state became in effect a supplier of cheap indigenous labour. The paternalistic reflex of the state was to institutionalise and control those it sought to protect. This reflex also reflected Social Darwinist principles because distinctions were drawn between ethnic groups, and the degree of protection was tailored to considerations about 'degree of civilisation'.

Real differences between ethnic groups were thus created. Each ethnic group was subject to specific restrictive and protective legislation and policies. Aborigines, Torres Strait Islanders, Polynesians, Japanese, and Papua New Guineans therefore faced different sets of choices and constraints in their workforce participation. The responses to these choices were understood as 'racial attributes', such as the tendency among Aborigines to abscond from luggers. I have argued that these responses were neither racial attributes nor wholly due to cultural differences between these groups, but attempts to come to terms with the conditions facing each group. The rate of production depended crucially on the personal motivation of the skilled workforce—divers and skippers. The motivation of indigenous workers to perform well was severely curtailed by the paternalistic embrace of the Queensland government.

In order to explain the ethnic stratification of the labour market it is not enough to say that it was a result of racism. To hold up racism as a self-evident explanation is to treat racism as an independent variable which itself requires no explanation. Racism does, however, require explanation.

Social Darwinist theory was not unequivocally drawn upon to comment on race relations. It did not serve as an encompassing ideology, but as a doctrine with scientific status it was frequently used to justify and entrench the political, economic and cultural dominance of whites. Ann Curthoys points out that very rarely was reference made to the position of Aborigines and that of Chinese in the same context, at least not before the 1880s, although in both instances British cultural superiority was defended with reference to Social Darwinism.[116] If a cognitive link was not made between these two situations, then it is difficult to causally link prejudice and discrimination to the ideology which legitimated it.

Noel Loos, too, observes that European attitudes towards Aborigines in frontier warfare were rarely justified in terms of Social Darwinist concepts even if these concepts were familiar. He argues that the racism of the frontier differed qualitatively from that of the metropolis, in that at the point of contact, Social Darwinist concepts gave way to economic power constellations—a phenomenon Loos refers to as 'the pragmatic racism of the frontier'. Whereas expressions of relativity such as 'high state of civilisation', 'advanced several stages in mental evolution' and 'quite as intelligent' had great currency at the level of policy advice, the 'practical men'—those in the industry—used terms such as 'cunning', 'reliable', 'indolent', or 'superstitious', to indicate the suitability of various groups for certain jobs. There is much less a sense of ranking and evolution in such terms, and more of unadulterated xenophobia.[117]

This 'pragmatic racism of the frontier' also characterised European attitudes towards Asians. Asians normally occupied an intermediate position between black and white, but if they threatened white economic dominance or political control, they could generate greater hostility than 'less civilised' groups. Thus the *Boomerang* found 'Kanakas' less objectionable than Asian labour because 'they leave their labour and money behind them when they depart' without opening floodgates of immigration or developing a vested interest in Australia.[118] Such positions were not validated by reference to a hierarchical ranking of races. In fact, resistance towards Japanese was based on a fear that they had superior qualities for the industry. The discourse of Social Darwinism was used to manipulate policy-making according to the labour requirements of the industry. In other words, evolutionary doctrine served as the justification for economic power constellations, and at the same time helped to cement such constellations by guiding policy.

That racism was manifested differently in different situations suggests that it was not ordered by the relatively coherent ideological paradigm which Social Darwinism represents but by particular economic relationships.[119] The strong link between South Pacific trading and the emergence of Queensland's bêche-de-mer and pearl-shell industry fits well with this view. At first the industry's demand for labour was crucially shaped by the model of South Pacific trading where the greater utility of imported labour over local indigenous labour had already been demonstrated by experience. Far greater control could be exercised over workers at work camps (shore stations) than if they resided with their families and worked on their own islands. The freedom to import south Sea Islanders was strongly and successfully defended by the industry. The somewhat greater esteem which they were awarded in turn helped to define the inferior position of local Aborigines.

Bain Attwood refers to 'the making of the Aborigines' in the sense in which E. P. Thompson analyses 'the making of the working class' —as a historical, dynamic process, an interaction between social structure and belief systems under the concrete conditions of colonialism. The colonial policy was to exploit the human and natural resources of non-capitalist economies on the basis of unequal exchange relationships. It required an imbalance of power and status between colonised and coloniser. The state aided the construction of ethnic groups defined by their access to power and status within that system. In other words, it was part of the colonial agenda to create, or underline, racial and ethnic differences, and to cast such differences in a hierarchical order. This hierarchical ordering suited the economic and political requirements and was supported by a belief system which could draw on scientific doctrine for its justification.

2

The Eclipse of an Alternative Production Strategy: the Torres Strait Lugger Scheme

Just as any history of Torres Strait would be incomplete without reference to the pearl-shell industry, so an examination of the pearl-shell industry inevitably entails a discussion of Torres Strait Islander society and its administration by the Queensland government. For a time, a decentralised lugger scheme in Torres Strait permitted flexible subsistence and cash production as an alternative to the commercial fishery based at Thursday Island, which was already beset by resource and other problems.

The Papuan Industries Limited was a philanthropical business scheme which had all the makings of a viable alternative production strategy. It was based on co-operative ownership of luggers, and exploited resource areas over which the owners had traditional rights and therefore a certain responsibility for resource conservation. As a supplement to a subsistence economy, the scheme was capable of flexible specialisation. Trochus, pearl-shell, bêche-de-mer, ornamental shells, dugong, crayfish and fin fish could all be gathered from the same luggers with minor technical adjustments. They were also used for transport and communication. This scheme was gradually transformed by the Queensland government into a mass production enterprise, essentially because it was viewed as an inefficient imitation of the private enterprises operating on the mass production model. The transformation of the lugger scheme and the tightening of paternalistic control over the Torres Strait are aspects of the same development. The resistance offered by Torres Strait Islanders was directed against both processes.

A closer look at the development of this scheme provides a sense of the acculturation processes involved in the 'making of a working class' as described by E. P. Thompson. We see the progressive alienation of workers from the means of production, the barriers to productivity encapsulated in the incomplete transition to consumerism, and the emergence of a collective, oppositional consciousness.

Torres Strait Islanders became an unfree proletariat under conditions of internal colonialism. Colonialism has been the focus of several other explanations of Aboriginal–European relations, first by C. D. Rowley, who distinguished between 'settled' and 'colonial' regions in Australia to explain regional differences in race relations. This kind of analysis has since become known as the theory of 'internal colonialism'. Internal colonialism only differs from colonialism in that the colony is not 'a distinct territorial entity which is spatially detached from its imperial metropolis'. The colonising group occupies the same territory as the colonised group, and exercises political domination, cultural oppression and economic exploitation.[1]

A particular characteristic of internal colonialism is the exploitative articulation between capitalist and non-capitalist modes of production, which tends to erode the non-capitalist economy. Jeremy Beckett analysed this process with reference to the Torres Strait pearling industry. The subsistence economy of the islands enabled participation in the cash economy at extremely low wages, and the colonial administration aided this exploitative arrangement by restricting movement into a free labour market on the Australian mainland. However, cultural adaptations among the Islanders, the high labour requirements of the industry, and the active encouragement of wage labour by the administration, gradually eroded the subsistence economy which was at the basis of their participation.

Becket argues that the administration both prodded Torres Strait Islanders along into capitalist production and subjected them to a paternalistic kind of bondage. From the 1890s to the 1960s, practically all employable Torres Strait Islander men were employed in this industry, and the lugger scheme was the solid pillar of Queensland's Aboriginal policy in Torres Strait. The decline of the pearl-shell industry was a calamity for the indigenous people of the far North. While the administration's protective stance cushioned them from the immediate blow of the industry's collapse, it left them no structure for progress. Beckett reflects:

Henry Dan prepares for helmet-and-corselet diving on board the *Paxie* during a Commonwealth Fisheries survey of shell-beds, 1956. The cumbersome diving suits were cut back for greater mobility.

The tender (Don Boota) and crew wait on the *Phyllis* while the diver is submerged, 1950s.

Sammy Bowder on the *Phyllis* assists as diver David Guivarra resurfaces, 1950s.

Georgie Wallis and Sammy Bowder clean pearl-shell on the *Phyllis*, 1950s.

It might be said that the marine industry carried the Islanders to the threshold of the industrial world and left them there. They had become a part-time proletariat, with all the contradictions that such an idea implies. They were drawn from their subsistence activities by the lure of consumer goods, only to be forced back on these activities again.[2]

The historiographical difficulty of reconstructing a balanced view from official documents is strongly evident in this chapter. Oral history provides an important check on the perspective of the administration, which cannot stand as an unquestioned account of events. Official documentation, however, provides a chronology of events which is absent from oral records, and which is necessary for an understanding of the policy shifts surrounding the transition of the lugger scheme. Besides, the often defensive tone of Protectors' reports adds a colour of its own to the unfolding of events.

In the ethnographic literature, the Torres Strait is divided into three regions on the basis of linguistic, socio-cultural, and geological distinctions: the eastern, western and central islands.[3] All Torres Strait islands were drawn into the mother-of-pearl industry, but their involvement varied in intensity and effect according to the cultural significance of agricultural and maritime subsistence activities on each island, the strength of South Sea Islander influence, and different administrative practices on each island. This distinction is particularly evident in the contrast observed by Beckett between Badu in the west and Murray Island, an eastern volcanic island.

When the pearl-shell industry developed in Torres Strait during the early 1870s, the eastern islands were outside Queensland's territorial limits and their inhabitants were legally Pacific Islanders. For the colonial administration, Murray Island was always a 'trouble spot'. Several bêche-de-mer fishers sought refuge there, employing indigenous people in swimming-diving, and the industry there went unsupervised. Pacific Island missionaries, also largely unsupervised by the London Missionary Society, established a 'theocratic rule' on the first mission station in Torres Strait.[4] It was from here that resistance to the paternalist control emanated. Murray Islanders went on strike in 1913, again refused to work on the company boats in 1921, and instigated a regional strike in 1936, after which they did not re-enter the scheme. They led the demand for relaxation of the paternalist rule of the Queensland government, and were the first to enter the mainland labour market in 1947. More recently, they declined the Queensland government's deed of grant in trust over their land, and instead filed a historic land rights battle in the High Court which resulted in the renunciation of the legal doctrine of *terra nullius* (unoccupied land).

The Murray Islands (Mer, Waiar and Dauar) were the centre of the Malu-Bomai cult, with power distributed by membership of a secret society, and even today Murray Islanders continue to hold fast to cultural traditions, with some asserting that the cult is still alive.[5] According to Beckett the attitude which characterises Murray Islanders is openness to new things combined with a determination to adapt them into their culture:

> According to the mythology, just about everything came from somewhere else, even the original inhabitants and the dugong-shaped hill that dominates the island of Mer, not to mention the twin deities, Malu and Bomai . . . When Europeans began coming the Meriam seemed equally receptive. In 1802 Matthew Flinders found them friendly and eager for trade . . . The Meriam strategy was to domesticate what they accepted. Just as Malu and Bomai had been contained within fetishes and confined within shrines, so iron was integrated into the subsistence economy and foreigners were adopted and assigned kinship statuses. Of course, once colonisation began in earnest, domestication was a matter of mitigating intrusive forces rather than neutralising them, and in the long run the Meriam must be judged to have been fighting a losing battle. But out of this battle they developed a sense of domain that was theirs from time immemorial, which they could and should defend against all comers.[6]

On this fertile island, gardening was of great importance. The government teacher stationed on Murray Island observed in 1908 that

> in initiating their young men into manhood, they teach them that they are not to interfere in sea-work, but that they must look after the land. They regard it as a lazy man's work to fish . . . They look down on the men to the west; they ridicule them and call them fish-eaters.[7]

This assessment is corroborated by ethnographic accounts. Those who held positions of power on Murray did not engage in marine activities. Beckett observes that Murray Islanders participated in the cash economy in a disciplined way, in order to obtain commodities which in turn enhanced agricultural productivity. They participated in pearl-shelling in large numbers when it was profitable and withdrew *en masse* when it was not. Certain cultural traditions were actually enhanced by the state's tight control over earnings. For example, compulsory deductions were made from wages in favour of the mothers of crew, and, since marriage feasts and bridewealth relied on the distribution of garden produce, the authority of elders was thereby strengthened.

Badu developed differently under the strong influence of the pearl-shell industry. Before colonisation, Baduans relied on the collection of wild fruits and legumes (yams and tubers) more than gardening, supplemented by marine produce. They were already used to long absences from home for hunting and raiding. By 1884, two pearl-shell stations had been established at Badu Island, and in 1905 it became the centre of Papuan Industries Ltd (PIL) which established plantations on which Badu Islanders were employed. The PIL also employed a Macassan, a Malay, and several Pacific Islanders who married local women. South Sea Islanders were not under the authority of the Department of Native Affairs, and were therefore not supported on other islands, but on Badu they enjoyed as much support as Torres Strait Islanders from the PIL. The PIL did not discriminate between South Sea Islanders and indigenous Torres Strait Islanders: all were referred to as 'Papuans', and all were to be evangelised. This facilitated the integration of South Sea Islanders into the community. The son of the Samoan Tipoti Nona became a dominant political leader who was largely responsible for the commercial success of pearling on Badu after the 1936 strike. Beckett links the ease with which this successful skipper could become a political leader on Badu to the cultural traditions of the Baduans who followed the Kwoiam cult. This cult was centred on Mabuiag so that the cult leaders on Badu had little executive power, and the 'mamoose' appointed by John Douglas soon gave way to elected councillors who did not need to be indigenous Baduans.[8]

The official appointment of a mamoose on each island represented a kind of self-government in Torres Strait which Douglas used to ward off the administrative infringements of the 1897 Protection Act. The 'mamoose' was assisted by elders as councillors and a staff of native police. Government teachers were stationed on the larger islands and acted as superintendents. Their formal function, apart from teaching, was as clerk and treasurer of the native courts, able to advise the court but without formal authority in the rulings, but in practice they wielded great influence as the representatives of the Queensland government. These teachers discouraged 'idleness', and encouraged participation in the workforce. They exercised considerable discretion in their administration of the islands, and implemented local regulations through their influence over councils.

This 'indirect rule'[9] further underlined regional differences in the way in which Torres Strait Islanders became involved in pearl-shelling, as local councils were able to encourage or resist recruitment into the commercial fishery, or opt for community-based participation.

Until 1904 recruiters had free access to all islands, and did not require a recruiting licence. Torres Strait Islanders were not only cheap to employ but could be employed seasonally or occasionally as required, and released to their communities, where they supported themselves through subsistence activities. The annual fluctuations in workforce participation in Table 2 indicate just how unreliable was the employment on wages boats (commercial boats).[10]

For those working on wages boats the accumulation of debt often presented a problem because crew could draw on their wages during their term of employment by getting clothing, tobacco and other commodities from the slop chest. It was quite usual to end up in debt at the end of the season, until slop chest deductions were no longer recognised by the Protector, to whom all wages were due, in 1912. To indicate the scale of slop chest deductions, the ruling average wage for Torres Strait Islanders was £2 a month in 1901, but after slop chest deductions their average wages credit was £5 a year (the average credit for mainland Aborigines was £2). The commodities drawn from the slop chest were priced exorbitantly, but for indigenous crew the slop chest represented the liberty to buy commodities without the supervision of the Protector.

Another way of participating in the pearl-shell industry was the 'truck system'—renting luggers from Thursday Island pearl-shellers. The owner claimed one-third of the gross proceeds, and the man in charge was responsible for all expenses, including licences. Renting afforded the option to purchase, but often boats were lost through debt. There was also some distrust of these business dealings. Jacob Susan from Rotumah, who had lived on Darnley since 1888, lost the two boats he rented from Burns Philp through debt in 1907. He felt that Burns Philp were cheating him when he sent shell through them to the London market and received news that nothing more was coming to him after the initial £70 advance payment. Indigenes who rented luggers were exempted from the licensing requirements of the 1881 Pearl-Shell Act. Several South Sea Islanders who had married locals, and their descendants, took advantage of these exemptions and rented boats from Thursday Island pearl-shellers, but indigenous Torres Strait Islanders did not, until 'company boats' were introduced. These were acquired on hire purchase by Torres Strait Islanders under a lugger scheme, and intensified the workforce participation of Torres Strait Islanders.

TABLE 2   TORRES STRAIT ISLANDER PARTICIPATION IN THE PEARL-SHELL INDUSTRY

	On wages boats	On company boats	Number of company boats
1900–01	336		
1901–02	192		
1902–03	306	60	1
1903–04	n.a.	n.a.	6
1904–05	n.a.	n.a.	n.a.
1905–06	38	n.a.	17
1906–07	183	n.a.	18
1907–08	181	n.a.	20
1908–09	262	n.a.	n.a.
1909–14	n.a.	n.a.	33
1914–15	n.a.	n.a.	21
1915–16	n.a.	n.a.	21
1916–17	264	240	22
1917–18	277	265	20
1918–19	298	254	26
1919–20	318	250	10
1920–21	190	168	n.a.
1921–22	252	240	n.a.
1922–23	237	350	20*
1923–24	242	350	28
1924–25	220	350	15*
1925–26	216	350	39*
1926–27	131	400	30
1927–28	n.a.	400	19*
1928–29	n.a.	430	16*
1929–30	n.a.	450	24*
1930–31	112	480	n.a.
1931–32	232	390	21*
1932–33	181	386	26
1933–34	198	370	26

Table 2 cont'd

	On wages boats	On company boats	Number of company boats
1934–35	194	459	26
1935–36	147	316	21
1936–37	240	328	25
1937–38	n.a.	n.a.	n.a.
1938–39	n.a.	378	26
1939–40	n.a.	300	25
1940–45	n.a.	n.a.	n.a.
1945–46	100	600	32
1946–47	110	n.a.	40
1947–51	n.a.	n.a.	33–25
1951–54	n.a.	600	n.a.
1954–57	n.a.	n.a.	23–20
1957–58	n.a.	255	23
1958–59	341	295	23
1959–64	n.a.	n.a.	15–16
1971			2**

Source: Annual Reports of the Chief Protector, *QPP*
  * Boats trading to Badu
** Source: Beckett 1977: 96

The company boats

From 1904 to 1930 the lugger scheme was jointly operated by the Papuan Industries Ltd and the Department of Native Affairs (DNA) and its predecessors. These two institutions did not share a common vision, and there was evidently a degree of competition between them from the beginning. In the annual reports of the Chief Protector, no reference is made to the PIL's involvement in the lugger scheme until 1912, whereas histories of the PIL claim credit for the scheme for the PIL.[11] The term 'company boat' derives from reference to this trading company, but denoted both luggers rented from the PIL, boats purchased through the PIL, and boats purchased through the DNA. In 1930 the DNA took over the PIL operation, and this merger has further blurred the distinction between the PIL's involvement in the lugger scheme and that of the DNA. Of the sources referred to in this study, only Beckett briefly mentions that there were two parallel agencies involved in the lugger scheme.[12]

The lugger scheme was initiated by Reverend Fred Walker. He was stationed for the London Missionary Society (LMS) in the Western District of Papua, spanning the Gulf, Torres Strait and Fly River area. From 1896 to 1901 he had engaged in island trading and evangelising together with his brother Charlie in New Guinea, in competition with Burns Philp who held a virtual trading monopoly in the area. He objected to the kind of large-scale commercial development which turned indigenes into wage labour, dependent on a single monopolistic employer. For example, he observed with dissatisfaction in 1894 that the British New Guinea syndicate acquired 250 000 acres at the favourable price of 2s an acre for plantation farming and mining. In the same year, he began to seek support for his idea to form a Christian trading company to engage in trading and plantation farming and to provide technical training. He felt that an alternative industrial development could protect indigenous rights to land and labour by 'the promotion of independent native enterprise and the creation of innumerable small peasant proprietors all along the coast'.[13] In 1897 Walker helped the Mabuiag Islanders to buy a boat, as a first step towards this goal.

The role of the churches in industrialisation was a topical issue. The churches saw some value in replacing 'lost traditional occupations and culture with worthwhile and concrete activities'.[14] But should their involvement in industrial education go to the extent of commercial interest? Walker pointed out that similar schemes were operated by the Church Missionary Society in Uganda (The Uganda Company Ltd) and by the Free Church of Scotland (Scottish Missionaries Industries Ltd). He attempted to interest the LMS by describing his scheme as a supplement to traditional missionary methods, 'an outflanking movement on a large scale by which . . . the enemy will ultimately be driven from the strongholds he at present occupies and the triumph of Christ be secured'.[15]

Walker clearly intended his scheme not as a complement to commercial imperialism but as a rival to it. He fully intended to disadvantage non-Christian traders by organising alternative production around the mission stations. The LMS feared considerable resistance from commercial traders, realising that the scheme would compete directly with Burns Philp. Fearing a consequent loss of contributions, the LMS refused to antagonise vested commercial interests. The LMS directors justified this stance with reference to their christianising mission: if indigenes were started 'on the road to money making, they would be led to greed and avarice'.[16] Walker was required to resign from the LMS in order to begin his scheme. The company was to be conducted 'in avowed alliance with the LMS' but on strictly business lines. The LMS did not go further in its support than to wish him well, and this lack of support did not augur well for Walker's efforts to raise capital in Britain.[17]

After these deliberations the PIL was finally incorporated in 1904 as a limited liability company registered in Queensland, with a capital of £23 904 subscribed by British businessmen, among them Cadbury and Lever Brothers. Walker had aimed at a starting capital of £50 000, and in 1912 a second prospectus was issued entitled 'The Appeal of the Backward Races to the Business Man', which brought the capital to £30 000.[18] As a business investment, the PIL was unattractive. The *Torres Strait Pilot* expressed a critical view:

> From a business point of view it is difficult to see where the shareholders in the Company are going to gain any benefit, in view of the possibly small profits against the heavy risks . . . The natives pay nothing for the numberless small expenses incidental to acquiring these boats; but will be charged 5 per cent. interest per annum upon the purchase price until it is paid off . . . The only profits which can accrue to the Papuan Industries Ltd., will be in the matter of supplying stores.[19]

To prevent speculation in shares, they could not be sold without the company's prior approval. The maximum dividend was set at 5 per cent, but no dividend would be paid until a reserve fund of 5 per cent of paid-up capital was accumulated. In fact no dividend was ever paid. By 1926 the net profit amounted to a mere £1680.[20] It is therefore not incongruous to refer to the PIL as a philanthropic business scheme.

The company established small coconut and rubber plantations on the Binaturi River and acquired 406 acres on Badu Island at £1 2s an acre from the Queensland government to establish its headquarters and a trading station.[21] By 1912 over 1200 acres of land had been leased on the West Papuan coast and in Torres Strait. Profits from the plantations were slow to come, and to tide over the time until the plantations became productive, the company concentrated on trading. It restricted its operations to Torres Strait and two or three stations in the Western District of Papua. It encouraged rubber plantations with free gifts of seedlings in order to generate future trade, and bought copra from several islands. At the PIL headquarters on Badu alcohol was banned, and the trading store was commended as 'the grandest thing ever done for Torres Strait Natives'.[22] It prevented the Torres Strait Islanders from spending the money they earned from the company boats in the Thursday Island hotels. (They were not permitted to stay overnight on Thursday Island until after World War II.) Chief Protector Roth expected that the PIL headquarters at Badu 'will be highly beneficial both to the natives and to this department',[23] but subsequent Protectors did not share this view. The PIL had 'a bad press' because Walker had already irked Burns Philp in New Guinea. It was reported that because missions were financed from free gifts, mission traders had an unfair advantage. Moreover, it was alleged that by allowing the Islanders to enter into debts, the missionaries were forcing them to join the mission's religion.[24] According to one of his sympathisers, Walker was the 'best hated man in New Guinea'.[25]

By 1906 the PIL had a fleet of six ships which were rented to Torres Strait Islanders. In order to encourage them into bêche-de-mer fishing and pearl-shelling, the PIL sold luggers to Islanders on hire purchase at cost price, charging 5 per cent interest. They were required to sell their shell to the PIL and purchase their stores from the PIL, an arrangement similar to the policy pursued by Burns Philp. Several South Sea Islanders, who had settled in Torres Strait, took advantage of the scheme. Edmund Pitt, the son of Douglas Pitt from Jamaica, was renting two boats from Thursday Island pearl-shellers and one from Walker, with option to purchase, which was licensed in Walker's name. A Lifu Islander on Darnley Island, named Coco, also rented a boat from Walker which was licensed in Walker's name because 'I could not go into Thursday Island myself to get a licence, because my boat is too small'.[26] The PIL also provided luggers to Torres Strait Islanders on a kinship basis, in which case the transactions were conducted through the local Protector. The PIL advanced half the purchase price, or sometimes a larger proportion.

But before the PIL became active, the Queensland government officials at Thursday Island took up the initiative floated by Walker, and the first 'company boat' was the *William*, bought in 1903 by Murray Islanders from Farquhar (Queensland Pearl Fishing Company), for £100 at 10 per cent interest. Douglas arranged the sale of shell at Thursday Island and Protector Bennett advanced £30 from the Aborigines Protection Account, which had been started in 1902 from wages due to lugger crew who absconded or died during their term of employment. The income from this lugger was £125 in the first year in pearl-shell and bêche-de-mer, of which about £30 was required for fitting out, sails, and gear. Douglas and Bennett supported the indigenous enterprise because the Mabuiag Islanders had been 'treated badly by European traders on the truck system'.[27]

This move was so successful that within a year, as the PIL commenced operations, Murray Islanders (from Mer and Dauar) had cleared three boats, the *William, Barb,* and *Gelam.* In the first two years, sixty Islanders had earned over £1000. Mabuiag and Boigu Islands also bought boats with small advances from the Aborigines Protection Property account. The local Protector, O'Brien, reported that he arranged storage and sales of shell at Thursday Island, supervised the purchase of food and gear, settled the accounts, and handed over the remaining cash and a balance sheet to a 'head man' in a sealed package. The seal was broken at a public meeting on the island, and the proceeds distributed among all males and females, although swimming-divers received a greater portion, and the balance sheet was interpreted by the schoolchildren.[28] This description gives a harmonious gloss on the procedure. Comments made by Torres Strait Islanders who left school twenty years later cast some doubt on the capacity of the classes of 1905 to interpret the balance sheets: 'We had no education to check the scales, we knew no arithmetic, subtraction, addition. If we brought up 5 or 7 tons and the price was, say £155 per ton, we might get, ah, £5, or £6? Just pocketmoney'.[29]

But the Protector was defending his commitment in the face of criticism from the southern press that the benefit of these boats was not apparent. O'Brien continued:

> One very tangible benefit has been that the earnings of the boats have enabled the natives of several of the islands to avert the food famine which would otherwise have been consequent on the failure of the crops during the year. Last year was a very dry year on all of the islands of Torres Strait, and several applications for relief to you would have been necessary on behalf of some of the islands had it not been for this source of revenue. As it was, applications for 1 ton of flour each for Darnley and Badu Islands were approved by you. These applications would have been unnecessary if these islands had had their own boats.[30]

In early 1906 the price of pearl-shell plummeted and 200 Torres Strait Islanders were suddenly out of work because several pearl-shellers laid up their luggers and others had moved their fleets to Dutch waters. This gave a great boost to the lugger scheme as the administration sought to pick up the slack. By the end of the year there were seventeen company boats, of which five had already been cleared of debt. The participants were Murray (Mer and Dauan), Mabuiag, and Boigu, now joined by Yorke, Yam, Coconut, Darnley, Badu and Moa. Hammond, Stephens and Saibai were applying for boats. About 170 Torres Strait Islanders were employed on company boats, which had cost between £100 and £200 each. By 1907 the number of company boats had risen to twenty. The sale of produce amounted to £2992, and the cash disbursed to Torres Strait Islanders, after all compulsory deductions, purchases of gear, stores and food, was £282. It became the aim of every island community to own at least one company boat. By 1908 Mabuiag had paid off two boats costing £170 each within two years. Murray and Badu had two boats each; Saibai owned three.

From the Islanders' point of view the scheme was a great success. They took pride in their company boats with the characteristic black-and-red-striped railings. The boats carried the names of their respect-ive islands (*Miriam, Erub, Mabuiag, Badu, Yama* etc.), of landmarks on the islands (*Gelam*) or of totemic groups (*Wakaid, Argan*). On most islands young men continued to work for wages, while the company boats were staffed by older and married men who were more reluctant to stay away for long periods. The scheme offered a degree of economic independence and an opportunity to manage their own affairs and business. The Yorke Island schoolteacher thought that

> the Papuan Industries Limited has been very good to them . . . They get pearl-shell when they can, and, of course, they [the luggers] help them to get food. They catch a large amount of dugong and turtle. They get all kinds of marine produce when they can get it.[31]

While the scheme was unprofitable for the PIL, it largely fulfilled Walker's aims. In 1908, giving evidence to a Royal Commission, Walker said that there had been no need for government relief since the scheme had started. Pearl-shelling on company boats became a cottage industry which was labour-intensive and relied on the most simple technology—swimming-diving with goggles—rather than dress-diving with an air pump. All company boats were sailing ves-sels, supplemented by rowing dinghies. The goggles were made by the swimming-divers themselves, and some also wore rubber-soled shoes. There was no danger of divers' bends; the only fear of the swimming-divers was sharks. The benefits of the vessels were not confined to independent participation in pearl-shelling. The luggers were used for hunting expeditions to secure dugong and turtles and for inter-island visits.

It was frequently observed that once the luggers were paid off, Torres Strait Islanders worked less hard to earn a profit with them. They made an extra effort to gain as much profit as possible in the shortest possible time to pay off their luggers to rid themselves of their debts, and then integrated their luggers into a combined cash production–subsistence economy. This use of the luggers was seen by the administrators as the obvious failure of the entire lugger scheme. By 1908, when a royal commission investigated the industry, the mood of administrators had swung from initial enthusiasm to gloom.

From Yorke Island, it was reported that they worked well until the boat was clear, 'but now they humbug a lot, travelling round to the different islands'.[32] The teacher at Darnley Island disbursed penalties as a work incentive: 'Nothing, it seems will move these people—not even fines and imprisonment—to look after their boats and go to work'.[33] The schoolteacher at Murray Island also complained of the waning incentive to work after the boats were cleared:

> they want to get possession of the boat just as an ornament. They like to see the boat at anchor in front of the village, and to be able to say 'That is our boat' . . . I have tried to induce them to continue at the work, but without much success. During the first twelve months they did work well, and cleared the boats. At that time I had the men working according to a time table, so many men going out to work at each tide; but after they got their boats clear they began to think that they were their own masters.[34]

Torres Strait Islanders used the paid-off boats to maintain or improve their lifestyles. On Murray Island the effort petered out when there was an abundant harvest. The 'company boats' that were clear were placed in charge of the elders for intermittent bêche-de-mer fishing, while the younger men signed on again on wages boats. On Saibai, pearl-shelling was done by the younger men who did not have gardens, whenever the water was clear, but the main effort was directed towards house construction with the proceeds. The councillors aimed at a separate house for each married couple. Mabuiag entered upon a display of wealth when its commercial ventures were successful. The Islanders were building a church and gave 3000 coconuts to the PIL for carrying cement for the church. They also presented 7000 coconuts to Moa and 4000 to Badu. The government teacher despaired: 'they give it away instead of selling copra', which was fetching £14 a ton.[35] Evidently the Torres Strait Islanders were pursuing different aims from those of the Protectors. This incomplete acculturation into the capitalist work ethic was explained in terms of innate characteristics:

> But here, the predominating characteristic of the aboriginal race asserts itself, and immediately they know the vessel is no longer in debt, all incentive to work is gone, the catch of the fish decreases, and the vessel is neglected. As instance of this, the catch of marine produce in 1906 was £2,756, and, in 1907 £1,587.[36]

The negative assessments of the lugger scheme were at times tied into other issues. For example the teacher at Yam island reported in 1910 that the company boat was working very unsatisfactorily—most of the crew were spending their time playing marbles. He did mention that the weather had been bad, but blamed the councillors for this 'indolence' and suggested that a new council should be appointed. At the heart of this suggestion was the fact that the Samoan missionary teachers, who held considerable sway over the council, were in open contest with the government teacher, arguing that their authority, deriving from God, was much greater than that deriving from the government. In 1912 the missionary teachers were expelled because of immorality and 'keeping a dirty house'.[37] The negative assessment of the lugger scheme also coincided with significant changes in personnel, with the result that the privileged treatment of Torres Strait Islanders over mainland Aborigines was eroded.

Pronouncement of failure

Douglas, the driving force behind self-government of Torres Strait Islanders, died in 1904, and was replaced by Hugh Milman. In 1906 Chief Protector Roth was replaced by Richard Howard. Roth had been less insistent than his successors on indigenous participation in the workforce. When Thursday Island Protector Bennett suggested in 1903 that the government should take over recruiting for the pearl-shell industry, Roth opposed the proposal, whereas Howard immediately seized on the idea of a central labour depot in his first annual report as Chief Protector in 1906.

The local protectorship at Thursday Island also changed, from George Bennett (1897–1904), who had helped to establish the scheme, to Charles O'Brien (1905–7), who was still quite enthusiastic about it, to John Costin (1907–8). Costin also held the office of shipping master and pearl-shell inspector. He sought to reintegrate Torres Strait Islanders more fully into commercial pearl-shelling. For example, whereas the previous Protector, O'Brien, had barred Japanese bêche-de-mer captains from fetching water at Murray Island on their way down the Barrier Reef in order to prevent recruiting there, Costin permitted it again. It was well known that since the recruits were signed on at Cooktown and the boats worked all the way down, this arrangement provided the skippers with one month's free labour. Costin also relaxed the regulations governing indigenous employment so that crew could 'oversign', that is, sign on again for a further year without returning home first, 'in order to keep as many natives employed in the fishing industry as possible'.[38] This relaxation of rules led to an increase in desertions, and the requirement to return crew to their home before signing them on again was reimplemented in 1921.

With these changes in personnel, the paternalistic rule of the Queensland government was gradually implemented over Torres Strait Islanders, and the co-operation between the PIL and the Queensland government became uneasy. It was at this time that government teachers and Protectors started to voice the concern that the lugger scheme was a failure. Walker felt that the scheme had been organised, under the supervision of the Protectors, on a wrong footing. The proceeds were distributed by the island elders without recognition of merit of the individual divers. He thought an individual basis would be more successful than the 'communistic' approach, because often the swimming-divers did not get any take-home pay at the end of a trip: the takings were 'impounded' towards the debts accrued in running the boats. He felt that even if it was a financial failure, the scheme was worth preserving as a principle because it advanced the business knowledge of Torres Strait Islanders: 'The lugger scheme can become the basis of social improvement and progress'.[39]

The PIL and the DNA differed substantially in their attitudes towards indigenes. The PIL regarded them as fully autonomous entrepreneurs with property rights over the luggers, which they bought on the time-payment system. It sought to secure the trade from these luggers for its Badu store by contractual relationship. The local Protector opposed this contractual relationship. For the

Protector, the 'natives' were wards of the state, not the fully responsible legal entities of a business relationship. In the eyes of the Queensland government, they had no land rights, no rights to their labour, and no rights of property. When Costin was asked 'When a boat has been paid for, to whom does it then belong?' he replied that 'it is vested in the Protector as trustee for the natives'.[40] The Torres Strait Islanders, on the other hand, clearly presumed property rights over their luggers. They understood that once the vessels had been fully repaid, these were their unencumbered property. The DNA approached the question of ownership with delicacy:

> The island fishing boats are the property of the tribe, and used for the general benefit. The mamoose is nominally in charge as representative of the village, and is responsible to the Chief Protector of Aboriginals for the proper care of the vessel and the disposal of the produce earned, through the Protector at Thursday Island, and the equal distribution of the nett proceeds. The Protector at Thursday Island takes charge of all such produce, sells it by public auction or tender, devoting 50 per cent of the money to the payment of interest and redemption, another smaller percentage to repairs, renewals, purchases &c., and the remainder is either handed to the mamoose or his agent, or expended by the Protector for the general benefit.[41]

While it was asserted that the vessels were the property of the Islanders, these were unable to dispose of the produce in a free market, nor were they, as wards of the state, entitled to the proceeds. After they paid off their debt, the Protector continued to 'give them as much direction as when they are in debt to the Department'.[42] He even threatened to take their boats away, and actually impounded one boat, because they had incurred a debt with Thursday Island stores. The government teacher at Mabuiag testified that indigenous people had become more restricted in their spending since Costin's arrival: 'when Mr. O'Brien was here he paid half the money to them and they spent it themselves; but since Mr. Costin came here he has altered that, and he had the handling of the whole money—he pays them what sums he thinks proper'.[43]

Costin, with the support of Chief Protector Howard, brought Torres Strait Islanders fully under the 1897 Protection Act. In order to prevent them from spending their money on alcohol at Thursday Island, Costin opened a bank account for each man signed on for wages boats. They needed permission from the Protector to draw small amounts of cash, and could only draw on their accounts at the island stores.

Howard's policy was to encourage wage labour and to control the wages in order to make the administration of Aborigines self-sufficient. In response to Hugh Milman, the Government Resident at Thursday Island (1904–08), who found it 'both harsh and un-necessary' to enforce the 1897 Act in Torres Strait,[44] he explained that

> in most instances deductions varying from 20 per cent. to 50 per cent. only, according to intelligence, are made from the wages earned, the balance being paid to the boy direct and expended by him at his own sweet will . . . Provided the Protector is satisfied that the aboriginal re-quires the money for his own use and benefit, he is allowed to draw in moderation such sums as he may need, even to the whole of the account, if the circumstances justify it.[45]

Opposition to this paternalism was played down ('they are easily discontented if they think there is any cause'). This tightening of control also caused resentment on the mainland: residents from McIvor River and Cape Bedford approached the Chief Protector in 1907 with the message that they could look after themselves.

Costin thought that although the vessels were used to tide Torres Strait Islanders over 'hungry times', their net effect was negative, because they incurred debts for repairs. He therefore resisted any extension of the system, and placed difficulties in the way of the PIL. For example, he insisted that their luggers observe the same licensing requirements as wages boats. Indigenes were exempt from licensing fees and from the requirement to sign their crew on the ships' articles. Walker claimed these privileges on behalf of the in-digenes who were renting the fifteen PIL boats, arguing that they were co-operatively run, so that there were no employees, and that they were working on the home reefs of the Islanders in charge. Nevertheless, Costin satisfied himself that the concessions under which the PIL had been operating had not been recorded in writing anywhere, and insisted that all PIL boats take out articles and sign on all their crew. Five PIL boats were laid up as a result. Moreover, Costin required that the produce from all luggers acquired under his auspices be delivered to the government store at Thursday Island rather than to the PIL store at Badu. Walker protested: 'The chief point in connection with our company has been to keep the natives from Thursday Island, but the Government have blocked us in our purpose by compelling the natives to go to Thursday Island to sell their shell and get their supplies'.[46] In 1912, eleven boats sold their

Bully Drummond displays a coral-encrusted pearl-shell on Duffield's *Jennifer Jill*, 1949. He is wearing the divers' flannel, worn underneath the diving suit. The cap prevented hair from falling over the face during diving.

Thursday Island Harbour, 1900, the centre of the pearl-shelling industry in Queensland

Swimming-divers with goggles, usually made by the divers from tortoiseshell, 1917

shell to the PIL store at Badu and ten to the DNA at Thursday Island. In 1913, twenty-six boats dealt with the PIL and seven with the DNA, and from then on about half the fleet dealt with each depot. It was not until 1921, during the slump which lasted until 1930, that the Queensland government transferred its business to the PIL store at Badu.

Costin was hostile towards the PIL, which he saw as a wealthy company backed by 'influential men with plenty of money'.[47] The PIL, however, sought to distinguish itself from commercial pearl-shellers by its benevolent trading attitude. It offered prices slightly above the price obtained at Thursday Island, and submitted its records to Costin for inspection to demonstrate that they were dealing fairly. Costin concluded from the accounts that 'the natives were getting the better of them'.[48] Because Walker felt it was important to project this benevolent image, he was particularly irked when Mabuiag Islanders complained that they were being exploited by the PIL, who made profits on their shell and offered low prices. He reacted by barring Mabuiag Islanders completely from the Badu Island store.

Costin refused to accept the argument that the lugger scheme was beneficial for Torres Strait Islanders. He sought to erode the PIL's advantages, and to force Islanders back into wage labour, arguing that they were 'better off' working for wages. On wages boats they were earning between £2 5s and £2 10s a month plus food, whereas on their own boats they made only about £1 5s a month. By simple calculation it was thought that it was 'more advantageous for the natives' to be employed at £2 a month than to run their own luggers, on which they could not earn £24 a year.[49]

The manager of Burns Philp, Joseph Mitchell was of quite the same opinion: it was 'better for the natives' to work for pearl-shellers, because they would earn higher wages, and because 'all coloured men do better with a little supervision. They work better'. He also suggested that whites should be in charge of all Torres Strait Islander boats. With this suggestion Mitchell sought to eliminate both the competition from the 'company boats' and that of the Japanese, at a time when the Queensland government sought to implement the White Australia policy in the pearl-shell industry. Pearl-shellers felt that the government had monopolised Islander labour with the lugger scheme, and that company boats had an unfair advantage because they did not need to sign on and discharge crew, and no limits on the number of workers were imposed. Because wages boats needed to provide food for the longer voyages, the pearl-shellers argued that their costs of production were higher. Their position was supported by data supplied by the Sub-Collector of Customs at Thursday Island.[50]

The context of these criticisms was that at this time the industry was in an environmental crisis which heightened competition. Pearl-shell was getting scarce, and the pump boats started to encroach on the shallow grounds near the islands, if they saw swimming-divers successfully harvesting shell. Some skippers of pump boats used underhand measures to keep the competition from swimming-divers at bay. They threw grease or dirt into the water to attract the sharks, in order to force swimming-divers off the grounds. (Sharks were of little concern to dress-divers, because they could be scared away with air bubbles.) Swimming-divers, in turn, sometimes muddied the water to hinder the dress-divers.

One Murray Islander summed up the benefit of lugger-ownership to Torres Strait Islanders: 'The boats were our only highway'.[51] Only in the late 1960s were aerodromes built, flying doctor services introduced and sisters stationed on the islands. The luggers meant communication and transport, access to the means of production in an enveloping cash economy, and a vehicle for subsistence production. They were a symbol of prosperity. These considerations were absent from the Protector's assessment of the commerical viability of the scheme. In order to remain productive, the vessels needed to be maintained. A season spent unproductively meant a season in debt, even if the purchase price had been cleared.

Instead of accepting the Protectors' generalised pronouncements on the success or failure of the scheme, it is advisable to take account of the ways in which luggers were worked on the different islands. A 'snapshot' at around the year 1910, when the scheme was considered a failure, reveals a varied but generally prosperous position with some setbacks. In the first enthusiasm about the scheme, boats had been acquired by island communities which were too small to staff them on a commercial and permanent basis. For example the population of Adolphus Island was so small that it was not listed in any of the annual reports. In 1910 the *Martha* of Adolphus Island had run into debt and was auctioned by the DNA, leaving a bad debt of £60.

Mabuiag Islanders embraced the scheme and largely withdrew from wages boats. In 1910 the wages Mabuiag Islanders earned on commercial boats were £100, while the company boat had earned £500 for a population of around 250. Only twenty-one men worked on wages boats in 1912. The government teacher wrote, 'I do not know what the natives would do if they had not boats'.[52]

On Saibai the island court devised a new punishment for offences: forced labour on wages boats. The councillors opened a store on the island, and when the island experienced a drought and serious food shortage in 1912 it was overcome without assistance. In 1910 the company boats earned £119 for a population of about 250.

Moa Islanders were lucky twice with pearls. In 1912 and again in 1915 a pearl was found realising £255 and £425 respectively, more than the income from pearl-shell and bêche-de-mer, which was £205 in 1912 for a population of about a hundred.

On Murray Island most young men (about fifty) were working on wages boats, and entering pearl-shelling rather than bêche-de-mer collecting. Murray Islanders were also holding Saturday markets, attracting many Japanese customers from Thursday Island. The government teacher was unimpressed with the 'spurious effort' on company boats and found that the men 'required continual encouragement and supervision'.[53] The *Miriam* had earned £182 in 1908, and the Komet tribe of the island bought another lugger in 1911. The *Barb* had been sold by the Protector in 1908, and the hull of the *William*, which had sunk in Darnley harbour the previous year, was sold also. The population of Mer and Dauar was about 400.

On Darnley Island (population 220 in 1908) the *Erub* was the subject of inter-tribal dispute and was left abandoned for three months in 1910. In the following year Home Secretary Appel visited and encouraged the Islanders to recommission the boat, whereupon the government teacher 'told them to get to work' on it.[54] They did so reluctantly and worked irregularly, and in 1912 the teacher pressured the men into signing on again with the wages boats. Several South Sea Islanders resident on Darnley were renting bêche-de-mer boats from Thursday Island pearl-shellers. Gradually these 'individually owned boats' were also entering into the Protectors' discourse, being referred to for the first time in 1913.

In 1916 the total earnings of Torres Strait Islanders from the pearl-shell industry amounted to £9089: £4730 from company boats and £4395 from employment.[55] These figures do not bespeak a financial failure. The Protector was dissatisfied with the returns, because he compared the boats to those of the pearl-shellers which served only a single, commercial purpose.

Tightening control and resistance

The administration normally took credit for the success of the lugger scheme, but if there were problems with it, the indigenes were blamed. For example, when the boats trading to Badu obtained good results in 1916, a local Protector remarked that 'this excellent result is mainly due to the efforts of the Government teacher, Badu, who exercises a supervision over all boats trading to that place'.[56]

In 1912 an Island Fund was established, to which each island had to contribute in proportion to its earnings. 'The object of the fund is to promote a spirit of independence among the people . . . without asking monetary assistance from the Government or any individual.'[57] In times of drought the islands could now draw on this fund. (The Aboriginal Provident Fund established in 1919 as sickness and unemployment insurance was the extension of this scheme to mainland Aborigines who were not on reserves, and in 1928 an East Coast Fund was also established.) Also a boat insurance fund was started to substitute commercial insurance which only covered for total loss of a vessel.

In 1912 the local Protector reported that most boats would be in credit at the end of the season:

> This satisfactory position was not easily attained, as most of the natives do not worry about being in debt, and resented our efforts to place them on a sound footing. In course of time they realised we had no intention of being turned from the object in view, and resigned themselves to the inevitable.[58]

Torres Strait Islanders did not welcome such constant interference in the management of the company boats, and Murray Islanders led the way in protests. In 1913 the local Protector William Lee Bryce reported:

> Every endeavour is made to persuade all able-bodied islanders to engage in profitable employment, and, as usual, all sorts of excuses are put forward for not doing so. There is no scarcity of work at a fair wage, but this year many are standing down, and will probably remain unemployed, as the boat owners are endeavouring to obtain men from Papua. Some allege the institution of the Island Fund is their objection, others openly stated they proposed waiting until wages are increased.[59]

It was not simply that wages were controlled, but the Protectors sought to resettle island groups for administrative convenience. For example, in 1912 Coconut and Hammond Islands still had no school, and therefore no government representative. Torres Strait Islanders were eager to gain access to formal education for their children, and the administration used this leverage to draw them into its ambit. The eighty Hammond Islanders wanted to go to Prince of Wales Island, but the Protector suggested Moa; the sixty-three Coconut Islanders wanted to go to Sue Island, but the Protector suggested Yorke, where schools already existed.

Schools fulfilled a dual function in the acculturation of Torres Strait Islanders. They entailed the allocation of a superintendent, and they also inculcated work habits without giving young Islanders 'ideas above their station'. This hidden curriculum was made quite explicit in annual reports. Lee Bryce 'discouraged higher subjects'[60] and reserve education was 'of purposely not too high a standard'.[61] Islanders were kept in a carefully orchestrated state of educated ignorance until they learned about the standards of the outside world during World War II, and demanded more than 'an educational set-up that provides little incentive to the individual to become other than a manual labourer or a worker in the pearl-shell industry'.[62]

The discontent of Torres Strait Islanders, who were 'learning to labour', is apparent in the Protector's 1915 report. This report makes reference to the 'bad influence' of South Sea Islanders in Torres Strait, who were exempt from the provisions of the 1897 Act, and therefore did not come under departmental authority:

The past year was marked by a strong feeling of unrest among the people, which manifested itself in refusals to work when good employment was offering, and, in a few places, by open disregard of departmental authority . . . They have a very good idea of the limits of our authority, and, while willing to obey all directions that can be supported by the Acts and Regulations, strenuously oppose attempts to improve their condition which are not within the four corners of legislation relating to aboriginals . . . For many years officials and others interested in the welfare of the islanders have endeavoured to persuade all able-bodied men to engage in congenial employment, or work their own boats in a systematic manner. In a few instance these efforts have been successful, but, unfortunately, in most places results are not encouraging, particularly so in the eastern group [where nature provides fairly bountifully] . . . As we are endeavouring to gradually raise a strong healthy race to a higher plane, it is the duty of these people to take the utmost advantage of the facilities provided for them . . . In some quarters this procedure would be termed 'slavery', but any person who possesses an intimate knowledge of the people and the subject will think otherwise. The islanders have not yet reached the state when they are competent to think and provide for themselves; they are really overgrown children, and can best be managed, for their own welfare, as a prudent parent would discipline his family.[63]

This paternalistic attitude has been sharply perceived by Torres Strait Islanders: 'The government leads us like little children, but in time you let little children go. The government should let us go'.[64]

The apparent failure of the lugger scheme, therefore, was essentially the failure to permit an emerging working class the expression of its consciousness. The administration wanted Torres Strait Islanders to enter into a cash economy as wage labour—but not as free wage labour. In time, Islanders would clamour for access to a free labour market, and citizenship rights so that they could negotiate the sale of their labour power. The tension between cash economy and subsistence economy was exacerbated by an administration which encouraged wage labour on the one hand and clung to a restrictive paternalism on the other. The DNA was instrumental in creating conditions of internal colonialism in Torres Strait.

In 1914, with the start of World War I, the shell market was closed. The income of Torres Strait Islanders dropped from £5373 in the previous year to £1558. This is an indication of the value of the pearl-shell industry (wages boats and company boats) for the Islanders' economy. In this crisis, the utility of the company boats was strongly apparent: they were used to gather bêche-de-mer as a cash income, and to fish and hunt turtle and dugong to keep up a food supply.

The prices for gear and repair materials rose to prohibitive levels—a yard of canvas, normally 1s, now cost 6s. Under these conditions lugger maintenance became difficult. Islanders started to acquire dinghies, from which women and elders could collect marine produce, and tended to use the company boats simply as transport for produce. Because the upkeep of the boats was neglected, the administration took punitive action, reallocating boats and issuing warnings that returns needed to improve. At Darnley, only one man was allowed per dinghy, and everyone had to report to the government teacher how much time they had spent on the dinghy and how much they had caught.

In 1912 a pearl-sheller sent a trial consignment of trochus shell to Japan, and trochus quickly became an alternative export to pearl-shell in the Australian industry. As trochus is accessible to swimming-divers, this was well suited for company boats, who gained access to the trochus market for the first time in 1915. Trochus-fishing imbued the industry with new vigour. But Torres Strait Islanders continued to express their resentment of the administrative grip. In 1919 Protector Gilson Foxton cryptically reported that 'several troubles of a serious nature amongst the natives, owing to the lack of communication, have had to be held over'. In 1921 the Murray Islanders struck for higher rates. They were dissatisfied with the administrative control of their earnings.

> When it is pointed out that the compulsory banking deduction averaged, say 50 per cent. at the most of the total wages earned, and of that deduction nearly 60 per cent. was returned to the owner in clothes and other benefits, it will be seen that the hardship alleged is somewhat overstated.[65]

In 1922 Cornelius O'Leary replaced Foxton as local Protector at Thursday Island. With this change, the local Protector increasingly assumed the function of a merchant. O'Leary was well versed in current prices and knew the market opportunities. He reorganised the boats according to market potential, directing them to fish for trochus, bêche-de-mer, black-lip, or gold-lip pearl-shell, as opportunity dictated: 'A persistent driving power is needed behind the native; and while it is left to the crews to work at their own sweet will the vessels will never show the results which with firm handling and regular supervision, should be attainable'.[66] Reporting of the success of the luggers became more businesslike, and seasonal decline was more likely to be explained in terms of weather and market conditions than to be blamed on 'native indolence'. For the company boats 1924 was a record year, and catches were excelled again in 1925, 1926, and 1927. Company boats now had agencies in Cairns and Cooktown. Saibai and Badu Islanders performed particularly well. The *Wakaid* made a name for itself, always in close competition with the *Saibai*; and the *Wakemab* produced excellent results (12 tons of shell on an 8-ton cutter). The scheme was now operated as a business enterprise, and its success measured in those terms. The proof of success were wages comparable with master boats.

The Eastern Islanders were reluctant to engage in the industry on this basis. In 1931 Murray Islanders laid up their two luggers because shell was fetching low prices. This strategy ran counter to the business expectations of the Protector:

> The Murray Island boats are dismal failures amongst those of the Eastern Islands. It has been found difficult to persuade these people to leave their home reefs, and they seize upon any pretext for returning from the working grounds and remaining home. For the New Year the Murray Island boats have been placed in charge of Jacob Gabey, erstwhile teacher at Yam, who has instruction to work down the coast.[67]

The Island Industries Board

In 1922 Walker was unsuccessful in raising any further capital for the PIL, and retired because of failing health. In the meantime, William Hodel, a Thursday Island pearl-sheller, had joined the staff of the PIL in 1912, and supported the Protector's objectives. The friction between the two institutions eased. The DNA began to use the PIL's Badu store instead of requiring its luggers to come to the Protector at Thursday Island. The wife of the new manager, J. C. Harman, helped to establish boy scouts, rovers and girl guides at Badu, a movement which quickly became popular. Darnley Islanders formed a group of sea scouts. In 1927 the PIL acquired a boatslip at Thursday Island, where Torres Strait Islanders were trained in carpentry and boatbuilding. The slip produced a hundred dinghies in two years, underselling the Japanese by £1, and breaking the Japanese monopoly over boatbuilding on Thursday Island.

After Walker's departure the PIL continued to operate for a further eight years, but in 1930 it fell victim to the depressed markets in rubber, coconut and pearl-shell. Its plantations in Madiri and Daru were sold to the Unevangelised Fields Mission, and the Queensland government took over its Torres Strait operations as the Aboriginal Industries Board. In 1939 this became the Island Industries Board (IIB). The administration gradually increased its control over the luggers, and in 1952 looked back on the PIL phase as an 'unorganised system of co-operation'.[68]

The local Protector became the manager of the IIB. There was no longer a pretence that the company boats belonged to kinship groups on the islands. They were reallocated at the discretion of the IIB manager according to the performance of crews in order to maximise efficiency. In 1933, for example, the *Manu* was transferred from Poid village (Moa Island) to Mabuiag, the *Mabuiag* was given to Boigu, the *Roma* transferred from Murray to Badu, the *Naianga* from Badu to Darnley, and the *Erub* from Darnley to Yam. No longer were the balance sheets interpreted by the schoolchildren, or the profits distributed by the island elders: wages were credited to the crew's passbook, and the returns were handled by the Protector, and neither the captains nor the councillors ever saw the balance sheets. This caused considerable distrust of the Protector's accounting methods.

> *Adai* and *Adiana* were the Murray Island trochus boats under the State government. They took it off us and gave it to another island when they said it was in debt even though at first everybody had paid so much to put the money together to buy it . . . They kept the books, you had no proof.[69]

Murray Islanders continued to distance themselves from the company boats, while Badu emerged as the showcase of the Strait. The Protector handed out trophies to the crew with the best catch each season and Badu crews continued to win them. Several island stores were opened where residents could obtain standard lines of commodities without having to come into Thursday Island. The stores were a further incentive to participate in the cash economy because purchases could only be made against credit in a passbook.

Participation in the pearl-shell industry had now become a firm tradition in Torres Strait. It provided status ranking and was the main avenue of cash income. Employment on pearl-shell boats was ranked higher among Torres Strait Islanders than swimming-diving for trochus and bêche-de-mer, so that employment on wages boats was more valued than participation in company boats, unless one could become the skipper of a boat, a leadership position which was highly valued, and entry to which was awarded on the basis of kinship position. 'Most of the lads elect to follow the occupation of their fathers and engage as learners in the fishing fleets. A number enter as pupils for the teaching service and the native clergy.'[70]

As a matter of fact, there was not much choice. The islands of Torres Strait were now government reserves, and movement between them, and particularly to the mainland, was restricted. For inter-island visits, a permit from the government teacher was required, and Torres Strait Islanders were not permitted to stay on Thursday Island overnight, so that they were barred from employment in the commercial centre. As soon as they left school, the young men started to work on the company boats, or if they were lucky they were signed on at Thursday Island: 'there was nothing else to do'.[71]

A 1934 amendment of the Protection Act brought mixed descendants of Aborigines under the Act, so that the South Sea Islander descendants in Torres Strait were now also under departmental authority, and their business included in the reports to the Chief Protector. Many non-white residents of Thursday Island, and the descendants of South Sea Islanders, expressed considerable opposition to this extension of powers. They had always considered themselves as free agents, often pitying those who were 'under the Act' for the way in which they had to queue in front of the shipping master to ask permission to draw some of their wages. 'They tried to make us like the Aboriginal. But we were a mixed race of people, Irish and everything, Malay, Filipino, Portuguese, how can you put them under the Act?'[72]

'Natives on strike'

With the takeover of the lugger scheme by the Queensland government, interference in management increased. The Protectors were now fully committed to the scheme. It was the Protectors' scheme, not the Islanders': the company boats were 'the boats controlled by the Department for the benefit of the natives . . . the property of the Department'.[73] The Protector made his annual rounds to each island signing up crew for the company boats. Torres Strait Islanders became increasingly disaffected and started to protest that wages on company boats were below those earned on wages boats. Many Aborigines on wages boats were earning higher wages than Torres Strait Islanders on their own company boats, while funds from the Torres Strait region, which was now financially self-supporting, were diverted towards the support of mainland reserves. The control of all personal incomes was particularly irksome—the crew only received 'credit' to draw on the island stores.

In response to this criticism, the Protector asserted that even though income on the wages boats was higher *per capita*, the total income from company boats exceeded that from wages, and that anyhow, it was the only, and therefore the best, alternative they had. The very argument that had been used by previous Protectors to demonstrate the failure of the lugger scheme, while the PIL was involved and the work was largely self-directed, was turned on its head when the administration was in control of the scheme. 'Although there is a temporary revulsion by the natives to work on the "company" boats, there is no system that meets their needs better.'[74] There were now between twenty-five and twenty-seven company boats employing some 400 men, or three-quarters of the total Torres Strait Islander labour force.

The revulsion referred to by the Chief Protector was not temporary: on New Year's Day of 1936 Torres Strait Islanders began a strike which lasted for four months.[75] They refused to work on the company boats, and the entire fleet lay idle. Local Protector McLean was unpopular, and O'Leary, who was now the Department's deputy chief director and stationed on Palm Island, returned to Thursday Island to help McLean in his efforts to persuade the men back to work. At a meeting on Murray Island, the men refused to listen and jumped out of the windows of the schoolhouse where the assembly was held. The Islanders challenged the administration to take the boats back: 'Take them, we lived here before the boats came here . . .'.[76] It was an open contest. One Badu Islander described to Nonie Sharp how the strike was carried across the strait:

> Well in that time there was a cargo boat used to sail. It was a boat called *Darton* and the skipper was called M——, old M——, he was the skipper. When he goes to Murray Island the things they decided there they sent as a message with him to bring up here. When he calls at some of the islands like Central islands, then come [*sic*] down to Badu, he let us hear the message on the island of Badu. Then when he takes cargo to Saibai, Dauan and Boigu he takes the message and tells them. So that strike was going one week. So when Mr. McLean goes round all the islands this time, he goes to Murray Island first. They do it there: they jump through the windows. Then when he comes here we give him a surprise: the strike was happening here too; we give Mr. McLean a surprise . . . That strike's been coming to us by old M——, skipper of that cargo boat. When he sails through Torres Strait, whichever island he comes to he yarn there with them. Cargo boat of Aboriginal Industries Board carrying cargo and taking messages. [Laughter] Carrying cargo and loading messages . . . ![77]

The experience of the strike differed somewhat from island to island. There were no regional leaders, and each island submitted its own set of claims. Because disaffection with the system of remuneration was the common theme of these demands, the press reported it as a strike for higher wages. But the Torres Strait Islanders were not a fully fledged proletariat; they did not yet accept their alienation from the means of production. They objected to the loss of control over their luggers, and suggested various strategies of addressing this grievance. Yet control of the lugger scheme was the one central demand which the administration would not yield to. Torres Strait Islanders did not gain control of their wages and passbooks.

A Saibai Islander described the strike:

> In 1936 during the strike I was still in school with Mr Bryant. They broke windows in the store . . . I saw them talk to the superintendent about not getting enough money, they asked him where all the money was going. I didn't speak much English, I only heard what the Island men were saying [among themselves]. The strike lasted one or two [seasons], and they went out on the boats again, but still the same State Government, the Director of Native Affairs, were the ones we had to deal with . . . People disagreed with the government. They wanted family boats and debunk those boats where you worked for small wages. But still the government weighed the shell. It looks like they cheated. They didn't let you know how much it weighed. They [Islanders] told each other how much each got when they came out of the white man's office.[78]

Another Saibai Islander made the same points: distrust of the administration's accounting and the aim to control personal earnings:

> We sold [the shells] at Badu, [to] Mr Walker of IIB. I worked for Mr Walker as carpenter there. He helped the Island people, but when the Department took over they ran it differently and took the money altogether . . . We struck in Saibai at the same time. We argued with the white teacher for a fair go for our wages. It lasted for months . . . Before that all the shell was counted together. After that, each counted their shell . . . We still got our money into the passbook. DAIA ran the business at TI.[79]

Police and DNA staff were stationed on the islands to deal with the strike, and in February thirty 'leaders' were gaoled at Badu, because the school bell—timekeeper and pacesetter on the island— had been removed. Badu was seen as the weakest point in the chain of resistance, because it had always been the centre of company boat pearling and its results were exemplary for Torres Strait. Two Badu councillors were the only two of about 400 Islanders who did not support the strike. In February four boats were manned at Badu. In March, Stephens and Darnley Islanders signed on again with pearl-shellers while Murray Islanders continued to hold out and their company boats were withdrawn. In April Saibai and Boigu still with-held their labour from both company boats and wages boats.

O'Leary began to reorganise the company boats by gradually limit-ing their number, granting some concessions, and choosing families to whom to award boats. From now on the boats were referred to as the 'DNA fleet', and they were awarded to families, not island communities. Darnley and Murray Islanders no longer participated in the scheme; they went into the employ of pearl-shellers. Badu again became the exemplar of success in the reorganised scheme, the pride of the administration. A Badu Islander remembered proudly:

> Badu Islanders worked hard. Murray and Darnley got lazy, they had to move them. We got more money than any other island. The government gave us a plaque. Uncle Tanu always got most trochus-shells, and my father always came second.[80]

Nonie Sharp, who has examined the strike episode in depth, sees its greatest significance in the emergence of a regional identity: the strike was 'the first act of the Torres Strait Islanders as one people'.[81] The strike was played down by the administration, but Sharp has unearthed its wider significance. It was directed at the paternalistic rule of the Queensland government, rather than at wages or employ-ment conditions on the luggers. This is obvious from the demands made, and from the concessions gained as a result of the strike.

The most immediate result of the strike was the abolition of the 'Boo' or time-whistle on all islands. Captains were now supplied with a copy of the boat returns. On the strength of their solidarity, based on a newly emergent regional identity, Torres Strait Islanders gained significant concessions towards a larger measure of self-government. The councillors were charged with selecting crews and captains, and captains were responsible to the councillors. The Island Fund was now called island tax in recognition of the business basis of pearl-shelling. Permits for inter-island visits were no longer required, and the first conference of all Torres Strait councillors was held on Yorke Island in August 1937. The longer-term results of the strike were manifested in the 1939 protection legislation, where separate Acts dealt with the administration of Aborigines and of Torres Strait Islanders, formalising what Sharp calls the policy of 'indirect rule' for Torres Strait. The island councils were charged with the functions of local government, and indigenous courts were legally recognised.

World War II and its effects in Torres Strait

With the approach of war in Europe in 1938, trochus became practically unsaleable, and the price for pearl-shell fell below the cost of
production. Five hundred Islanders were engaged in pearl-shelling
and its ancillary industries. The Pacific war brought commercial
pearl-shelling to a standstill. In 1942 the larger vessels were taken
over for defence purposes, and the smaller ones immobilised because
of the threat of Japanese invasion from the north. Eight hundred
Torres Strait Islanders joined the armed forces as soldiers and sailors,
mostly in the Torres Strait Light Infantry Battalion, and the scout
movement proved valuable as a nucleus of civil defence. Torres Strait
Islanders in military service were paid at two-thirds the rate of white
soldiers. All over Queensland, Aborigines were formed into work
gangs in essential industries. Pearl-shelling was conducted on a small
scale during the war by Islanders, not for export but to supply the
military authorities who required the shell for trading in New Guinea
and for use in prismatic compasses and as uniform buttons. In March
1942 Thursday Island and several indigenous communities were
evacuated.[82] The wartime experience made a very deep impression
on Torres Strait Islanders. Contact with white Australians and some
black Americans 'opened their eyes' about the world outside the
Strait. A Saibai Islander described the changes brought about by the
war:

> Army people came, every island had two signallers. [Normally] only the
> big islands with stores had radios but during the war each island had
> radio and two white signallers. They taught islanders to operate the
> telephone, wireless, trucks. We learned all our knowledge from the army;
> before we knew nothing. It was proper hard strict law; no Island people
> allowed on Thursday Island. After the war now you find us all over
> Australia, in the railways. The army unlocked the gate. Education was
> increased. Wages came up.[83]

Having fought side by side with whites, the Torres Strait Islanders'
expectations were raised that after the war they would be treated as
equals. The Protector noted these raised expectations:

> Most of the Islander ex-servicemen received their discharges during the
> year and from their association with Australian personnel they had as-
> sumed a changed outlook on life, completely altering in many ways their
> way of living as compared with pre-war days. They had seen how the
> European people lived, their style of buildings and dress, mode of living

and habits. To meet this change the Board [IIB] has had to alter its outlook also to some extent. With money in quantities which they had never before possessed, the Islanders abandoned their desire for cheap articles and were asking for good clothes, more manufactured food as against their own native products and, above all, building material in order to erect dwellings on the European style.[84]

At the end of the war, the IIB purchased and demolished 164 army buildings in order to erect European-style houses. Many Torres Strait Islanders were now receiving Commonwealth government social service payments, which, together with the income from military allotments, created an 'unprecedented prosperity'.[85] Under the direction of two pearl-shellers, Torres Strait Islanders were formed into expeditions to retrieve the luggers which had been left at New Guinea. Others that had been sunk at Thursday Island were now recovered:

> With the money from the army our families bought the boats. We bought the *S.S. DONA* [that stands for] Sinking Ship Director O'Leary Native Affairs . . . *Dona* was a family boat. We bought it from Farquhar; it was *Sheila* before. It had been sunk at TI, we raised it with drums, it was covered with sand and mud.[86]

Postwar reconstruction was aided by a boom in the trochus market from pent-up demand. Because trochus is accessible by swimming-diving, without diving gear, the conditions for the DNA fleet were favourable, particularly since pearl-shellers had great difficulty in re-entering the industry because of a scarcity of usable luggers. In 1947 the private fleets numbered nineteen vessels and employed 110 Torres Strait Islanders. The IIB headquarters were transferred from Badu to Thursday Island where they are today. Torres Strait Islanders were stationed in labour barracks on Thursday Island to help rebuild Thursday Island. The IIB was determined to take the leading role in the industry now. It recommissioned forty luggers, and prepared to equip them for dress-diving, to train Torres Strait Islanders as dress-divers, and began to build a slipway on Thursday Island.

In order to make indigenous people self-supporting, the Protector sought to foster indigenous industries so that Aborigines would not be 'a burden on the taxpayer'.[87] The DNA was therefore strongly opposed to attempts by pearl-shellers to reintroduce Japanese divers. Torres Strait Islanders were now financially dependent on the industry because they could no longer fall back on subsistence activities. Torres Strait was 'independent of Government assistance other than that provided to any white community'.[88] Torres Strait Islanders and Aborigines made up 90 per cent of the industry's workforce, and many Torres Strait Islanders were divers, tenders and engineers, and doing very well. They now demonstrated that they were as good as Japanese divers. One Islander diver recorded a catch of 22 tons in the 1951 season—the highest recorded catch by a Japanese diver on a comparable boat had been 13 tons.

The DNA was now fully committed to the mother-of-pearl enterprise. In 1949 Chief Protector O'Leary moved his office to Thursday Island to become manager of the IIB. (The Chief Protector's position was now referred to as the Director of the sub-department of Native Affairs, DNA.) It was no longer the Islander's lugger scheme, but a business conducted by the DNA. As manager of the IIB, the Director became preoccupied with business management. He was well versed in current prices and market prospects. He realised that dealing on a contract basis was preferable to selling by auction. In 1950 he entered into contract with South Sea Pearling Co. (Gerdau) for the season's catch of up to 200 tons of pearl-shell (the previous year's catch had been 141 tons), and with Brown and Dureau (also agents for Gerdau) for up to 500 tons of trochus (the previous year's catch had been 180 tons). The businesslike attitude also extended to employees. Low yields were no longer blamed on indigenous indolence: 'It can be accepted as an established fact that fluctuations in production as between one year and the other cannot be regarded as the fault of the diver and his crews'.[89]

This remarkable turnaround in attitude was an expression of the commercial approach to the enterprise. The DNA had invested a tremendous amount of energy in the project, and the administration of indigenous people in the far North was organised around the pearl-shell industry. The DNA director observed that

> independent pearlers can withdraw from the industry as market fluctu-
> ations compel such action, but the Board cannot retreat from its under-
> taking to see that the Island worker . . . is protected in the years to come
> in an industry which he has done so much to establish.[90]

The transformation of a co-operative lugger scheme, capable of flexible production, into a mass production enterprise was now complete.

The final crisis

The postwar boom did not last long. One Saibai Islander described the brief honeymoon:

> [Before the war] trochus was very scarce and hard to get. Then war was declared. After the war we bought family boats from DNA and the shell prices came up to £700 to £1000 a ton. There was plenty of shell. It lasted only a couple of years, then the prices dropped again until now.[91]

By 1949 the Protector expressed 'grave concern for the future of the industry'.[92] There had been a dramatic drop in prices and overseas markets were uncertain. One overseas buyer (probably Gerdau) had offered £301 per ton of pearl-shell, a rate at which it was impossible to make a profit, according to the Protector, who warned that as a result the ruling wage scale was in jeopardy. In the following season these problems were compounded by bad weather, and several luggers were laid up. It was in the midst of this crisis that the Protector abandoned the traditional wages policy and permitted pearl-shellers to share the risk with indigenous crew:

> The conditions of employment of islanders in this industry are closely guarded and the insistence is that these workers should be employed on a profit-sharing basis, to ensure they receive a reasonable return and that an incentive is provided for these workers in a particularly precarious industry.[93]

The timing of this shift reveals a marked sympathy with the problems of pearl-shellers. The Protector annually negotiated the wage rates for indigenous crew with the pearl-shellers' association at Thursday Island, and several Islanders have explained that this was why their wages were so low. They felt that in an open labour market they could gain higher wages. In 1955 there was an exodus of Torres Strait Islanders to the mainland, particularly from the Eastern Islands. Murray Islanders gained a good reputation in railway construction and on the canefields.

In 1957 the trochus market collapsed, but the blow was cushioned for Torres Strait Islanders because the IIB had won a three-year agreement with Gerdau which expired in January 1960. The DNA fleet was now the largest on Thursday Island and was able to absorb the Torres Strait Islanders who lost their jobs with pearl-shellers.

The IIB started to diversify into other business activities. It marketed collector's shells and encouraged curio manufacture. Its stores supplied sewing machines, radios, refrigerators, and furniture. The motto was 'What can be produced is bought, what can be consumed is sold!'.[94] In 1961 the IIB started to sell ornamental shells to American, New Guinean, South African and Australian buyers. For the sale of trochus shell, it was now necessary to advertise through newspapers and overseas trade commissioners. By this means, the IIB won a further three-year contract with Kuhlenkampf & Co. Pty Ltd of Sydney in 1960. In 1961 the first pearl-culture farms were established in Torres Strait, on Friday Island and Escape River, heralding a new era. The emphasis shifted from the pearl-shell to pearls. Japanese technicians once again took the skilled positions in this industry, and about forty Torres Strait Islanders were engaged in unskilled work. The DNA luggers started to collect live shell to sell to the culture farms. Because of the timely diversification of IIB activities, the decline in the pearl-shell industry was not reflected in the IIB figures. By 1962 over 1000 Torres Strait Islanders had migrated to the mainland, and it became difficult to staff the luggers. Prawning, crayfishing, and turtle-farming became the new marine activities.

There were several steps in the transformation of the lugger scheme. It started off as the co-operative company boats which harvested the home reefs with simple technology, and served both cash production and subsistence economy. Walker's vision was to create an independent yeomanry of producers. The PIL scheme and its aims were somewhat out of step with policy developments, because its establishment coincided with a change in administrative personnel at Thursday Island, with the result that a new agenda of tighter regulation was extended over the Islanders. The friction between the PIL and the DNA, and the initial lack of DNA control over the scheme, led to a negative assessment of the entire scheme. Only four years after the scheme began, the local Protector pronounced it a failure, because Torres Strait Islanders displayed managerial shortsightedness by their failure to accumulate a capital reserve. Yet regional prosperity had improved so markedly that as early as 1908 the Protector was able to divert income from the Island Fund to the Aboriginal Fund. Rather than make an effort to train Torres Strait Islanders in business management and accounting, the DNA itself gradually assumed the management of the luggers, content to 'assimilate' Torres Strait Islanders as manual workers.

The DNA's criticism of the scheme was inspired by the vision of mass production as the paradigm of successful enterprise: it was expected that luggers should be used only for cash production, should be staffed all year round, and should continue to operate even when the prices for pearl-shell or bêche-de-mer declined. The success of the scheme was measured in terms of output, volume of production and value of cash return, that is, by direct comparison to the profitability of wages boats which worked year round (from February to December), exploiting large areas for a single resource. In this assessment, debts accrued for repair loomed larger than the relief of seasonal famine.

Pressure from the pearl-shellers coloured the assessment by the Queensland government. The Protectors were more intent on controlling than emancipating Torres Strait Islanders, and interpreted the policy of assimilation in the interests of employers. The company boats competed with wages boats in the raising of shell, but they competed with the government at a much deeper level: they were co-operatively organised and reaffirmed traditional kinship structures and traditional claims to land, sea, and resources. They offered a basis for assimilation without rescinding traditional claims. Resisting such indigenous autonomy has been the consistent policy in Queensland until very recently.

The administration of indigenous people in Queensland has been highly dependent on individual Protectors, because legislation permitted considerable discretion for the executive. After Costin's departure from Thursday Island the Department's assessment of the lugger scheme became less pessimistic, and the appointment of O'Leary as local Protector at Thursday Island in 1922 represents a further step in the transformation. With O'Leary's business-like attitude and the formation of the IIB in 1930 the scheme became a state enterprise without being accountable to Torres Strait Islanders. By the late 1930s, 20 per cent of Islanders' wages (now including South Sea Islander descendants) were channelled into the Protector's budget, and Torres Strait Islanders were not only self-supporting but funds were diverted into the support of mainland reserves. After World War II O'Leary expressed the DNA's commitment to the scheme by removing the DNA office to Thursday Island and assuming the title of IIB manager.

Gradually, the DNA had assumed ownership of the means of production. It acted as an employer of wage labour, determining what produce to obtain, and where, sending the boats as far as Mackay, and taking advantage of advanced technology. The lugger scheme was completely transformed into a mass-producing, commercial enterprise.

The greatest impetus for the company boats took place in times of crisis for the industry. The scheme took off on a large scale in 1906 when prices dropped and shell was also getting scarce. Immediately after the war, when pearl-shellers had difficulty in revitalising the industry, the DNA became the most active pearl-sheller, rebuilding boatslips and warehouses on Thursday Island. Diving equipment was purchased in the 1950s when the industry was already on the decline, never having completely recovered from the upheaval of war.

The pastoral and marine industries were the mainstay of indigenous employment in Queensland. When these two industries collapsed between 1960 and 1975, indigenous Queenslanders were thrown back on to state assistance. But with the introduction of federal social service payments in 1960, the incentive of the State government in devising new enterprises waned. A flurry of projects, mostly with federal funding, was half-heartedly supervised by the DAIA. Allan Dale analyses the failure of such projects as the external imposition of ideas on Aboriginal communities. Pearl-shelling and stockwork had become, over three generations, traditional occupations where sons followed in their fathers' footsteps. They offered an occupational identity, and release from reserve life. Those who witnessed and participated in this era are resigned: 'We have gone backwards'.[95]

A Matter of Convenience: the Japanese Dominance in Pearl-shelling

While local indigenous labour was employed for swimming-diving, gathering trochus and bêche-de-mer, and as crew on apparatus boats, the Japanese became the favoured ethnic group to be recruited into dress-diving and tendering, the prestigious occupations within the industry. From the 1890s to World War II, thousands of Japanese came to Australia to participate in the pearl-shell industry and were acknowledged as its backbone. They were renowned as the best pearl-shell divers in the world and they also introduced technical modifications to the diving industry: they gave Thursday Island luggers their characteristic design, introduced the 'half dress' (a diving suit cut off at the waist for greater mobility), developed methods for testing for the presence of pearl-shell on the sea floor, and constructed glass-bottomed tubes to find bêche-de-mer.

Several Japanese captains attained almost legendary status in the industry, such as Captain Kono (Kono Tesaburo) and Tomi Fuji (Tomiharu Fuji). The latter settled at Thursday Island and his family, like the descendants of other Japanese captains, continues to live there. So close was the link between Thursday Island and Japan that this tiny island has a name in Japanese, Mokuyo-to. Over 600 graves at Thursday Island cemetery bear Japanese names, some with posthumous Buddhist names, although the Japanese recruits generally professed to belong to the Church of England so that they could get buried at the divers' cemetery. Thursday Island contained a 'Japanese town' with boarding houses, a public bath, stores, and a brothel. All of these were destroyed during World War II by American troops, who used the building materials for barracks. Only the Japanese Club house remains on Thursday Island, inhabited by a Chinese family. From 1893 the Japanese became the largest ethnic group in the pearl-shell industry, far outnumbering Europeans at Thursday Island. By the turn of the century, all the luggers built at Thursday Island were built by Japanese craftsmen, and most boatslips were owned by Japanese. They were not only the most successful ethnic group in the industry but they also caused the most resentment, because of their numerical dominance and because of the entrepreneurial competition which they presented to pearl-shellers. There was no State government department to administer this ethnic group, as there was for indigenous labour. Their administration was an international issue, for which after Federation the responsibility fell to the federal government—a Labor government whose policy was to expel coloured and Asian indentees. The pearl-shellers insisted that Japanese were indispensable for the fishery, and by a curious twist of argument their continued presence came to be accepted as quite within the spirit of the White Australia policy. The singular exemption of the pearl-shell fishery from the White Australia policy allowed the Japanese to further entrench their vested interest in the industry at the expense of locally available native labour.

These developments pose several questions: why did the Japanese become dominant? Why did pearl-shellers prefer them? How was their presence dealt with ideologically? What motivated them to work here despite adverse regulations, exploitative arrangements and squalid working conditions? These can be answered to some extent from interviews with former Japanese divers and crew, and the works of several writers provide much of the background to what follows.[1]

Early arrivals, 1876–90

For several centuries Japanese fishers sailed to China, Indonesia, and the Pacific Ocean—Guam, Palau, the Gilbert Islands and New Ireland. The Japanese ruling elite was receptive to the ideas promulgated by Western missionaries, but as the imperialist aspirations of Western nations were increasingly understood as a threat to Japanese sovereignty, Japan closed itself to the Western world in 1637, for 200 years. The Bakufu edict imposed the death penalty on Japanese attempting to leave the country, and all Western missionaries and merchants were expelled.[2] In 1854 Western traders were again permitted to set up business in Japan as a result of American military force. In 1866 the Japanese government for the first time issued passports to authorise overseas travel for Japanese, and Japanese workers began to be signed on as crew by British captains. One of the first Japanese consulates in the British Empire was established in Melbourne in 1879 to protect Japanese seamen from excessive exploitation in the world of capitalist colonialism which they were newly entering.

The first recorded Japanese diver in Torres Strait was Nonami Kojiro from Shimane Prefecture, arriving in 1876 at the age of about 25, who learned dress-diving from a Malay. Several other former Japanese sailors also became Torres Strait pearl-divers or crew, and performed so well that Burns Philp & Co. started recruiting discharged and impoverished Japanese sailors in Hong Kong. The Japanese first arrived in numbers in the 1880s when pearl-shellers started to recruit in Japan directly. In late 1884, a hundred Japanese were at Thursday Island, and in 1885 the Honorary Consul at Melbourne went to Thursday Island to hear grievances. The Japanese foreign ministry had reservations about Japanese employment in Australia, particularly after some men had returned to Japan and a Tokyo newspaper gave an unfavourable account of the working conditions on Thursday Island. Beri-beri was rife because the unbalanced diet provided by the pearl-shellers, and there were some casualties from racial conflicts. To curb the flow of migrants, the Japanese foreign ministry simply prohibited contracts which provided for the employer to cover the cost of passage, so that it became difficult to recruit divers—the passage cost more than the annual Japanese wage of about ¥40. The number of Japanese at Thursday Island dropped slightly from 200 in 1886 to 170 in 1890, and pearl-shellers again recruited from Hong Kong and Singapore, as they had in the 1870s.

Pearl-shellers were eager to employ Japanese as divers. It is possible that after having been sheltered from participation in the outside world for so long, those Japanese who volunteered for overseas contracts were among the most enterprising and adventurous, being reputedly more daring than Pacific Islanders, Filipinos or Malays. It is not that the Japanese recruits were somehow predisposed towards participation in the industry. An eyewitness in 1883 described their miserable introduction:

> In the early stages they were in dire straits. Among them were people who had never been in a boat in their lives. Seventy per cent were seasick. When aboard, their limbs ceased to answer. If there were any waves at all, they collapsed in the morning and remained in this condition all day. It was exactly as if we were taking the sick to sea . . .[3]

But on the whole they performed so well that pearl-shellers started to favour them over other types of labour, and their numbers at Thursday Island continued to increase. (See Table 3)

The profitability of pearl-shelling depended crucially on the work ethic of the divers. The remuneration system offered financial incentives for the diver, but not for the crew, to increase the catch. The divers' lay (payment per ton according to tonnage) either depended on the price realised at sale or was agreed to by annual negotiation. The diver was responsible for the rations, repair of equipment, and wages, and the pearl-sheller provided for the boat, equipment and boat repairs. The diver therefore shared the risk of loss when shell-beds were becoming depleted, weather conditions were unfavourable, or the prices dropped.

Until 1891 the Japanese were merely one of the ethnic groups employed in the industry, and the Japanese government continued to take a negative attitude towards emigration to Australia. In that year, however, a new Foreign Minister was appointed who encouraged emigration and later became a founder of the Colonists' Society. Japanese merchants began taking an interest in the migrant labour movement and facilitated worker migration with group finance. Groups of Japanese migrant workers were financed by private individuals who advanced ¥100–130 for each member. By now the shallower grounds of 10–20 metres had been depleted and pearl-shell was obtained from depths of 35–40 metres. Diving had accordingly become more dangerous with increasing mortality rates.[4] The emigrants were required to take out a life insurance policy for the benefit of the creditor, and each member vouched for the whole group, so that peer pressure ensured that the advances were paid off. After repaying the principal, usually within one year, 40 per cent of the combined overseas earnings of a group was due to the creditor. David Sissons has estimated the compound interest from such an investment to have been at least 27 per cent and up to 106 per cent.

TABLE 3   JAPANESE PARTICIPATION IN DIVING AT THURSDAY ISLAND (1895–1940)

Year	Total	Japanese	Others
1895	242	120	122
1896	269	139	130
1897	304	179	125
1898	331	211	120
1899	362	331	31
1900	390	234	156
1901			
1902	319	239	80
1903	354	252	102
1904	357	282	75
1905	367	291	76
1906	173	157	16
1907	180	174	6
1908	174	172	2
1909	155	142	13
1910	160	150	10
1911	190	172	18
1912	200	171	29
1913	175	168	7
1914	158	154	4
(no figures available for years 1915–24)			
1925	183	181	2
1926	143	143	0
1927	172	171	1
1928	212	212	0
1929	214	214	0
1930	95	95	0
1931	52	52	0
1932	103	103	0
1933	94	93	1
1934	95	94	1
1935	185	162	23
1936	246	211	35
1937	265	238	27
1938	246	232	14
1939	233	226	7
1940	195	175	20

Source: Reports of the Inspector of Pearl-Shell and Bêche-de-Mer Fisheries, Thursday Island, *QVP*

As a result of this commercialisation of Japanese migrant labour, the Japanese population at Thursday Island increased rapidly from less than 100 in 1892 to nearly 500 in 1893, to over 700 in 1894, overtaking the European population at Thursday Island.[5] The influx led to an oversupply of labour, and wage rates at Thursday Island dropped. In 1894 over 100 unemployed Japanese entered the mainland labour market. They created a further niche for Japanese indentees in the sugar plantations. The collective organisation which enabled their immigration also formed the basis for business opportunities once they arrived. Japanese formed combines and became the proprietors of luggers, and Japanese brothels in each Australian pearling port (Darwin, Wyndham, Cossack, Fremantle, and Thursday Island) provided finance for the purchase of luggers and slipways. This meant that the Japanese started to stand in competition with, instead of in the service of, the pearl-shellers. The threat of their commercial creativity was compounded by their sheer numerical presence at a time when the northern outpost was considered vulnerable to foreign incursions.[6] Legislation to restrict their entrepreneurial freedom was not yet in place.

John Douglas and James Clark claimed that the whole pearl-shelling industry was passing into Japanese hands, at a time when only eight of 183 luggers at Thursday Island were actually Japanese-owned. The business community at Thursday Island was fearful of the Japanese competition. A Japanese visitor in 1893 observed:

> The whites are beset with fears which they cannot put aside . . . In the course of my visit to the Island I often heard that the more influential among the natives [white Australians] were discussing what would happen in circumstances such as the following—if we invested big sums and set up large agencies there; if we exported shell to London without going through middle-men; or if our government sent several hundreds more of us there. It was obvious that our latent strength was causing fear among the Island's principal merchants and shopkeepers.[7]

The pearl-shellers were keenly aware that the only hold of white Australians over the industry was their control of the means of production. The labour power was non-white, and the pearl-beds were situated largely outside Australia's territorial limit. The commercial solidarity of the Japanese was therefore a serious threat. From the 1890s to 1916, pearl-shellers were engaged in a series of arguments with federal and State governments. The pearl-shellers wished to permit the employment of Japanese on the one hand, while curtailing their role in the industry to that of a dependent workforce on the other.

The resistance to Japanese dominance

As it became apparent that the Japanese were entrenching their position in the industry by making inroads into lugger-ownership, pearl-shellers no longer unequivocally supported their presence. They agreed that some kind of check was needed on their participation in the industry, and government officials at Thursday Island were inclined to support the pearl-shellers. John Douglas wrote: 'I am most decidedly of the opinion that all boats in this Fishery should be owned by British Subjects and that no boats except those belonging to British Subjects should be licensed'.[8]

Douglas called for a 'radical cure' of the Japanese problem, arguing that 'the distinction of colour and creed should not exist for us, so long as we secure the rightful ascendancy of our race'.[9] In other words, so long as white dominance was assured, there was no need for racial hatred. Douglas suggested that 'coloured aliens' should be denied permission to recruit indigenous labour. This would have prevented the Japanese skippers from taking control of the luggers. But Chief Protector Roth reminded the Government Resident that this was unlawful, as only Chinese were barred from obtaining recruiting licences under the 1897 Protection Act. Besides, Queensland was the only Australian colony which had endorsed the Anglo-Japanese Treaty of Commerce and Navigation which accorded Queensland exports to Japan beneficial treatment, and prevented Queensland from placing such restrictions on Japanese. Despite this, as local Protector of Aborigines issuing recruiting permits, Douglas decreed that all non-British applicants had to submit a written request for recruiting permits.[10]

On the advice of Douglas, the Queensland government began to voice opposition to the flow of migration from Japan and appealed to the Japanese government to restrict immigration to Australia. The flow of immigrants slowed, but not enough to alter the population trends at Thursday Island. In 1897 there were 1000 Japanese engaged there, almost double the number of European residents. Of

231 licensed boats, 22 were owned and 46 rented by Japanese with option to purchase, so that almost one-third of the pearl-shell fleet was in Japanese hands.

In response to the threat presented by Japanese commercial interests, a commission of inquiry was appointed in March 1897. Chaired by John Hamilton MP, the commission lent an open ear to pearl-shellers, merchants and officials at Thursday Island, and recommended restrictions on the operations of Japanese. As a result, the *Pearl-Shell and Bêche-de-mer Fishery Act 1881* was amended in December 1898 so that aliens could not rent boats or be issued boat licences.[11] This amendment was the first legislative attempt to fix the position of Japanese in the pearl-shell industry, by excluding them from ownership of the means of production. It was precisely the kind of race-ranking exercise which inspired labour radicals to insist on a White Australia policy. William Kidston condemned the amendment as hypocritical:

> It is the recognition that there are and there ought to be two races in Queensland—one a privileged race having all the rights and protection of the laws, and the other an alien serf race, not permitted to do the best they can for themselves—and only permitted to live here if they will work and make profit for someone else.[12]

The reference to aliens rather than Japanese in the amendment was made at the insistence of the British government, which was an ally of Japan. Nevertheless, the amendment was openly directed against the Japanese, and it was the government's intention that Asians would be excluded from naturalisation so that they could not circumvent these restrictions by taking on citizenship. In addition, the Queensland government considered the introduction of an immigration restriction act. Meanwhile any Japanese entering the State had to get special approval from the Queensland government, and all applications for entry of Japanese were rejected until October 1900. During this time other non-white groups, particularly Filipinos and Torres Strait Islanders, were beginning to be employed, and the number of Japanese on shipping articles declined from 576 to 318 between 1898 and 1901. In 1900, responding to pressure from the Japanese government and from pearl-shellers, the Queensland government began to allow replacements of Japanese to the level of 1898, but requests to introduce new crew members were only agreed to if they were made by white pearl-shellers. The government position therefore was the one desired by pearl-shellers to protect their interests. Japanese were barred from lugger-ownership and prevented from working in any capacity other than on pearling luggers, while avenues for pearl-shellers to tap the overseas cheap labour pools were kept open.

White Australia: an exception that confirms the rule

After the federation of the Australian colonies, immigration became the concern of the new federal government, which placed immigration restriction high on its list of priorities. The federal government was more removed than the Queensland government from the interests of the pearl-shellers, and made several attempts to implement the substitution of foreign with white labour. Still, employees in the pearl-shell and bêche-de-mer industry were exempted from the provisions of the Immigration Restriction Act of 1901. The federal government initially accepted the 1902 population of coloured persons as a ceiling up to which replacements could be made and granted additional permits for new boat licences in order to allow the industry to grow, but a Senate resolution of 1905 restricted the immigration of non-whites to replacement of departing workers.

Workers for the pearl-shell industry were only allowed into Australia if they were under a contract of indenture (normally three years). The recruits were issued with an identification certificate showing their handprint and two photographs which was only valid for the purpose of diving in Australia. The employer covered the cost of passage and deposited a bond with the Queensland government to ensure that indentured labourers did not penetrate the mainland labour market; they were therefore a captive workforce. This arrangement again served the needs of the pearl-shellers while at the same time heeding the pressures of the White Australia policy which was now high on the political agenda of Labor forces.

Former indentees described the procedures: they registered their interest with one of their relatives in Australia, and waited until one of the captains recommended them to a pearl-sheller. Requests for labour (translated into English as 'letters of calling' or 'summonses') were sent by pearl-shellers to recruiting firms in Japan such as the Kobe Industrial Immigration Company or Morishima Immigration

Company in Kushimoto, a large landholder. The recruits were assigned to 'free pensions' in Kobe, that is, the immigration companies paid their expenses in special guesthouses. The firms arranged for medical examinations, the signing of contracts and the issue of identity papers. Recruits had to testify that they were going of their own volition. The contract of indenture spelled out in great detail the requirements of each worker. It contained stipulations concerning the quantity and variety of food dealt out as rations, number of meals, mealtimes, the standard and size of sleeping quarters, working hours, the mode of payment, holidays, and so on. (These specifications were similar to those provided for by the *Pacific Islanders Protection Act 1880*, and South Sea Islanders who were indentured for work on Queensland sugar plantations were required to sign similar contracts.) Such contracts were meant to safeguard the recruits from exploitation, but they were a mere formality, and the workers themselves accepted that the company was not bound by them. When they arrived at Thursday Island, the workers signed a different contract with the employer:

> We signed two different contracts. One at Kobe which was negotiated between the two governments—this was just a formality, so that we could leave Japan. The second contract was signed when we arrived at Thursday Island; it was a contract between the workers and the company. It was not a matter of cheating. Our elders had described to us what to expect.[13]
>
> . . . when we arrived [at Thursday Island] we signed another contract, because conditions on the boat were different . . . The Kobe contract was a mere formality. It had been negotiated between the Japanese and the Australian governments, it was just a showpiece.[14]

The actual treatment received by indentured workers depended not on written agreements, which were made to satisfy government regulations in the country of origin and in Australia, but on their access to social and political power. Chapter 2 has shown that the most powerful political support of indigenous people, the Department of Native Affairs, pursued its own goals in representing native employees *vis-à-vis* white employers. Unlike the indigenous participants in the industry, the Japanese were able to draw on several sources of social and political power. The Japanese government was highly conscious of its reputation in the Western world and therefore sought to protect its *emigré* nationals from exploitation by placing

conditions on employment agreements, and by consular representation in Australia. It also sent observers into the Western countries
who independently reported on the working and living conditions of
Japanese abroad and on ways in which Japan could simulate Western
production methods.[15] The Anglo-Japanese alliance provided further
protection, because Japan could influence decisions made in Australia through its British ally. But the most effective source of power of
the Japanese at Thursday Island was their social organisation.

Around the turn of the century shell-beds were becoming depleted, so that luggers had to go further afield and the work became
more difficult. In 1905 Hockings and the large Clark fleet left for
the Aru Islands in Dutch New Guinea. The departure of over 100
boats and about 500 men meant that the Thursday Island fleet was
reduced almost by half. Clark argued that the federal government's
restrictions on recruiting had caused a shortage of labour and the
severe slump which the industry was suffering in 1906. This was
evidently untrue, since the departure of the floating stations left over
300 South Sea Islanders unemployed who had sheltered at Thursday
Island from the provisions of the Immigration Restriction Act.

The resource crisis placed downward pressure on wages on Thursday Island. Japanese divers demanded to be issued free diving dresses,
as had been the practice on floating-stations. They organised a strike,
to which the pearl-shellers responded with a lockout. But since few
other trained divers were available, the Japanese gained an increase
in remuneration. Out of 165 divers licensed at Thursday Island in
1908, 164 were Japanese, and anti-Japanese feelings ran high.

The Queensland government evidently saw a need to assist the
ailing industry, and attempted to settle the problem of coloured
labour at the State level. A further public inquiry in 1908, chaired
by Brisbane portmaster John Mackay, sought to devise strategies to
replace Japanese with white or indigenous labour. The list of arguments against Japanese employment in the industry was long. Not
only did they hold a monopoly over diving, the fact that they out-
numbered Europeans in Torres Strait was considered a defence risk.
John Bleakley of the DNA argued that they contributed nothing to
Australian wealth because they sent their savings home. The Thursday Island merchants argued that the Japanese were the cause of the
depression at Thursday Island because they imported their own food
and bought provisions at their own shops, even forcing their crew
to spend money in alien instead of European shops.

During these hearings, a division of interest between shore-station owners and floating-station owners became evident. Floating-station owners tended to support the notion that the Japanese were indispensable, whereas shore-station owners felt that with sufficient financial incentive from the government, they could be replaced. Floating stations were more highly capitalised and had larger overhead costs. All provisioning and equipment was borne by the company, which therefore paid a smaller lay on the shell procured by each diver. On floating stations, all shell was opened on the mother schooner in the presence of a white supervisor, and any pearls found were claimed by the company, while shore-station owners had no means of supervising the operations of their boats, or the opening of the pearl-shell. The skipper was in complete command of the boat, responsible for provisioning, recruiting, and wages. It had become the practice for the divers to claim any pearls found on shore-station boats.[16] With the extra income from pearls, estimated at £8000 per annum on Thursday Island, shore-station employment had become more remunerative for divers, with the result that floating-stations had experienced a shortage of divers.

Shore-station owners felt the entrepreneurial dominance of their Japanese skippers, which left them little control over the luggers. Several Japanese skippers flew the Japanese flag on the boats, which were formally owned by white pearl-shellers, and were registered in Queensland. Hockings remarked that 'the present boat owner is not the master of ceremonies he previously posed to be upon the ruling of what are supposed to be his shelling affairs'.[17]

The floating-station owners, notably Clark and Hockings, defended the qualities of Japanese divers. Clark argued that 'the best diver in the world for getting shell was the Japanese', and that it took a special gift for recognising shell on the sea floor.[18] He referred to a 'special faculty' for finding shell, similar to Aboriginal tracking skills. The Japanese were a cheap labour force, and they were hardworking. The aim of the large companies was to continue employing Japanese, but restricting their number to that required by pearl-shellers, and their role to that of a dependent workforce.

The hope of the shore-station owners to gain some concessions from supporting the removal of Japanese from the industry was well founded. The Royal Commission sought to encourage small, independent white entrepreneurs by limiting the number of boat licences to five for each owner. Its aim was to place the industry on a stable and sustainable footing. It recommended a complete restructuring program for the industry, establishing a training school for divers, and gradually replacing coloured divers with whites.

John Mackay hoped to recreate the former state of the industry, before Japanese divers arrived, when white owner-operators had small stations on the islands of Torres Strait. It was suggested that small owner-operators could combine pearl-shell farming with tropical agriculture, turtle-breeding and dugong-hunting. The commissioners repeatedly drew the comparison of pearl-shell fishing with fishing off Brittany or in the North Sea, and witnesses agreed that pearl-shelling in Torres Strait was far more agreeable. Some years later Mackay actually suggested this career to European fishers and had to revise his opinion because they scorned the idea. The witnesses, who personally remembered the beginnings of the industry (one of them was Yankee Ned Mosby of Yorke Island), differed greatly in their estimates of the numbers of former white divers, and possibly overestimated the number in retrospect.[19] Despite contrary evidence from several witnesses, the commissioners held fast to the notion that white divers had been pushed out of the industry by the massive entry of Japanese which had begun in 1891, and that they would once again be attracted into diving if the Japanese were held back and better incentives offered.

The commission's recommendations and massive 355-page report were ignored by both State and federal governments. A complete restructuring was too costly, and the industry too economically insignificant to warrant the high degree of financial and regulatory state involvement it required. Moreover, the division of powers between State and Commonwealth complicated the issue of reform. The State administered the fisheries, whereas the Commonwealth was responsible for immigration and customs.

The federal Labor government was strengthened by the 1910 elections and it now attempted to rigorously implement the White Australia policy by removing the Japanese from the pearl-shell industry. In 1911 instructions were issued that after July 1913 only five Malays per lugger could be indentured, and only if the diver and tender were both white men. Even those pearl-shellers who had supported the replacement of Japanese with white divers had done so with the proviso that the industry receive State support similar to the bonuses awarded to the sugar industry for the introduction of white workers. The Mackay Commission had recommended the phasing out of Japanese labour within the framework of complete reform based on financial and scientific assistance. The Western Australian government joined pearl-shellers in objecting to these instructions, because it felt that Broome depended entirely on the pearl-shell industry for its existence, and pearl-shellers were arguing that without the Japanese there would be no pearl-shell industry. In response to the protests from pearl-shellers, the federal government initiated the Bamford Royal Commission in 1912 to investigate 'the preponderance of the Japanese'.[20] The introduction of restrictions on Japanese divers was deferred to 1915, and then to 1918, and finally abandoned as the result of the Bamford inquiry.

Japanese nationalism had become increasingly aggressive, and Japan started to offer military resistance to the imperialist claims of other nations. Signs of this attitude were the Sino-Japanese war over Korea (1894–95) and the Russo-Japanese war over Manchuria (1904–05), as a result of which 'Japan became the first Asian nation to prove its superiority over a Western power'.[21] Although Britain had allied itself with Japan to resist Russian imperialism, Australia, Canada, and America started to fear Japanese expansion and curbed Japanese immigration. In a climate of animosity towards Japanese in Australia, sectional interests in Queensland were using the White Australia objective without sharing its philosophy with the labour movement. An Australian Fisheries Association, a loose collection of small owners, mainly of bêche-de-mer luggers, was formed in 1906 to combat Japanese boat-ownership by dummying.

> The only object that we in the north have in view is to keep the ownership of the boats and the diving operations in the hands of white men . . . The association was formed in every way to advance the interests of white as against coloured fishermen . . . The AWU is 'out' for a White Australia, and is opposed to the employment of any alien labour, whereas we do not object to the employment of aborigines, Papuans, or any Polynesian labour, as boats' crews.[22]

This interest group felt that the dominance of the Japanese in the industry was threatening, and it sought to replace them with white divers. In this objective they were aligned with the Australian Waterside Workers Union, whose members at Thursday Island were some former white divers and wharf labourers who would have liked to try their luck in the industry. They were so certain that suitable white divers could be found that they placed an advertisement in the southern press inviting white divers to apply for positions at

Thursday Island, while the 1913 Royal Commission was sitting. Unfortunately for their case, the response was not encouraging as not one reply was from an experienced diver. This alliance of interest criticised the division of responsibilities in the administration of the industry between Commonwealth and State authorities, and suggested that the industry be controlled entirely by the Commonwealth, because it expected that the Commonwealth government would be more amenable to excluding Japanese. The larger owners represented by the Pearl-Shellers Association, on the contrary, suggested that the State take control over the industry, since it was 'more in touch'.[23] Both the Western Australian and Thursday Island Pearl-Shellers Associations made submissions to this effect.

The pearl-shellers were sceptical of the potential of white divers, but nevertheless made some luggers available to the federal government for an experiment. The superior merit of white divers was tested by recruiting nine British certified deep-sea divers who were familiar with the Navy's staging techniques. Three died from divers' paralysis and the others gave up, and, according to James Clark, none of them had raised more shell than an untrained Asian try-diver. This experiment was subsequently often referred to as the ultimate rebuttal of suggestions that white divers could carry on the industry. Some doubts, however, were raised about the validity of the experiment, suggesting that the divers had been sent to work on a patch which was already depleted.

The question of the disappearance of white divers from the industry was re-examined, and there was actually a consensus among all parties that they had not been 'squeezed out of the industry' by Japanese, as the 1908 inquiry had been willing to accept. John Mackay himself, who had chaired the earlier commission, now thought that alcoholism had been the cause for the failure of white divers. James Clark said that they had left the industry because they tended to buy luggers and found it unprofitable. Even those who painted a grim picture of the 'yellow peril' admitted that white divers had caused their own demise by their drinking and gambling habits:

> White men do not go in sufficiently for combination. They are too jealous of each other . . . It is largely the fault of the white men themselves that they have become as weak as they are in Thursday Island. While they were gradually becoming weaker the Japanese were insidiously creeping into the industry.[24]

Although the general contention among officials was that the Japanese would thwart any attempt to introduce white divers, there was no evidence that the Japanese had actively resisted the employment of white divers in the past in Queensland. Nevertheless, the Japanese were in fact so dominant in the industry that their anticipated reaction was a major consideration in the experimental introduction of white divers. If they struck, the industry would be at a standstill. Moreover, some owners of bêche-de-mer boats feared that coloured crews would desert if they were not under the charge of a Japanese skipper.

In its final report in 1916, the Bamford Commission rejected the notion that white Australians could replace coloured divers. As in the sugar industry, the replacement of coloured with white labour would have meant an increase in production costs, but unlike sugar, mother-of-pearl was a luxury item already in danger of substitution by other materials, and there was no domestic market. This meant that the increased cost could not be passed on to the market without endangering the industry as a whole. Moreover, the Bamford Commission pointed out that white divers were not attracted to the industry because of the harsh working conditions and health risks. The annual death rate of divers was over 10 per cent, while the Queensland death rate was 1.1 per cent.[25] It was argued that white men could not be exposed to these health risks:

> the limit of a pearlshell diver's working life is from five to seven years, and then he too often retires with a legacy of paralysis, rheumatism, or pulmonary disease which materially shortens his life, and too often leaves him a mental and physical wreck.[26]

The federal government now accepted that pearl-shell diving was not a suitable occupation for whites:

> Having carefully weighed the evidence ... your Commissioners have decided that diving for shell is not an occupation which our workers should be encouraged to undertake. The life is not a desirable one, and the risks are great, as proved by the abnormal death rate amongst divers and try divers. The work is arduous, the hours long, and the remuneration quite inadequate. Living space is cramped, the food wholly preserved of its different kinds, and the life incompatible with that a European worker is entitled to live.[27]

This was the argument which had long been used to plead for an exemption from the White Australia policy: 'It seems to me that the lives of the strongest and best of our workers—and these only may engage in diving—may be employed with greater advantage and profit to the Commonwealth than in the pearling industry'.[28]

Two authors have considered the relevance of this decision for the White Australia policy. J. P. S. Bach argued in 1956 that if the White Australia policy was to secure a high living standard, and was based on a 'well-developed social conscience with regard to the social status of the worker', then the exception granted because of the self-interest of influential pearl-shellers discredited the entire objective. Because of their access to cheap labour, pearl-shellers lost touch 'with the realities of normal Australian industrial conditions', and the creation of a coolie class undermined the moral authority of 'White Australia': 'the Commonwealth laid itself open to charges of insincerity when it allowed aliens to enter the country as workers, but refused them the right to share in the material rewards of their labours'.[29] Bach wrote at a time when the White Australia policy was being practically eroded by a massive influx of postwar immigrants from Europe, but had not been officially abandoned.

Lorraine Philipps, on the other hand, argues that the exception confirmed the rule. The 'moral authority' of the policy never did extend to non-whites. It did not aim to improve the position of Aborigines, for example, nor, for that matter, of women. The decision to exempt the industry was based on the consideration that diving was dangerous and harsh, and exposed divers to 'racial contamination' from close association with coloured crew. Once it was accepted that crew would never be white, it was found much preferable to engage alien divers—if they could be kept in dependence on white employers. 'It is thus evident that administrative developments with respect to the shelling industry strongly reflected the policy objectives of White Australia.'[30] Philipps argues that a commitment to the White Australia objective was the major determining factor in the decision.

However, it is apparent in the evidence given to the Bamford Commission that pearl-shellers were simply threatening to leave Australia altogether, so determined were they to continue employing Japanese divers. Both Australian and overseas fleets could register under the Dutch flag of convenience and harvest the grounds from Merauke in Dutch New Guinea (or from Dutch Timor instead of Broome), as the large Clark fleet had been doing since 1905. Like Social Darwinist terminology with respect to other coloured workers, 'White Australia' arguments had been successfully used by employers to demonstrate the unsuitability of diving for white Australians.

David Sissons explored the party-political background of this policy shift. When the federal Labor government gained a majority, it was committed to turn coloured, especially Japanese, divers, out of the industry. Shortly after it appointed the Bamford Commission, a conservative government was elected in May 1913. There were some changes in the personnel of the Commission, which held over its final report until the end of World War I, but the final report did not add anything of significance to the progress report of 1913. The decision to exempt the pearl-shell industry was made in the last weeks of a Labor cabinet.

The decision did not reflect party-political shifts, but may have been influenced by international pressures, from Britain and Japan. During World War I Malayan and Papuan labour was often in short supply and the government was cautious not to offend Japan by discriminating against Japanese. The Treaty of Versailles confirmed a prewar agreement between Britain and Japan, when England supported Japan's claims over the German Micronesian islands north of the equator (Marianas, Caroline and Marshall Islands), and Japan supported Britain's claim over the German islands of Samoa, New Guinea and Nauru south of the equator. Japan used the leverage of this military alliance during World War I to protest against Australian anti-Japanese attitudes and unsuccessfully sought the incorporation of the principle of racial equality into the peace covenant, against Australian resistance.

The federal government was therefore faced with opposition from Britain and Japan, as well as with the threat from pearl-shellers to take the industry offshore. Moreover, the authorities began to realise that much of the shelling industry was carried out in waters outside the territorial 3-mile limit, so that Australia had no actual jurisdiction over the pearling grounds. The government preferred to continue allowing the use of coloured labour in order to retain some jurisdiction over the industry, to retain the revenue from it, and to be seen to be supporting an Australian industry.

The only further government action to restrict Japanese dominance was to limit the number of indentured men from the same ethnic background to a maximum of five on the same boat. This restriction was implemented in 1923 after Japanese had taken to the streets during annual wage negotiations (see below p. 120). It aimed at ensuring that a whole crew could not consist of Japanese. The figure permitted two divers, two tenders, and a cook to be from the same ethnic background as a concession to the relationship of trust between divers and tenders, and to their culinary idiosyncrasies. Nevertheless, the number of divers from other nationalities continued to dwindle, and from 1925 to 1934 all but one of an average of 126 divers licensed at Thursday Island were Japanese, and from 1935 to 1940 Japanese made up some ninety per cent of pearl-shell divers licensed at Thursday Island (see Table 3).

The social mechanisms of Japanese success

Federal attempts to curb the Japanese dominance were directed at limiting the number of entrants into the industry. But it was not so much their numerical dominance as their virtual monopoly of the divers' role which gave the Japanese industrial strength, and their social organisation was instrumental in making the period of indenture financially successful despite the temptation to drink and gamble, a vice shared by all ethnic groups in the industry.

The inexorable appropriation of the diving role by the Japanese was due to the practice that it was the prerogative of the head diver to nominate new recruits, who were usually relatives of the diver. The result was that rather than placing a check on the dominance of Japanese, the ceilings applied to the entry of Japanese entrenched their appropriation of the diving role through nepotism. Because kinship ties were a prime criterion of recruitment, a Japanese boat crew formed a close-knit group which imposed strict behavioural norms on its members. The new recruits were generally assigned to the captain who had nominated them. Normally they worked as cooks for a year, and then progressed along an informal career ladder as enginemen, tenders and try-divers, before becoming divers. The role of diver itself carried certain privileges and considerable prestige, both while in Australia and at home, and it was the aim of every recruit to become a diver, so that pearl-shelling was more than a short-term financial attraction, it was a career path. A lugger captain was in total command of his crew, who were like personal servants for him: 'We were the inferiors of [Captain] Kono. He could order us to wash his clothes. The youngest on the ship worked for the eldest. You rowed him ashore and picked him up again if he wanted to go to a movie . . . It is a very lowly experience'.[31] A Japanese diver

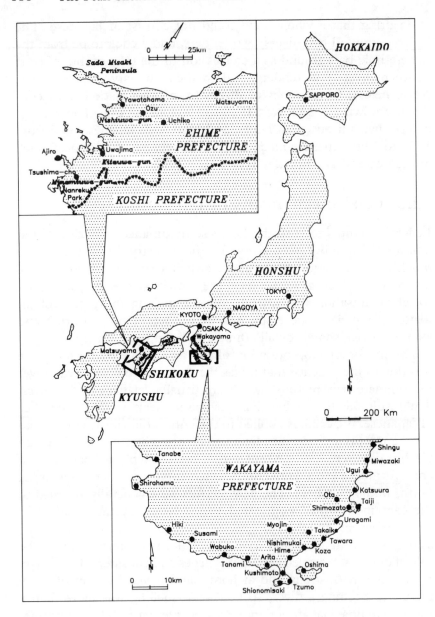

Map 3   Recruiting areas in Japan

explained the discipline on board: 'Living on a lugger was similar to military service, with strict hierarchies and lines of command. The captain was obeyed at all times. It is a Japanese tradition to live in a hierarchy'.[32]

Divers who were in charge of boats had a high standing in the industry. The head divers stayed in boarding houses referred to as Iyo House for those from Ehime Prefecture (Iyo is an older term for Ehime), or Susami House, Kushimoto House, Izumo House, etc. named according the village of origin of its residents from Wakayama Prefecture. The Japanese crew normally stayed on the luggers but used the boarding houses for recreation, and also stayed there during the lay-up season from December to March. New recruits were nominated by head divers who normally recommended someone whose family was familiar, so that particular villages had long-standing links with specific recruitment destinations.

Most pearl-shell divers at Thursday Island came from Ehime and Wakayama Prefectures (see Map 3). Their villages are perched precariously on the extremely narrow coastline between rugged mountains and rocky shores, and the connecting road which threads through them is at times hewn into the rock. Competition for arable land is fierce, and the villagers eke out an existence with a combined fishing-farming economy. Before World War II, Wakayama had no infrastructural link with Tokyo, and had therefore no access to the Japanese domestic market for its produce. An inward-looking economy developed. Tokyo was further away in the imagination of these villagers than was Thursday Island. To the young boys, who at age 17 had been neither to Tokyo nor abroad, the distances involved were merely conceptual. In some villages it was common for the more enterprising among them to go to Thursday Island if they had the chance, whereas other villages looked to America or Brazil to escape the narrow career opportunities and poverty at home.

Some senior Japanese captains and businessmen fulfilled the role of *oyakata*, or patriarchal employer, for groups of Japanese. They handled the money and transmitted savings of the younger crew, issued work clothes, and stipulated the standard of dress required to go to town. The young recruits had a great degree of personal dependence on such leaders.

> I was under the care of Yamashita Haruoshi, the president of the Japanese Club. He was in his 40s or 50s and took care of everybody, also concerning the wages. He sent my money home, I never had any

money. We had no need for spending money. Even clothes were supplied by the elders . . . The only money I needed was for postage stamps. The money I sent home might have been 200 Yen per month, but I really can't remember, because I never saw the money, only the receipts. We never doubted Yamashita, he was like a father.[33]

Yamashita was a storekeeper on Thursday Island.

The first diver gave our pay directly to Yamashita, four times a year . . . Yamashita sent my money home. I bought clothes with the pocketmoney. I needed a white shirt and pants if I wanted to go to the movies. Yamashita made sure we kept good appearances if we went to town, no shorts were allowed. We didn't need clothes to work, only if we wanted to go to the movies or drinking.[34]

A divers' club, or *Doshi-kai*, was formed in 1917. It has come to be referred to as the Japanese Club, but it was actually a fraternity of divers to which Japanese crew did not properly speaking belong. The *Doshi-kai* led the annual negotiations with the master pearlers in which the price of shell was agreed. The wages of the Japanese crew then depended on the price of shell as determined during these negotiations and on the tonnage raised.

Because of the consultative nature of wage-fixing procedures and the *oyakata*-style social organisation, militant industrial action was not generally considered a fruitful avenue among the Japanese. Head divers felt bound by the annual negotiations, and crew considered it a matter of loyalty to abide by the conditions negotiated by the head divers.[35] Nevertheless, there were exceptions. The reports of the Department of Harbours and Marine referred to the fact that in 1919 'much time was lost through labour troubles'.[36] In February 1923 the wage negotiations at Thursday Island became deadlocked, and 400 Japanese marched to the house of Mr Adams, the manager of Burns Philp. According to Thursday Island officials, they shook the house and threatened Adams, while police watched helplessly.[37] It was rumoured that the Japanese contemplated the assassination of two pearl-shellers. The police magistrate found the local defence insufficient and asked for reinforcements from the Department of Defence. The wages dispute lasted until August and received considerable attention. HMAS *Geranium* investigated the incident and found that the Japanese had behaved in an orderly way and that their demonstration had not been directed against the townspeople. The Defence Department concluded that this was a purely industrial disagreement which should be handled by the State in order to prevent it from becoming an international incident. As a result the number of indentured men from the same ethnic background was limited to a maximum of five on the same boat. In 1929 Japanese divers again achieved a rise from £95 lay per ton to £105 through industrial action.[38]

Further reference to industrial action is made in the report of the Department of Harbours and Marine for the year 1934–35 which says that temporal dissatisfaction of divers regarding their terms of agreement led to a slight delay in the start of operations, and that some employers dismissed their Japanese divers and laid up their luggers, recommissioning them later in the season with Malay divers. This response by employers to industrial action broke the almost absolute monopoly the Japanese had exercised over the role of diver since before World War I. (This trend is reflected in Table 3.) The renewed attempt to replace Japanese with indentured Malay divers coincided with the arrival of Japanese-owned fleets in Australian waters.

The Japanese were reputed to be hardworking. The lay system offered financial incentives for divers to maximise the catch. The way in which responsibility was shared between the owner and the diver virtually indemnified pearl-shellers against loss on the working of the vessel, and it was the head diver who bore the risk of loss when conditions were unfavourable. The onus was on the Japanese themselves to make the endeavour profitable. Diving was only possible in clear water from late March to December, avoiding the North-West monsoon and springtides.[39] The only way to increase the catch was to attempt more and longer dives while conditions were favourable. This exertion increased the risk of bends in an already perilous occupation. The workday normally extended from dawn to dusk. If bêche-de-mer were caught, the work went on through the night: 'you had no time to sleep, you have to make money, see? . . . By the time all of the fees were subtracted there was nothing left if you didn't have a good tonnage'.[40]

The Japanese would take turns to navigate at night, so that as little time as possible was lost in moving from one shell-bed to the next. The workday on diving boats started in the small hours of the day: 'As a cook I got up at 2 or 3 a.m., made a yeast dough, cooked rice and miso soup, then baked the bread. The divers were down before sunrise'.[41] It is said of one skipper that he slept on deck instead of on his bunk, in order not to become too lazy. With this kind of motivation, the Japanese made an attractive workforce in an industry which relied substantially on the performance of the divers to increase profits. Their primary orientation was towards their home and families. While they were here, they were prepared to take risks and content themselves with difficult working conditions. A pearl-sheller said, 'I do not think you would ever get white men to put up with the life they would have to live on luggers'.[42]

Generally speaking, the Japanese were a transient labour force, but several of them stayed for extended periods, 'oversigning' at the expiry of their initial three-year contract. Still, even those who stayed most of their working lives thought of themselves as temporary visitors at Thursday Island. One Japanese diver who spent sixteen years there between 1927 and 1946 called Thursday Island his second home, but he nevertheless said that 'it was money we wanted, so we could eat'.[43] Another former diver explained:

> If you were a diver and saved your money you could return to Japan quickly. All the young men wanted to be divers . . . That's why there were many accidents among young divers, they wanted to make money fast. It is a Japanese trait to be greedy. We want everything quickly. The Chinese would bury their bone on Thursday Island and make a fortune, but the Japanese are not like that, they want to go home again quickly.[44]

Most of them were sending money home to support their families, and if they did not have enough money they would seek an advance on their wages and indebt themselves. These are the terms in which Japanese described their earning capacity:

> If I worked as a cook for two years I could build a big house, it was big money for a 17-year-old. In Japan it would take you fifty years to earn that sort of money.[45]

> One month's pay at TI was as much as the mayor of Susami got. We were earning that at age 16, 17, making money like a high-school principal.[46]

> There was no income here. You could only be a fisherman, farmer or carpenter, and on TI you earned twice as much.[47]

> The Shionomisaki divers were first-class divers. They earned more than TV stars.[48]

The prospect of accumulated savings and high earnings was the prime motivation for Japanese recruits. In 1890, ten Japanese on their way back to Japan won £22 500 in the Melbourne Cup sweepstakes. Their return as rich men contributed to a rush from

Wakayama Prefecture to a land of bounty and promise. One pearl-sheller referred to this incident in 1913:

> In the early days there was no restriction on their introduction, and there were several successful Japanese divers, who had obtained a few pearls. A great impetus was given to the inrush of Japanese to Thursday Island by the good fortune of a Japanese syndicate, which drew Carbine in a Tattersall's sweep when that horse won the Melbourne Cup. The prize money amounted to £22,000. A lot of that money went to Japan. Most of the single men who were members of the syndicate went home at once, and the fact that these men had plenty of money led others to come here ... The win ... had an important influence in inducing Japanese to come to the island. They had no conception of how the money had been obtained. All they knew was that their friends had come home with a lot of money and they at once concluded that Thursday Island was a good place in which to make money.[49]

Four of these men were from Wakayama Prefecture, and a local historian described how upon their return they displayed their wealth through gambling and frivolous spending. Only one of them invested wisely: 'he bought whole mountains of cedar trees. He was a good man. [He did not gamble.] He used all his money to buy mountains in Shionomisaki, Koza, Shingu, and he became the biggest mountain owner, the richest man in the area, and sent his children to university'.[50]

A Japanese observer gave this impression of the reaction of Japanese villagers to the display of wealth brought from Australia:

> At Shionomisaki, for example, almost the whole village went *en masse*. It is said that things have reached the stage where, in estimating a man's worth, instead of enquiring whether he has made any money, they ask whether he has ever worked in Australia, and that the same question is asked when marriages (or the adoption of an heir into a family with no son) are being negotiated.[51]

According to one Japanese observer in 1894, it was not unusual for the emigrants to send home ¥100 per annum even in their first year. The average annual wage in Japan was around ¥40 at the time.[52] In 1913 the average yearly savings of Japanese were estimated at £40 each.[53] However, a comparison of wages at this time indicates that the Japanese had to work hard for their financial advantage over those who stayed at home.

In 1913 a Japanese fisher could expect to earn £1 1s a month (about £12 12s per annum). As crew on a pearling vessel, according to one employer, he could expect to earn between £3 and £3 10s per month (£27 to £31 10s per annum, working for nine months in the year).[54] According to the Japanese interpreter at Thursday Island, wages were lower, however, at £1 10s a month for the first year of recruitment, rising to £2 a month in the third year, that is never more than £24 per annum (if working for twelve months), and as little as £13 10s, which was little more than the average income of a fisher in Japan. A diver, on the other hand, might expect to earn as much as £120 per annum, and a tender £72. These rates were not high enough to attract white divers—the equivalent Harvester wage in Brisbane was £123 10s per annum.

The savings which some recruits sent home were enough to fully support their families. Many substantial houses were built from Australian earnings in the Japanese villages from where the recruits came. Some returned recruits were able to purchase a farm or a fishing boat with their savings to improve their social and economic position. 'But the lasting effect of immigration was education for their children . . . They wanted them to be teachers, doctors, and so on. Even the nieces and nephews were sent to school. Shiono-misaki is famous for its high level of education.'[55]

The houses built from Australian savings are monuments of the success of former 'emigrants'. Even today former pearl-shell divers enjoy the status of minor celebrities in Japan, comparable perhaps to our Anzac veterans. A *Mokuyoto-kai* (Thursday Island Club) was formed in Wakayama and erected a monument at Thursday Island in 1979 in honour of the Japanese divers who had died there. One family whose brother had died at Thursday Island contributed ¥2 million to the monument. The Japanese press remains receptive to news items relating to former Arafura Divers. A Japanese historian of the industry said that even the white women at Thursday Island would lift their hats if a diver passed them on the streets.[56] Whether or not it can be taken literally, this kind of statement underlines the image of these divers at home.

The Japanese motivation to participate in the industry was strong. Recruits came from impoverished areas of Japan where a stint in Australia not only made a big economic difference to their future life but also gained them considerable prestige, particularly if they had managed to become a diver. These were incentives to work hard, and the work ethic was further enhanced by the strong social links which existed between divers and their crew. The industrial strength which their monopoly of the diving position afforded them was used by the Japanese to defend their privileged position at Thursday Island.

The postwar resumption of pearl-shelling

In December 1942 all Japanese in Australia, including those who were indentured, were sent to internment camps in Hay, New South Wales, and Tatura, Victoria, for four years, until 1946. They saw themselves as civilians and felt protected in the knowledge that they were not, properly speaking, prisoners of war. When they were released from Hay, the Japanese arrived back in war-torn Japan with their Australian savings, which should have been the foundation for a prosperous future, but rampant inflation rendered their fortunes worthless:

> All our savings were in the bank, and the banks simply closed. When we got back we came with nothing. At home they said we should have bought things, goods, but we brought our money with us and it was not worth anything.[57]

> My savings had been confiscated by the Australian government and they were getting interest. I was supposed to build a house with it, but all you could buy with it when I got back was two tatami mats.[58]

After World War II, pearl-shellers sought to resume the employment of Japanese divers. But the Torres Strait Islanders allied themselves with the Australian Legion of Ex-Servicemen and Women to resist the reintroduction of Japanese. The Director of Native Affairs argued strongly that pearl-shell diving ought to be reserved for Torres Strait Islanders.

> The population of Thursday Island, white and coloured, and the Islanders of Torres Strait and aboriginals on Cape York Peninsula are in the main dependent on the marine industry, viz. pearlshell and trochus-shell, for a livelihood. From this industry are the corollary undertakings of shipwright, blacksmith, carpenter, storekeeper, &c., but without the pearling and trochus industry . . . Thursday Island as a town would be nonexistent and the Islanders and aboriginals would be in a particularly difficult position industrially. It is therefore natural that every effort to further this industry must be taken to permit the continuation of this outpost of Australia as a unit in the life of a nation and for its ultimate defence . . . These Island workers . . . regard the ocean as their domain, the birthright of their race.[59]

Some local sections of the ALP joined in the protest. To satisfy Australian pearl-shellers without offending anti-Japanese sentiments, the indenture of 106 Okinawans was permitted in 1958. Okinawa was an American mandated territory, so that it could be argued that the recruits were not actually Japanese people.[60] Government sources described the Okinawans as industrious but lacking experience. During the first season three of them died and some were repatriated. Pearl-shellers remember this experiment as a disaster, and Torres Strait Islanders who were engaged in the industry saw the arrival of this workforce as a hilarious reversal of prewar relations: 'they didn't know anything—*we* had to teach *them*!'.[61] The Okinawans were re-patriated before the expiry of their contracts; only six of them stayed at Thursday Island and married local women. Hal Hockings, who employed thirty-two of them, related his experience with the Okinawans:

> They wouldn't allow the Japs in but they allowed the Okinawans in. That was the downfall of the pearling . . . It cost a lot of money [to rig up the boats], and they got hardly any shell . . . The Okinawans were dying off with bends, they didn't know anything about staging. They were dying like flies (about 12 or 14 died—not nearly enough), and all went on strike. They all came inshore and refused to go on the boats . . . Those who didn't go on strike (well) we had to lay up the boats anyway, because we had to feed them and they weren't picking up any shell. (Five out of our six boats were laid up.) . . . We sent them home as soon as we could but we didn't have the money to send them back, it just about broke us. It was dreadful.[62]

In Okinawa the offer of a diving job at Thursday Island came at an opportune moment in the midst of generally high levels of un-employment. Several foreign governments were advertising employ-ment opportunities abroad. Some of the recruits were fishers, some had dived for trochus, and some were salvage divers, but none had done pearl-shell diving. Most importantly, unlike the prewar Japanese recruits, the Okinawan recruits had not been socialised into expectations by local Japanese recruiting agencies and kinship struc-tures. They found the equipment outdated and felt that their contracts had not been honoured. Obviously the Okinawan recruits had not been initiated into the two-contract system which was the entrenched practice at Thursday Island:

> The agreements were very good, but when we arrived in Australia things were different. We had been promised that the boats would be ready with first-class gear, but no gear was set when we arrived, and we just

After World War II, almost anything that could float could be used for trochus-shelling, including Bill Kirkpatrick's *Australia*, a former mudbarge, shown here with skipper Joe Hartland and Torres Strait Islander crew, Townsville, 1954.

The Torres Strait Islander crew of the *Wondai* unload trochus shell at Paxton Wharf, Townsville, 1954.

Jimmie Sailer, former crew member of the trochus boat *Australia*, on top of a heap of trochus shell after grading, Townsville, 1954

The crew of the *Wondai* grade trochus shell, Townsville, 1954: (clockwise) Wano Ano, Jimmie Sailer, unknown (standing), Douglas Pitt, Jacob Susan, Jardine Kiwat, Jack Ossier, Kepnie Day.

stayed at TI for several months. Okay, we didn't know the Australian water. We were seamen but we didn't know about pressure. They had promised a pilot for each boat to show us. It was supposed to be very deep pressure, thirty fathoms [54 m] or more. It was important to have good gear. You need two compressors in case one engine breaks down [but there was only one on each boat] . . . The company supplied food but it was all rubbish, sometimes just two tins of meat for the whole crew, and rice. According to the agreement we were supposed to have plenty of tucker and meat. But the company was greedy like that. That's why all the boys went on strike.[63]

The 'new chums' from Okinawa also did not understand the grading system applied at Thursday Island, and felt deceived when much of the shell they raised was discarded, and the remainder graded according to quality and size. They found it impossible to keep track of the wages calculations. They were on wages of £20 a month plus a bonus if they raised more than 10, 15 and 20 tons, the bonus depending on the grade of shell.

My countrymen who went to Broome and Darwin made good money, because they got paid on whatever tonnage they brought in . . . At Darwin and Broome there was a set price per ton . . . It was very hard. We didn't speak English, we couldn't fight the company. We were like prisoners . . . We felt cheated, but we couldn't go to court. These people could have told the court anything, and I think in any country the court has to stand up for its own people. We didn't have an ambassador, our government was American.[64]

Only when the experiment with Okinawan divers failed did the pearl-shellers resort to local labour as dress-divers, and found, somewhat to their surprise, that 'they were marvellous'.[65] The people they employed were mainly mixed descendants of Malays, who had been exempted from the Aboriginal Protection Act. They also worked on a lay system, and adopted the same disciplined attitude as the former Japanese skippers had. The young divers were as reckless as the Japanese had been in risking their lives to increase the catch.

The insistence of pearl-shellers on the reintroduction of Japanese after the war demonstrates that the success of Japanese in the role of divers came to be considered as a kind of innate capacity for diving. Even Okinawans, who had never previously been engaged in pearl-shell diving, were expected to be more suited than the locally available labour.

Far from being a kind of innate capacity, the success of Japanese as divers was due, in the first place, to the conditions under which they participated in the industry. The lay system of payment offered an incentive to maximise the catch in order to increase their earnings. This system of remuneration encouraged a vested interest of divers in the industry, and the career structure offered a further incentive to work hard. The relative poverty at home made the money earned in Australia attractive, and the recruits hoped to earn enough money in a short time to enable them to improve their position at home upon their return. The building of a substantial house, the acquisition of a farm, or the purchase of a boat, which their savings afforded them, meant upward social mobility for returned divers. They were disciplined by their tight social organisation marked by kinship recruitment, *oyakata* figures and *doshi-kai* representation. Their near monopoly of the diving role enabled them to confer the benefit of employment in Australia to the male members of their extended families. Their social cohesion enhanced their discipline and reliability, attributes which Australian employers valued highly. Because of their positive attributes, Australian employers found the Japanese essential to the industry and insisted on their continued entry. The reputation of the Japanese divers became a self-perpetuating label favouring the conditions under which they could manifest such attributes. That the industry was exempted from the White Australia objective was an admission that it could not be carried out by white Australians, an admission which became embarrassing when Japan claimed rights for its citizens to pursue the industry without Australian assistance outside the 3-mile limit.

4

Losing Grip: the Japanese Challenge to an Australian Industry

In the 1930s Japan displayed some technological precociousness *vis-à-vis* its 'advanced' neighbours. Its fleets fished in the offshore waters of Dutch and British colonies, and in Australian, American and Canadian waters. These fishing efforts were consolidated under the auspices of the Japanese state into a technologically advanced, highly capitalised and efficient industrial activity which took advantage of the vagueness of international definitions of sovereign rights on the high seas. The question of extra-territorial powers of contiguous states became urgent.

Challenging Australia's implied claim to the pearl-shell beds in the Great Barrier Reef Province, Japanese fleets started to harvest here. Together with the earlier inroads into lugger ownership by Japanese, this new challenge called into question the self-conception of the industry as an Australian one. State personnel wondered whether the industry was not more beneficial to foreign interests than to Australians and whether it was possible, or indeed worthwhile, to protect such an industry.

In several instances Australian territorial boundaries had been extended in order to bring Australian pearl-shelling activities under Australian jurisdiction. But the Japanese challenge required such territorial expansion to be justified internationally, with the result that the debate over the industry in Australia was transported into the realm of national rivalry, with the Commonwealth government claiming jurisdiction over the entire continental shelf in the postwar era.

Dummying: the erosion of white dominance

The 1898 amendment of the Pearl-Shell and Bêche-de-Mer Fisheries Act prohibited the issue of boat licences or renting of boats to aliens, so that it became the preserve of white pearl-shellers, apart from a few naturalised Asians, to own luggers. But the Japanese competition for boat-ownership was not extinguished by casting it into illegality. The legislation created the phenomenon of dummying, the nominal ownership of a boat on behalf of Japanese for a fixed rent or share in the profits. Dummying took several forms. 'Verandah pearlers' lent their name to a licence for a weekly payment, and these luggers were crewed fully by Japanese. Some Japanese syndicates bought luggers on hire purchase from storekeepers. These advanced the purchase price, sold supplies of food and equipment and bought shell at current prices. Clark and Burns Philp, as well as several smaller merchants, were known to lease vessels to Japanese with option to purchase. If the divers for whom they held the licence departed, or fell behind in their payments, the deposit on the hire purchase was forfeited, and ownership of the lugger reverted to the licensee. This arrangement indemnified the nominal owners against any loss on the operation of the vessel.

The distinction between dummying and the *modus operandi* of the industry was very fine indeed. Representatives of the business community at Thursday Island alleged that 'the whole system of working amounts to dummying' and strongly supported the exclusion of Japanese from the industry altogether.[1] Reg Hockings, a leading pearl-sheller owning floating stations, felt that Japanese who worked on a lay and retained the pearls found, thereby had an interest in the boat, so that the practice of shore-station owners, who did not claim the pearls, contravened the spirit of the 1898 amendment.

Dummying was more profitable for the Japanese than employment under the normal agreements, and placed upward pressure on wages and conditions:

> Shortly after the leasing of boats became illegal by special regulation, boats were worked under 'private agreements', the diver becoming responsible for the tender's and two crew's wages—an amount about equal to the rent previously charged for the lease of a boat . . . When one owner was not checked others followed suit under pressure from their divers.[2]

It became the practice to grant cash advances to divers in order to attract them. Clark advanced £10 000 in one season. Floating-station owners found it difficult to recruit divers, because their divers were not allowed to claim any pearls found. Japanese working under such 'private agreements' tended to sign on their three shipmates, all of whom could dive, at a nominal rate of 1s a month in order to evade the duties charged for divers' licences, and then shared the proceeds equally.[3]

Dummying was a difficult charge to prove. The only proof of ownership required for the issue of a boat licence was a declaration under the Pearl-Shell and Bêche-de-Mer and Merchant Shipping Acts. The Sub-Collector of Customs, who issued the licences, had no authority to investigate ownership. He could report to the port-master as the relevant State authority, but both pearl-shellers and public servants were reluctant to raise the issue of dummying. Since the onus of proof was on the prosecution, the 1898 amendment was in fact unenforceable without the co-operation of the pearl-shellers themselves.

One case of dummying in Cairns was closely examined by the 1916 Royal Commission: in 1906 three boats had been built by some Japanese who subsequently approached several Cairns businessmen to act as a dummy-owner in order to procure a boat licence. When the person who had repeatedly been named before the Commission as dummy-owner was questioned, he contested that he had merely acted as a creditor in the first instance, but when the Japanese could not meet their debt, ownership of the boats was transferred to him. His loan was used as a deposit, and the remainder of the purchase price (£500 each for two boats) was to be subtracted from the profits the boats were earning. The Japanese who had built the boats were engaged on a lay basis and were in charge of the two luggers. The licensee had no receipts of the transaction, and very little idea of the working of the lugger. Although the case was an unambiguous in-stance of dummying, it only differed from the normal working of the industry, as far as could be ascertained, in that the sellers of the boat and the divers engaged on them were the same people. Since no evidence which could have got a conviction could be procured, the commissioners finally dropped the matter. One witness, who applied a liberal definition to 'dummying', concluded that 'ninety-nine per cent of the boats are dummied because although the boats are registered in the names of white men, there are now no white men in the pearl-shelling industry'.[4]

Dummying enabled the Japanese to entrench themselves in the management of pearl-shelling despite the 1898 amendment. They became more self-assured, even flying the Japanese flag as a matter of course on the Queensland-registered luggers. Pearl-shellers were increasingly willing to look upon dummying as a serious problem, as it was felt that the Japanese were closing ranks against them. According to official reports, Japanese steamers had started to buy shell from Japanese divers who worked for 'verandah pearlers' and shipped it to Kobe at cheaper freight rates than those available to Thursday Island pearl-shellers. There had also been cases where shell was transferred from a number of hired luggers to that which performed best, so that the best lugger was quickly paid off while the other luggers were returned to the owners.

Japanese divers also used the differences between floating stations and shore stations to their advantage. Floating stations, being more highly capitalised and incurring greater running expenses, offered £25 per ton of shell, while shore stations, which off-loaded much of the risk on to divers, paid £80 a ton. Apparently shore-station divers were buying shell from divers employed on floating stations for £40. This kind of solidarity between Japanese divers was in fact a response to dubious practices by pearl-shellers, who had started to debit divers by holding them responsible for the losses incurred during bad seasons.[5] This meant that instead of receiving their lay when bringing in shell, their share of the revenue would be used simply to service this 'debt'. At the end of 1912, Farquhar's divers, for example, had accrued a 'debt' amounting to £2700 and insisted that all such debts were written off. The pearl-shellers had no legal claim over such accumulated 'debts' and the indentees were legally entitled to be discharged at the expiry of their contract.

Boat-ownership was the single tenuous link which made the industry an Australian one, and pearl-shellers started to fear for their monopoly, with local public servants echoing their concern. The Bamford Royal Commission questioned the pearl-shell inspector about these fears in 1916:

— As coloured aliens only are employed in the industry, what difference would it make if boat licences were issued to aliens?
— The white man, I should think, would then be forced completely out of the industry.

— But is not the white worker out of it already?

— Certainly.

— Then, if licences were granted indiscriminately to coloured aliens and white people alike, would the present white boat-owners also be squeezed out of the industry?

— I think so, because the profits of the existing white owners would be still further reduced [and] the Japanese would induce their fellow-countrymen to forsake their white employers and dive for them.[6]

The Japanese monopoly over boatbuilding at Thursday Island also became an issue. All of the Thursday Island boatslips employed Japanese for boatbuilding, and some slips were owned by naturalised Japanese. The characteristic lugger design, by which a Broome lugger could be distinguished from a Thursday Island lugger (see Glossary), was due to Japanese improvements on the standard model, according to local requirements. It was held as a general truth that the Japanese had displaced white carpenters by working for lower wages, but that they now 'want almost as much as the white men'.[7] In fact white carpenters were earning 15s a day, while Japanese shipbuilders were employed at 5s a day.

Although disunited over the strategies, pearl-shellers were unanimous in seeking legislative assistance in controlling the Japanese vested interest in the industry. Faced with various proposals to attract white divers into the industry, however, the commissioners began to wonder: 'Do you think it would be worthwhile for the Commonwealth to make a sacrifice in order to establish an industry in which only two out of every ten men employed would be white men?'.[8] In the event, as we have already seen, this question was answered in the negative.

The question of territorial powers

The vested interest of the Japanese in the industry was powerful, and most of the pearl-shelling grounds were actually outside the 3-mile limit. The only hold Australia had on the industry, therefore, was that boat licences were reserved for British subjects and the fact that Thursday Island was a convenient pearl-shelling port. If the Japanese were alienated from Australian employment, it was possible that they would seek to establish their own pearl-shelling industry in extra-territorial waters, for example on the Great Barrier Reef.

Queensland acquired extra-territorial powers over the seabed resources of Torres Strait and the Great Barrier Reef in 1888, when the Federal Council at Hobart[9] had adopted Queensland's *Pearl-Shell and Bêche-de-mer Fisheries Act 1881* as the *Queensland Pearl-Shell and Bêche-de-mer (Extra Territorial) Act 1888* in which the entire Great Barrier Reef and Torres Strait province was described as Australasian waters, except for waters 3 miles from low-water mark around any island which came under Queensland territorial jurisdiction under the *Queensland Coast Islands Act 1879*.[10]

The Federal Council Act was intended to enable Queensland to collect licensing duties from vessels operating in these waters, but these powers referrred only to British subjects and British vessels (Section 19). One witness to the 1913 Royal Commission expressed this concern:

> Queenslanders were at one time under the impression that the power of the State extended to all waters between the mainland and the Barrier. The Japanese showed us distinctly that they are largely extra-territorial, and that we certainly could not keep out of them a vessel under a foreign flag.[11]

He was referring to a recent incident where a Japanese diver was charged with the murder of one of his coloured crew but the case was suspended because his defence counsel argued that the court had no jurisdiction, since the incident took place at a point 3 miles distant from any island, and therefore in extra-territorial waters. The matter was not referred to the Supreme Court, so that the question of extra-territorial waters had not been settled.[12]

This line of defence was not an original argument, however, and it was not 'the Japanese who showed us distinctly' that the pearl-shell grounds were largely outside the jurisdiction of the State. James Clark and Reginald Hockings had successfully used the argument in 1907 in order to circumvent a newly introduced income tax in Queensland. Earlier, Clark had attempted to use the same argument in Western Australia, but in order to defeat his submission the authorities there obtained an extension of extra-territorial powers in 1889 to Ashmore, 180 miles from the coast. Clark argued that this 'was the reason the limit of the Colony was extended to bring us under the jurisdiction of the Government'.[13] (This meant that all the waters off Western Australia in which the pearl-shell fishing was taking place were recognised as Australasian waters by the Federal Council.)

Australia had in fact no jurisdiction over alien ships within the extra-territorial limits (that is in the Great Barrier Reef), but its jurisdiction had never been tested. Practically all the pearl-shell raised was from extra-territorial waters.

Poaching, or the entry of unauthorised vessels into territorial waters, was widespread in the pearl-shell and bêche-de-mer fishery. The Macassan fishers, who had visited the north-west coast for centuries, continued to do so despite legislation to stop their annual visits.[14] The Clark fleet continued to harvest the Darwin pearl-shell beds in 1933 while it was registered in Dutch New Guinea, and was therefore technically also poaching. Australian-registered vessels, too, frequently entered foreign territorial waters. When a Wyben company boat from Thursday Island was arrested in New Caledonian waters, the Burns Philp fleet manager protested that the captain had acted in defiance of specific instructions. One Japanese captain from Thursday Island claimed he had been blown off the Queensland coast when he was arrested in the Solomon Islands. The Morey Company boat *Mildred* went to New Caledonian waters repeatedly, even though its Aboriginal crew was not permitted outside Australian waters.[15] From interviews among former pearl-shell divers and crew it is apparent that poaching was a regular activity of the Australian-registered luggers.

In the 1930s, twenty years after the Bamford Royal Commission realised how vague Australia's jurisdiction over its pearl-shell beds was, the fears of alien intrusion were substantiated. Japan had become the sole importer of Australian trochus shell, and Japanese firms now sought to participate in the primary production of the shell by sending their own vessels to harvest pearl-shell. The Arafura Sea had become an attractive destination for Japanese pearl-shell boats and by 1933 they were also coming down the Barrier Reef as far as Mackay and the Swain Reefs, to collect trochus shell, bêche-de-mer and anything else that might be useful, outside the 3-mile limit of Queensland waters.

The consolidation of Japanese pearl-shelling

The Japanese economy was highly cartellised and directed to a significant degree by the state. Craig Littler recapitulates that following the 1868 Meiji Restoration, the state became the initiator of industrialisation. In 1880 most state-owned factories and mines had been sold to a handful of favoured families, called the *zaibatsu*, who controlled large conglomerates of companies through interlocking directorships and strategic marriages. During this phase of industrialisation the *oyakata* system of employment emerged: in the absence of a free labour market, independent labour contractors recruited and supervised employees. The state continued to be the largest investor, contributing a greater share of national investment activity than any industrialising state in Europe or North America, until the 1930s, when a third phase of industrialisation commenced during which the *zaibatsu*, like Mitsui controlling 150 firms and Mitsubishi controlling nearly 200, came to dominate the Japanese economy.

By 1934 well-financed companies such as Mitsui and Seicho Maru[16] used the Japanese mandated territory of Palau as a base for their fleets to harvest shell off the north Australian coast. There was also much Japanese fishing in the New Guinean districts of Manus, New Britain, New Ireland and Kieta. These vessels were staffed by adventurous fishers from Formosa and other outlying islands of Japan. In 1934 Japanese raised 200 tons of shell in the Arafura sea and on the Australian extra-territorial pearl-shell beds, in 1936, 750 tons, and in 1938 Japanese vessels collected 3459 tons of shell compared with the Australian production of 2543 tons. Australian pearl-shellers protested that 'another five years will see the Japanese in possession of the whole business'.[17] The fleets were supported by research vessels making surveys of the ocean bed, and ichthyologists studied the growth of pearl-shell and experimented with pearl cultivation and the artificial development of shell-beds in Micronesia. This was vastly different from the way the industry was carried on in Australia, where hand-pumps were still in operation in 1940. In other words, at this time Japan was already exploring the potential for sustainable production, and concentrated its efforts on the much more valuable pearls rather than pearl-shell.

A representative of Mitsui diplomatically broached the topic of Japan's contestation of Australia's sovereignty over the pearl-beds in 1936. The *Sydney Morning Herald* reported: 'Since Australian pearling boats employed Japanese as divers, he hoped that both countries would co-operate in the pearling industry. Japanese pearling interests were only too willing to give any help to Australians.'[18]

The Japanese fleets were more than covering their domestic mother-of-pearl demand with the trochus and pearl-shell they were raising. In 1936 Mitsui contracted their entire yield of pearl-shell to the Otto Gerdau Company, the world's leading mother-of-pearl importer in the United States, so that Japan entered the world market as a major producer of mother-of-pearl, challenging Australia's leading position.[19] United States imports of mother-of-pearl reached an all-time high of 10 000 tons in 1937. By 1938 the foreign markets for pearl-shell were severely glutted, and marketing was difficult in the face of the tense international position in Europe and Asia. Japanese fleets were not subject to the controls applying to Australian-owned vessels. They disregarded the restrictions which had been placed on the raising of chicken-shell and did not contribute to Australian revenue in taxes, licences and duties. They sold to the United States below Australian production costs. Their entry into the field subverted the solidarity of Australian pearl-shellers, who engaged in price-cutting, selling at prices that scarcely covered expenses. The pearl-shellers clamoured for a subsidy to be able to compete with Japanese prices, arguing that they were at a disadvantage by paying import duties on material required for the operation of the fleets.

The state continued to play a directing role in the Japanese economy. Government and semi-government organisations encouraged Taylorist scientific management and rationalisation through 'mass production, standardisation and the elimination of waste'.[20] The state's role in co-ordinating private economic actors was particularly evident during times of war. In 1938 the state presided over a reorganisation and co-ordination of Japanese military, political, cultural and economic activities. The clamour for a 'southward drive', which had previously been confined to nationalist extremist groups, became nationally respectable, and the government sought to resist the 'trading encroachment by Western powers'. Immigration restrictions overseas at the time aggravated population pressures in Japan, and high protective tariffs in several Western nations undermined its trade. At the advice of the government, the companies operating in the South Sea combined into a single company, the Nippon Shinju Kabushiki Kaisha, and accepted a catch limit of 30 tons per sampan.

The amalgamation of pearling fleets constituted a significant strengthening of Japan's vested interest in the pearl-shell industry. In March 1939, in the face of severe marketing difficulties, Japanese representatives again suggested a co-ordination of Japanese and

Australian fishing efforts on the basis of the previous season's pearl-shell exports to the United States, proposing that Australia contribute one-third and Japan two-thirds of the total production. Although this proposal reflected the actual export capacity of the two countries, it was anathema to the Australians.[21]

From competitors to enemies

Since the early years of the century Japanese luggers had been observed fishing for mother-of-pearl, trochus and trepang on the Great Barrier Reef. Foreign vessels were not bound by the size limits on shell applying to Australian vessels, and the Japanese had access to a much more varied market in sea produce than the Australians, who only exported bêche-de-mer and mother-of-pearl. The Japanese vessels were even more vigorous resource-raiders than the Australians. The independent entrepreneurial activities of Japanese in Australia met with deep distrust. They challenged white dominance so that justifiable fears were overlaid with racist denunciations: 'when they go over a reef they are like a cloud of locusts, and leave nothing behind them, not even a clam shell'.[22]

Sightings of Japanese sampans had always been associated with rumours about sounding the reef and Endeavour Strait, and the fact that Japanese captains employed in the pearl-shell fleet painstakingly updated charts, which they kept to themselves, led to periodic reports of Japanese espionage. For example, in 1909 the Bishop of North Queensland wrote to the Department of External Affairs:

Bishop's Lodge
Townsville,
Queensland.

May 20th 1909

Private and Confidential

My dear Atlee Hunt,

There have been a great many vagrant rumours in N.Q. about Japanese beche-de-mer boats systematically taking soundings of the reefs and channels in our waters. We have a beche-de-mer boat in conenction with our mission station at Yarrabah, and this week I questioned the Captain, a *highly* intelligent Torres Strait Islander called Douglas Pitt, as to whether he has seen anything in this way. I was surprised to find that he had done so [and] frequently, but only in one case could I get any definite evidence. A big boat of about 40 tons, he said, manned altogether by Japanese, and called the 'Defender' was for some months hanging about the *outside* of the reef between Cooktown and Townsville. Small boats were sent out day after day sounding near the barrier reef. They apparently took no steps to hide the charts they were using as our boat was manned entirely with aborigines, but perceiving once that Pitt had noticed the chart they asked him not to talk about the matter ashore. I have no doubt as to Pitt's veracity.

I am in doubts as to whether this information is of any use, but if you consider it is worth showing to the Minister of Defence please do so. It has occurred to me that our aborigines may be used as 'scouts' along the coast so long as the Japanese do not consider them worth noticing. As you know a Yarrabah boy is many points ahead of the ordinary black both as regards intelligence and reliability.

If what I have told you is of no use please tear this letter up.

Yours very sincerely[23]

External Affairs replied that it was well known that the Japanese government had maps of Torres Strait which were far more detailed than the Australian Admiralty charts. It was not considered useful to conduct a detailed survey of the reefs, because the reef was constantly changing, and the survey itself would take ten years to complete. At any rate, the Australian navy did not have officers with the requisite training.[24]

The Thursday Island harbour master also reported in 1911 that three naval officers were among the Japanese working in the fleet. But the Chief of Police, who said that he was 'on intimate terms with the Secretary of the Japanese Club', denied the truth of the statement, saying that a few of them had taken part in the Russo-Japanese war, and were excellent navigators. Rumours of espionage were persistent—it was even suggested to send 'a Chinese disguised as a Japanese' to live and work with the Japanese pearl-shellers.[25]

The appearance and yearly increase of Japanese sampans in extra-territorial waters in the 1930s started another wave of anti-Japanese protest in Australia. Queenslanders considered these sampans to be poaching, but action could only be taken if they fished within territorial waters. They often entered territorial waters to obtain wood and water, but if they claimed to be in distress their request could not be refused. Concerns were raised about their interaction with Aborigines, particularly at Bathurst and Melville Islands.[26] When a Japanese vessel was boarded by customs officials at Cape Tribulation in 1934 the crew was found to be armed with rifles. Possibly this was because in 1932 five Japanese on a sampan had been killed by Aborigines at Caledon Bay on 17 September 1932.

The Japanese poachers created considerable media attention for provocative behaviour. One sampan was reported to have taken 3 tons of gold ore from Possession Island as 'ballast' despite protest from the prospector. Another report referred to a group of fourteen campers being so disturbed at Cape Upstart by Japanese sampan crews in December 1935 that they felt compelled to retreat to another site. However, the Low Island lighthouse-keeper objected to a newspaper item which reported him as saying that the Japanese had made a nuisance of themselves. He corrected the statement by saying that the Japanese who had landed conducted themselves in a gentlemanly fashion.[27]

Very few fishers ventured into the reef at that time, but there were some encounters with island residents. Claude and Harold White, who were living at Percy Island (1921–65), asked the Department of External Affairs in 1935 how they should react to Japanese sampans which were calling at the island. They were repeatedly visited by the *Taicho Maru* with thirty-one crew as well as by other boats, and wanted an open letter from the department to warn them off the island.

> Harold: Just before the war, we had the Japanese in with sampans. They were alright, but they got a bit cheeky at times. My mother had a cockatoo and they wanted it so badly, we had to put it away or they would have pinched it. We had gelignite for removing stumps etc. The Japs saw it and wanted it to blow fish up. We had to hide it. We couldn't stop them because under federal government regulations they were allowed to land as shipwrecked sailors for wood and water.
> Claude: We were very nervous about the Japs. We had no patrol boats and nothing. We couldn't have a personal war with them.
> Harold: They broke the laws in all ways. They got undersized shell, they'd take anything . . . Before that the pearling luggers had [indentured] Japanese . . . They were fine people.[28]

A resident of Dunk Island complained of Japanese arrogance and thought they were well aware of the impotence of Commonwealth authorities. A resident of Brampton Island (1934–60) also met the Japanese with considerable distrust:

> a Japanese 'research ship' pulled up on its way to New Caledonia. They came in with a sick man and anchored three miles out of port. [They asked us] to bring the sick man ashore. We wouldn't bring him ashore unless they gave us a bond of £100 in case he went missing. They [didn't pay it and] sailed away during the night.[29]

It is possible that an emergency was sometimes feigned to be allowed to enter territorial waters.

With the approach of World War II, fears that the presence of Japanese vessels constituted a defence risk intensified. The Sub-Collector of Customs at Thursday Island remarked, 'I regard every Japanese in Australia as a potential spy'.[30] The WA district naval officer raised the issue of 'a recent manifestation of interest in the north of Western Australia by Japanese'.[31] A Japanese firm was apparently buying large numbers of Sir John Kirwan's book *An Empty Land*. Such news struck at the heart of Australian fears that the underpopulated North was an open invitation for foreign invaders. One 'Japanese destroyer' reported in the press in April 1932 was found by Secret Intelligence to be merely a schooner which tendered for the Seicho Maru Company's pearling fleet near Bathurst Island.

At a higher level, the Japanese activities in the Great Barrier Reef province were considered with much less concern. An inspector of the Brisbane Investigation Branch thought that the Japanese presence had only commercial significance. The Director of Intelligence in the Defence Department also ascribed the reef surveys to economic need in response to population growth, rather than to territorial expansion. He considered the twentieth century an era of espionage, not all of which was on behalf of official circles, an explanation also given by Japanese attachés.[32]

While federal and State governments were deliberating on the responsibilities for northern patrol, the lack of such a patrol made Australia appear vulnerable. If the industry which sustained the northern settlements was left to other nations, Australia's north was open to economic as well as military penetration. The Commonwealth finally commissioned a patrol vessel to deal with illegal fishing in 1936. This patrol, on the *Larrakia*, turned into an embarrassment when it fired on a Japanese fleet outside the 3-mile limit.[33] By 1939 the *Vigilant* patrolled northern Queensland waters, and the Northern Territory was patrolled by the *Kuru* and *Larrakia*. These were found ineffectual in preventing the unsupervised landing of Japanese boats on the coast, but aerial surveillance was too costly.[34] One author remarked at the time that the Japanese sampans had become 'for the Australian public a sort of concrete symbol of the Japanese "menace" ', so that the political significance which was attached to Japanese poaching was out of proportion to the economic importance of the pearl-shell industry.[35]

This was precisely the issue addressed by an interdepartmental commission on Japanese poaching in 1939. The most pressing question, 'whether the pearling industry in Australia was of sufficient economic or national importance to warrant the taking of steps by the Commonwealth Government for its preservation', was answered in the affirmative:

> As to the value of the pearling industry, the Committee is of the opinion that, although the beds within Australian territorial waters (with the possible exception of those adjacent to Thursday Island) have practically been depleted and the operations of the Japanese vessels now take place in waters outside the territorial limits of the Commonwealth, the industry is of sufficient economic and national importance to justify active steps for its preservation. The district surrounding Broome is dependent upon the pearling industry and the cessation of pearling operations near this area would probably result in the collapse of the town, leaving this portion of the Australian coast largely uninhabited. From a strategic point of view alone, such a state of affairs would be undesirable. Thursday Island and adjacent islands are economically dependent on the fishing industry. There is also a fleet of 22 boats based on Darwin, a port of great National importance. Altogether there are 142 Australian vessels operating in and adjacent to Australian waters, directly employing 1,941 persons.
>
> The indications are that the Australian industry is languishing and the position is jeopardised by the growing Japanese competition. Although recently a considerable measure of financial and other assistance has been given by the Commonwealth Government, it is felt that, unless additional steps are taken to afford it protection and some basis of economic security the industry will in a few years disappear, leaving the whole fishing field in the Northern and North Western waters of Australia to the Japanese.[36]

It was the defence value of the industry, rather than its economic value, which made it worthy of the attention of the federal government. Moreover, the illicit landing on the coast by Japanese sampans also raised the concern that smuggling, the importation of disease, intercourse with Aboriginal people, and the illegal landing of immigrants, might be taking place. Because the extra-territorial powers conferred by the Federal Council Acts of 1888 and 1889 were confined to British subjects, the federal government could only effectively police territorial waters against foreign fishing. There was still no patrol in Western Australia; patrols were, moreover, costly and inefficient. The federal government therefore felt powerless to deal with the issue unilaterally, unless an agreement with the Japanese

The *Placid*, at Cooktown wharf, painted in the Bowden colours—white with black railing. Originally a Bowden boat, it was still engaged in trochus-shelling in 1965. The boat's new owner George Snow stands amidships with 'Cyclone' and Sesai Esmail.

The *Dalia*, originally a Bowden boat, was used both for pearl-shelling and trochus-fishing and even made the occasional voyage to New Guinea to gather bêche-de-mer (Engineers' wharf, Thursday Island).

Luggers at the Burns Philp jetty on Thursday Island during lay-up season; the Japanese inscription gives the date as the Taisho era (1912–25)

Pearl-shells and pearls displayed with other fine household ware at Mrs Muller's store, Cooktown, 1898.

government was entered into to control the movements of Japanese on the Australian coast and to impose output restrictions and conservation measures. Such a bilateral agreement, however, would have been an admission of weakness, and the Prime Minister's Department advised against it.[37]

The fact that Japanese bombs were dropped on the three pearling centres of Australia—Darwin, Broome and Torres Strait (Horn Island)—could be understood as a vindication of the Australians' fears. On the other hand, these centres were used as military installations and therefore presented a strategic target. During interviews conducted in 1987, one Japanese diver admitted that when mines were placed in Torres Strait, his uncle Horimoto marked the mines on his charts,[38] and a Japanese historian confirmed that pearl-shelling and fishing ships

> were requisitioned by the Japanese navy as spy ships to Palau, the Philippines, New Guinea, Borneo, Java, etc. They carried cargo and personnel, and made charts of the foreign ports, noting where water, bananas, potatoes, and so on could be obtained. They were instructed to do so three years before the outbreak of war. I spoke to one of the captains myself.[39]

In 1942 the Japanese indentured labourers were interned as enemy aliens on instructions of General MacArthur, because their intimate knowlede of the northern coast was considered too valuable to be permitted to filter back to Japan.[40] In April 1945 their status was changed from that of internees to 'Prisoners of War/merchant seamen', which meant that they ceased to be immigrants and could not claim protection under the Immigration Acts.[41]

Postwar pearl-shelling on the continental shelf: sharing Australia's resources with Japan

After World War II, the political reorganisation of the world system was accompanied by the extension of territorial claims over the seas. The aggressive prewar activities of Japanese fleets had alienated several national governments, and during the peace treaty negotiations in San Francisco in 1951 the question of international fishing rights featured prominently. In 1945 the United States asserted its jurisdiction over the resources of its continental shelf in order to secure oil resources. This was the first time that the geological concept of 'continental shelf' found power-political application. Mexico, Argentina and Peru followed suit, and the United Nations' International Law Commission began to formulate an international fishing rights code on the basis of this new concept.

During the peace treaty negotiations early in 1951, Australia proposed an agreement on fisheries with Japan which would bar Japanese from fishing on the continental shelf. Japan declined to enter into such an agreement, but offered to apply the same conservation measures on its fleets in Australian extra-territorial waters as were enshrined in Commonwealth legislation. No such federal legislation existed. In the following March the Australian government enacted the *Fisheries Act 1952* and the *Pearl Fisheries Act 1952*.[42] These acts placed the control over extra-territorial fisheries in the hands of the federal government and allowed Australian waters beyond territorial limits to be declared 'proclaimed waters' in which fishing could be restricted in order to conserve stocks.

Japan attracted heavy foreign investment, particularly in the military and luxury industries. Pearl-shell and pearls were part of this luxury industry, so there was expansionary pressure on the industry. The Gerdau Company of New York resumed its business relationship with Japanese pearl-shelling companies. In February 1953 it was learned that the Shinjugai Sihui Company was preparing to send a fleet of Japanese pearl-shell fishing vessels to the Arafura Sea.

Australian pearl-shellers protested that this highly efficient fleet would cause overproduction of mother-of-pearl on the world market and exhaust the shell resources within a few years. In order to postpone the arrival of the fleet, Australia entered negotiations in April 1953 to reach the type of bilateral agreement that had been envisaged by the peace treaty on the issue of Japanese participation in the exploitation of swimming and sedentary fish. During these negotiations the Australian government realised how vague the formulation in the peace treaty was, and Japan skilfully exploited its bargaining position. The United States and Canada had already negotiated agreements with Japan before the peace treaty had been finalised, and Australian negotiators began to feel that Australia had been 'left out in the cold'. Under Section 9 of the treaty Japan was required to enter negotiations over fishing rights with allied powers, but this clause did not require Japan to conclude agreements![43]

Pearl-shellers sought to resume the employment of Japanese divers. The Queensland government opposed this on the grounds that Torres Strait Islanders were available to continue in the role of divers, and in the Northern Territory, too, Aborigines were being trained as divers. Of the State governments, only Western Australia supported the reintroduction of Japanese divers. Western Australian Senator Scott reiterated the well-worn argument of the pearl-shellers: 'I wish to make it plain, so that there can be no mistake in the future, that the Japanese are the only people capable of bringing shell to the surface'.[44] In spite of popular protests, a group of thirty-five Japanese was permitted to work for the Streeter & Male and Morgan companies of Broome in the 1952–53 season. The Japanese government, however, declined passports to the group, because Japanese luggers were still refused entry into the northern Australian waters.

The Japanese negotiators were careful not to enter into an agreement with Australia which acknowledged any Australian sovereignty over its continental shelf. Australia's bargaining position was that foreign vessels would be allocated areas and catch limits and would observe the size limits in force under the *Pearl Fisheries Act 1952*. In other words, the foreign vessels would operate under Australian laws on the continental shelf. But Japan insisted, as it always had done, on the freedom of the high seas. In particular, it refused to accept an allocation of fishing areas, since it was obvious that Australia intended to allocate to the foreign vessels those pearl-shell beds which were deeper and more difficult to reach.

The negotiations languished until Japan succeeded in reaching an agreement on the departure of the Shinjugai Sihui fleet under a provisional regime, for which it accepted all the conditions placed by Australia on the entry of the fleet. The fleet left Japan on 13 May 1953 and arrived 60 kilometres north-west of Bathurst Island on 5 June. It had been allocated an area of 1440 square kilometres. On 10 August the Japanese fleet left its allocated area to enter areas fished by Australian luggers in order to fulfil its catch quota. This breach of agreement was a challenge to Australia's claim to control foreign pearl-shelling operations in its extra-territorial waters.

Negotiations broke down and an amendment to the *Pearl Fisheries Act 1952* was passed in September 1953 as a formal assertion of Australia's authority over its continental shelf.[45] The crucial clauses introduced in this amendment explicitly applied the Act to foreigners, and extended the definition of Australian waters as waters that are above the continental shelf. In addition, the Governor-General now proclaimed certain areas as restricted areas, and the Pearl Fisheries and Fisheries Acts came into operation on 12 October 1953. Australia now claimed jurisdiction over its continental shelf. Queensland Senator Byrne declared in Parliament: 'It cannot be denied that Australia dealt very fairly with Japan up to the time the negotiations broke down, and we now have no alternative but to adopt the procedure outlined in the bill before the house'.[46]

The amendment which adopted the term 'continental shelf' was only made to the Pearl Fisheries Act, not the Fisheries Act—the doctrine was incorporated into Australian law in the context of the pearl-shell dispute with Japan. The continental shelf doctrine acknowledged the sovereign rights of coastal states over the natural resources of the seabed and subsoil of their continental shelves, as well as the prescriptive rights (established by tradition) of other states, but made these subject to regulation by the coastal state. This meant that foreign vessels would be subject to legislation by the coastal state. So far the doctrine had only been applied to mineral resources, but Australia now applied it to sedentary fishing.[47]

These extraordinary attempts by the federal government to protect the pearl-shell industry took place not because of any economic significance[48] attached to the industry, but with a view to international rivalry. The defence value of the industry was stressed because there was no regular patrol of the North either by sea or air. There was considerable public support for a strong stance against Japan, and the opposition parties fully supported the government on the issue.[49]

Rather than agree to operate under Australian legislation, Japan proposed to submit the dispute to the International Court of Justice and prepared to become a party to the court's statute. Australia's legal advisers were not confident of the outcome of such litigation and counselled the government to seek a political solution. The continental shelf doctrine had never been applied to sedentary fisheries, and the prewar activities of Japanese fleets in the pearl-shell beds in question weakened Australia's historical argument. Besides, the industry was languishing and did not serve well to demonstrate the use of the extra-territorial resources by Australians.

Australia was very concerned to appear reasonable in international public opinion, particularly with a view to the pending case before the International Court of Justice. In May 1954 a further provisional regime was agreed. A fleet of twenty-five luggers with a mother ship and a research vessel were assigned specified areas outside the 10-mile limit of the Northern Territory. The fleet carried 145 divers (five per vessel) and was allocated a catch quota of 1000 tons of pearl-shell. They were accompanied by an Australian Fisheries inspection ship to ascertain that catch quotas and size limits were observed. Apart from the annual negotiation of assigned areas, which continued to be a bone of contention between the two governments, the Australian Fisheries observers considered the provisional regime to work well—except that it did not conserve the pearl-shell stocks, which was the declared intention behind the entire government concern over the industry. In fact, Austalia could only exercise such discrimination against the Japanese as this regime constituted if it was for the purpose of maintaining the fishery.

By 1956, after three years of Japanese fishing under the provisional regime, it became apparent that the pearl-shell resources were not as plentiful as had been presumed. The Japanese fleets had been assigned the outer pearl-shell beds of the Northern Territory, in order to place the onus on them to survey new beds. However, no new beds were found and the Japanese had not been able to fill their quotas. Their catch was declining annually and it was obvious that the twelve-year rest which the beds had had since the war had no lasting effect on stocks in the face of high-technology mass extraction. In the allocation of areas to the Japanese fleet, political caution rather than an attitude of resource husbandry guided the restrictions imposed on the Japanese fleet:

> The scale of operations of the last three years reduced stocks to such a degree that the rate of recovery has been considerably retarded . . . Australia . . . has virtually been forced to allow pearling in areas of the Northern Territory Division at a higher rate than is prudent by conservation standards in order to appear reasonable before international public opinion and especially the International Court of Justice.[50]

Although it had been agreed in principle to submit the dispute to the International Court of Justice, neither party wanted to appear as the plaintiff who would bear the onus of proof. Once a decision was made by the court, it would be compulsory for both parties to comply with it. In view of the uncertain outcome of the litigation both governments saw an advantage in resolving the dispute as a bilateral agreement.

Negotiations progressed slowly until the Japanese again displayed great diplomatic skill in forcing the issue in June 1956. The United

Nations were planning an international conference on fishing rights, and it was expected that such a conference would lend much greater weight to the authority of coastal states over their continental shelves than a legal decision would do. In June 1956 Prime Minister Menzies saw the Japanese Ambassador before leaving for the United States and Japan. After his departure the ambassador approached the Department of External Affairs and created the impression that Menzies had foreshadowed a resumption of bilateral negotiations and the signing of an agreement on pearl-shelling while in Japan. This impression was created merely by asking whether the Australian government 'had anything definite in mind', and was no doubt helped along by the personal style of the Prime Minister.

Although the Australian negotiators were inclined to stall, the hint of an imminent resumption of negotiations led to the hurried formulation of a new bargaining basis during the Prime Minister's absence. His staff were at a loss to speculate what promises Menzies might have made to the ambassador, but nobody on the Australian side doubted that the Prime Minister had made a certain commitment. Australia ceased to insist on the allocation of separate fishing areas. It offered port facilities to Japanese vessels and required the shell raised by Japanese fleets to be exported from Australia in order to secure foreign currency earnings. This closely followed a proposal made by the Gerdau Company. The attractiveness of this proposal was that it meant that Japanese fleets acknowledged Australia's sovereignty over the continental shelf by obtaining Australian fishing licences.

Eventually Japanese-owned fishing and pearling fleets were permitted into Australian waters north of 22nd degree latitude (that is, north of Onslow in the west and Mackay in the east), with certain restrictions on area and catch, and Queensland pearl-shellers were also allowed to get divers from Okinawa. The federal government sought to justify this decision to the Australian public with reference to the War Dead Mission (the repatriation of dead bodies), and Japan became a trading partner for Australia, placing large orders for beef, and exporting motorcars. Japan also obtained the rights to fish for tuna in the Great Barrier Reef province.

In Japan, a clear distinction between sending fleets to Australia and sending indentured men into the employ of Australian pearl-shellers did not filter through to popular consciousness. The celebrated role of the deep-sea diver, now assisted by modern technology in the procurement of wealth, took centre-stage in media reportage. The highly publicised departure of pearl-shell fleets in 1953 was understood as a mere continuation of a traditional activity.

For all the grandstanding to conserve the pearl-shell industry—the assumption of legal control of extra-territorial fisheries, the extension of jurisdiction to the continental shelf, the preparations to settle the pearling dispute before the International Court of Justice—the Commonwealth in fact did nothing for the industry. It did not intend to start patrolling, and the States were still to carry out licensing of vessels and divers. The assumption of federal control of the offshore fishery was purely nominal in order to extend the Australian government's sphere of influence.

Just as the restrictions placed on Japanese whaling did not conserve whales, the restrictions placed on the Japanese fleet did not conserve the pearl-shell stocks. Their formulation was subject to a political process with little scientific input. They were based on optimistic assumptions about undiscovered beds, unsupported by scientific evidence. The beds had not been surveyed. The catch quota of 1000–1250 tons was imposed on the basis of a few prewar takes, and on the observation that the beds had had a twelve- or thirteen-year spell. The areas which were allocated to the Japanese were chosen with a view to compel them to prospect for pearl-shell, rather than with the aim of conserving certain areas. When the shortage of shell became apparent, the restrictions were relaxed instead of tightened. By 1956, the Japanese fleet was allowed in all but one sub-area of the Northern Territory beds, and into Western Australia. The postwar ideology of unlimited growth could not be challenged by ecological alarm bells—a shortfall in resources was interpreted as a challenge to exploit more vigorously.

The entrenchment of a Japanese vested interest in the pearl-shell industry had been facilitated by sectional interests in Australia. Boat-dummying had been carried on with the co-operation of some pearl-shellers. The Japanese contestation of Australia's exclusive use of the pearl-beds relied on arguments and strategies pioneered by the Australian pearl-shellers themselves. Moreover, the industry's exemption from the White Australia policy was an admission that Australians were unable to conduct it. The Japanese involvement seriously challenged the conception of pearl-shelling as an Australian industry.

The reaction of pearl-shellers to Japanese competition in the 1930s was also ill-suited to defend the industry. Japan participated in the primary production of shell by sending its own fleets, and in the face of highly organised Japanese competition, Australian entrepreneurs displayed weakness and disunity. Instead of exercising disciplined solidarity to overcome the problems caused by a saturated international market, each sought to increase their market participation.

The challenge to Australia's sovereignty over the Great Barrier Reef in the 1930s revealed an inadequacy in the legislative protection over resources considered to be Australian. Previously, pearl-shellers had enjoyed the support of government officials echoing their arguments in Brisbane. But in this case the Queensland government was unable to come to their rescue. The issue had to be resolved in the international arena, by the federal government. The federal government's interest in the industry was therefore crucial in determining the level of support the industry would receive. The fishery was languishing and required considerable state assistance for restructuring after the war. The dominant role of the Japanese raised the question of just how 'Australian' the industry in fact was, and, if its benefits were accruing to aliens more than to Australians, whether it was worth protecting by state intervention. But these considerations receded into the background as the issue became one of debate between two nation-states. The Japanese government, always closely involved in the affairs of its private economic actors, entered the stage as a dominant player. This was the decisive new development that dictated the stance taken by the Australian government.

In the postwar pearling dispute with Japan, the federal government postured strongly on behalf of the industry, but its interest in the industry derived from the issue of territorial claims, and not from the economic significance of the industry or a sincere effort to conserve it. Geo-political rather than domestic-economic reasons provided the incentive for action. The pearl-shell industry again became the fortuitous occasion for the gradual extension of territorial boundaries. But while the pearl-shell industry was the issue over which this territorial extension was argued, the government in fact did nothing to aid the ailing industry. Next to the political significance of controlling Japanese fishing operations on the continental shelf, the conservation of the industry and its resources was a subsidiary consideration, and this reordering of priorities was sorely felt by the industry.

5

Resource Use and Management

As we have seen, the pearl-shell industry was modelled on the mass production paradigm and based on resource-raiding. These two strategies set the industry on a collision course with the natural environment. When the mass production model is applied to the primary sector as 'mass extraction', it is understood (see Introduction) as a method of production which aims to generate and maintain the largest posssible volume of output. This is done by exploiting large areas for a single resource, and by intensifying the productive effort through organisational and technological means.[1] Success is expressed in terms of volume and value of production, as in the secondary sector.

In the mother-of-pearl fishery, the productive effort was successively intensified by the introduction of diving apparatus, air-compressors, and motor-powered vessels. Innovation was not an attempt to save labour but a response to declining resources in the easily accessible locations. Incidentally, it was in the area of organisation that the greatest advances were made, after the initial breakthrough to dress-diving. The increase in lugger size and crew size, concomitant with longer voyages, and the advent of floating stations, owed as much to a proliferation of hierarchical delineation and a formalisation of managerial control as to mere technological advances. Arguably, the same is true for mass production in the secondary sector. Stephen Marglin argues that it was not the introduction of technology but the work discipline and supervision which accompanied its introduction that led to higher productivity.

Mass production is typical of the secondary sector, which is not directly faced with natural resources. Consequently this strategy holds no blueprint for the important question of how to deal with limited natural resources; it neither fosters, nor is it incompatible with, resource husbandry. Despite a common commitment of state and industry to the mass production paradigm, the use and management of resources were therefore open to contestation.

Pearl-shellers had recourse to the colonial strategy of resource-raiding. From their own statements their resource-raiding attitude is undeniable, and it is here that they parted company with governments. 'Resource-raiding' refers to a production strategy which operates on a 'depleted yield basis'[2] relying on territorial expansion for its continuation. This had been fostered in earlier industries, such as the sandalwood trade, from which the pearl-shell fishery had evolved, by the concurrent imperialist expansion of the state. If resources declined in one area, the industry moved on. Such a strategy is typical of the colonial frontier. The solidification of colonial empires made resource-raiding problematic: governments became interested in retaining the fishery within certain territorial confines, and this required a reorientation of production strategies towards sustainable use.

The pearl-shellers held fast to the 'tried and tested' strategies: shell-beds were intensively harvested until they became unprofitable, and luggers moved further and further afield. Fleets were registered under foreign flags of convenience and the area exploited stretched ever further into extra-territorial waters. Technological innovation was used to facilitate this territorial expansion rather than to stabilise production levels at sustainable yields. Under these conditions, the industry reached its natural limits to growth around the turn of the century. A protracted resource crisis, coinciding with the Great Depression of the 1890s, sparked off a long chain of government attempts at regulatory intervention which will be reviewed below.

From its inception, the fishery's rate of resource exploitation caused concern. As early as 1870, Queensland government observers feared an exodus of vessels from Torres Strait to the north-western coast as a result of overfishing. In a letter of 1871, the Government Resident, Henry Chester, identified the problems which were to beset the fishery throughout its history:

For some time past no new patches of pearl-shell have been discovered
. . . it is not improbable that after a few months' rest places that are now
exhausted will again pay for working, but not upon a large scale. Patches
like those on Warrior Reef are not likely to be again met with, and
already there are signs of a general exodus of the pearl fishers to the
North West coast of Australia. The diving apparatus with which several
of these vessels are supplied, and from which so much was expected,
have proved comparatively useless owing to the way in which the shells
are scattered . . . Every week renders it more certain that the fishery is
nearly at an end as far as large vessels are concerned; although it may
for a time continue to yield a living for a few engaging in it on a humble
scale.[3]

As a gloomy prediction for the fishery's survival, these comments
were more than a little premature. In the event, technological improvements, fleet reorganisation, and imperialism permitted much
further territorial expansion. (The 'large vessels' referred to were
10 tons.) Nevertheless, the analysis of the problem was succinct.

Chester's letter raises three important points. First, the fishery
started off as a highly capitalised effort intent on mass production.
It harvested intensively and focused on a single resource, unlike
beachcombing where individuals confined themselves to a small area
and gathered a variety of produce with a minimum of capital out-
lay—the 'humble scale' referred to in the letter. This alternative
method of exploitation was widely practised along the Queensland
coastline. Success was qualitatively expressed, as independence and
sustainability, and in standard-of-living parameters.[4] The crucial difference between these two production methods is that one is aimed
at subsistence the other at market production. Since the pearl-shell
fleets were owned by international and metropolitan companies, the
choice between these two methods was foregone. Still, alternative
production strategies aimed at market rather than subsistence production were available. Some of these were not classifiable as mass
extraction as defined here, and were used for pearling in other parts
of the world (see pp. 183ff.).

Second, technological improvements quickly became necessary to
sustain that method of production. Within three years, several vessels
had been equipped with diving apparatus. Third, if technological
improvements did not improve production, territorial expansion was
resorted to: the 'exodus' of large fleets to newly discovered beds.
These three points serve to underline that the mass production

strategy was at stake rather than a steady production output. A collective choice of the kind which Sabel and Zeitlin refer to was made in favour of one strategy over the other, with the (cautious) consent of the government representative who was aware of an alternative strategy (the 'humble scale').

A profile of productivity

For its first twenty years, the industry operated fully on the model of colonial trading stations. The island-based shelling stations were organised from Sydney and staffed with South Sea Island and other imported labour, under the supervision of a few white managers. The growth strategy during this period was territorial expansion. Two new developments in the 1890s introduced a dynamic element of growth: the Japanese, bringing with them personal ambition and an *oyakata*-style middle management (see pp. 117ff.), became a steady supply of cheap and reliable labour; at the same time, floating stations were introduced to Torres Strait. These two important organisational innovations intensified the productive effort and launched the fishery into the model of mass production. The obvious effect was that fishing activity flourished, the number of boats, men, and firms proliferated, and the fishing grounds were further expanded. The less obvious effect was a steady decrease in relative productivity, which meant that catch per unit effort[5] declined. From 1890 to 1913, the industry was at its most dynamic. It was also the subject of no less than five official inquiries. The consequence of industrial growth was resource depletion.

Once the Tutu Islanders revealed the location of the shell-beds, it took approximately one year to exhaust the supply. The patch which Banner began to harvest in 1868 yielded a record of 2500 pairs of shell in one week; the largest shell weighed almost 6 kilograms. But when Chester visited eighteen months later, three boats brought in only 100 pairs each in one week, and it was presumed that the 'patch was nearly worked out'.[6] More beds were discovered, but the yields of the early years were never to be repeated. The remainder of the fishery's course was the futile search for a repetition of that first extraordinary harvest.

The Commissioner of Fisheries reported 'considerable depletion of the most readily accessible fishing grounds' in 1890.[7] It had been common for some time to gather shells of 3–3.5 kilograms, of which 300–400 pairs made a ton, but now it was common to collect shells of just over 1 kilogram, of which 600–700 pairs were required to make a ton, which took one month's work; and even shell of 1 kilogram was collected (800–1200 pairs to a ton). By 1905 a shell of 5 kilograms was considered monstrous.

Official reports made ample references to resource depletion. But this was not the industry's only problem, so that other explanations for the troubles were always at hand. Although there were no systematic inspections of the resource over time it is possible retrospectively to test, and support, the claim that the fishery suffered from resource depletion. Appendix II demonstrates an inverse relationship between fishing intensity and relative productivity. Moreover, each productivity peak was immediately followed by a decline, suggesting that high productivity was at the expense of sustainability. There was a considerable productivity decline between 1890 and 1904, but despite the declining catch per unit effort, profitability increased. For the pearl-shellers, therefore, resource depletion did not cause fundamental concern. Their battle was mainly with governments, who sought to regulate their activities. Still, the figures indicate that the industry suffered three resource crises before 1940 (1898–1905, 1913–14, and 1930–32). While the Mackay Commission responded to the first crisis with proposals to restructure the fishery, the second solicited no appropriate response, because it was overlaid with the economic crisis induced by World War I. The third crisis, similarly, occurred in association with a demand crisis (see Chapter 6). The discussion of productivity in Appendix II indicates that the industry overcame its resource crises by contraction. The 'healthy' state of the resource from 1934 onwards was at the expense of the industry's magnitude.

Resource-raiding

Despite the obvious depletion of shell-beds, pearl-shellers had a vision of unlimited growth: there would always be other shell-beds; they only needed to be found. Faced with the suggestion that they were ruining the fishery on which they depended, the pearl-shellers expressed disbelief. The Mackay Commission presented evidence of declining returns per boat (see Table 4 in Appendix II), but for the pearl-shellers it stood to reason that 'the more people there are on the ground the more shell they will get'.[8] In estimating their profits in 1904, pearl-shellers still operated on the expectation of 4 tons per boat, an average that had 'not been realised for any of the past three years either at Port Darwin or Thursday Island'.[9]

A visiting scientist described the pearl-shellers as 'content to reap all they can of the harvest they have not sown . . . without the slightest care or compunction for the reapers that follow after'.[10] The Sub-Collector of Customs warned of imminent depletion because the shells harvested were so small as to threaten the reproductive capacity of the beds, but

> practical pearl-shellers receive his vaticination with equanimous indifference; and, in the light of thirty years' experience of the fisheries, during twenty-six years of which period the despoiling of pearl-beds was unrestricted by any size-limit, they predict an eternal continuity of the industry, regarding the natural supply as inexhaustible, without taking into consideration the additional possibilities of cultivation.[11]

Reg Hockings, one of the pearl-shellers, made a statement protesting against the homily of depletion in the Torres Strait beds:

> I have no fear of this coming about to the beds of Torres Strait. Natural protection has done its work successfully in the past, and will do it in the future . . . If the shell becomes thinned out it becomes unpayable, and consequently that portion is left, and the beds have an opportunity to recuperate.[12]

Hockings's position, that government intervention was unnecessary because the business became unprofitable before any patch was depleted, was taken by several pearl-shellers. For an industry which operates on a low level of profitability, there might be grounds for expecting a self-regulating mechanism.[13] Table 5 in Appendix II indicates, however, that the level of profitability was quite high, so that it was possible to 'flog a dead horse'.

The government did not share the pearl-shellers' vision of unlimited growth, because, unlike the fishery, the nation-state had territorial boundaries. To retain revenue from it, the fishery needed to be viable within these boundaries, and therefore shell stocks needed to be preserved. Queensland had already extended its boundaries twice (1872 and 1879—see pp. 34–5) to include the fisheries in its territory and had made an unsuccessful bid for the New Guinean coast in 1883. Hockings, who had just brought his fleet back from the Dutch Aru Islands, suggested that the fishery be separated into two divisions, one within the 3-mile limit, where the government could limit the number of boats, stipulate the ethnic background of employees, and lease certain areas; the other a 'free-for-all' division where floating stations from any nation could harvest at will. This was precisely the kind of territorial distinction the government did not wish to consider: it would have meant surrendering Queensland's claim over most of the pearl-beds.

Pearl-shellers stated bluntly that their goal was to run at a profit, not to preserve the fishery:

Mackay (Commissioner, head of Marine Department): Has the industry been carried on with any regard to its preservation?

Hodel (owner of 5 vessels): On one or two occasions the Government have closed areas, but in name only. They have never been effectively closed.

Mackay: People employing divers have had no regard to the preservation of the industry by their system of working?

Hodel: Absolutely none.[14]

Bennett (Commissioner, Sub-Collector of Customs and Pearl-Shell Inspector at Thursday Island): Have the grounds been worked with any regard to the preservation of the industry?

Clark (owner of 115 vessels): No; except during the time that Mr. Philp restricted the number of licences.[15]

Mackay: Can you tell us if they have been worked with any regard for the preservation of the industry, or have they been worked merely with a view to scoop up as much shell as possible without any consideration for the future of the industry?

Hayne (owner of 14 vessels): They have been worked to get as much shell as they could.[16]

Senator Bamford (Commissioner in 1913): when [you were] before that [1908] Commission you were asked whether your boats were worked with a view to securing the future of the industry, or making the greatest profit for the time being, and you replied that you were working them to get as much shell as you could. Are your boats still being worked on the same principle?

Hayne: Exactly.[17]

The pearl-shellers had an extremely low time-horizon, characteristic of colonial resource-raiders, and not untypical for Queensland producers into the 1960s. One pearl-sheller commented in 1956 that 'we pearlers are not interested in five years' hence. It is this seasons's markets that are important'.[18]

The techniques of mass extraction

The intensification of productive effort was both a competitive response to declining resources and the growth strategy of mass extraction. The introduction of underwater breathing apparatus in 1871 was the first technological breakthrough which enabled the industry to expand.

The diving apparatus Chester referred to in his 1871 letter was to become the standard equipment on luggers for decades. It was first supplied by the German firm Siebe & Gorman, and later by Heinke of London. It consisted of waterproof canvas and a copper helmet. Air was supplied by a manual pump operated by two deck-hands at a time. The lifeline was held by the tender to receive signals from the diver, who, by pulling and shaking the lifeline, signalled for more air, to be pulled up, or to pull up the shell basket. Depths of 15 fathoms (27.4 metres) were worked as soon as diving dresses were introduced, although most shell was obtained in shallower waters until the turn of the century, when the 20-fathom line (36 metres) had been exhausted.

With this equipment, the entire workday was organised around a single diver, and a new hierarchy on the luggers emerged in which the diver was dominant (quite unlike the swimming-divers who were under the supervision of a non-diving skipper). In 1912 permission was given to carry more than one diver per boat. Immediately several boats registered two or three divers, but because only one pump was carried, still only one diver could be submerged at a time.

For 'swimming-diving boats' 'in-charge' licences were issued, whereas 'pump boats' required 'diver's licences'. This distinction became as much one of prestige as of production method. The government's concern with the fishery was in the main about the more technologically advanced, more highly capitalised, more ef-ficient, and less flexible dress-diving which relied on Japanese divers.

The Heinke equipment from London became the favoured diving gear at Thursday Island, and despite considerable research and ad-vances in diving technology (powered by the European naval in-terests), the diving equipment used in the fishery remained resistant to change. In 1913, the mode of deep-diving was identical to that practised in the 1870s, while in Europe a prototype oxygen reserve tank, developed by Rouquayrol and Denayrouze, was used, referred to as 'steel knapsack'. Decompression chambers and other inno-vations (like the telephone contact with the ship available to British navy-divers) were not considered suitable in Torres Strait because of the strong tides.

For diving in shallower waters (up to 10 or 11 fathoms—18–20 metres), the divers themselves experimented with the diving dress to facilitate movement. They abandoned the dress and dived with the helmet and corselet only, in order to walk more easily, and it became the practice for the luggers to drift across the shell-beds while the divers were submerged. In about 1913 it became common for the divers themselves to drift across the beds pulled by the luggers. This posed the danger of the air pipe or lifeline being caught on coral outcrops or rocks, and led to terrible accidents. (Divers were not covered by workers' compensation.) Many divers died this way either from asphyxia, or, if they 'threw the helmet', from drowning. For this method of working, a lugger would stake out its field of operation with buoys, and it was expected that others would not trespass—although if shell was scarce the opposite reaction was often observed.

The only further modification of the diving dress was the final abandonment in 1960 of helmet and corselet diving in favour of the safer half-dress. This was used by the Okinawan divers and several Torres Strait Islanders, and improved the safety record of the fishery.

Most other innovations to the diving dress were unsuccessful. The early attempts at improvement were directed at shielding the diver from the water pressure at great depths to reduce the risk of divers' bends. A station manager for Burns Philp developed an armoured diving suit of copper, with an outer layer of canvas. It was unsuccessfully tested in Sydney Harbour in 1907 after ten years of design development. The high water pressure at 30 to 35 fathoms (54–63 metres) squeezed the canvas layer into the crevices and joints of the armour. He went on to develop a pneumatic dress in association with Dunlop, consisting of rubber tubes and covered with canvas which could be filled with compressed water to protect the diver from pressure more successfully than the air in the standard diving dress. In 1922 an early kind of hookah gear was tested to 48 fathoms (87 metres), described as a 'new Japanese diving apparatus' which required no dress or helmet, but a mask which covered only the nose and eyes. It was not considered useful because divers were exposed to sharks and the cold water, and suffered boils from the high salt content of the water. In 1936 the Austral Diving and Pearling Ltd launched a new type of diving dress, but the inventor contracted a severe divers' paralysis while testing it, and it was thought that he would never fully recover. SCUBA outfits (self-contained underwater breathing apparatus) were tested in the 1960s but were found unsuitable because the air supply was too limited for the time required to be spent under water. Staging alone could take several hours if diving to great depths.

The most important further development was the introduction of air-compressors to replace the hand-pump. This allowed several divers to be down simultaneously. Among the lugger crews, the distinction was made between stern diver ('head diver', 'number one diver') and second diver. The first ten vessels at Thursday Island were so equipped in 1920. In the 1940s these were replaced by propelling engines, which meant that the vessels could now be powered by the same motor which also drove the diving pump. Initially there were some problems with carbon-monoxide poisoning, because the air intake was installed below the exhaust pipe.[19] After World War II, Pilford compressors from Sydney and Jenbach compressors from Austria competed with the Heinke gear. Motor-powered vessels displaced the sailing luggers which had become the hallmarks of the fishery.

Together with the introduction of dress-diving, modifications were also made to the vessels themselves. To gain access to the deeper shell-beds, larger vessels were required to make the longer voyages.

In 1881 shell-beds were discovered in an area west of the chain of islands between New Guinea and Cape York. These were further and further explored and became the most permanent haunt for the Queensland-based fleets, referred to as 'Old Ground'. Old Ground was more exposed to the weather than Endeavour Strait and Warrior Reef. The 10-ton vessels were replaced by larger ones, from 15 to 18 tons, and up to 20 tons burden, and travelled together as fleets. The area of Old Ground harvested in 1897 was some 2500 square kilometres, the depths worked were 10–15 fathoms (18–27 metres). In 1875 the area referred to as Old Ground was well within Queensland's maritime boundary, but by 1902 it extended beyond them. In the 1940s the area of Old Ground stretched 96 kilometres to the west of Badu and 144 kilometres from north to south, covering an area of some 8700 square kilometres.

In 1875 the pearl-shelling areas were north of the Cape within maritime boundaries, just south of Somerset, and along the west coast of Cape York to Jardine River. In 1892 the areas included Old Ground, Princess Charlotte Bay, Darnley Island and Friday Island

Passage. Most shell was obtained from 8 fathoms (14 metres), but some divers went to 20 fathoms. In 1897 pearl-shell was found at Princess Charlotte Bay on the east side of Cape York. It yielded an inferior kind of shell, which may have depressed the price fetched for Thursday Island shell. A cyclone in 1899 destroyed sixty vessels, most owned by James Clark, and 300 lives were lost. After this disaster the area was abandoned as a popular pearling ground. When rich pearl-shell beds were discovered in Western Australia in the 1885–86 season, a large number of vessels (registered in Sydney) moved from Thursday Island to Western Australia. But the small sudden cyclones known as willy-willies presented a great risk there. A cyclone diminished the Western Australian fleets, and most returned to Torres Strait by 1890.

They brought with them a further innovation, the floating station. Fleets of 15–18 luggers were serviced by a large mother schooner (some schooners registered in Western Australia were 150 tons) which acted as storeship for the shell and disbursed provisions, transported by small tenders. While shore-station vessels made fishing trips lasting one month, the floating-station vessels stayed on the shell-beds for the entire season. The fact that the owners rather than the divers claimed the pearls diminished the income of divers. The responsibilities of the skippers were also reduced, from strategic decisions and recruiting to the day-to-day supervison of crew.

Between 1902 and 1903, the number of pump boats registered at Thursday Island increased from 175 to 200, and the number of floating stations from eight to nine, with schooners ranging from 69 tons to 132 tons. From 1904 to 1906 eleven floating stations operated out of Thursday Island. The luggers, ketches and cutters employed for the floating stations were from 8 to 17 tons. Many new vessels were being built, which were larger, more powerful, and more seaworthy than the older type. The inshore beds had become unprofitable, and the new grounds were more distant and exposed. Swimming-diving declined, and the floating-station system was now recognised as the most practical and economical.

The luggers were starting to go as far as Cairns to find shell, as well as poaching in New Guinean waters and the closed area outside Darnley. 'On the whole, the area from which shell could be obtained in payable quantities has contracted . . . and shellers must either look further afield for fresh finds or content themselves with smaller profits'.[20]

The floating-station system underlined a division of interest between the smallholders based on shore and the highly capitalised fleets. In almost every issue, from Japanese divers to shell size to the restriction of licences, this division was apparent, with the former expressing a nationalistic, anti-monopolistic, Laborite view and the latter representing the interests of international capital, more willing to experiment and to exercise the freedom of mobility according to political or economic expediency. One shore-station owner referred to the new system as 'the devastating (I refer to exhausting the beds) floating-station system, with its pernicious slop-chest, which saps at the very foundations of freedom in that its effect is the payment of wages in kind at the masters' prices instead of in cash'.[21]

This system was more profitable because no time was wasted in plying to port for provisioning and discharging shell, and the fishing effort was considerably intensified. It was observed that 'so far as the temporary profits of pearl-shellers are concerned, there is no question that the schooner system [floating stations] proved the most advantageous; but, having regard to the preservation and permanence of the pearl-shell as a national asset, it cannot be gainsaid that the system was most prejudicial'.[22] The floating stations afforded the added advantage that a white employee could supervise the divers and crew. One witness said that the floating stations 'are necessary to have proper control over the divers and to secure the pearls'.[23] Greater efficiency was achieved by intensified managerial control. The argument that technological innovation in the direction of centralisation of production served the purpose of managerial control is already familiar with reference to the emergence of factories.

This intensive fishing proved self-defeating, however, and before it could be prohibited because it caused depletion, it was abandoned in Torres Strait. In 1905, after fifteen years of floating-station operations, the first big resource crisis occurred. Business confidence was at an all-time low, and resource problems were compounded by the attempts of the government to restrict the recruiting of Japanese. Clark and his business associate Hockings moved their fleets to the Aru Islands to operate under the Dutch flag. It has been estimated that £80 000 worth of plant and perhaps £20 000 capital were thereby removed into foreign waters. The State's revenue from the fishery fell by almost half, from £19 098 in 1904 to £10 353 in 1906.

The Aru-based floating stations leased areas from the Dutch government, under the condition that local fishers were to be granted traditional fishing rights. According to Clark the liaison with the Dutch colonial officials was pleasant enough, because 'the Dutch are a small nation and not looking for trouble'.[24] But within a few years the floating stations had depleted these resources, too, and decommissioned several luggers. Clark sought to register fifteen of his 105 boats in Queensland in order to send one floating station into the Torres Strait beds. However, because the number of aliens allowed into the fishery had been restricted, it proved difficult to return to Thursday Island. The Clark fleet was unable to return, whereas Hockings, in business liaison with Clark, was able to register ten vessels and their foreign crew, apparently through personal contact with officials.[25]

The Mackay Commission examined the issue of ownership structure, and it was felt that large companies had a more detrimental impact on resources because they harvested more thoroughly. Even after Clark's departure in 1905, Queensland's fleets were more monopolistic than those at Broome or Darwin. In 1906, 58 per cent of boats registered in Western Australia belonged to owners of five boats or less, whereas in Queensland only 25 per cent of boats were registered by small companies, and none of these owned pump boats.[26] The 110 pump boats registered at Thursday Island in 1908 were all owned by six companies.

The Thursday Island pearl-shell fishery was characterised by a small number of companies with a substantial participation, whose involvement lasted for most of the duration of the fishery. A regular feature of interviews with former participants was a brief litany of well-remembered 'great names': BP (Wyben), Hockings (Wanetta), Morey, Farquhar, Cleveland, Carpenter, Bowden.[27] Ownership in the other two ports was more diversified, and no floating stations were registered at Darwin.

James Clark was the most dominant representative of the floating-station owners. He was variously referred to as the 'pearl king of Australia' or the 'oyster king of Australia'. Clark had entered oystering as a hobby, and by 1900 he rivalled the Moreton Bay Oyster Company, established in 1876 for the sole purpose of oystering on a large scale. He sold his oyster business to the latter in 1923.[28] In 1881 he entered the pearl-shelling business at Thursday Island as an employee of Frank Jardine, and then established himself on Friday Island. In 1885 he removed his fleet to Western Australia where he formed a partnership with Reg Hockings. In 1889 he returned his fleets to Thursday Island, until he went to Aru in 1905 with 115 luggers and took over concessions previously held by Arabian lessees. He formed the Celebes Trading Company with Dutch merchants, and became the Dutch Consul at Brisbane, an office later assumed by Reg Hockings. When the yield at Aru declined, and it proved difficult to re-enter the Australian fishery, he scaled down his pearling interests. In 1916 he was granted permission by the federal government to return with thirty-four luggers to Broome, though his primary interest was now oystering. He turned some of his luggers, as well as some Torres Strait and South Sea Islander employees, to that business at Hervey Bay and in Brisbane.[29]

The Mackay Commission proposed to discourage large companies by limiting the number of vessels to five for each owner (a reduction in licences per owner would be achieved gradually by disallowing vessel replacement). This shift to small-scale owner-operators had also been a key element in the reform of the sugar industry and was well within the spirit of Labor government policy.

The Commission may have been somewhat affronted by Clark's proposal to lease the entire pearl-shell area in Torres Strait from the Queensland government. He offered two arguments in favour of his suggestion: a long-term lease would provide the lessee with an interest in the sustainability of the resource; and a monopolistic pearl-sheller would be able to control supply, and therefore influence and stabilise the market for pearl-shell. He argued that small ownership was detrimental to the fishery because small operators were at the mercy of buyers. To counter any reservations against leasing marine areas, Clark argued that overseas governments were willing to lease shell-beds, and that the Queensland government leased oyster-beds. He estimated that the government earned £500 per annum from licences, and offered to pay £5000 per annum for a 25-year lease. The revenue from licences in 1908 was £1210, of which £862 derived from boat licences. Although Clark's figures were wrong, therefore, his offer was nevertheless financially attractive. The annual direct revenue from the fisheries was estimated at £12 000. At Aru, Clark paid $6000 for his lease. Clark had also been misled by the commonly used term 'oyster lease'. Unlike the NSW government, the Queensland government did not issue oyster leases, but only annually renewable licences to occupy, without tenure. The Queensland government did not yet consider maritime areas as something which could be owned, or leased.

In their report the commissioners condemned the idea of monopoly ownership, and gave no further consideration to this proposal. Clark's proposal raised an important issue, which the government was not prepared to consider. The main objection to periodic closure of areas for purposes of recuperation was that it was too difficult to police. The most rational action under those circumstances was to get to the closed area first, before the others arrived, to benefit from what little spell the beds may have had, and before the area had fully recovered and was reopened. It was evident that there was a problem in the private use of common resources: pearl-shellers knew that they were depleting shell-beds but did not care, because it did not pay to care, and they felt they could not afford to—unless, of course, the resource was also privatised.

The techniques to sustain mass extraction, then, relied more on organisational than on technological innovation to intensify production. Floating stations made highly efficient use of pump boats to expand the fishing grounds into extra-territorial waters. They also had an important side effect: by introducing different methods of remuneration and supervision, the ever-present competition for labour developed into a competition between two entrepreneurial types, and deepened a rift between the smaller owners and the larger, more capitalised companies. This rift remained with the industry even after floating stations were disbanded. Innovation, territorial expansion and fleet reorganisation were essentially responses to declining productivity.

The 'tragedy of the commons'

We have now cast the pearl-shell industry as one which embraced the mass production paradigm while clinging to colonial notions of unlimited growth where resource use was concerned. Mass extraction aims at a continuous output, whereas resource-raiding is an essentially itinerant strategy punctuated by periods of harvesting, depletion, and prospecting. The tension between these two strategies was at the expense of resource stocks, and this was only possible because the resource was a common, public resource, so that the individual users carried no private liability.

The explanation of resource use given here is a case-specific, historically grounded approach to the phenomenon which Garrett Hardin elevated to the status of a law, or inexorable principle, called 'the tragedy of the commons'. To illustrate the principle at work, Hardin referred to the exhaustion of the English commons.

According to Hardin, each private user of a common grazing area reaps the full additional benefit of adding one more head of cattle (+1), whereas the cost of over-use (–1) is shared by all. The individual cost of the additional overgrazing is therefore 'only a fraction of –1', and always less than the individual benefit. (What Hardin is actually referring to is the cost of grazing, not the cost of overgrazing.) Hardin argues that 'every rational herdsman' sharing the commons must come to the conclusion 'that the only sensible course for him to pursue is to add another animal to his herd. And another; and another . . .'.[30] The enclosure of the commons is inevitable, since 'freedom in a commons brings ruin to all'.[31]

This formula actually predicts the depletion of limited common resources under conditions of unregulated access (given a certain population density). Hardin argues that modern societies cannot afford such commons. The crucial characteristic of the commons is that access is not regulated, the commons are 'open to all'. This notion of the commons operates in a historical vacuum. As John Quiggins points out, the English commons were open only to a defined group of commoners, and the intensity of use was regulated by 'stinting' according to seasons. The enclosure movement was therefore not the creation of access regulations where none existed, but the replacement of one set of property rights with another, under political conditions which favoured private property over common property.

The dynamics of the tragedy of the commons rests not in the absence of access regulations but in the contradiction between common resources and their use for private gain. This is why the attempts of the state to insert itself with regulatory intervention have little success unless the contradiction itself is addressed.[32]

Privatising has been a frequent response to the tragedy of the commons. Privatising the commons presumably creates liability for the resource used. As in the manufacturing industry, which pays for its raw materials, the resource is no longer free of charge, and the cost of use is not shared. The externalities are internalised. Leases over reefs and islands represent this approach: the common seas are carved up into privately owned parcels. As a mechanism for resource management this approach is only effective if it does indeed create a liability for the resource, for example by making exhaustion more expensive than conservation.[33] Short-term leases are merely a suspension of common property status, not a resolution of the contradiction, since they permit lessees to swiftly deplete resources and then surrender the lease.

Again, it is the moment of choice which is important. The contradiction between private use and public resources is analogous to (but not identical with) that posited by Marxist dialectical materialism between the means of production (which are privately owned) and the social relations of production (where the production process is a social process). In both cases, too, the inherent contradiction might be understood as a phenomenon of historical dynamics, as a conflict which 'carries the seeds' of transition from one mode of production into another. The eventual resolution of both contradictions is possible by socialising the means of production.

A collective enterprise, such as the Papuan Industries Limited, must be immersed in compatible institutional conditions. Common property rights must be recognised, and defended, with a mechanism for redress, or compensation for infringements of the common interest. The recognition of a common interest of Torres Strait Islanders was anathema, for reasons quite unrelated to the resource issue. The administration was bent on denying pre-existing property rights, and the seas were seen as not property at all.

As a solution to the 'tragedy of the commons', socialising operates on the same principle as privatising. It resolves the conflict by internalising the externalities. John Quiggins suggests this solution for solving the problem of dryland salinity:

> Economists have generally taken a critical view of common property institutions. This is largely the result of sloppy terminology (in which 'common property' is equated with 'no property'), backed up by an uncritical acceptance of historical myths. In reality, common property structures involve well-developed rights of exclusion and use, and have outperformed private property rights structures in many agricultural systems.[34]

The experience of fisheries management suggests that the 'tragedy of the commons' is a phenomenon which occurs in historically specific instances of the shift from one mode of production into another, where the law limps behind actual developments. The mass production strategy required some self-regulatory mechanism of resource protection. Property rights are such a mechanism, but the state was slow in recognising their potential, and when it did, only private property rights were considered. Traditional use rights in fisheries are today an approach to socialising the use of commonly owned resources, granting special privileges for indigenous communities to practise traditional hunting methods.[35]

Attempts at husbandry and regulation

During the thirty years from the 1890s to the 1920s several Australian primary industries suffered from the problems caused by production strategies which relied on territorial expansion, now that most productive areas had been taken up. They also suffered from introduced pests. In order to continue its role as primary producer in the British Empire, Australia opted for intensified production with the help of scientific and technological innovation, increased capital investment and improved infrastructural provisions. Agricultural departments engaged research scientists and disseminated information, and applied science prospered in Australia.

For the pearl-shell industry, too, the state attempted to harness scientific advice in order to solve the worsening resource problems. The management tools used by the state to conserve pearl-shell stocks were closures of areas, size limits on pearl-shell, and even restrictions in the number of licences issued. The first legislative intervention which had some effect on resource management in the pearl-shell fishery was the *Pearl-shell and Bêche-de-mer Fisheries Act 1881*. It provided for annual licences of vessels and divers as a way of obtaining revenue from the fishery. Licensing also enabled the state to collect statistics for the industry so that general productivity trends could be observed. Thereafter, the keynote of the state's involvement in pearl-shell resource management was a succession of five public inquiries into the fishery. The radical reform proposals which emanated from these inquiries demonstrate that alternative models for the conduct of this fishery were available. Resource management was awarded a low priority, however, so that objections and barriers against its implementation were not overcome.

Saville-Kent and the enactment of a management package, 1890

In 1890 the marine biologist W. Saville-Kent, as Queensland Commissioner of Fisheries, conducted an 'Investigation into the bêche-de-mer and pearl-shell fisheries of Northern Queensland'. At this time it was the pearl-shellers who expressed concern, and who invited government regulation. The value of pearl-shell exports had steadily decreased from £94 152 in 1884 to £50 332 in 1888. Divers were bringing in shell weighing from 450 grams to as little as 150 grams a pair (spanning 120–150 mm across the outside diameter), of which it took over 6000 pairs to make a ton. Overseas buyers were protesting that such shell was 'practically valueless, as on attempting to strip it with machinery in the usual manner for trade purposes, no workable mother-of-pearl or nacre is left'.[36] In several countries, oyster-fisheries were failing because of overfishing, and this was understood by fisheries managers as a warning for the pearl-shell industry. The Commissioner held a meeting with pearl-shellers to canvass their opinions, and was anxious to demonstrate in his report the extent of industry support for his recommendations:

> The urgent need of a restriction being placed on the indiscriminate taking of small and imperfectly developed shell, so extensively practised, is recognised by all the leading boat owners, shelling station proprietors, and mercantile firms engaged in the fishery . . . By some of the members present it was also advocated that certain areas of the shelling grounds should be closed for a more or less extensive interval, so that they might have time to recover from their over-exhausted condition . . . The desirability of closing certain areas of the pearl-shelling grounds in order that they may have an opportunity of recovering . . . is fully recognised by several of the most prominent members of the shelling trade.[37]

It was suggested that the master of the government vessel, who was a former manager of one of the larger pearling stations, should be appointed as inspector of the pearl-shell fisheries under the direct control of the Government Resident at Thursday Island to supervise these restrictions. Saville-Kent reported that pearl-shellers also complained of the insecure tenure over shore stations and the heavy customs levy on rice, and that they recommended that pearl-dealing should be supervised by a licensing system.

Saville-Kent supported all of these suggestions. He proposed the closure of Endeavour Strait for three years and the imposition of a size limit on marketable shell. He suggested a minimum size of 8 inches (203 mm) measured across the outside of the shell, which corresponded to an inside nacre measurement of 6 inches (152 mm). Pearl-shellers had suggested 7 inches without specifying which measurement should be taken. The inside measurement was a more reliable indicator of maturity, but the outside measurement was suggested so that divers could easily determine the size while submerged.

As a result of this inquiry, the Pearl-Shell Act was amended in 1891 to incorporate all of Saville-Kent's recommendations. Provision was made to lease reefs, banks and foreshores. Longer-term shore-station leases were granted instead of the annual licences, and pearl-dealers' licences were instituted. Royalties similar to those in Western Australia were also imposed at the rate of £2 per ton of shell exported, a source of revenue mentioned, but not recommended, by Saville-Kent. An inspector of pearl-shell and bêche-de-mer fisheries was appointed to enforce the regulations of the 1881 Act and its amendments.[38] A size limit was imposed so that no shell smaller than 6 inches inside measurement was allowed to be harvested, except for the purposes of shell-cultivation. The Act also provided for the closure of areas to allow them to recuperate. The first closure was proclaimed in 1893, as a result of 25 fatal diving accidents that year at Darnley Deeps alone, where depths of up to 20 fathoms (36 metres) were being worked.

Saville-Kent saw as his greatest contribution the suggestion that the fishery be placed on a permanent footing by turning to the artificial cultivation of shell, as in the oyster industry. Saville-Kent demonstrated that pearl-shell did not migrate, as some pearl-shellers believed, and that live shell could be successfully transported. He transplanted some shells to the coral reef near Vivien Point at Thursday Island and observed their successful growth for six weeks, using the technique applied in the oyster-fishery. He expected that within three years they would reach the size of marketable shells. He anticipated a transformation of the fishery in the not too distant future, based on permanent leases and shore cultivation, largely dispensing with the need for deep-sea diving, and permitting the owners to claim the pearls found. The pearl-shellers were sceptical: 'Little or no credence was attached by them to the possibility, suggested by the author, of bringing in the shell alive and cultivating it artificially'.[39]

Nevertheless, Saville-Kent's efforts inspired James Clark to establish the Pilot Cultivation Company in 1892, which leased an area between Prince of Wales and Friday Island to conduct experiments in artificial cultivation. Between 100 000 and 150 000 5–6-inch shells were 'planted' (thrown overboard), of which 30 000 were successfully raised four years later at $6\frac{1}{2}$ to $7\frac{1}{2}$ inches. Stones were deposited in Friday Island passage to catch the spat (oyster spawn).

The other pearl-shellers strongly objected to the experiment, on the grounds that Clark's boats were permitted to raise shell below the 6-inch limit and would deplete the commonly used shell-beds. Their divers poached on the Clark lease, but convictions could not be procured: 'The Japanese were stealing our shell at night, and when we eventually caught them we were told by the District Court judge who tried the case that pearl-oysters were wild animals and that we could not get a conviction against men for stealing wild animals'.[40] One of the problems of the lease was that it entailed both sides of Friday Island passage, so that to prohibit entry on to the lease would have meant closing the passage to traffic. The area was subsequently declared a reserve.

There may have been some substance to the concerns expressed by the shore-station owners when they criticised the raising of small shell by Clark's fleets. These were not transplanted on to platforms as in oyster-cultivation, the method demonstrated by Saville-Kent, but simply dumped on the leased site. It was some time before a satisfactory transport method was adopted, something which Saville-Kent had achieved at the first effort. The practice resulted in a considerable mortality rate, and it is probable that the lease acted simply as a storage area for prematurely raised shell which was not allowed to be marketed. It was alleged that at a time when other boats averaged less than 1 ton of shell a month, Clark's boat yielded almost 9 tons.[41]

Pearl-shellers found the size limit imposed by the 1891 legislation unnecessarily stringent. Moreover, they argued, the minimum size did not serve to protect the smaller shell, because it referred to the inside measurement. The shells were opened on board of the luggers and if they were found to be too small they were simply thrown overboard. Pearls were more prolific in these smaller shells, and ironically 5–6-inch shell was fetching the highest price at the time. 'A spirit of irritation existed against the 6-inch gauge, which was considered to be unreasonable and unnecessarily oppressive, and irritation begat wilful rebellion. Shell under 6 inches across the nacre was recklessly raised, opened for pearls, and cast back as waste into the sea'.[42] In 1896 the size limit was reduced to 5 inches (127 mm) nacre measurement or $6\frac{1}{2}$ inches outside measurement, regardless of whether the shell was used for cultivation or export. The special privilege, designed to encourage cultivation efforts, was dispensed with.

The decision to relax the size restriction was made without scientific advice, and shortly before a further inquiry into the fishery was held. The decision resulted in a record catch the following year and an increase of 100 vessels thereafter, accompanied by a decline of 200 tons in the yield of shell.

The Hamilton Commission of 1897

In 1897 a Departmental Commission on Pearl-Shell and Bêche-de-mer Fisheries submitted its report. Heading the Commission was John Hamilton, who represented the northern entrepreneurs in the Queensland Parliament as Member for Cook, and who in 1905 participated in a public vendetta against Dr Walter Roth which led to the resignation of the Chief Protector.[43] The Hamilton Report was concerned with the preponderance of Japanese in the fishery, and resulted in the exclusion of aliens from boat licences. However, it also paid some attention to the potential for artificial cultivation, and to the size limit of shell.

After the recent reduction in size limit, the commissioners found pearl-shellers 'less inclined to grumble' than usual. Still, a few minor complaints were received apart from the dominant theme of Japanese managerial encroachment.[44] No amount of legislation could protect shell stocks unless it was enforceable, and the Commission therefore recommended the appointment of a floating inspector who would act like a goldwarden, and recommended Frank Jardine for the position, on the basis of his experience as inspector in the Burmese pearl-fishery. It was also recommended that some over-used areas should be closed, and that discoveries of new shell-beds should be rewarded by the State government. It was thought that the 5-inch limit should be retained, because, as Government Resident Douglas put it, the matter had been 'practically settled', meaning by the practical men in the industry, a term which conveyed considerable respect for their opinion.

The results of this inquiry were a further closure of Darnley Deeps because of the accident rate, and the exclusion of aliens from boat licences. In other words, it was deemed more important at this stage to make the fishery white than to make it permanent.

The turn of the century was a period when grave concern at the rate of resource exhaustion in the pearl-shell fishery was expressed by officials. Floating stations had arrived in Torres Strait. James R. Tosh, a British biologist, was appointed to the Queensland Marine Department in 1900. He supervised experiments in oyster-cultivation in the southern areas of Queensland, when the oyster industry was at its peak at the turn of the century. He strongly supported an experimental five-year closure of areas. He also suggested the closure of all deep-water areas permanently to serve as spatting grounds from whence the spat would be carried to the shallower grounds by ocean currents. He also advocated a return to the 6-inch limit, and a reduction in the number of boat licences. These views were endorsed in the Annual Report of the Marine Department in 1901.

The number of licences was frozen against strong protest from pearl-shellers. This restriction, imposed under the Conservative government of Robert Philp (1899–1903), was lifted in the first year of the Labor–Liberal coalition government (1903–07). (This first experiment with licence limitation in Queensland sank into oblivion with Fisheries administrators, who completely reinvented the wheel of limited-licence fishery in the 1970s.[45])

Other authorities, too, had lent their weight to the concerns expressed by Tosh. In 1899 the Glasgow biologist Stephen Pace, the pearl-shell inspector at Thursday Island (George Bennett), the Government Resident at Thursday Island (John Douglas), and the head of the Marine Department responsible for the fishery (T. Almond), agreed that unless some areas were closed for at least seven years, and the number of licences restricted, 'the industry will in all probability in a few years become extinct'. Endeavour Strait, which had been the most prolific ground, was 'now destitute of shell'.[46] It was now well accepted that the fishery was suffering from depletion of resources. However, on the question of reproductive maturity of pearl-shell there was still no scientific consensus, and therefore the question of the size limit was not re-examined.

Pressure on the shell resources intensified as the fishery grew. After the dramatic loss of fleets in the 1899 cyclone, the fleets exceeded their former strength within a year. The thirty-five pump boats lost were replaced by forty-nine vessels of a better design, and more systematic methods of working were adopted. Moreover, the bêche-de-mer and tortoiseshell fisheries had taken a downturn, and many of these vessels were turning to pearl-shelling by employing swimming-divers. There were more boats in the fishery than before, yet the quantity of shell landed had decreased.

The Dashwood Inquiry of 1902

Increasingly, luggers entered extra-territorial waters to fish for shell. One pearl-sheller estimated that 85 to 90 per cent of shell was obtained beyond the territorial limits.[47] The area of Old Ground fished already extended beyond Queensland's maritime boundary. The Comptroller-General of Customs, Judge Dashwood, was asked to determine how much of the pearl-shell grounds were within Queensland limits, and whether there was any substance in the suggestion that the industry could be lost to Queensland altogether by the fleets registering under different flags, particularly at the new Dutch settlement of Merauke.[48]

Dashwood found that the yield had been gradually diminishing during the previous five years, and that the fishery needed to be regulated if it were to remain a source of revenue for Queensland.

> Viewing the experiences in connexion with the pearl oyster industry in other countries, notably Japan and Ceylon, it is clear to me that it cannot be considered of a permanent nature, unless carried on under proper restrictions and safeguards. It is unquestionable that over-fishing has brought about the unproductiveness of pearl-shell beds in other localities, and, so far as one can judge, the same result will follow in Torres Straits if prompt measures are not taken to prevent them being so depleted that their recovery may be indefinitely delayed.[49]

Unlike Tosh, who wanted all deep-water areas closed permanently as spatting grounds, Dashwood recommended closure 'because of the risk to human life . . . or at any rate until there are appliances which will enable them to be worked without the deplorable loss of life'.

The Darnley Deeps closure (the area between Murray, Darnley, and Stephens Islands) had been imposed for the safety of divers. It was renewed for a further ten years in 1902, and smaller areas in the Great North East Channel were closed for two years.[50] The closure was renewed in 1905 against protest from shellers, and again in 1913. In other words, Darnley Deeps remained closed almost continuously from 1893 to 1916. However, there was no efficient patrol vessel, and poachers easily evaded the inspector's sailing vessel when it appeared on the horizon: 'Occasionally the Sub-collector of Customs went out in what was the most distinctively-rigged boat in the Straits, and the men could recognise it while it was yet miles from them'.[51]

The first reported prosecution for poaching on closed areas occurred in 1913, and the fine imposed was £5. Despite the almost permanent closure of Darnley Deeps, divers continued to harvest there illegally. By 1903 the Darnley grounds had been worked out to 20 fathoms, and on all grounds 'the 20 fathom contour is being steadily approached'. At this time it took about 1500 pairs of shell to make a ton of pearl-shell. The pearl-shell grounds, apart from Darnley, were now Old Ground (providing 34 per cent of the yield) the Warrior Reefs into New Guinea, Red Point on the north-west of Cape York, Orman Reef, and around Mabuiag, Moa, Badu and Mt Adolphus Channel. By 1908 the depth worked at Darnley Deeps was from 35 to 40 fathoms (45–72 metres). The pressure at 40 fathoms was such that staging took 40–60 minutes and divers could only stay for 2–5 minutes on the bottom. Still, the shell at these depths was so plentiful that it was considered worth the trouble. The closure of areas as an administrative tool was used to protect divers rather than to allow stocks to recuperate.

Experiments in artificial cultivation

Government officials continued to call for steps to encourage the artificial cultivation of pearl-shell, and for the reintroduction of the 6-inch size limit.[52] Pearl-shell stocks at Mergui (British Burma), Tahiti, Puamotu (Eastern Polynesia) and Panama were exhausted. Edible oysters were extinct in Spencer Gulf of South Australia and nearly extinct at Moreton Bay through indiscriminate fishing.

A federal Senate resolution in November 1905 again demanded government support, this time from the Commonwealth government, for scientific cultivation, in association with steps to implement the White Australia policy. However, the federal government took no action because the fisheries were under the authority of the States. The State government, on the other hand, did not commit itself to any course of action while the White Australia issue was under examination. The State government administered the fisheries through the *Pearl-shell and Bêche-de-mer Fishery Act 1881*. It issued licences and leases, imposed closures, size limits, and other regulations (such as regarding the nationality of eligible licensees), registered and inspected vessels, controlled the employment of indigenous labour, and undertook some policing of the grounds. The federal government controlled immigration, and therefore also had a role in the supply of labour, and it had the sovereignty over extra-territorial areas. This division of responsibilities impeded the management of the fisheries.

A short-lived cultivation experiment had been conducted in Beagle Bay by a Broome pearl-sheller, and James Clark had employed Stephen Pace on a three-year contract, with an annual budget of £1000. No reliable information was available regarding the life cycle, age of reproductive maturity and spatting periods of pearl-shell. Saville-Kent had estimated that pearl-shell took three years to grow to 8 or 9 inches, and five years to attain a weight of 5 or 6 pounds. Several pearl-shellers thought that a marketable shell was ten to fifteen years old. The growth observed on Clark's experiment supported the statement of an overseas scientist, Figuier, who thought a 6–8-inch shell must be between eight and ten years old. Clark's request for scientific assistance from the government had been endorsed by the Hamilton Commission without avail.

None of the pearl-shellers felt that Saville-Kent had contributed anything of practical value to the industry. He had succeeded in producing blister pearls, but pearl-shellers objected to the production of 'fake pearls', fearing for the reputation of the fine natural pearls. According to Mackay 'a lot of correspondence passes through the Department regarding the fishing, and I never heard Mr. Saville-Kent's name quoted'.[53] Saville-Kent was no longer in government employment, but continued to experiment with the artificial cultivation of pearl-shell in association with Lever Brothers. At first he experimented in Borneo, and in 1904 he transplanted shell from Torres Strait to two atolls in the Cook Islands (Suwarrow and Penrhyn) where only black-lip pearl-shell occurred naturally. The Torres Strait variety did not occur further east than the Solomon Islands. He had considerable difficulty in securing a contract for the transport of shell, apparently because the Japanese divers refused to carry live shell. He did not succeed in propagating the shell. Had these experiments been successful, the Australian fishery would have faced a further challenge.

Saville-Kent returned to Torres Strait shortly before his death in 1908, where he leased a bay area in Albany Passage at Somerset (near Wai Weer Island) for the Natural Pearl-Shell Cultivation Company, London, whose experimental station was managed by Bertie Jardine. Considerable knowledge of predators, reproductive maturity, and life cycle of the mollusc had been gathered. The station conducted experiments in pearl-cultivation and some blister pearls were produced.

In 1908 a Japanese patent for the artificial cultivation of spherical pearls was registered (see p. 190 below). The principles of pearl-production and pearl-shell cultivation were well understood, but their application in tropical waters continued to raise practical problems. The aim of pearl-shell cultivation was to render the perilous diving in open waters unnecessary. This meant that shell stocks on the leases had to be self-recruiting, but the strong currents carried away the spat. Saville-Kent and the Japanese researchers now concentrated on artificially cultured pearls, which opened up an entirely new avenue for the industry.

Clark, on the other hand, had arrived at the opinion that cultivation of shell was futile: 'I do not think it is necessary to cultivate at all. The world cannot use all the shell we can produce now without cultivation, and I am quite satisfied we cannot cultivate it'.[54] He abandoned his cultivation experiments after a few years, and the scientific insights gained from it were not disclosed. 'The reasonable inference is that they were unsuccessful.'[55] The company's relationship with its research scientist ended on a bitter note. According to the company management, he had been provided with every reasonable facility, but his work had been of no commercial use. Pace, on the other hand, said that he had not been provided with diving equipment, so that he could not observe reproductive activity. Moreover, he complained that despite the exceptional abundance of shell on Friday Island, his work had been 'constantly interfered with by the want of shell'. His contract gagged him from publishing the scientific observations he had made.[56]

In 1908 Hockings commenced experiments in association with Tosh. Hockings had visited overseas pearl-shell industries, and thought that nothing more was known overseas than in Australia about cultivating pearl-shell. After four years of experimentation, he expressed himself as 'hopeful' of success.

Pearl-shellers expressed somewhat greater confidence in Tosh than in Saville-Kent. He was renowned for his experience with oyster-cultivation, and became a professor of biology at the University of St Andrews in Britain. As the Fisheries Department's biologist, Tosh visited Thursday Island with a view to establishing a marine biology research station, and tenders had already been called when, ostensibly for financial reasons, the idea was dropped and Tosh recalled to Brisbane.

Most pearl-shellers still doubted the possibility of success in cultivation. The lengthy process of research and experimentation exceeded the patience of practical men, while the government did not support cultivation experiments against the resistance from pearl-shellers. The cultivation experiments were privately financed and conducted in secrecy. The success of one company in cultivating shell would have endangered the livelihood of the other pearl-shellers, who therefore offered every possible resistance, from pilfering to non-cooperation to lobbying against experiments. In Western Australia, the pearl-shell act was even amended in 1922 to prohibit pearl-cultivation, and A. C. Gregory, a large pearl-sheller of Broome, was prevented from employing a Japanese pearl technician.

The Mackay Commission of 1908

From 1902 to 1913 John Mackay was the head of the Marine Department as portmaster in Brisbane, and like other administrators at the time he expressed great concern for the permanency of the fishery. This period was characterised by the utmost concern about the fishery coupled with administrative paralysis and legislative inaction, because the unresolved White Australia issue overshadowed that of conservation. The package of management legislation enacted in 1891 had largely succumbed to pressures from the industry.

Seventeen years after its introduction, resource management was again given priority attention. In 1908 Mackay chaired the most exhaustive inquiry ever conducted into the industry.[57] The Royal Commission was briefed to suggest sustainable management strategies for the fishery. It was entitled 'Royal Commission into the working of pearlshell and bêche-de-mer industries of Queensland, with special regard to the following objects:—the working of pearl oyster beds in such a manner as to avoid depletion;—the scientific cultivation of pearl oyster;—the possibilities of encouraging white divers with a view to their gradual substitution for aliens'. Several of the witnesses called before this commission had had direct experience of the fishery since the 1870s.

The Commission submitted a comprehensive package of restructuring proposals. It attempted to subordinate the White Australia objective to an improvement of the fishery's internal structure, which would ensure that white divers would be attracted to pearl-shelling. The Commission's vision for the fishery entailed a very different production strategy based on small-scale (white) ownership, permanent settlement, resource husbandry, and the exploitation of a variety of resources: 'They might combine pearl-shelling and bêche-de-mer fishing, and cocoanut-growing where the opportunity offered'.[58]

The most urgent recommendation was to appoint a competent marine biologist as chief inspector of pearl-shell fisheries. In order to encourage the artificial cultivation of pearl-shell, research and teaching facilities were required. A School of Marine Biology, similar to the Agricultural College at Gatton and the Charters Towers School of Mines, was recommended. No cultivation leases were to be granted under existing regulations; but the foreshores in Torres Strait and as far as Cape Melville were to be reserved for long-term cultivation leases, on liberal terms, guarding against the creation of a monopoly.

In view of the depletion of resources, the export of bêche-de-mer was to be prohibited for two years, or until recuperation of stocks was demonstrated. The number of boat licences was to be controlled, and licensees restricted to five vessels per owner. No vessel larger than 25 tons was to be licensed, so as to prohibit floating stations. The permanent closure of Darnley Deeps and deep areas near Mount Adolphus was considered necessary, and the periodic closure of all grounds except Old Ground. Reinstatement of the 6-inch size limit was recommended. Finally, the rigid enforcement of regulations and the protection of cultivation areas required an effective patrol.

The Mackay Report solicited no action from either the federal or the State government. Licences had been restricted before the report was tabled. A bill was drafted along the lines of the recommendations, but not incorporating the proposals on marine biological investigation, and it was not submitted to Parliament. The Secretary to the Treasury (which controlled the Fisheries Acts) speculated that it may have been withheld by Cabinet because of the cost involved, because other more pressing matters needed attention, or because the evidence of depletion of beds was not conclusive.

Some of the proposals could have been implemented without legislation, such as stricter patrols of closed areas. Hockings observed:

I find that our laws are neither better nor worse than those of any other country in this regard, with the exception that in some lands those directly interested are given more police assistance, and the people themselves are more amenable to the law than some of our own people might be.[59]

But Mackay himself was not convinced that there was a danger of depletion. When questioned several years later, he felt that the deep-water areas (40 fathoms and more) could not be denuded, and that the north-westerly season provided an annual spell for the shallower beds. At any rate, by 1913 Mackay arrived at the conviction that the fishery could never be suitable for white men, and therefore felt that it was best left alone, since it was doing fine. This remarkable turnaround in attitude symbolises the general position of the state towards the industry. Having chaired the most comprehensive inquiry into the fishery, Mackay had a keen understanding of every aspect of the industry. His enthusiasm for reform had led him personally to try to recruit white divers in Europe. He had now resigned himself to the fact that pearl-shellers did not welcome radical change. Meanwhile, the fleet had been halved in numbers and the fishery continued to contract.

The Bamford Commission of 1913

A further exhaustive inquiry was conducted in 1913, this time by the federal government, to investigate means by which the White Australia policy could be implemented in the pearl-shell fishery (the fifth official inquiry into the issue since 1897).[60] An interim report was submitted in 1913 which dealt with resource management in the briefest manner and recommended the cultivation of pearl shell as a means towards that end. It proposed efficient patrolling and the prohibition of diving below 25 fathoms (45 metres) because of the danger to health.

The recommendations of the Mackay Commission on the arrest of shell-depletion were repeated 'without fully endorsing them'. Since the Bamford Commission reported to the federal government these proposals were of little relevance. They were included, nevertheless, because the commissioners advocated the cessation 'of the whole of the islands and reefs of Torres Strait' to the federal government, so that the industry could be wholly administered by the Commonwealth, particularly since most of the fishery took place in extra-territorial waters. (Since federation, Queensland patrolling officers could only exercise their authority within the 3-mile limit. The federal government, on the other hand, refused to patrol the extra-territorial fisheries, because fisheries were 'a matter for the States'.)

With the approach of war, the inquiry was suspended. The European pearl-shell market was closed, and pearl-shelling came to a virtual standstill. An experiment with British navy divers had failed to demonstrate that whites could successfully dive for shell. When they tabled the final report in 1916, the commissioners arrived at the conclusion that the fishery was unsuitable for white labour. As a result, any restructuring proposals—particularly any which would have met with resistance from both the State government and the pearl-shellers—were ignored.

The advent of trochus-shelling

During World War I, while the European shell markets were closed, America became the most important market, while Japan became a buyer of lower-grade shell. As a cheap alternative to pearl-shell, the first experimental consignment of trochus shell was shipped in 1912, and trochus-shelling quickly became part of the fishery. The shell grew on the shallow reefs and could be obtained by swimming-diving, so that its collection was more akin to bêche-de-mer fishing than to pearl-shell diving. Vessels now frequently shifted from bêche-de-mer to trochus collection and vice versa according to market opportunities and season.

By 1917 Thursday Island vessels went as far as Rockhampton to collect trochus, and the reefs were 'much depleted', the outlook not promising. Production decreased because overfishing had denuded the beds. A closure of trochus reefs was not within the powers of the fishing authorities under the pearl-shell and bêche-de-mer legislation.[61]

Dress-diving for pearl-shell, meanwhile, had resumed in early 1917. Only the shallow areas of Endeavour Strait were worked (6–9 fathoms, or 10–16 metres). Old Ground had not been visited for ten years because it was too exposed to the weather and quite depleted. In 1919 the pump boats again went to the deeper areas at great distances. Several small owners entered the industry in the early 1920s, and some vessels were now fitted with air-compressors instead of hand-pumps. There was some concern that the earlier experience of denudation of beds would be repeated, but no closures were enforced.

As far as pearl-shell was concerned, the fishery languished. Many shellers turned to trochus-shelling. In 1920 only 70 pump boats were registered, compared with 138 in 1910 and 341 in 1900. The prices obtained for pearl-shell were as low as £120 a ton, when it had fetched around £192 in 1910 and up to £200 in 1902.

In the 1930s the Australian federal and State governments took the initiative in encouraging marine industries, particularly coastal fishing and trawling, as a result of which fin-fishing became an important industry in Queensland, conducted as a full-time rather than a part-time occupation. In 1928 the Commonwealth Development and Migration Commission, CSIRO and State fisheries departments developed a strategy to foster coastal fishing and trawling by providing improved transport, distribution, and marketing facilities, and research into fish curing, oyster-cultivation, and the occurrence of sponges and food fishes. F. W. Moorehouse, a science graduate of the University of Queensland, was appointed marine biologist to investigate oysters, bêche-de-mer, pearl-shell, trochus and sardines, and was attached as scientific officer to the Great Barrier Reef Research Expedition of the British Museum in 1929.

As a result of the recommendations made by Moorehouse, a minimum size of $2\frac{1}{2}$ inch (612 mm) for trochus shell, measured across the exterior base of the shell, was enacted in 1931. This measure, somewhat belatedly introduced after a decade of intensive trochus-shelling, was the last act of resource management by the Queensland government before the industry declined. The 1936 report of the Department of Harbours and Marine indicated that trochus were scarce and the grounds were gradually being worked out. Marketing problems, rather than resource exhaustion, set the agenda for government intervention in the 1920s and 1930s.

In this reconstruction of the pressures for and against resource management, the course of the Queensland pearl-shell fishery may appear somehow inexorable. After all, governments did their best to manage the fishery without being authoritarian, and pearl-shellers also tried to improve the industry without cutting into their profits. How else could the fishery have been conducted? The Australian fishery did not operate in isolation; its operations present a contrast to types of management in other countries.

Pearl-shell management overseas

Despite the local abundance of pearl-shell, it was a relatively scarce resource known to occur only in a comparatively few, well-defined areas. The Australian mother-of-pearl production competed with, and overshadowed, other centres of production. There was a lively fishery in the Persian Gulf, more specifically in the Gulf of Serendib and at Sofala. The Bay of Bengal contained two fisheries, one in the Gulf of Mannar (between India and Ceylon) and one at the Mergui Archipelago (off the Malay Peninsula in British Burma). There were also small pearl-fisheries in China, Tahiti, Eastern Polynesia (Puamotu, Manahiki, Suwarrow), and the Gulf of Mexico (Panama), and freshwater pearls were found in the mussels of the Mississippi River.

In the East Indies shell was raised in the Timor Sea (Lesser Sunda Islands, Ambon and Celebes) in the Dutch East Indies, at Aru (Dobo) in Dutch New Guinea, at Samarai, and in the Arafura Sea. Japanese and Arabian fleets came to the East Indies. Australian-owned vessels also visited the East Indies, as well as raising trochus in New Caledonia and pearl-shell and trochus at the Philippines while it was under American control. Finally, Japan competed with Australia as a centre of pearl and pearl-shell production. *Pinctada maxima* is not found in Japan, but Japanese fleets fished overseas, and oysters and abalone were harvested in Japan.

After the turn of the century, the entire pearl-shell and pearl industry was in a resource crisis. The grounds at Mergui, Tahiti and in Eastern Polynesia were fished out. Reports of depletion came also from the Persian Gulf, the East Indies, China, Japan, and the Mississippi Valley. The Mannar fishery was sporadic and relatively insignificant. That leaves only the Philippines, Panama and New Caledonia unaccounted for.

A review of all these fisheries would be too far-reaching, because of the variety of political and historical contexts in which they were embedded. A juxtaposition of four of these fisheries, however, serves to point out the variety of possible management and production strategies, ranging from vastly alternative to quite similar approaches.

India–Ceylon: the ancient method[62]

The oldest known pearl-fishery was located in the Gulf of Mannar, between Ceylon (Sri Lanka) and India. It is thought to have commenced several centuries BCE and was known throughout the ancient world.[63] The pearl-fishery was located on both sides of the Gulf of Mannar, and the market was at Tuticorin on the Indian mainland. The Parawa, the traditional owners, whose wealth depended on the fishery, guarded the beds against infringements. Parawa headmen inspected the banks, recruited the divers and superintended the fishing operations. Muslims, who are thought to have migrated from the Persian Gulf pearl-fisheries and who were known as Lubbais, also settled in the area and engaged in pearl-fishing.[64]

The traditional pearl-fishery was not a regular or annual event. Rather, it was an irregular mass festival and trade fair, at which the whole harvest was reaped. Since pearling was the production of wealth, and not a subsistence activity for the traditional owners of the pearl-beds, it was not conducted with a view to regularity. On the contrary, their relative scarcity was instrumental in maintaining the value of pearls.

It is likely that colonial rule exerted pressure on the pearl-fishery to produce greater (taxable) wealth, which was the main purpose of the secular Portuguese administration. In 1658 it was reported that the inhabitants of Mannar Island had become impoverished because the 'oysters have migrated and are to be found on the coast of Tuticorin'.[65]

During the Dutch rule (1658–1796) seventeen pearl harvests were recorded, sometimes in successive years. The harvest which took place in 1700 was described in detail. Before a harvest was conducted, the pearl-beds were tested by sending out ten or twelve vessels from each of which several thousand oysters were collected in different localities. If the yield of pearls from this sample was promising, a public announcement invited far-away merchants, the deputies of rulers, and the public to a harvest which lasted for several months, during which a lively market was held.

Each fishing boat had five large diving stones, on which the divers stood, in order to descend, as the stones were quickly lowered into the water. The diver was burdened with a rope which secured a shell-basket or net, and also served as a lifeline by which communication was possible. As soon as one diver was pulled up, another went down. The oysters were opened after a few days, and the pearls graded by shaking them through a series of colanders with different-sized holes.

The Parawa and Lubbai divers had separate boats. Complex negotiations and political alliances determined the privileges to be granted to local rulers by assigning them diving stones, and the rate of contribution from Parawa and Lubbai divers was fixed in advance. In the 1708 harvest nearly 400 of $4321\frac{1}{2}$ stones—or the season's work of 800 divers—were allocated in advance as tributes (the half stone means that it was not fully crewed). Of the participating divers 4760 were Christian Parawas, 3103 were Muslim Lubbais and 780 were Hindus. The image of 8643 divers, let alone the supporting crew, 864 captains, and armed escorts, descending on an area is almost beyond imagination. The highest number of men (not only divers) ever officially engaged in the Torres Strait fishery (over a far larger area) was 2509. Meanwhile, it must be supposed that the multitudes on shore, including the families of crew, merchants, and onlookers, far surpassed that number.

This account is dwarfed however, by an earlier one, written in 1685, which estimates the number of participating boats at between 4000 and 5000, with eight or nine divers and ten to twelve crew each. The number of people thus referred to is 72 000 at the minimum. The pearling boats were accompanied by armed men to guard against Malabar pirates. This account, too, describes the testing of shell-beds, by three boats collecting 1000 oysters each. The pearl-beds were at 5–7 fathoms (9–12.6 metres), and divers could remain submerged for the duration of 'two credos'. The proceedings lasted from four o'clock in the morning to four o'clock in the afternoon, announced by gunfire. The season went from 11 March to 20 April. Meanwhile, for nearly two months, 'the merchants assemble and hold a splendid fair; there are magnificent tents and all sorts of merchandise of the most valuable kind are to be had there, as vendors come from all parts of the world'.[66]

The Dutch Administration participated only indirectly, by selling the fishing rights. In the 1740s, the Dutch East India Company began to question the value of the pearl-fishery (to the company). Its officers were apparently unable to buy pearls, because this required expert knowledge. The company earned duties and licences from the fishery, but feared that the extensive trade fairs accompanying it undermined its trading monopoly. During a lean period in the 1730s, speculation arose as to the cause of depletion. The Dutch Governor of Ceylon argued that depletion was a natural phenomenon, but the vested interest of the company necessarily dims the objective value of his assessment:

> experience has shown that the banks have lain fallow for a much longer time than has as yet been the case on this occasion . . . Indeed there are many natives who pretend to give reasons for the failure of the banks, and who say that the multitude of persons forced there against their will have ruined the banks, whilst others looked to their own profit too much.[67]

The Company decided to reorganise the fishery by renting out the beds to a single lessee, to prohibit the public festivities accompanying it, and to withdraw the privileges of local rulers. One harvest was attempted under these restrictions in 1746, but in the following three years some privileges were granted again. Thereafter, no harvest was held for nineteen years, possibly, as Hornell speculates, because of the political rivalry with local rulers. Between 1800 and 1900, twelve harvests were held, five of them in consecutive years. This gives a mean interval of eight years between harvests, both during the Dutch and the British administration.

After the British occupation in 1796, traditional privileges were finally withdrawn. The British Government claimed two-thirds of the entire catch. This was done by dividing the unopened shells into shares and auctioning them, so that an expert knowledge of pearls was not required in dividing the catch. The Mannar fishery remained orientated towards pearls. The shell was of inferior quality and used only for lime. As a result of serious concerns about the sustainability of the pearl fishery in the late nineteenth century, the British administration placed emphasis on artificial cultivation. It assumed complete control of the fishery through an administrative body employing a scientific officer, which imposed seasonal closures: 'The boats go out to work under the supervision of a Government steamer. They start and cease work at a given signal; and they can only work upon the areas indicated by the Government officer in charge of the fishery'.[68] The pearl-bed administrators periodically inspected and tested the banks, accompanied by the hereditary chief of the Parawa only as a token gesture. The Parawa remained responsible, however, for recruiting.

Burma: the British colonial method[69]

The pearl-shell fishery in the Mergui Archipelago of the Bay of Bengal commenced in 1891, when a Queensland pearl-sheller, Mr Chill, pointed out the value of this resource to the British colonial government. The Mergui Archipelago was divided into five 'blocks' or districts, and pearl-fishing rights for the blocks were auctioned. Frank Jardine, of Somerset, became pearl-shell commissioner and assessed the beds in 1893–94. Under his supervision, the leased beds were 'recklessly exploited' for a decade. In 1900 a licensing system for diving pumps replaced the leases for pearl-shell, while the 'block' auctions continued for rights to collect trochus, bêche-de-mer, arc shell (spoon shell, *Pteria* sp.) and green snail (*Turbo* sp.). Apart from the licence fees or lease, no taxation or royalty was raised.

The history of this fishery is very similar to that of Torres Strait. First, the shallow areas were exhausted which were the employment of indigenous swimming-divers, the Selongs. The return from swimming-diving decreased year by year until it was 'practically nothing' in 1906. Second, divers for pump boats were indentured Japanese and Filipinos, most of whom had prior experience in Australian pearl-shelling. There were also some Malay and two Chinese divers, while the Burmese were not considered suitable for dress-diving. Third, the fishery required the clarification of maritime boundaries between Siam (Thailand) and British Burma (Myanmar). Fourth, trochus-collecting was introduced as the pearl-shell declined in the shallow areas. The first reference to trochus collection was made in 1900 (1912 in Queensland). Fifth, the Mergui settlement practically owed its existence to the pearl-shell fishery. The colonial officials concerned with the area echoed the concerns and opinions of the pearl-shellers. It was argued that the south-west monsoon, which interrupted fishing from April to September, was a natural closed season which allowed beds to recuperate and acted as 'an effective barrier to depletion'.

The fishery had reached its peak within four years of commencement (340 tons of mother-of-pearl in 1894, and an average yield per boat of 6.5 tons), and then set course on a downward trend (90 tons of mother-of-pearl in 1905, and an average yield per boat of 1.1 tons), which pearl-shellers sought to compensate with increased fishing intensity (the number of boats continued to increase). In 1907 the fisheries administrator actively sought to encourage territorial expansion of the fleets, particularly to the Moskos Islands, as resources noticeably declined in the Mergui area.

Periodic closures were not considered, because of the cost of policing involved (and further taxation would 'attack the existence of the fisheries'). On the contrary, it was felt that the fishery could support

150 pump boats instead of the 76 licensed in 1907 (the greatest number of boats recorded had been 80 in 1905). A much greater calamity than declining resources, it was argued, would be 'the abandonment of the industry by a large number of owners'. It was admitted that 'the Mergui pearl fisheries have in the past proved more remunerative for individuals than they are to-day, but still they bring a large measure of its prosperity to Mergui and no small profit to the owners'.[70] The resource depletion had not made its mark on profits, because of lucky pearl finds and fluctuating shell prices. The revenue earned from the industry also continued to increase due to a proliferation of lease-types (for example sub-leasing of trochus-shelling rights within an area leased for trepanging), and because in the scramble for more fishing areas the lessees bid each other up at the annual public auctions.

There was even less concern for the sustainability of the resource than in Australia. The opinions expressed by local officials about the pearl-shell fishery at Mergui were merely an expression of the interests of pearl-shellers. Pleading 'economic hardship', these evidently sought to avert an increase in taxation as well as discouraging regulatory intervention. That protective intervention was unnecessary was demonstrated by the substantial profits which could still be made. The contradictory nature of these statements detracted little from their acceptance. The available figures demonstrated declining average productivity, but were not presented in such a way as to make that point.

The Mergui pearl-shell fishery lacked the countervailing interest of settled colonists and the pressures for conservation which were brought to bear on the Australian fishery in the interest of a White Australia. While revenue was increasing, the colonial government saw no need to expend effort or expense on the industry. Mergui was a resource-raider's paradise, and by 1908 it was generally considered to be depleted. It was later extended to the Nicobar and Andaman Islands.

The East Indies: the Dutch colonial method

In the East Indies, foreign vessels, particularly Australian and British (from Mergui), poached in the Dutch-controlled waters, even with nets, which was highly detrimental to resource stocks. But in 1898 the Dutch presence in western New Guinea was formalised, a post at Merauke established, and the Dutch colonial authorities[71] granted pearling leases to foreign monopolies in order to earn revenue. The colonial administration judiciously policed the leased and common maritime areas, to keep away poachers.

The first legislation to protect the Dutch interest against poachers was passed in 1893, which banned all foreign pearling except those fishing by permit. The licensing fees were in proportion to the number of diving suits used. The luggers did not need to be registered under the Dutch flag (a substantial saving compared to Australian-registered luggers), and were assigned leases outside the 3-mile limit. The only proviso was that indigenous fishers must be allowed to exercise traditional fishing rights in the leased areas. Permission had to be obtained from the local sultan or rajah, and a compensation paid to him. In 1902 the legislation was sharpened. A fixed amount of $6 per vessel per month was charged. Refusal to pay led to confiscation of equipment and shell, and the fines imposed were $160, a two-year prison term, or seizure of the vessel. 'Unsatisfactory behaviour' earned the pearlers a gunboat escort out of the Dutch waters (a treatment once administered to the Clark fleet). Warships were patrolling as far as Tanimbar, Ambon, and the Moluccas, and trespassers were confronted by warships or local trading vessels. This was at a time when the Macassan fleets from the Dutch colony still regularly visited the North Australian coast to gather trepang.

The recruitment of indigenous labour was controlled in a similar manner to the Australian restrictions. If they were shipped overseas they were signed on and paid off at their home port. Until 1900, when Socialists became dominant in the Dutch Parliament, forced labour was part of Holland's colonial policy, and particularly at Koepang in Timor, indigenous labour was readily available.

The experience of the Clark fleet, which went to Aru in 1905 and sought re-entry into Queensland by 1908, suggests that under this regime, too, the fishery was operated on a depleted yield basis.

Japanese pearl culture: an entrepreneurial approach[72]

Since the Meiji Restoration in 1867, pearl-fishing had become a traditional female activity at Omura Bay (Nagasaki), Nanao Bay (Ishikawa Prefecture) and Ago Bay (near Toba, in Mie Prefecture). Some women supported their families with pearl-fishing while husbands assumed domestic duties. In the 1880s the pearl-bearing oysters became depleted, and in 1888 a self-confessed eccentric merchant, Mikimoto, of the ascendant *chonin* class (merchants), formed a village co-operative[73] at Jinmyo Mura (near Toba) to experiment with pearl culture. The Chinese had for centuries produced miniature mother-of-pearl Buddhas by implanting a small embossed metal piece into oysters which was enclosed in nacre by the oyster. The principle of pearl growth was therefore well known, but pearl-culture had not succeeded. In 1893 Mikimoto achieved the first success in cultivating semicircular pearls (blister pearls), and in 1896 he took out a patent for their cultivation for ten years. In 1898 the first commercial crop of semicircular pearls was harvested at Tatoku Island, where twenty female swimming-divers were permanently employed. (In the 1930s this number was still the same.) In 1905 round pearls were produced for the first time, and in 1908 the process was patented.[74] A further breakthrough was the cultivation of several pearls in the same oyster, and techniques were developed to lengthen the lifespan of the oyster, so that the pearl could mature longer.

Mikimoto used royal connections to create a European interest in his pearls, and was aided by scientists at universities and fisheries departments in Japan (there was a Pearl Faculty at Ise University). He extensively used trade fairs and world expositions to market his product, and established jewellery factories in Japan and retail shops overseas. Initially, there was considerable resistance in the European market against 'artificial pearls'. In order to maintain a high profile for this new product, Mikimoto destroyed low-grade pearls, once in an ostentatious demonstration outside the Chamber of Commerce, where he burned $25 000 worth of inferior pearls in 1933. To guard against natural disaster, particularly octopus infestations and the Red Tide (a periodic algal growth explosion), pearl-culture farms were set up also at Omura (Kyushu), Nanao (Ishikawa), Tanabe (Wakayama) and Okinawa in the 1930s. In the 1940s a pharmaceutical company was added to the pearl empire which sold crushed seed pearls as calcium phosphate for medicinal purposes. Mikimoto is the biggest 'success story' in the history of pearling. The company's display rooms in the Gin'za, Tokyo's central shopping district, are among the spectacles for the tourist in Tokyo.

A review of overseas fisheries brings the Australian approach into some perspective. Two of the fisheries reviewed above were concerned with pearls. The ancient method was based on jealously guarded traditional ownership. At Mannar the stocks were permitted to build up to abundant levels, often over more than a decade, and then the rich harvest was reaped with a tremendous intensity of fishing effort which exhausted the beds. The fishery had a central place in the community's political life. Pearls were the major source of wealth and power, and their relative scarcity, augmented by over-fishing, enhanced their value. Moreover, the opulent display of wealth which accompanied the fishery, and the rarity of the event, added to its reputation. Overfishing was an instrument of market management. It differed from resource-raiding in that it did not rely on territorial expansion and was not guided by a philosophy of un-limited growth.

In Japan, pearl-fishing was not embedded in traditional political structures as at Mannar. It was an individualised, female activity, conducted as a regular source of income. The absence of political integration, and the expectation of continuity, provided the frame-work for an entrepreneurial intitiative to make the harvest predictable by resource husbandry. With this shift, the fishery became an in-dustry, but not one that was based on mass extraction. Productivity was increased by maximising the resource potential. Technological innovation was not used for territorial expansion but to intensify the productivity of the already available shell (cultivating several pearls per oyster and lengthening their life span). Industrial growth was achieved by forward integration. Shops and manufacture were added to the company before production plant was increased, and this was done not by increasing the size of the existing plant but by adding new farms in various locations as an insurance against natural dis-asters. At the basis of this growth strategy was the concept of a limited resource.

There is a great contrast between the ancient method at Mannar and the entrepreneurial approach in Japan. But they had three key elements in common, which distinguished them from the Australian production strategy. The first was the concept of resource-owner-ship. In Japan, the resource was subject to private property regu-lations by means of permanent leases. At Mannar, the resource was collectively owned, and user rights were subject to complex political negotiation between the Parawas, the Lubbais, and their respective patrons.

The second element was the concept of scarcity, which might be understood as an effect of ownership. The Japanese production strategy was based on the expectation of a continuous, steady output, so that resource scarcity had to be overcome. Husbandry techniques were developed to guard against scarcity and became the central philosophy of production. In the case of Mannar, on the other hand, periods of scarcity and abundance were culturally constructed by means of intensive harvest and closure. By this means, scarcity was integrated into the culture, and was part of the production process.

The third distinguishing element was the concept of luxury. In the Japanese case, quality control and controlled level of output maintained the status of luxury for the pearls produced. Also, a considerable effort at image management was made by using royal connections and through display of wealth. At Mannar, too, an international reputation was enhanced by the presence of royals and the display of wealth, while the long periods of scarcity maintained the status of luxury for the pearls.

The other two fisheries reviewed are more similiar to the Australian fishery, in that they were concerned with pearl-shell, and they were both colonial enterprises, that is, not conducted by native residents except on a small scale. In stark contrast to the ancient method, where the fishery was inextricably linked to the political structure, state and industry must be considered as separate actors in the colonial fisheries. The colonial state earned revenue from the industry through leases and licences. No income tax, export duties, or registration fees were raised. In other words, the state assumed territorial rather than managerial functions. It sold property rights (as leases) and granted rights of entry (as licences). It did not intervene with a view to sustainability, either in the form of resource management or marketing aid. Pearl-shell was a raw material for export in a typical colonial centre–periphery network.

For the fishery, this colonial framework meant that resource-raiding was still possible, unfettered by territorial boundaries. The pearl-shell centres (Aru, Kupang, Mergui) were a port, not a permanent home for the pearl-shellers. The fact that both of these fisheries were conducted on the basis of leased areas, and that resource depletion resulted in both cases, suggests that privatising the commons is not a sufficient condition for sustainable resource use.

Despite the strong parallels between these two colonial models and the Australian fisheries, there are also significant differences. The Australian governments made some comparatively interventionist overtures. The significant difference which may explain the interventionist stance of the Australian governments is that between conquered colonies, exploited as a source of wealth, and settled colonies, where the government represented a local electorate. Where settlers engaged in production for export, they were both colonised and colonisers. That they were colonisers is abundantly clear from the dispossession of indigenous people, and from the way in which they referred to Britain as 'home'. The ethos of the colonists permeated their culture. However, they were also colonised in the sense that they were the dependent producers in the colonial trading network. In that function, they had residential interests with a view to greater permanency than unsettled resource-raiders. Their elected governments had a legitimate role to play in resource management. For the Queensland pearl-shellers, and even more so for the business-people of Thursday Island, for example, it was important that shell was found in the Torres Strait area rather than in some other British dependency. A whole community of merchants, workers, and, not least, government officials anchored the pearl-shelling interest to this particular area. The Australian state therefore had not only a pecuniary interest in the industry, as the colonial governments did, but also a certain mandate to attempt to render the industry sustainable.

On the face of it, there were ample attempts, both from governments and pearl-shellers, to institute some form of resource management in Australia. On closer inspection, however, these appear ineffectual and half-hearted. In the contrast with the overseas case studies presented, the concept of settlement colony explains both why the state had a certain interest in managing resources with a view to permanency, and why there was so much resistance to these attempts, since resource-raiding was the tried and tested means for conducting a collection industry in the colonies.

Resource-raiding as a strategy to supply mass production was a recipe for decline. As the resource was being overtaxed, relative productivity declined and in turn solicited a self-defeating intensification of productive effort until the natural limits of growth were reached. Although it was accepted that certain shell-beds were exhausted, the industry insisted that territorial expansion rather than resource management was the solution to productivity crises. The industry's response to its first major resource crisis was contraction, and the industry's structural problems remained unaddressed. The pearl-shellers were reluctant to embark on resource husbandry because cultivation leases represented a new enclosure movement.

Sustained by the vision of unlimited growth and expansion, they saw no need to privatise the common resource, to pay for, and be individually liable for, its regeneration.

The state, on the other hand, territorial by nature, did not share this vision. It was in the state's interest that the fishery should flourish within set territorial confines. It was therefore not by accident that the period when the fishery was at its most vibrant was also the time when it was most intensively subjected to official inquiry. The government's attempts to manage pearl-shell resources with size restrictions, closures, and restrictions on licences fall into the period from 1891 to 1908, the period in which the industry underwent its first resource crisis.

When bold legislation was introduced along the lines of Saville-Kent's suggestions it was apparently thought that the regulations had the support of the industry. However, the industry was divided between large companies, mostly floating-station owners, and smaller pearl-shellers, mostly shore-station operators, and a conflict of interest within the industry flared up over shell-culture experiments. The 1891 management package was gradually dismantled, and henceforward the legislators took care to test pearl-shellers' opinions before passing new laws. But in its attempt to solve the 'tragedy of the commons', the government also pursued its own set of political goals—the establishment of a 'yeomanry' of small pearl-shellers and the implementation of the White Australia policy. This agenda overshadowed the resource issue, particularly with regard to the Mackay and Bamford inquiries. A shift of the industry towards cultivation (which in the event did not occur until the 1960s, arising out of another crisis) could have solved both the resource problem and the labour issue.

In the 1930s the fishery contracted, and resource use ceased to be its dominant problem. From now on, the government's involvement in the fishery was mainly in the area of marketing and financial assistance. In the 1950s the government's concern for the industry shifted to debate in the international arena, as we have seen in Chapter 4.

6

The Last Thing on their Minds: Marketing

The pearl-shell fishery links into several dominant themes of Australian history. The quest for pearl-shell played a significant role in the development of the far North and the formation of northern State boundaries. The treatment of Aboriginal populations, the administration in Torres Strait, and Australia's relations with Japan were all affected by the fishery. The end-product of this industry, which had such far-reaching ramifications, was buttons—a somewhat mundane destination for the precious shell. Some pearl-shellers were apparently unaware of the market for which they produced. The manager of Burns Philp's Wyben fleet had always thought that pearl-shell was used 'for inlaid work on revolver handles, knife handles, umbrella handles, and so on', and expressed surprise when he was informed by the royal commissioners in 1908 that 90 per cent of pearl-shell was used for buttons.[1]

The final link in the chain of the pearl-shell industry's weaknesses was that the industry produced entirely for an overseas market, over which it had no influence and about which pearl-shellers had only spurious information. Moreover, as a luxury item, pearl-shell was more sensitive to economic downturns than staple exports, although the degree of that sensitivity was frequently overstressed. The exporting procedures were handled by a few overseas buyers who advanced money to pearl-shellers, and these 'middlemen' exerted considerable control over the market, both on the supply and on the demand side.

In the face of an oligopolistic market, the most serious weakness of the pearl-shellers was their disunity. The industry was characterised by a competitive individualism: pearl-shellers tended to distrust leadership and reject authority. This attitude made it difficult for larger companies or governments, or, indeed, industry associations, to take a lead in organising or co-ordinating the fishery. Only under extreme pressure was a short-lived solidarity ever achieved, and the actual market strength of Australian producers—the world's largest source of pearl-shell—never manifested itself as market power: the ability to control marketing and stabilise prices. From the 1920s to the 1940s marketing was the most serious problem of the industry.

The pearl-shellers generally understood themselves as primary producers without any role in marketing or production. Australia's colonial position as dependent producer for the needs of Britain's industrialisation was deeply ingrained in the imagination of producers. Pearl-shellers displayed a negative attitude towards suggestions of domestic manufacture. It was far more convenient to leave those things to the people who 'knew best'—and who were invariably overseas. State officials were reluctant to impose solutions on an uncooperative industry, which generally resisted regulatory intervention and state-led innovation. State support was therefore restricted to monetary assistance to prop up an ailing industry rather than aimed at the active restructuring and facilitation of a market which several public inquiries had proposed. As a result, the marketing weakness of the industry was never properly addressed.

World War II represents a watershed in the industry. The federal government of the postwar era was committed to establishing a broader manufacturing base and, drawing on the powers acquired during the war from the State governments, took a leading role in postwar reconstruction and national economic management. It assumed responsibility for the management of the extra-territorial fishery, which became largely the domain of Japanese fleets. The domestic pearl-shell industry was economically devastated after the war, and gradually emerged with a transformed ownership structure based on a large number of inexperienced pearl-shellers. Their fishing activities were confined to shallow waters, and concentrated on trochus shell. There was a brief flurry of activity: a button factory was even set up in Cairns. For a moment it seemed as if the fishery could become a truly Australian one. But technological innovation overtook the industry. The combined effect of the development of plastics for buttons and of pearl-farming displaced the rough, laborious and perilous pearl-shell industry. The new industry, pearl-culture, was again not an Australian-controlled industry.

As Chapter 1 showed, the earliest pearl-shell stations in Torres Strait were financed by large companies, mostly based in Sydney. These companies acted as exporters of shell, with the pearl-shellers as dependent producers. Firms like Burns Philp, Paddon and Godeffroy acted as financiers for the share-trading captains, and exported the shell via Sydney. As a lasting result of these early arrangements, the Torres Strait shell continued to be referred to as 'Sydney shell' on the London market. In the 1870s there was a keen market for pearl-shell, and good shell fetched from £320 to £400 a ton.[2] By the 1890s Torres Strait production had stabilised around the 1000-ton mark, and prices averaged at £125 a ton.

As more pearl-shellers entered the industry in the 1890s, overseas buyers were able to assume a more influential role. Small owners were unable to withhold shell from the market and depended on the price offered by the buyers. They were also less able than large companies to curb production if there was an oversupply. All Australian shell was sold in London, and from there distributed to manufacturers, mainly on the Continent. The industry was now at the zenith of shell-production, and entered the first of the three resource crises traced in Appendix II. Pearl-shellers started to think about alternative markets such as the Far East, in order to compensate with better prices for declining productivity. Australians were already the main producers of mother-of-pearl. In 1906, for example, 99 per cent of shell imported by London came from Australia and Aru (19 per cent from Thursday Island, 43 per cent from Western Australia and 37 per cent from Clark and Hockings at Aru). From 1903, small amounts of shell were sold in other markets, and the United States emerged as a second major market. The Hong Kong and Japanese buyers purchased the lower grades of shell, while the better shell went to the United States and London. There was almost no processing of pearl-shell in Australia, although this had variously been suggested and there were two short-lived attempts at it.[3] Australian textile producers, including some large firms in Brisbane, imported shell buttons, mostly from Japan.

Button manufacture overseas

The processing of pearl-shell involved several separate processes and produced much wastage. Most of the left-over shell was discarded, and uses for scraps developed only gradually.[4] The entire production process was mechanised, using specially designed machinery driven by steam or electricity, or 2–3 horsepower engines. Some smaller workshops used 'pedal power'.

A 1917 account of the production in Iowa and Illinois, the centre of the American pearl-button industry, illuminates the processes involved. The first step in button-production, and also the most labour-intensive, was cutting (sawing) the blanks. This was done only by men, who occupied the best-paid position at about US$8–10 per week. This process mainly took place in small sheds which were outbuildings of private homes or workshops. Only a few large factories reserved their ground floor for cutting blanks and conducted the finishing processes on the upper level.

The sawing produced a fine dust, and some cutters protected their nose and mouth with cloth. In a few large factories, air ventilation systems were installed to exhaust the dust. The powder was almost pure carbonate of lime, suitable for fertilising clay soils or polishing metal, but there was no ready market for it. The cutting of blanks produced the greatest wastage of shell. In the case of the Mississippi shell, the wastage was estimated to be as high as 90 per cent; for higher-grade shell it was estimated at around 50 per cent. The small shell fragments were used in road construction by local councils, and most manufacturers were glad to be rid of the waste—some even paid to have it taken away. One innovative manufacturer treated the shell scraps further to produce uniform fragments with rounded edges, which were sold as poultry feed additive.[5]

The finishing of blanks was done in manufactories. First the blank was 'dressed', which meant grinding the back of the blank on an emery wheel to make an even surface. In the American industry, this was done by 'boys' at US$4.50–7 a week. The grinding machines were the most expensive single piece of equipment used in the process. The further processes were done by 'girls' (girls and women), earning from US$3.75–6 a week. The blanks were 'faced' to shape the front of the button, giving it its central depression. Then two or four holes were drilled before the buttons were polished with the action of a chemical fluid in wooden tumblers. Next, the buttons were washed and dried, sorted and graded, and then sewn on cards and packed in boxes.

Birmingham was the British centre of shell-button production, and there, too, the large factories employed mainly women and girls as cheap labour.[6] But blanks were cut by putting out work, using the cheapest available labour, as in Germany: 'in lots of villages in Germany women who have small machines, which cost only a pound or two, cut out the buttons in their own homes and send them on to the manufacturer. Under that system they work very cheaply'.[7]

Japanese and American manufacturers entered into shell-button production with cheaper types of shell after the turn of the century. A lively industry developed rapidly in the Mississippi area around the freshwater mussel, after a tariff barrier for buttons of 25 per cent *ad valorem* was imposed in 1890. A German immigrant with prior experience of pearl-shell manufacture in Hamburg, J. F. Boepple, pioneered a factory in Muscatine on the Mississippi in 1891. By 1898, eleven factories and thirty-eight saw works (where blanks were cut) in Iowa and Illinois employed 1434 people. Button production became one of the major industrial activities of that area, supporting the mussel-fishery which employed several hundred people, and many machine shops specialised entirely on making and repairing the machines used in button-production and diving.

> There was naturally some difficulty at first in putting on the market buttons made from our native fresh water shells, but the demand was rapidly developed, as the quality and price of the buttons became known, and at present Mississippi River Buttons are sold in every State and Territory and in Canada. It is reported that orders have recently (1899) come from England.[8]

A similarly spectacular success was experienced in the Japanese shell-button manufacture. Japan quickly became the sole buyer of Australian trochus shell, after the first commercial shipment of trochus in 1912, and supplied most of the Australian demand for shell-button. The European and British shell-button producers felt the pinch of this competition from cheaper materials. That such an enterprise was not set up around the Australian shell-production was a serious omission. The Australian shell-fishery remained wholly dependent on exporting raw shell, despite increasing difficulties with overseas marketing.

Marketing problems

Price instability was a major obstacle to the industry's prosperity, to which pearl-shellers invariably referred when faced with the proposition to employ white divers. In 1896–97 pearl-shell prices dropped to a low £70 a ton, while in 1912 the average price at Thursday Island was as high as £200. A docker's strike in London had caused a shortage of shell, with the result that some shell sold in London for £530 a ton. But even without such externalities, prices varied greatly, not only from season to season but from one bi-monthly auction to the next during seasons, and between different grades of shell. The average price of shell used for year-to-year comparisons glosses over such variations.

Generally, Australian shell fetched higher prices than that from other producing countries, and Torres Strait shell was considered to be of higher quality than other Australian shell. In 1908 Torres Strait shell was graded into four classes, from Very Best shell to Poor Quality, but by 1913 the grading system had changed to six classes from AA to E. Broome and Darwin shell each formed their own class, with some variations in the quality of Darwin shell. There were also seasonal variations in quality, so that producers found it difficult to secure advance contracts. The shell was auctioned in London because pearl-shellers were unable to deliver shell 'as per sample'. This meant that they were never quite certain of their returns.

These variations in quality also posed a problem for buyers. According to a report about the American market for pearl-shell, prepared by the Australian Trade Commissioner to the USA, 'buyers at Australian fishing grounds work on different ideas as to the significance of the nominal grades'.[9] In other words, grading was unreliable and inconsistent. The absence of a nationally uniform and reliable grading system impeded rational planning.

A further marketing difficulty was that demand was fairly inelastic: it did not respond readily to price fluctuations. This was evident in the production trends of the different pearl-shell centres in Australia, which tended to cushion each other's variations. For example, from 1900 to 1906, Torres Strait exports were on a downward trend, which was compensated by increased exports from Broome, Darwin and Aru.[10] The centres of production, even within Australia, competed with each other to satisfy an inelastic demand.

Pearl-shellers offered three explanations for their marketing difficulties, all of which were credible in terms of market theory. What was not questioned, however, was the attitude of pearl-shellers, which was the greatest obstacle to a remedy.

A luxury commodity

It was widely understood that pearl-shell catered for a luxury market, so that it was vulnerable to economic downturns. However, while it was true that some pearl-shell buttons were at the upper end of the market, much of it was used for standard production. Buttons were also made from other types of shell (abalone and mussel) and from leather, horn, semi-precious stone, glass, metal, wood and casein. According to a market report in 1917, there was a large regular demand for D and E grade shell for low-priced staple buttons. AA and A grade, and some B grade shell, was used for fancy buttons. These grades were presumably somewhat sensitive to fashion. B and C grade shell was bought by novelty[11] manufacturers, and the demand was limited and seasonal. Demand for novelties and high-grade buttons was vulnerable to economic downturns.

Pearl-shellers emphasised the fashion-dependence of their industry, and offered this as an explanation of the drastic price fluctuations from which it suffered. The Comptroller-General of Customs expressed this view after a cursory investigation into the industry: 'As to the value (of pearl-shell), it is not so far as I can ascertain regulated by the supply. It depends wholly and solely upon the fickleness of fashion, and is liable to very extreme fluctuations'.[12] Herbert Bowden, a pearl-sheller at Thursday Island, recalled that when a fashion in ladies' winter jackets with huge buttons was launched in New York, it created a keen demand for Aru shell, whereas the introduction of many small buttons running along ladies' sleeves raised the market for high-grade pearl-shell from all centres.

It is difficult to believe, however, that the bulk of pearl-shell was affected by such short-lived fashion trends. If between 80 and 90 per cent of Australian pearl-shell was used for buttons, most of the production must have been in standard *lignes* (button sizes), which were used for shirts and blouses, up-market manchester and lingerie. The instance referred to by Bowden, where a particular fashion had a specific effect on Aru shell, is much more likely to have resulted from a three-year contract with Clark's Aru fleet. In truth, Australian pearl-shellers took little interest in the processing and uses of pearl-shell.

Insignificance of output

That all pearl-shell was exported unprocessed to London was understood by pearl-shellers as an unalterable fact. Some were convinced of the insignificance of their industry in terms of the world market. One pearl-sheller argued in 1913 that 'our output is so small, we could not secure the attendance of buyers at local sales'.[13] In that year about a quarter of the world's production came from Thursday Island.

Pearls themselves, on the other hand, attracted overseas buyers to Thursday Island to such an extent that it had been found necessary to introduce pearl-dealers' licences with residential restrictions. At Thursday Island, pearls were considered a by-product of the industry, 'diver's perks'. Only in times of recession did the pearl-shellers look for ways to claim the pearls found, but generally they had no part in marketing the pearls, and Hockings wanted it understood that he was a pearl-sheller, not a pearler. If buyers came to Thursday Island for the side-product of the industry, the fear that overseas buyers might ignore this centre of production was surely unfounded.

Dependence on the market 'at Home' was the last thing to worry Australian producers—on the contrary, it was reassuring. Enjoying favoured supplier status in the British Commonwealth, Australia serviced the needs of British industry and commerce, without yet suffering the effects of the unbalanced economic structure typical of dependent colonies. Pearl-shellers were content to confine their involvement to primary production, and reluctant to involve themselves beyond that role.

Oligopoly

The most frequent, and also the most convincing, explanation of marketing difficulties was that pearl-shellers faced an oligopolistic buying environment. The Bamford Commission was informed in 1913 that a few buyers controlled the market and price of shell, and interrogated several witnesses, who all agreed that they were not operating in a free competitive market, without being able to point to any specific instances. It was understood that the market was manipulated by 'a ring of buyers' who secured long-term contracts in order to speculate.

It was observed that in periods of high shell-production, these buyers curbed their purchases to depress prices. It was also alleged that they manipulated demand by withholding certain grades of shell from the market until their prices dropped. This created, on the one hand, a demand for those grades of shell which were less favoured by manufacturers, and led, on the other hand, to price-cutting among producers. Alternatively, the buyers might enter long-term contracts for shell and then cease buying from other sources, creating a shortage which forced prices up, so that they profited from the fixed price of the shell under contract. Buyers passed on inflated prices to the manufacturers, but not depressed prices. The curious result of these manipulations was that while shell prices were strongly fluctuating in the producing countries, they were fairly stable in the manufacturing countries. One disgruntled observer wrote from America: 'Prices have been the same to manufacturers, whether the shell cost £90 over the scale or £250'.[14] The image which emerges from these descriptions is one of small competitive producers and small competitive manufacturers at either end of the production chain, linked by oligopolistic buyers who determined prices.

These descriptions are entirely valid. But the power of the middlemen did not depend on mutual agreement and sinister manipulation. The financial dependence of producers on the buyers ensured that the latter assumed a powerful position. Not only the producers were dependent on buyers to arrange sales and grant cash advances for rigging up luggers for the next season, but so were 5000 manufacturers in America and Europe. Most of these had neither the capital nor the storage facilities to buy shell in large quantities, and bought fortnightly or even weekly. Where cutting blanks was done by putting out work, the buyer leased the necessary machinery to the workers. The dealers sold shell on credit, so that they acted as financiers both for the producers and for the manufacturers, a role which banks would not take, because pearl-shelling was not considered an acceptable risk. The better they controlled the market, therefore, the better the buyers could bear such a risk.

There can be little doubt that buyers dominated the market. But it is useful to remember also that the portrayal of the sinister machinations of oligopolistic buyers served to vindicate various attempts of the large pearl-shelling companies to gain control of the industry's output, in a political climate where Labor in government strongly condemned monopolistic control.

Strategies to cope with marketing difficulties

Each of these explanations gives a slightly different emphasis, and a number of strategies were attempted to deal with marketing problems.

Sheltering with the giants?

The larger companies made several attempts to stablilise prices by acting as agents for smaller producers. Burns Philp in particular saw a need to regulate overseas markets for pearl-shell and sandalwood, but the efforts of Mitchell, the manager of Wyben Company (BP) in this direction met with little success:

> A few years ago the Torres Straits pearl-fishers combined with those of Western Australia, and we held our shell in London in order to obtain a price which we considered would cover the cost of production. After holding the shell for a considerable time, and incurring a good deal of expense for storage and so forth, we had to sell, and came to the conclusion that we should have done better had we sold in the first instance. The speculators were too strong for us.[15]

Mitchell pointed to the buyers' oligopolistic control of the market as an explanation for the failure of this producers' cartel in 1905. However, the short-lived attempt at combination was considerably weakened by the competition between Burns Philp and Clark. The latter had a stronger involvement in Broome and Darwin than Burns Philp, and wished to be put in charge of the marketing of the combined pearl-shell output in London. Moreover, the cartel was formed at a time when pearl-shell stocks were so depleted that half the Thursday Island fleet had left for Aru, that is, under highly inauspicious circumstances.

Shortly after Mitchell's statement, Burns Philp made a renewed attempt to counter the buyers' strength with restrictive trade practices. A 'Pearlshell Convention' was formed in 1913 with the aim of holding a reserve price for the shell. The three-year agreement gave Burns Philp control of two-thirds of the world production of shell sold in London, marketing all of the Aru shell, the output of all save one Thursday Island pearl-shellers, and 65 per cent of the Broome shell, as well as some shell from Tahiti. (Both Clark and Burns Philp claimed to have instigated this cartel.) But with the outbreak of World War I the London market closed, and the convention was suspended, never to be renewed. Burns Philp was caught with £250 000 worth of pearl-shell stockpiled in London, on which advances of £90 000 had already been paid. Storage and insurance costs were mounting until in 1915 three-quarters of the stock was sold in New York. Again, the explanation given by Burns Philp for the failure to sell the shell before the outbreak of war, was 'the antagonism of the large Dealers'.[16] Pearl-shell prices at the time were already very keen, after a season of exceptionally high prices.[17] Buyers may have had good cause to resist a pearl-shellers' cartel which aimed to drive prices even higher. Pearl-shellers, for their part, had equally good cause to combine, since, as we have seen, 1913 was again a time of resource crisis at Thursday Island.

Such spurious efforts, undertaken under the stress of crisis, and resulting in failure, only confirmed the smaller owners in their distrust of the large companies. How well founded that distrust in fact was is revealed by a glimpse from inside Burns Philp. In 1909, Burns Philp attempted to combine the large pearl-shellers at Thursday Island with overseas buyers in a single company. James Burns expected that the company would consist of 'half a dozen of the big shell men & we can come in with them & wipe out the smaller fry'.[18]

The 'smaller fry' continued to feel that they were at the mercy of the large companies both here and overseas, who were scheming to keep them in a state of financial dependence: 'We were infants, businesswise, dealing with multi-million dollar corporations: the old boys, city boys, Wall Street boys. And we here in Australia: "she'll be right", just as long as we were making a quid . . . Only in the aftermath when you're lying down do you see what's been happening'.[19]

The pearl-shellers' marketing position was weakened not only by the division between small owners and large companies but also by the competition between the Australian centres of production. The following extract demonstrates how deeply ingrained were the rivalries between different producing centres. At the very moment when he called for solidarity, James Clark, who was working from Aru, expressed resentment of the other centres:

We are not united out here, or were not until lately; and, therefore, they at Home have got shell for anything they liked to give us. Three or four years ago, however, we made a contract with the buyers in London for our own shell at £170 a ton for three years, and they forced the shell up and made a profit of £42 000 a year—we did the work and they made the profit. In consequence of having our shell in hand, they could force the market up, *and Thursday Island and Western Australia have been having a good time for the last three years at our expense,* sharing, as they did, in the increased prices.[20]

Models of co-operative marketing to offer an alternative to the hegemony of single firms were not yet available, so that the efforts of pearl-shellers to strengthen their position *vis-à-vis* buyers were embedded in competition and suspicion. Like Burns Philp, Clark insisted on the necessity of opposing the 'ring of buyers' with a 'ring of pearl-shellers':

> That is what we should do—we should pool the shell. We have always been told that we could not get more than a certain price; but that is nonsense, in the face of the fact that at Home the price was forced up to nearly £500 a ton . . . about this time last year. These men have shown us that the shell is worth a good deal more than we were led to believe it was. The contract ran out last May . . . and . . . the buyers . . . slumped the shell by . . . £130 a ton; and they came in January and promised us another fall of £30, or £160 a ton. We were not out to take a licking like that sitting down, although these people, of course are financially strong.[21]

As a countervailing strategy, Clark proposed to take out a monopoly over the Queensland shell-production (see Chapter 5). Such posturing could surely not instil the confidence of small owners in this company's leadership.

Producer solidarity: the Torres Strait Pearl-Shellers' Association

To stand up to a controlled market required above all producer unity. The producers needed to monitor and co-ordinate the quantity of production, the rate of export, the quality of grading, and they needed a co-operative marketing mechanism to negotiate prices, store shell, get contracts, and maintain a reserve price. In essence, they needed to construct different institutional arrangements. Their competitive individualism—expressed as rivalry between different centres of production (Broome, Darwin, Thursday Island, and Aru), and different types of producers (swimming-diving and deep-diving operations, floating stations and shore stations, verandah pearlers and full-time pearlers, large companies and small owners)—prevented the emergence of lasting defensive institutions.

The industry at Thursday Island did have a Pearl-Shellers' Association, but its purpose was to deal with employees. It led the annual round of wage negotiations with the Japanese divers' representatives (the *Doshi-kai*) and with the Protector of Aborigines as the representative of indigenous employees. Beyond that it was unable to act as a mouthpiece for the interests of pearl-shellers, because on a whole range of management issues (ownership restrictions, employment of white divers, closure of areas) the interests of large companies were contrary to the interests of small owners, and the concessions to change each was willing to make differed widely. Even questions like the cultivation of shell and domestic button-manufacture were divisive. Their common interest, a desire for higher prices, was not enough to unite pearl-shellers.

The Torres Strait Pearl-Shellers' Association was a voluntary association with no means to enforce any policies across the industry. It frequently released statements of concern through the local newspaper, the *Torres Strait Pilot*, which were sometimes picked up in the southern press. It also endorsed the overseas visit of some members to collect information about marketing. But such activities were marginal. The association was more concerned with day-to-day activities, and intent on sailing well-charted waters. One of its former secretaries expressed this attitude when asked why the association had not explored new marketing strategies, particularly new uses of pearl-shell to reduce the fashion-dependence of pearl-shell: 'I don't think that was a mistake. It [the industry] has been going for 100 years'.[22] Clearly, the association did not see its role in planning, management, research and advice, or in industry leadership. It did, however, manage to form yet another short-lived attempt to pool the shell, in 1925, when Burns Philp and Dalgety's were appointed as sole agents for the combined output of the association's members. Burns Philp and Dalgety's advanced £120 a ton at 6 per cent interest, and charged 2.5 per cent commission on gross sales. However, the pearl-shell market had now shifted to New York, whereas Burns Philp dealt through its London office where sales were poor. The two-year contract was not renewed. Burns Philp's London manager complained that 'the Association display a desire to "run with the hare and hunt with the hounds". They desire to sell their Shell to the dealers, and at the same time to the manufacturers'.[23] This comment suggests that the pearl-shellers were not united behind the association's decision to sell through Burns Philp. After this experience, most Thursday Island pearl-shellers entrusted the Gerdau Company of New York with their shell, and Burns Philp gradually withdrew from marketing pearl-shell.[24]

Domestic button-manufacture: a role for government?

The first official reference to a marketing problem was the remark about price fluctuations made by N. E. Lockyer, the Comptroller-General of Customs, in 1904.[25] Lockyer considered manufacturing pearl-shell buttons in Australia, but concluded that it was not possible to nurture a domestic manufacturing industry with high tariff walls, as had been done in the case of sugar mills. Moreover, he was advised that 'it was utterly impossible to secure the Australian shell. The market is so controlled that we cannot buy pearl-shell here'.[26] Lockyer's investigation of the pearl-shell industry had been an afterthought during a visit to Thursday Island which was primarily concerned with customs matters. He spent little time on the issue, gathering opinions from a few key figures in the industry and its administration.

The 1908 Mackay Commission again interrogated some pearl-shellers about the issue of processing shell in Australia. But even with the suggestion of government assistance, most pearl-shellers did not consider the establishment of button-manufacture in Australia feasible. Very few had taken an interest in the issue of marketing and manufacture, but most gave a negative assessment of the potential for domestic manufacturing.

The most persistent objection made was the small size of the domestic market. This was a rather invalid objection, since there was nothing to prevent a domestic factory from exporting buttons, at a considerable saving of freight costs over the export of un-processed shell. A further objection was the changing fashion which affected the demand for buttons. This difficulty could have been overcome by restricting operations to the cutting of blanks for export, leaving the finishing processes to overseas manufacturers. The third objection referred to the high wage rates in Australia. This objection was made by the very men who employed indigenous and indentured labour far below the Australian standards of remuneration.

Herbert Bowden had investigated the issue of button-manufacture at some depth, and advised against an attempt to produce in Australia. He argued that the full range of shell types was not available here, so that it would be difficult to keep up with changing fashions. The success of the Japanese and American production described above, based entirely on a single type of shell in each case, invalidates his objection. Bowden himself was in the process of buying a failed button factory in Noumea, which employed time-expired convicts.

He intended to supply Sydney and Melbourne producers of cheap clothing. Perhaps a government-assisted factory in Australia would have interfered with his plans.

As a result of the negative response by pearl-shellers, the Mackay Commission did not take up the issue of marketing in its report, although 21 per cent of that year's output had been withheld from sales, so that a marketing problem was already apparent. The same was true for the 1913 Bamford Commission. There was a widespread belief that because of the powerful influence of buyers an Australian factory would be unable to secure shell.

After World War I, the Commonwealth Department of Repatriation investigated the possibility of manufacturing pearl-buttons in Australia to generate employment for returned soldiers.[27] Because of the considerable wastage involved in cutting button blanks, it was estimated that freight costs could be halved by cutting blanks prior to shipping.[28] Moreover, cutting blanks would have tended to standardise the quality of exports. Most importantly, it would create employment and produce value added—the price difference between buttons and raw shell was enormous: if a ton of buttons was worth £1232, the raw shell was perhaps £200. Shipping and handling the shell roughly doubled its cost.[29]

Both the Department of Industries and the Department of Repatriation were convinced that some manufacturing industry could successfully be built around the pearl-shelling activities in Australia. In response to overseas inquiries, one Canadian manufacturing family even offered to immigrate, bringing all necessary equipment, and supervising production as manager. The offer was relayed to James Clark and apparently ignored.

At the end of World War I, after two exhaustive inquiries into the pearl-shell industry, the issue of domestic manufacture had not been addressed in any systematic way. For example, while it was true that many pearl-shellers were so indebted to buyers, through advances, that they were not at liberty to sell to others, this was partly because they could not obtain advances from banks or anywhere else. If an Australian factory had been set up with government assistance, it would have been possible to offer similar advances in order to get contracts. It was true that the domestic market was too small to encourage manufacture in Australia by means of an import duty on pearl-shell products, as it had been done in the sugar industry. On the other hand, the possibility of exporting pearl-shell, either as a finished or semi-processed product, was ignored. The assumption that a domestic factory would only produce import-substituting commodities, and not compete on the overseas markets, was firmly grounded in the industrial policy orientation of the time.

The American ascendancy

From around 1904, most Australian shell was processed in America, but was still sold through the London market. The first direct consignment of shell to New York took place in 1903, and this became a constant, if insignificant, supply route in 1906. Herbert Bowden had been to the United States, and it is quite possible that the American interest in Australian shell had been augmented by his visit. 'When I was in America, I could have sold all the best shell we produce. They do not want the low grade shell; they have not time to deal with it, because their own sweet-water mussel shell meets all their requirements.'[30]

London lost its formal dominance in pearl-shell buying as a result of World War I. The London market halved its intake of Australian shell in 1914, and practically closed in 1917. Thereafter American importers dealt with the producing countries directly instead of buying through London. Australia consequently became the major supplier to the American market, and the United States market became the world's dominant shell market.

But the relative strength of Australia as a supplier of shell did not translate into market power. The quantity and price of shell exports were unpredictable. After a careful analysis of the available import and export data on shell, the Coombs Commission arrived at the conclusion that the period from 1919 to 1939 showed no overall time trend whatsoever. That is, export markets for shell were not gradually expanding or contracting, but simply fluctuating.

There were, however, strong correlations between the Australian production and American imports. The Coombs Commission found that the production of shell buttons in the USA did not depend on supply levels but on American domestic conditions. The volume of supply did not affect shell prices, rather, the average price for Australian shell closely followed the wholesale price index for textiles in the USA. Australian producers were, in other words, extremely dependent on the American shell market.[31]

It is well known in pearl-shelling circles that the New York market was strongly dominated by a single firm, the Gerdau Company.

Gerdau had a decisive role in the institutional arrangements in the Australian industry. Many former pearl-shellers still remember Alan Gerdau, who professed to have a special relationship with Thursday Island, which he often visited. Several of them were financially dependent on him, and resented that dependence. Gerdau had an interest in stabilising the level of production and controlling the price of pearl-shell.

The company exerted considerable influence on Australian government policy regarding the industry.[32] Like Burns Philp before, Gerdau pursued a policy of bringing as much of the world's pearl-shelling output as possible under its umbrella. The company continued to dominate the shell market into the 1960s. For example, in 1954 Gerdau handled 90 per cent of the Australian, and all of the Japanese production of shell. While frequent reference is made to Gerdau in departmental records and by former pearl-shellers, Kuhlenkampf of Hamburg and Friedlein in London are not widely known as shell-buyers.[33] Gerdau occupied a similarly influential position in the marketing of coffee (from Brazil), sugar (from Cuba), and pepper in the United States—colonial raw materials produced with cheap labour. The company's pearl-shell interests constituted only about 10 per cent of its business, but Alan Gerdau assured Thursday Island pearl-shellers that he would continue to market their shell 'even if it costs me thousands'.[34] With the shift of the pearl-shell market from Britain to the United States, marketing started to be recognised as one of the industry's problems.

Institutionalised marketing: federal intervention

World War I provided the framework for an unprecedented level of government intervention in the private sector. The federal government fixed prices for several essential commodities, and applied controls on the marketing of a range of primary produce, while the Queensland government set up a chain of State enterprises. During the Great Depression, the federal government began to use its external affairs power to regulate several export industries by establishing overseas marketing boards for dairy products, fresh fruit, canned fruit and dried fruit.

In the pearl-shell industry, too, government concern shifted from labour issues to marketing problems. In the late 1920s the Great Depression in Europe made its mark on the industry. As luxury items, pearls and at least some grades of pearl-shell were highly susceptible to economic downturns. Australia contributed around 85 per cent of the world production of pearl-shell (2250 tons) with an export value of £500 000 per annum. In 1927 the price for pearl-shell dropped to £130 a ton, and below production costs. Pearl-shellers appealed to the federal government for help.

Marketing, or the dominance of monopolistic overseas buyers, was now seen as the foremost weakness in the industry. Federal Parliament was informed that 'those engaged in the production of pearl shell in Australia have for many years been suffering severely at the hands of Continental and American purchasers . . . they have been handicapped by the adverse influence exerted in the Continental and American markets'.[35] The Commonwealth established an overseas marketing board to stabilise prices. The board was comprised of a government representative and two elected representatives of the Western Australian and Queensland–Northern Territory industry respectively. In the election of industry representatives each vessel represented one vote, so that in effect the franchise was awarded according to wealth. Several Labor members protested against this arrangement, but acquiesced because it reduced the danger of aliens being elected. At any rate, similar legislation already existed for other export produce. The board acted as the exporting agent for the pearl-shellers. Other exporters now required licences from the board which could be made subject to conditions imposed by the board.[36] As soon as prices recovered, however, pearl-shellers resented this arrangement, and the marketing board was disbanded before the crisis was truly over.

Voluntary output restrictions: the buyers organise producers

During the Great Depression the problem of slackening demand was amplified by increasing shell-production. In mid-1929 rich shell-banks had been discovered in Western Australia (about 60 kilometres south-west of Wallace Islands), and the year's harvest brought a record national output of nearly 1500 tons. In January 1930 overseas buyers urged Thursday Island shellers to curb their output. Large stocks were being withheld from an already flooded market. The pearl-shellers agreed to limit their catch to 850 tons.

The market continued to be very unstable. In 1931 mother-of-pearl prices varied from £63 to £115 a ton. The Torres Strait Pearl-Shellers' Association announced a further reduction, to 350 tons, and similar output restrictions were agreed upon in Broome and

Darwin. Thirty boats (out of 109) were laid up at Thursday Island and several hundred indentured employees were repatriated. For the 1932 season the output limit was raised slightly to 460 tons (shared by ninety-one boats) by agreement with the overseas buyers; and in 1934 and 1935 the production limit was 750 tons (between ninety-three boats). There were still large shell stocks at Thursday Island. The prices were £105 to £115 a ton.

The pearl-shell inspector now expressed concern that the output restriction agreements gave Gerdau a virtual monopoly over the shell produced. This observation was astute, but poorly timed, considering the severity of the crisis. As a matter of fact, the voluntary restrictions were not adhered to. For once it would have been beneficial for Australian producers to rally behind the strength of the buyers. The crisis was not the result of market manipulations, and a controlled supply was essential in maintaining prices.

Return to competitive individualism and the end of an era

By 1936 the crisis was considered to be over. There were no further shell stocks at Thursday Island, prices had increased, and the output restrictions were discarded. But the return to competitive individualism was premature. A further threat for the pearl-shell industry was already emerging, with the entry of Japanese fishing boats into Australian waters in 1934. For the next few years the industry's troubles were blamed on the energetic fishing efforts of the Japanese. In 1938, the Inspector of Pearl-shell and Bêche-de-Mer Fisheries reported that the foreign-owned boats were swamping overseas pearl-shell markets.

Overproduction and shrinking markets
While it was true that the market was flooded, it was misleading to portray the Japanese as the sole culprits. The Japanese output—much of it from Australian extra-territorial waters—was on a meteoric rise from 8 tons in 1932 to 3840 tons in 1937 (overshadowing Australian production), but meanwhile the total Australian production also continued to rise from 1419 tons in 1932 to a peak of 2854 in 1937. The Dutch East Indies production curve followed a similar pattern with its peak in 1936. The combined output from

Australia, Japan and the Dutch East Indies rose from about 2000 tons in 1932, to 7653 tons in 1937. The rising production figures are indicative of the knee-jerk reaction of producers to poor marketing conditions: increased output and price-cutting. Without an institutional safety net, which a marketing board and reserve price scheme could have provided, pearl-shellers were exposed to the full force of the demand crisis induced by competition.

The trochus market had been less affected by the Great Depression. Trochus buttons were far cheaper than mother-of-pearl buttons, and were not considered a luxury item. During the mother-of-pearl crisis, about 88 pearl-shell luggers had been fitted out to fish for trochus and also to collect bêche-de-mer, for which demand was also good. By 1936, trochus had become scarce because the grounds had been 'gradually worked out'. As trochus output declined and prices rose, trochus priced itself out of the market, and a large stockpile accumulated at Thursday Island. In 1938 the trochus market was described as 'practically dead', as Japan, the almost exclusive buyer of Australian trochus, prepared for war.

In 1938, at the eve of World War II, the pearl-shell inspector reported that the outlook for the industry had never been so bleak. Buyers had not renewed their contracts, so that several pearl-shellers, who were dependent on advance credits from buyers, had no means of recommissioning their luggers. Bêche-de-mer was now practically unsaleable, so that all three industries were simultaneously affected by the marketing crisis, which was 'beyond the powers of solution by the local pearl-shell association or the administration'.[37]

Government assistance

The Thursday Island police magistrate and pearl-shell inspector O'Leary (who was also the trouble-shooting Protector of Aborigines after the 1936 Torres Strait Islander strike) conducted an investigation on behalf of the Queensland and Commonwealth governments. Again, marketing was recognised as the most pressing problem in the industry. It was found that there was 'little uniformity among pearlshellers' who engaged in price-cutting to sell their shell. Despite the Queensland Labor government's distrust of monopolies, the investigators recommended collaboration with foreign producers to stabilise the market. They recommended monetary grants to boat-owners because ruling prices scarcely covered the costs of production.

State and Commonwealth governments started to assist the industry with grants and loans. The first distress grant of £10 000, shared equally by the federal and WA governments, was awarded to the Broome industry after a cyclone in 1935. It was argued that Broome suffered especially from the Japanese competition. In 1938–39 the Commonwealth Bank advanced £64 000, jointly guaranteed by the federal and State governments, and the WA government also provided seasonal advances of £8000 to recommission luggers and pay crews. In Western Australia, over twenty-six boats were advanced up to £300 each. The State governments were reluctant to intervene with massive regulation, and the federal government's attempt to impose a marketing board had failed. The only role for government now was to prop up the industry with monetary assistance. But with the onset of war the marketing problems intensified to such a degree that this assistance failed to rescue the industry.

In 1940 Japan entirely ceased buying Australian trochus, and the European factories ceased buying mother-of-pearl. All Australian mother-of-pearl went to American manufacturers, while the low-grade shell (about 318 tons) was sold on other Asian markets. In 1941 trochus exports from Thursday Island dropped to 50 tons, and 300 tons were stockpiled at Thursday Island. Only sixty-five boats remained in the industry in Queensland.

Ironically, in the midst of this crisis, which pearl-shellers claimed eroded their profits, one of them resorted to technological innovation to improve production. In 1940, ten vessels were 'fitted with propelling engines instead of obsolete compressor engines'.[38] Shortly afterwards, the luggers were confiscated by the Navy.

The resurgence of trochus-shelling

After World War II, the pearl-shell industry was transformed: the Japanese divers were no longer available, and Torres Strait Islanders gradually replaced them, with the lugger scheme taking up a prominent position in the pearl-shell industry. Just after the war, the shortage of luggers and materials severely handicapped the pearl-shell industry. Not until 1949 was it considered to have 'considerably rehabilitated', using improved equipment, and increasing its average catch per boat. Bêche-de-mer fishing was not resumed, but there was a massive shift to the less dangerous, and less capital-intensive, trochus-fishery, which did not require complex equipment and deep-diving experience. A number of the old established companies withdrew from pearling. Carpenter, Cleveland, Farquhar, Hennessey, Sinclair, Wyben (BP), and Hodels were no longer operating. Arthur Sullivan's Morey Company was bought by Bowden, which now became the largest company, managed by Jack Dunwoodie.[39] Of the new names which appeared in the industry, the best-known were Shipway and Jones, Northern Waters Pearling Company (Lucas and Greene), Active Pearling Company (Arnold Duffield), Waitoa Pearling Company (Lance Fulward), Aucher Pearling Company (Jack Zafer), Ken Grayson, and Johnny Witts. Many returned soldiers and fishers drifted in and out of the trochus-fishery, employing a variety of vessels, from submarine-chasers to vehicular ferries—almost anything that could float could be used to collect trochus. Trochus was found on the reefs rather than in Torres Strait, so that the fishery became decentralised. About 200 trochus boats operated out of Mackay, Townsville, and Cairns, as well as from Thursday Island.

Fishing, too, became a dominant industry, undergoing metamorphosis from a part-time, local activity to a full-time, regionally integrated source of employment. As a result, the Great Barrier Reef province became the resource base for a broader range of commercial enterprise. In order to establish a viable fin-fishing industry, the Queensland government had established regional fish-marketing boards in the 1930s. These guaranteed a fair price for the catch, and granted advances for the fitting out of vessels. They offered refrigerated storage and processed the fish, experimenting in smoking, curing and filleting. On-board filleting, pioneered by 'Snowy' Whittaker, was facilitated by these favourable institutional conditions. The Fish Boards launched advertising campaigns, using commercials, nutritional information posters, and recipe cards. One very successful campaign popularised mackerel, which was not considered a desirable food-fish outside coastal Queensland. In 1952 the CSIRO established a Fisheries Division in order to support the industry with research and surveys.[40]

After World War II, there was a growing awareness of the importance of marketing. The market for raw materials started to shrink as industrialisation in Europe became less materials-intensive. Australia also began to establish an import-substituting manufacturing base in order to reduce dependence on the export of raw materials. This period of growth and construction, aided by more centralist State–federal relations, had a lasting impact on Australian ideology. It fostered an optimism which lasted into the 1980s, when it came under siege from environmental and economic pressures on governments, producers, and consumers to 'think globally'.[41]

The Northern Australia Development Commission

At the end of the war, all the familiar issues in the pearl-shell fishery were again canvassed: whether Japanese should be allowed to re-enter the industry, whether Torres Strait Islanders could be trained as divers (considering their 'intelligence beyond the capacity of mainland natives'), whether the fishery could employ whites (such as returned servicemen), whether domestic button-manufacture should be engaged in, and whether the resource could be protected. At the Premiers' Conference in January 1946 the Queensland Premier requested an inquiry into the prospects for the industry. The Northern Australia Development Commission was set up under the leadership of the Director of Postwar Reconstruction, Dr H. C. Coombs. At this time, Labor held office both in Queensland (1932–57) and at the federal level (1941–49).

The Coombs Commission described the pearl-shell fishery as 'one of the most important single units of Australian marine industries', with great dollar-winning value.[42] Dollar-winning meant American dollars—particularly desirable since the Bretton Woods agreement had turned the US dollar into the currency of international exchange. The Commission recognised the problems faced by the industry, but also saw great potential. The overriding argument in favour of aiding the industry was that Broome and Thursday Island depended on these fisheries. There was much pent-up demand for shell after the war, and the shell-beds had recuperated. The commissioners feared that this advantageous position would quickly be eroded if the industry returned to its prewar patterns of competitive resource exploitation. Again, a comprehensive package of proposals was developed to restructure the industry.

The result of this investigation was, at best, a general acknowledgment of the importance of the industry, and a commitment in principle of the federal government to assist it. The approach at restructuring which eventually followed the inquiry was piecemeal rather than vigorous, and too slow to have an impact. By 1949 the impetus of postwar demand had been spent, and none of the Commission's recommendations had been put into effect.

Concerning labour problems, the Commission recommended training arrangements both for the new pearl-shellers, who were mainly ex-servicemen with little or no fishing experience, and for Torres Strait Islanders. The question of the reintroduction of indentured labourers was left open, but the Commission thought that the potential of white and indigenous workers should be tested first. In order to improve living conditions for crew, the introduction of standards for the size and design of luggers, and standard equipment, including radio-telecommunication sets, was recommended, and a return to floating stations was proposed in order to access the more remote fishing grounds.

In 1952, after a public meeting at Thursday Island, the Queensland government granted £1500 towards establishing a training school for indigenous divers.[43] The federal government was asked to match that sum and to supply a diving tutor. A diving tutor could not be procured, however, and the board charged with establishing the training school disbanded. In 1957 a former navy diver was employed to train pearl-shell divers, but the training scheme now had little priority. In the following year the indentured Okinawans arrived.

To prevent exhaustion of the resource, biological studies and reef surveys were recommended to determine the carrying capacity of the reefs. The federal government was to assume responsibility for extra-territorial fisheries, where most of the fishing was now taking place. This assumption of responsibility took effect with the *Pearl Fisheries Act 1952* in the course of the pearl-shell dispute with Japan (see Chapter 4). Shortly afterwards the CSIRO began experiments in pearl-shell and pearl-cultivation at Thursday Island, and the Queensland Department of Primary Industries co-ordinated a survey of shell-beds.[44] In order to rehabilitate the industry, it was urged that the Navy disclose the location of requisitioned luggers, and that loans or seasonal advances be made by Commonwealth and State governments for some years. Several luggers were retrieved from the New Guinean coast by Torres Strait Islanders, but monetary assistance from the federal government was not easily obtained.

In order to control marketing, the Commission endorsed the Queensland Premier's suggestion of an Australian Pearl-Shell Pool as a marketing and consultative organisation consisting of State and federal officers and industry representatives. An economic survey of market prospects, and the consideration of new uses of by-products of the industry, such as trochus meat, clam and other shells was also recommended. It was not recommended to set up a button factory in Australia, because of the small impact that such an industry would have on the quantities of shell sold. Instead, it was proposed to cut blanks for export, under the auspices of the Island Industries Board. This was the second time that such a proposal was submitted by federal government agencies in the course of postwar reconstruction. Again, no moves were made to follow these suggestions and diversify the industry from one which exported only raw materials to one which also exported semi-processed commodities. Instead, the private sector repeated an earlier initiative in setting up a button factory which produced finished buttons, for the domestic market only.

Experiments in domestic button-production

Burns Philp had started the first experiment in button-production in 1931, when the federal government established a protective tariff barrier for pearl-shell buttons. The tariff was withdrawn in the following year, and casein buttons, an early type of plastic which did not withstand boiling, became the major activity of Pearlbutton Manufacturing Co. Ltd. The quantities of shell processed were minute, about 40 tons in eight months.[45] In 1938, the shell stock was valued at £20, whereas the casein stock was valued at £2893. A new wages award made the business unprofitable, and Pearlbutton Manufacturing merged with G. Herring & Co., producers of ribbons, binding and fashion accessories, to become Herring (Australia) Pty Ltd. This new company continued to produce mother-of-pearl buttons, but discontinued this line after a few years, because of the competition from cheaper Japanese imports.

Herring was a dynamic company which diversified and contracted according to opportunities, by means of subsidiaries and holding companies. During World War II it supplied the whole wartime requirements of the allied armies in dials used for prismatic compasses. Its range of buttons, marketed as Beutron, were mostly casein-based until the late 1950s, when new developments in synthetics-production were explored. The company acquired Australasian and Far Eastern rights in several synthetic pearl-shell substitutes. It also extended the market for its plastics for other uses. One of its products was Liquid Envelope, used for mothballing battleships and aircraft, and with a range of civilian applications. Herring extended into New Zealand (1948), Hongkong (1954) and Japan (1959). Their major competitor in Australia was General Plastics, which produced Beaucaire buttons.

General Plastics set up another pearl-button factory in Cairns in 1952, in association with five local businessmen with an interest in pearl-shelling. General Plastics wanted to offer a full range of buttons including pearl-shell. The company traded as Pearl-Shell Industries Pty Ltd. The local businessmen understood the factory as a pilot plant, apparently unaware of the previous efforts of Burns Philp and Herring. The company was capitalised at about £10 000, 'a fairly substantial investment'.[46] The Gerdau Company of New York arranged for the importation of machinery. The factory employed fifteen people and was set up in one part of a shed which also housed a pineapple factory at Smith's Creek wharf. The factory produced to the specifications of General Plastics, who provided the market. It only used mother-of-pearl, not trochus shell, to produce up-market buttons, such as for tuxedos, or the well-known Country Life brand of sports shirts. Most of the shell used was the best Broome shell. Contrary to the concerns expressed previously, the manufacturers experienced no difficulty in obtaining shell.

The operating budget was based on publications from the Continent, but because of the lack of expertise, greater losses were incurred in the cutting of blanks from the raw shell. Compared with the recovery figures from the Continent, there was a 40 per cent shortfall in recovery. Also, the blanks were split manually to achieve a uniform thickness, and in this process, too, losses were greater than expected. (Splitting blanks is not considered economical any longer.) One of the owners said in retrospect that 'a minor contributing factor to our failure was that the bulk of our machinery was second-hand, from Central Europe'.[47] After two years, the investors withdrew from the project and the factory went into liquidation. Another entrepreneur, Don Hing, bought the plant and continued to operate for a further two years. His failure is ascribed to the difficulties posed by the obsolete machinery.

The failure of both factories must be ascribed to the problems of an infant industry struggling against the competition from cheaper imports, without tariff protection. It was not justifiable to protect an industry which operated on such a small scale that it neither satisfied the domestic demand for pearl-shell buttons nor created much employment. Nor did it offer a significant outlet for the Australian shell, which should have been its *raison d'être*. As the pearl-shellers had predicted, but for different reasons, the production of pearl-shell buttons was not viable in Australia. The suggestion of the Coombs Commission, a midway solution between reliance on the export of unprocessed shell and the local manufacture of buttons for a domestic market, was ignored. Yet the cutting of blanks for export has carried the trochus industry of several small island nations into the 1990s.[48]

Synthetic buttons displace mother-of-pearl

Throughout the 1950s, shell prices were very high. In 1953 pearl-shell fetched £570 a ton; in 1954 it was still as high as £499, and trochus had risen to £190 a ton. Trochus prices continued to rise until in 1958 they reached £260 a ton, compared to £392 for pearl-shell. Trochus in fact priced itself out of its market niche. Moreover, production was unsteady as the shell became again depleted: 'one man scarcely got one tin of trochus per day, it wasn't economical'.[49] It was impossible to achieve a steady, low production of perhaps 2500 tons. The fears of the Coombs Commission were fully realised.

In this climate of unsteady supply and high prices, those who were concerned with the marketing of shell, particularly Gerdau and the large button-manufacturers, invested in the development of synthetic substitutes for pearl-shell. Casein buttons became brittle with repeated boiling, whereas buttons made of natural shell withstood wear and tear and retained their lustre. One of the new products developed in the 1950s was Tecpearl, made by Rochester Button Company in the United States, one of the world's largest producers of buttons. Another polyester pearl patent was sold to Herring Australia by a Dr Vogt of Cologne in 1957. A perspex material (methyl methacrylate), developed by Elhardt & Company in Germany, was used for handles on brushes, umbrellas, and shaving brushes, as well as for buttons. With these new products, the Australian button-manufacturers pushed into new markets. Herring subsidiaries supplied the United Kingdom and Australia, Hong Kong and New Zealand. Herring eventually took over Beaucaire, and merged with Butterick and Vogue Patterns as Beutron Plastics in 1969.

In 1956 Gerdau demonstrated the resilience of these new materials at Thursday Island: 'we boiled it for six hours and it still looked like shell'.[50] Pearl-shell had lost its competitive edge over synthetics.

'The bottom dropped out of the market'

The trochus-fishery was affected first by the introduction of the new synthetics. A number of trochus operators and divers shifted to pearl-shelling before leaving the industry altogether. 'Every boat went into trochus from 1952 to 1956. But everything flopped when plastics came out in 1956. The pearl-shell industry survived because of certain fancy buttons sold in Hamburg, and then because pearl culture started in the 1960s'.[51]

The irreversible deterioration of the pearl-shell market, particularly the market for trochus, was experienced as a sudden collapse after the introduction of synthetic substitutes. The cataclysmic nature of this deterioration is captured in the remarkable similarity in the choice of words which former divers used to describe it: 'the bottom dropped out of the market', 'the bottom fell out', or 'the market fell out'. The explanation for the decline of the industry given at the time was obviously one which hinged on marketing, rather than resource problems.

However, there are a few hints that marketing was not the only factor in the decline. Keith Bradford had already shifted his operations to New Guinea in 1953: 'The industry collapsed completely, one man scarcely got one tin of trochus per day, it wasn't economical. The boats went back to pearling'. 'Blue' Bedford, on the other hand, continued trochus-shelling until 1958, when he, too, turned to pearl-shelling, but withdrew after a while. The IIB boats continued trochus-shelling for several years with poor results. In 1968, when thirty-one boats brought in 1 ton of trochus shell, this part of the industry was pronounced dead.[52]

Pearl-shell was also affected by the introduction of plastic buttons. In response to the competition from plastic buttons, American importers combined with pearl-shellers and the federal, Queensland and WA governments in 1959 to launch an extensive sales promotion campaign overseas to emphasise the prestige value of genuine mother-of-pearl dress accessories and novelties. (A similar campaign was undertaken to promote 'Pure New Wool'.) But the demand for mother-of-pearl continued to decline. In 1961 the American importers, the virtual lifeline of the Australian producers, drastically curbed their purchases. That year the Japanese fleets made their last excursion to the Arafura Sea. Shipway and Jones laid up their boats because shell was unsaleable. Some pearl-shellers continued to

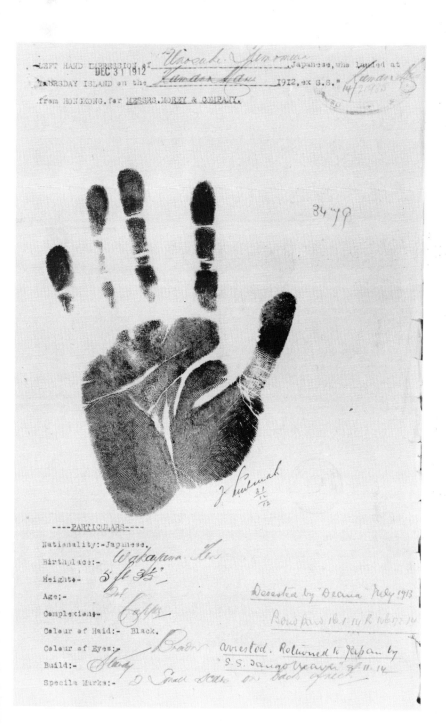

A passport of indenture for Unosuke Shimomura, 1912

Takenaka Yasuichi from Miwasaki ready for dress-diving, Burma, 1956; at forty-nine, Yasuichi was unusually old for a diver.

operate, exporting to Asian and European markets, but operating costs were too high to return a profit in the face of the downward pressure on prices induced by the competition from plastics. The largest company, Bowden, went bankrupt in 1960. Hockings sent his Okinawan labourers home and wound up the family business established in 1898. He went into the employ of a newly established pearl-culture farm.

From the Great Depression to World War II, marketing was the foremost problem of the industry. The demand crisis was exacerbated by the pearl-shellers, who reacted to it by intensifying their fishing effort, and was compounded by the resulting resource crisis from 1930 to 1932. This period of overproduction, with a concomitant fall in prices, was followed after the war by a period of volatile output. Manufacturers and buyers became more committed to the development of synthetic substitutes than to maintaining pearl-shell in the market. With that shift of commitment, the industry lost not only its traditional market niche but also its sole marketing stalwart.

The marketing problem of the pearl-shell industry might be characterised as the lack of forward integration between production and marketing/consumption. This is a familiar pattern in colonial systems of the international division of labour between specialised mass producers on the periphery, and consumption, distribution and processing in the centre. Very little attempt was made to break out of this pattern of dependence despite the fact that it became noticeable just after the turn of the century that the interests of those who dealt with the marketing and processing of the shell were not congruent with the interests of the producers.

The most obvious point of discord was the price of shell. A consistently high price would have been advantageous for the producers, and a consistently low price would have been advantageous for the manufacturers. The buyers, on the other hand, mediating between the two, were able to use drastic price fluctuations to bind both producers and manufacturers, by giving seasonal advances. This arrangement helped to cement centralised, oligopolistic distribution systems, making it both difficult, and less urgent, for producers to widen their markets.

The structure of the marketing channels, too, was therefore a point of latent discord. Buyers sought to control as much as possible of the shell output, whereas an open, geographically diverse market would have been more beneficial for the producers in the long run. For example, there was a market for pearl-shell in the Middle East where mother-of-pearl was used for inlay work and rosary beads, but Australian producers had no direct access to it. Instead, button-manufacture remained the single driving force behind demand schedules.

This narrow range of end-uses was a further touchstone in the division of interests between producers and distributors. The distributors were not marketing pearl-shell, they were marketing button material. This distinction became starkly obvious in the 1950s, when the very firms who had been buying and marketing pearl-shell were those who helped to develop synthetic materials to replace it.

Why, then, did this colonial division of labour persist? It persisted, first, because the division of interest was not recognised. Pearl-shellers had little insight into marketing, so that the degree to which price fluctuations were caused by fashion trends, or by oligopolistic manipulation, was uncertain.

Second, it was entrenched by institutional conditions. The financial dependence of producers on the buyers was both a cause and an effect of the weakness of defensive institutional arrangements, such as government-led marketing or strong industry associations capable of leadership, financial support, and marketing muscle. Buyers presented themselves both as a gatekeeper to that market and as a defence against financial uncertainty. They already occupied the niche which the federal government sought to fill with a marketing board, or which could have been filled by an industry association.

Third, this financial dependence, in an atmosphere of inelastic demand, explains much of that competitive individualism which characterised the industry. Producers were competing with each other for the share of a relatively fixed market. This meant that producers, and centres of production, were in real, and felt, competition with each other, and buyers were therefore more successful in regulating the output of the industry than governments or the industry itself.

The entire industry was based on colonial models of production. Previous chapters have discussed how the use of cheap indigenous and indentured labour and resource-raiding practices also persisted beyond the colonial era. Orientation to the market in Britain and later the United States was another manifestation of that colonial model.

7

Beyond the 1960s

The collapse of the mother-of-pearl market launched the Torres Strait region into a new era. In 1960 several pearl-culture licences were issued at Thursday Island. The restructuring, so long overdue, now took place under duress, at great economic cost to the pearl-shellers. The industry underwent contraction, and pearls rather than pearl-shell became its product. What emerged was an industry which had resource husbandry as its focus, and which could control its output. But it was not an Australian industry.

The pioneering work in pearl-culture of Japanese companies now paid dividends for Japanese investors. Pearl-culture relied on Japanese know-how, employed Japanese technicians, and was mostly financed by overseas capital. In 1962 there were forty Okinawans employed in the pearl-culture farms at Thursday Island. The Australian mother-of-pearl produced bigger pearls than Japanese oysters, and was an attractive investment for Japanese and other overseas companies.

Several pearl-shellers helped to establish pearl-culture farms in junior partnership with overseas investors. Denis George, with ten years' experience in experimental cultivation on Packe Island, was recruited by Mikimoto. Hockings became manager of the Goode Island farm of Australasian Pearlers, a Melbourne company with Japanese participation. Shipway and Jones ceased pearl-shelling in 1960 and became partners with Gerdau in the South Sea Pearling Company. Jack Zafer partnered a Japanese company in the Aucher Pearling Company, and Duffield became part of the Cape York

Pearling Company, with British and Iranian participation (Boris Norman and the sister of the Shah of Iran were among the partners). Gerdau participated in at least three culture farm ventures, Pearls Pty Ltd, South Sea Pearling Company, and the Nippo Pearl Company in Western Australia.[1]

The cultivation areas were still not self-recruiting (nor are they today), and live shell had to be obtained from open waters. But because emphasis had shifted from the shell to the pearls, not as many molluscs were required as for pearl-shelling. By 1964, twelve pearl-culture stations operated out of Thursday Island, and expansion was limited by the scarcity of live pearl-shell. The demand for live shell was the only support of the pearl-shell luggers, most of which were owned by the IIB. In 1968, 431 tons of pearl-shell, mostly live shell, were procured, and sold at an average of $1493 a ton.

Another disaster struck the industry after the oil tanker *Oceanic Grandeur*, carrying 58 000 tons of oil (58 million litres), struck an uncharted reef in March 1970. An exact assessment of the spill could not be made, but it was estimated that a million litres were spilled in two separate leaks, the larger one occurring during rescue operations. This was the 'first major oil spillage in Queensland'[2], and a timely warning about the hazards of oil-drilling on the reef, which was the subject of wide public controversy at the time, but on the whole, the spill was considered to be minor. For example Craig McGregor wrote for overseas readers, 'fortunately a catastrophe could be prevented: another tanker was able to take over a large part of the freight, and a calm sea enabled the dispersal of the oil blanket before it could cause much damage'.[3]

Locally, the accident was viewed differently. The oil spill was treated with Gamlen, a detergent which breaks the surface tension of the water to allow the oil—and the detergent—to sink to the bottom. Soon afterwards, the pearl-culture farms suffered huge oyster mortalities from a rare disease. Only two culture farms survived the epidemic.[4] Sales from pearls tumbled from $260 000 in 1969 to $37 000 in 1973 and Australian employment fell from 160 in 1970 to less than 60 in 1971. The pearl farmers sought compensation for the losses they sustained, but a causal link between the accident and the epidemic which killed the pearl-shell could not be established. The epidemic had been due to stress, but it was argued that such stress could have been caused by overcrowding the shell, for example during transport. Gamlen was a highly efficient detergent, used in ports, and not suited for open natural conditions. It was afterwards taken off the market. Ironically, it had been because of the pearl-culture farms that dispersal of the oil slick was deemed necessary. This accident and the compensation claims of pearl-culture farmers caused a deep rift between administrators and the industry. It is remembered with considerable bitterness by those who were involved.

Many Torres Strait Islanders turned their trochus-diving experience to crayfish-diving, which was becoming a lucrative industry. A dinghy could collect 100 kilograms of crayfish tails worth $1500. With the emergence of this new industry, pearl farmers were finding it increasingly difficult to recruit Torres Strait Islanders for the procurement of live shell, and these positions are now mostly taken up by Papua New Guineans. In 1985 only two boats and forty men were engaged in bringing in live shell.

The pearl industry now at Thursday Island is insignificant both in economic terms and in terms of regional prosperity, although there are indications that it may gain in value. In 1985 it produced $1 million worth of pearls, whereas the Western Australian pearl-culture farms, led by the successful Paspali company, produced a value of $40 million. In 1990 the value was $5 million and $60 million respectively. Indonesian, Malaysian and Burmese pearl-farms now offer a keen competition with cheaper labour, but Australian pearls have a very high international reputation. According to Haemen Mendis (nephew of the well-known Thursday Island pearl-dealer Nissie Mendis) a string of 23 Paspali pearls recently sold in New York for a record price of $3.4 million. There are now five pearl-culture farms in Torres Strait and a pearl-shell hatchery at Escape River (near Turtle Head Island) where pearl-shell is reared from spat, which is still not possible in the strong tides of Torres Strait.[5]

Demand for mother-of-pearl has also revived. In the 1970s a renewed commercial interest in natural products carried over from the leading fashion houses of Europe to the manufacturers of clothing in Taiwan, and trochus buttons were again sought after for the up-market ranges. One Queensland exporter was able to obtain some trochus shell from itinerant trochus-gatherers in 1972 for $450 a ton,[6] which he sold for $600 a ton. A former pearl-sheller returned to full-time trochus-fishing in Queensland in 1978. Employing ten divers, the Cairns region was fished out in one year. By 1980, three boats worked in trochus south of Mackay. Two of these harvested over 300 tonnes for two years. The trochus stocks had replenished themselves, and sixteen men easily gathered 2 tonnes of shell a day. The world production of trochus was estimated at between 3000 and 5000 tonnes annually, and demand exceeded supply, particularly after New Caledonia introduced stringent controls on its trochus-fishery in 1983 because of depletion. Prices were very high, and increasing sharply, from $1200 in December 1982 to $1795 in July 1985. By 1986 trochus was sold at $3.50 to $4.00 a kilogram, or $4000 a tonne.

Several of the former divers were eager to return to the industry. But it became increasingly difficult to resume trochus-fishing. The entire barrier reef had been declared a marine park (with World Heritage Listing in 1981), and the Great Barrier Reef Marine Park Authority (GBRMPA) had been established as a federal management agency for the reef in 1976. By 1983 all major sections of the marine park had been declared and zoning plans were in effect for all sections in August 1988. GBRMPA's publicity material emphasises sustainable resource-use practices with the slogan 'Ours to use wisely'.

The Torres Strait Treaty with Papua New Guinea, ratified in February 1985, declared Torres Strait a protected zone and guaranteed traditional fishing rights. It is administered by the Torres Strait Protected Zone Joint Authority (PZJA) consisting of the Primary Industries ministers of the Commonwealth and Queensland governments. It consults with Commonwealth, Queensland, and Papua New Guinean fisheries officials and scientists through a management committee, and with industry representatives (Queensland Commercial Fishermen's Organization, QCFO), and Torres Strait Islanders (Island Co-ordinating Council) through an industry and Islanders consultative committee. Its tasks are both management and conservation of fisheries, particularly of dugong and turtles.

At the State level, the Fisheries Service had been transferred from the Department of Harbours and Marine to the Department of Primary Industries, in order to draw on the management experience of primary industries. The Queensland Fish Management Authority (QFMA) was established in 1982 as a quasi-autonomous non-government organisation with industry representation. It is the licensing authority for all fisheries (except pearls, oyster, coral and shell-grit), issuing fishing licences, boat licences, and marketing licences. The administration of fisheries is now divided between the QFMA and the DPI. The Fisheries Act of 1976 introduced master pearler's licences, corresponding to master fisherman's licences, issued by the Fisheries Branch of the Queensland Department of Primary Industries.

The managing authorities had developed a far stronger commitment to sustainable yield practices than to fostering infant industries.

> When I came back and wanted to re-start trochusing, I had only obstacles put in my road by the government and authorities. If you want to go into trochus now, today—you can't. You have to go to the Department of Primary Industries Fisheries Service, to the QFMA, to the Torres Strait Joint Venture [sic] Authority, and to GBRMPA. Because none of them know anything about it whatsoever, the answer is invariably 'No'.[7]

Keith Bradford spent a considerable amount of time and energy in obtaining the necessary permits and licences. His account of the requirements is a vivid testimony to the bewilderment of applicants who sought to re-enter the trochus fishery in the 1980s. He assumed that the master's ticket he required was a master fisherman's licence from the QFMA. He had found out that in order to get it he had to first pay his fees as a master fisherman to the Queensland Commercial Fishermen's Organization, and that the number of master fisherman's licences was frozen to prevent overfishing in the prawn fishery.

Despite the factual discrepancies of Bradford's account, the gist of his statement was quite true. Trochus licences were restricted to a few experimental permits. To complicate the issue, trochusing was now administered as a completely distinct fishery from bêche-de-mer collecting, because the latter is a food-producing activity. If he wanted to collect bêche-de-mer, he did require a master fisherman's licence from the QFMA. In that case he also required a Prescribed Goods Order, and a 'registered establishment number' for his curing facility (a vessel or workshop) from the Commonwealth Department of Primary Industry, under the Export Control Act (No. 47 of 1982), and needed to satisfy a range of criteria established by that department to control the processing of foods for export.

The divisions of responsibility between State and federal departments also caused confusion. Until 1981, applicants had to get licences from both State and Commonwealth departments if they wanted to fish inshore as well as out on the distant reefs. The Commonwealth had responsibility for certain extra-territorial fisheries (such as the tuna fishery, in which Japanese participated to a large degree), whereas the States administered fisheries within territorial waters, as well as those outside them which were not administered by the Commonwealth. The responsibilities for offshore fisheries (conducted outside territorial waters) were redefined in a 1981 amendment to the 1976 Fisheries Act. It was a mirror legislation to that passed by the Commonwealth and all other States. It now depends on the specific fishery to be pursued as to which department must be approached.[8]

Several Torres Strait Islanders are keen to return to the industry as owner-operators, but find it difficult to wend their way around these complex management regulations. Does one raise a loan first, or obtain the master's ticket first? Does one apply for the fishing licence before obtaining the boat, or after? In order to compete for the limited number of bêche-de-mer fishing licences, the applicant has to supply the identification of the vessel, and demonstrate effective marketing arrangements. But in order to obtain orders from importers, one needs to supply samples—one must have been fishing already.

Whereas the commercial fishers have well-developed structures, such as the QCFO, to inform themselves of administrative innovations, there is no comparable information dissemination network for those wishing to enter, or re-enter, the trochus and bêche-de-mer fisheries. Most of these applicants, moreover, are in isolated locations, literally 'a thousand miles away' from Brisbane. There are no guidelines through the maze of licensing and regulating authorities, and applicants generally find that they face a bureaucratic nightmare.

Torres Strait Islanders see owner-operated trochus-fishing as a viable alternative to the large-scale fishing which characterises the prawning industry. There is some itinerant trochus-fishing from dinghies, and the Darnley Island community proposed to re-establish a trochus enterprise with Aboriginal Development Commission aid. They see the revival of trochusing as a promising future prospect for their people. 'No-one should depend on handouts. I want to train people, my experience is going down the drain . . . We extend our fishing rights 200 miles out but who will work it? All the experience goes down the drain'.[9] Some Torres Strait Islanders, who live in mainland towns and are therefore not linked into the representative structures of Torres Strait communities, have spent years negotiating with funding institutions and lobbying for an entry into the industry.

Meanwhile, the older men are dying, or feel they are getting too old: 'These days are gone now. Wilkie Nuwaki and me are left, but the others are too old. The young ones don't know which trochus shells are good or bad. A multi-million dollar industry lies under the water but nobody knows how to do it'.[10]

The GBRMPA commissioned a feasibility study of the trochus industry which estimated that an annual yield of 500 tonnes was sustainable. This would mean a fairly lively industry without the excessive fishing which had resulted in depletion in the past. The study proposed a lower size limit of at least 80 mm, and an upper size limit of 125 mm across the base of the shell, to ensure that shells reached maturity before being harvested. It was also suggested to limit the number of divers to fifty (based on an aggregate annual yield of 10 tonnes of shell per diver). A feasibility study of bêche-de-mer found that 'the abundance of commercial species of bêche-de-mer on the Reef was considerably lower than on reef areas in other parts of the world which support commercial fisheries'.[11] This survey resulted in the allocation of parcels of 3600 square miles (one grid square on the navigation charts). The Department of Primary Industries issues several experimental bêche-de-mer permits subject to annual review. Area allocation as a management tool was also adopted for the small number of trochus licences. These restrictions were felt to be a death-knell to the industry:

> Any applicant is limited to a 60 by 60 mile square within which there are already declared marine parks, you are limited to 50 tonnes, which you won't get in that limited area, so they successfully wiped out pearling, trochus and bêche-de-mer . . . At the moment trochus and pearl-shell is in world demand. The prices have never been higher. I get telex after telex begging for the stuff, but it's impossible to get because of the restrictions.[12]

When he first went trochus-fishing (1946–49), Bradford fished only around 50 tons a year. But he argues that it was because his operation was too small that he had to leave the industry, and that it is not economical today to operate on such a small scale.

> You can't just get any boat and go out and get some trochus. You need a boat with a carrying capacity to make a container load which is 16 tonnes. It needs to accommodate 12 men with room for on-board processing. You are looking at a boat of roughly a quarter of a million dollars. To outlay capital and get a crew organized to fish 50 tonnes of shell is ludicrous.[13]

Bradford operates on an estimate of $1500 a ton, that is, $75 000 for 50 tonnes. (Although prices were considerably higher at the time of interviewing.) He pays his divers $5000 a season, so that the wages share is perhaps $60 000. He argues that unless he can expect to fish at least 200 to 300 tonnes a season (a turnover of $300 000 to $450 000), it is not viable to go trochus-fishing, and not worthwhile applying for a licence.

When the first experimental licences were issued, Torres Strait Islanders were offered preference for fishing in Torres Strait itself, but declined, since the commercial collection of trochus shell is conducted mainly along the Great Barrier Reef. In 1990 the area allocations were replaced with a quota allocation of 25 or 50 tonnes per licence, with the total catch limited to 150 tonnes in Torres Strait and 375 tonnes on the east coast. This means that a maximum of twenty-one licences can be granted, and the total catch limit has been raised to 525 tonnes. Torres Strait Islanders were offered first option on a number of licences, but initially argued that they should not need to compete with commercial trochus-fishers for the limited number of licences, since traditional fishing rights are now anchored in legislation.

For Torres Strait Islanders, who have participated in the fishery since the 1860s, pearl-shell, bêche-de-mer and trochus-fishing has become part of their tradition. (It was this notion of tradition which was used in the pearl-shell dispute with Japan to claim Australian prescriptive rights in the pearl-shell fishery on the continental shelf.) However, the notion of tradition which legitimates special rights for traditional users, refers to non-commercial, subsistence activities of indigenous cultural relevance. Tradition, when referring to indigenous people, therefore refers also to a mode of production. This contestation of the term 'tradition' led to a showdown in March 1991, when two floating stations, crewed by Torres Strait Islanders, illegally fished for trochus in a protected area, and incurred the 'largest fine ever imposed for breaching a marine park zone'.[14]

Torres Strait Islanders no longer have a subsistence economy to fall back on. For several decades, theirs has been a 'transfer economy' relying on government assistance. To become independent of social service transfers, it would seem that they need to establish economically viable industries to compete in a cash economy. However, this does not mean that they need to imitate and recreate the production strategies of the past.

On the strength of the experience of the past, GBRMPA does not consider collection industries to be viable in the long term except on an occasional basis. Warwick Nash, the marine biologist who has been concerned with the biology and management of trochus, proposed that hatchery rearing of trochus might be possible to replenish suitable reef locations with juvenile trochus. However, under current restrictions the industry's expected value is $2 million annually.[15] The management committee advising the PZJA considered whether it was not better economic sense to let the industry decline than to revive it.

None of the management authorities involved is willing to tolerate a return to the old resource-raiding practices. In a rejoinder to Bradford, the former director of the Queensland Fisheries Service commented that considering the marginal economic significance of the industry, and unanswered questions about the level at which yield was sustainable,

> all authorities felt that if we can't get enough information and resolve the other control problems, everyone will be better off not exploiting these resources until we have the knowledge and control mechanisms to properly manage them . . . Because we all know what has happened in the past, the answer is invariably 'No' until we are sure that the controls can be adequately addressed.[16]

Government authorities are no longer committed to this industry. With sustainable resource-management philosophies firmly institutionalised, the industry, which relied on resource-raiding for its viability, is treated with suspicion, and large-scale fishing practices are not allowed to be reintroduced. Again, the state plays a leading role in defining the choice of production strategies. In this instance, the role of the state is highly visible and in conflict with the entrepreneurial will.

8

Explaining Decline: the Role of the State

The three structural weaknesses of the pearl-shell industry were not all equally prominent throughout the century of pearl-shelling reviewed in this book. Problems with the nature of the workforce, the resource-use strategies, and marketing surfaced with greater or lesser urgency at different periods, and none of these was satisfactorily resolved. The 1880s and early 1890s were, no doubt, the heyday of pearl-shelling. The fishery was expanding and vibrant, and gained its place in the national consciousness as a valuable economic activity. Torres Strait, which had been at the margin of the South Pacific, became part of Australia so that the fishery could be supervised, and legislation to administer the fishery was introduced.[1] To contain the worst excesses of labour abuse, rules governing the employment of Pacific Islanders and Aborigines were imposed. These, on the whole, accommodated the needs of the industry.

The first crisis in the fishery was reached around the turn of the century because of overfishing and resource exhaustion. This crisis transformed the state's involvement, from labour regulation and revenue-raising to attempts at reforming industrial strategies. A string of public inquiries sought to introduce artificial cultivation of shell, the replacement of indentured with white and local labour, and the breakdown of oligopolies. The resource crisis was eventually overcome not by state intervention but by contraction of the industry as the fleet was halved.

The new agenda of state involvement itself heightened a further problem—the Japanese dominance. Not only were the Japanese encroaching on the managerial prerogatives of white pearl-shellers but the possibility of immigration restrictions loomed over the industry for almost twenty years, causing considerable investment uncertainty. The three largest companies associated with the fishery withdrew or scaled down their involvement during this period.[2]

When the question of Japanese indentees was finally settled in favour of the pearl-shellers at the end of World War I, marketing started to assume greater proportions as a central problem. The international shell market had shifted to New York, and the established marketing channels became obsolete. During the 1920s shell-collection was conducted at the limits of the resource capacity. The resource pressure was eased by the slump in demand during the Great Depression. The industry entered the World War II period in a disorganised condition, suffering from overproduction and Japanese competition.

After World War II, the labour problem bounced back into focus. With the mass withdrawal of the Japanese, there was no trained workforce of divers. Moreover, the recruitment patterns of the past caused a reluctance to employ local, indigenous labour as divers, since the employment utilities of different ethnic groups had become proverbial, and were understood as racial attributes. The resource problem, still unresolved, continued to hinder a steady, reliable output, and marketing, still modelled on the old principle of raw materials exported through oligopolistic channels, was the final stumbling block for the fishery.

That the fishery survived as long as it did now appears more surprising than that it collapsed. What had sustained it? There were the seasonal advances from the buyers to tide pearl-shellers from one year to the next. Some luggers were used for sixty years, so that after the initial investment, running expenses could be kept low. The Japanese had been an efficient workforce, working with outdated equipment. These factors certainly helped the industry. Still, the financial survival of the industry was due above all to its continued access to cheap labour. Employment was seasonal (from March to December) and not secured by the normal industrial legislation (award wages, workers' compensation). The industry, in other words, was sheltered by the state.

The industry's exclusion from the provisions of the White Australia policy was a momentous concession. Without it, the industry would have taken on quite different forms, possibly not based on mass extraction. We have also seen how the state helped to construct conditions of internal colonialism in Torres Strait. Islanders were pressured into wage labour on luggers. Their movements were restricted, and lugger work became a condition of access to the consumer goods available from island stores. The Islanders were also encouraged to continue tending their gardens (farming was introduced to islands where it had not been a traditional activity), so that they could fall back on subsistence activities during the lay-up season. DNA officers mediated contact between employers and employees; they negotiated on behalf of the Islanders, and issued recruiting permits. The state of internal colonialism guaranteed the industry's access to cheap, dependent labour.

At first the PIL scheme subverted the agenda of dependence. The co-operative luggers became means of subsistence production which allowed pearl-shelling to be integrated into traditional kinship structures and trade relations. They afforded access to Western commodities without turning Islanders into wage labour. This scheme was gradually appropriated by the DNA and transformed into a state enterprise, imitating the production strategies of commercial pearl-shellers. The transformation of the lugger scheme is not only significant in its effects on Torres Strait Islanders themselves; it also constituted the suppression, by the state, of an alternative production style for the industry. In a world 'that might have turned out differently', the lugger scheme could have lured the cheap indigenous workforce away from the pearl-shellers (as these often claimed it did) and provided the material independence and the legal arguments to secure priority rights in traditional fishing zones. A network of co-operative enterprises exploiting a commonly owned property could have emerged, resolving the paradox of depletion referred to as the 'tragedy of the commons'. It is doubtful that the white pearl-shellers at Thursday Island could have subsisted under such circumstances.

In the event, the state resisted the emancipation of indigenous people, both out of a deep-seated racist paternalism which was guided by Social Darwinist principles, and because it represented a settler colony. The colonial design was to draw indigenes into capitalist relations under white patronage. Colonial states defended economic power constellations which ensured white dominance.

Settler colonies had their own internal contradictions, the effects of which have lingered beyond the formal colonial era. Inspired by the colonial vision of unlimited markets and resources on the one hand, they also had a certain interest in permanency. This interest was expressed by the commissions of inquiry which sought to produce a solution for the industry as a whole. The state tried to stem the inexorable 'tragedy of the commons' by regulating access with licence restrictions, size limits, and shell-bed closures. I have suggested that this approach is by nature piecemeal since it does not address the contradiction between common resources and their use for private gain.

The idea of artificial cultivation on permanent leases went some way towards addressing that dilemma. The state made a sustained attempt to foster cultivation as an alternative production strategy, which could have sustained both the resource and the mass production paradigm for the industry. However, the lengthy process of research and development necessary to adapt known cultivation techniques to tropical conditions far exceeded the time-horizon of pearl-shellers.

Pearl-shellers competed with each other for labour, for shell, and for access to an oligopolistic market with inelastic demand. Their competitive individualism hindered the emergence of collective institutions which could pool resources for experimentation and innovation, and thereby aid a long-term planning orientation. The competitive, individualistic industry resisted long-term vision and change. After World War II, all the old problems resurfaced, with all the old arguments. The centre–periphery relationship of marketing, the employment of indentured aliens and cheap indigenous labour, and the resource-raiding attitude became colonial hangovers.

Whether the state should continue to shelter the industry now became the subject of intense debate, particularly on the reintroduction of Japanese divers. The weaknesses of the industry were well recognised. Rather than forcing it into new strategies, a limited number of Japanese were allowed to be reintroduced so that the industry could re-establish itself on the familiar patterns, and lay claim to the resources on the continental shelf. Within a decade, the postwar bonanza had run its course.

The state reacted to a variety of domestic and foreign pressures both from the industry and administrative bodies. It was sensitive to demands from the industry but also pursued its own goals (territorial expansion, the White Australia policy). Moreover, national rivalries had a deep impact. Distinct phases in the industry's history are marked by the establishment of the northern outpost, World War I, World War II, and the pearl-shell dispute with Japan. The state played a significant, though passive role in the industry, and its supportive stance helped to sustain the production strategies practised by the industry.

Just as there were differences of opinion and interest within the industry, so the state also was not a monolithic entity with a uniform policy. A range of State and federal agencies were involved in the administration of the pearl-shell fisheries, with often conflicting views and intentions. Within these agencies, individual officers strongly influenced decision-making.

During the first, island-station phase of the fishery (to 1885), the government officers stationed at the outpost were stout advocates of the fishery. Many of them directly participated in it, and all of them were dependent for their position on the perceived importance of that outpost and on the prosperity of the fishery which was its economic mainstay. As a result, the advice received by governments closely mirrored the demands of the pearl-shellers. During this period, the sphere of influence of Queensland officials was extended over the fishery by means of the northward extension of Queensland's territory and the 1881 Act. The pearl-shellers, for their part, gained reductions in licensing fees and several exemptions from labour regulations.

The Goverment Resident's annual reports to the Home Secretary and the annual reports of the Chief Protector were substantially concerned with the fishery and continued to keep the fishery in focus for the Queensland administration. Douglas and Roth were forceful figures with considerable discretion in the local implementation of policy. They pointed out problems with the fishery and suggested acceptable solutions. Douglas kept Torres Strait Islanders outside the ambit of the Aboriginal Protection Act and took it upon himself to impose labour regulations. He represented pearl-shellers' views on size limits, cultivation, and various other matters. With the abolition of the position of Government Resident in 1912, the industry lost one of its direct regular lines of communication with Brisbane.

Changes in personnel within the Department of Native Affairs (DNA and its successors[3]) had a noticeable impact on its relationship with the industry. The first Chief Protector of Aborigines, Roth, imposed somewhat stricter labour legislation for the industry but generally endorsed lugger work, while Howard strongly encouraged

The Japanese cemetery at Thursday Island. A second memorial (centre) was erected in 1979 by the Mokuyoto-kai (Thursday Island Club), which consists of some thirty returned divers in Wakayama, as it was felt that the restoration of all the graves would be too difficult.

The Japanese Club on Thursday Island on Culture Day (birthday of the Meji Emperor), 3 November 1910

A breakthrough in the stalled bilateral negotiations permits the first fleet of Japanese pearl-shelling boats to enter the Arafura Sea, 1954. The fleet's departure from Kushimoto was celebrated and widely reported in the press.

it. Under Howard's direction the industry was granted easy access to Torres Strait Islander and Aboriginal labour, while subsequent directors and protectors gradually drew the focus of Torres Strait Islander pearl-shelling away from wages boats, favouring employment on company boats. The voice of this department had shored up much interest in the fishery, although it did not unequivocally support the industry. After World War II, the interests of the department were in open conflict with the wishes of the pearl-shellers, who wanted to reintroduce Japanese indentees.

With the appointment of the first inspector of pearl-shell and bêche-de-mer fisheries in 1891, another State government agency assumed some responsibility. For the sake of convenience, it will be referred to as the Queensland Fisheries Service (QFS[4]), although like the DNA it underwent a series of transformations in structure and name. The position of pearl-shell inspector was usually assumed by the local Protector of Aborigines. This arrangement strengthened the authority of Protectors and distanced the QFS from the affairs of the industry. Thursday Island became a training ground for careers in the DNA.[5]

The influence of the QFS on the fishery also depended on individual officers within it. These were the marine biologists who took a special interest in pearl-shell cultivation, W. Saville-Kent (1890), James Tosh (1900), Frank Moorehouse (1928), and Portmaster John Mackay. These people had a strong commitment to the fishery, but were critical of its resource-use strategies. It was from here that radical reform proposals emanated which met with opposition from the pearl-shellers.

After these early efforts, the QFS exerted little influence over the pearl-shell fishery. The position of pearl-shell and bêche-de-mer inspector became a parochial and somewhat quaint position within the QFS. Among the uncharacteristic tasks of a fisheries inspector were the protection of labour and of two species of tree (coconut palm and 'beauty leaf' *Callophyllum inophyllum* which grows on beaches). In fact, QFS personnel had 'very little idea of what was going on at Thursday Island'.[6] Fishing in Queensland was a small-scale, mostly part-time activity. Until intensive prawning started in the 1960s, fisheries and their administration were not a serious political or economic issue in Queensland. The QFS was a weak department, suffering from frequent reorganisation. For a few years it was even part of the DNA (then DAIA). The department which held most promise to make the pearl-shell fishery sustainable sank back into a passive role in its administration.

Customs, which became a federal responsibility after 1900, also had a direct interest in the fishery. It collected export revenue and customs on imports of gear and foodstuffs (particularly rice for the Japanese workforce). The extension of pearl-shelling into extra-territorial waters, and the possibility of losing customs revenue if the fleets registered under foreign flags of convenience, caused some concern for the new department. It headed two inquiries into the pearl-shell fishery (by Dashwood in 1902 and by Lockyer in 1904). These reports lent their weight to the opinions expressed in other departments. Thereafter, this department, too, confined itself to routine administration.

After the flurry of activity generated by the industry's first resource crisis, only the DNA retained a lively interest in the industry at the State level. A renewed wave of government interest commenced in the 1930s with the arrival of Japanese fleets and market saturation. The shift from resource problems to marketing issues increasingly brought the fishery into the ambit of the federal government.

The Commonwealth commissioned three voluminous reports of the fishery. The first of these, the report of the Bamford Commission (1913–16), was to herald radical changes, but concluded with the exemption of the industry from the White Australia policy. The Northern Australia Development Commission (Coombs Commission, 1946) reaffirmed a general commitment to the industry. The industry's economic contribution had always been of regional importance. After World War II its significance had diminished, but it still had a central part in regional economies. The fishery had some economic, and much geo-political value, having contributed significantly to the development of the far north of Australia and to the northward extension of Queensland's boundaries. The Coombs Report helped to shore up federal support for the industry despite the fact that the industry did not offer employment to white Australians, did not supply a domestic market, and its benefits for indigenous people were doubtful. Against the advice of the Queensland government, which was counselled by the DNA, the federal government permitted the limited reintroduction of Japanese workers. Rather than force restructuring, therefore, the government complied with industry pressures. External Affairs had to justify the Australian claim to the pearl-shell beds, and the Commerce Department was in close consultation with Gerdau, who was regarded as the only stabilising influence over the pearl-shell market. The pivotal agencies within the Commonwealth government were therefore not reacting to pearl-shellers themselves but to pressures and advice from overseas interest in the industry. The Commerce Department commissioned a study by John Bach to counter the Japanese argument that they, rather than Australians, had started the pearl-shelling industry in Australia (still a popular myth in Japan, only false if taken literally in an argument about historical precedent). Bach wrote an extensive history of the pearl-shelling industry in which he condemned its production strategies and lent some justification to the Japanese interest in it.

The Australian pearl-shell fishery was weak, the large companies had departed from it, and thorough change had always been paralysed by divisions among pearl-shellers. The DNA, one of the last of the Queensland departments to have an active interest in the industry, had its own luggers and disagreed with pearl-shellers about the resumption of prewar strategies. The Japanese no longer sought employment in the Australian industry but sent their own luggers, challenging Australia's claim over the pearl-shell beds. The federal government responded to overseas interests and pressures rather than domestic industrial ones. Radical restructuring could not be expected under those circumstances.

Once the industry had collapsed under the weight of its own structural weaknesses, there were no longer any influential counter-pressures to inhibit a gradual reorientation in fisheries management principles towards sustainable practices. Even Gerdau, who also contracted the Japanese shell, and had started to finance research into boilable plastics as an alternative material, had ceased to have a compelling interest in supporting the Australian industry. By the time the trochus-fishery was revived on a small scale, new management structures and philosophies were already entrenched. The arguments which had previously solicited government support— economic contribution and defence value—no longer applied.

Current management principles are vindicated with reference to the demonstrated failure of mass production strategies for collection fisheries. However, the lessons of the fishery had been evident long ago and by themselves were not sufficient to bring about reform. New institutional structures enabled a replacement of the mass production paradigm with the philosophy of sustainable yield management. A different set of political pressures has made indigenous collective claims over traditional fishing zones possible. Fisheries managers are now forcing the re-emerging industry to shed its colonial baggage and any visions of a 'multi-million dollar industry' under the sea. Pearl-shelling, trochus-gathering and bêche-de-mer collecting are now defined as 'collection fisheries', that is, activities not amenable to mass production, and with no necessary prospect of continuity.

Government agencies are increasingly sensitive to traditional use rights and under some public pressure to make allowances for cultural practices. It appears now that in order to generate official support for a trochus-fishery, Torres Strait Islanders will need to distance themselves from exploitation strategies based on depleted yield. A new niche for commercial creativity may well exist in embracing a cultural identity which defines itself through co-operative ownership, mixed subsistence and cash production, and a conserver ethic drawing on husbandry experiments, that is, an approach inspired by flexible specialisation rather than mass extraction.

This shift in outlook was not caused simply by a 'scientific discovery' of resource exhaustion. As the Introduction argued, changes in attitude and a reordering of economic priorities are essential for the successful implementation of solutions. Without a substantial change in the socio-economic circumstances of the industry and in larger political pressures and values, the 100-year survival of the industry might have been viewed as a success.

Appendix I

The Network of Early Stations

Figure 1 shows the ties of partnership and ownership between the island-based pearl-shell and bêche-de-mer stations in Torres Strait from 1862 to 1885. These ties have never been widely recognised and were reconstructed from incidental references to vessels, owners, stations, or captains engaged in the fishery. Demonstrating these linkages is therefore somewhat laborious, and the evidence for the ties between stations is explained below. The illustration indicates the persons in whose names vessels operating out of island stations were registered, and (in brackets) the greatest number of vessels registered in any one year.

Explanation of Linkages:

A   Between 1868 and 1870 Banner used the vessels *Pakeha* and *Julia Percy*, belonging to Towns, and *Bluebell* (belonging to Paddon) on Warrior Island, the first pearl-shelling station in Torres Strait (Chester 1870; Shineberg 1967:App.1).

B   The Warrior Island station was continued after Banner's death in 1872 under the name of Merriman. Bain indicates that Banner worked for James Merriman of Sydney. (Bain 1982:45; Aplin 1875; de Hoghton 1880).

C   After Paddon's death in 1861, his partner C. Edwards formed a new partnership with J. Frazer to establish the first bêche-de-mer station in Torres Strait, on Albany Island in 1862. Edwards also used the *Melanie*, used for recruiting in the Pacific and for prospecting, and *Kate Kearney*, both registered by Towns. This station was removed to Darnley in 1865. Other vessels associated with the *Melanie* (Capt. A. McAusland) and *Kate Kearney* were the *Challenge*, the *Western Star* (Capt. J. Hastings, 1872), and the *Storm Bird* (Hastings 1875). J. Hastings was also an old

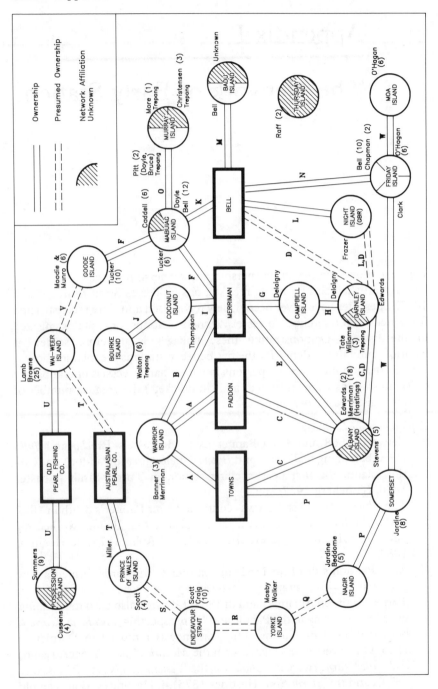

Figure 1   Networks of ownership and partnership between island-based pearl-shell and bêche-de-mer stations in Torres Strait (1862–85)

sandalwooder, who went into the employ of Merriman. (Shineberg 1967:passim; Moresby 1873; Jardine 1.1.1872, 20.7.1872; Aplin 1875)

D   Frazer, Edward's partner in the Albany station, also skippered the *John Bell* (Aplin 1875).

E   In 1877 Merriman & Co. had 21 luggers registered at Thursday Island. Their station was at Albany Island, managed by Hastings 'a snug fishing station . . . one of the most enterprising, and I believe I may add, one of the most successful of those who are engaged in the fishery' (Douglas, 8.12.1877 and Heath, 1875 in Prideaux 1988:146, 159) (Merriman's Warrior Island Station was still operating. Ware and Brown, who had five vessels registered in 1877, also acted for Merriman. In 1873 Ware had bought two impounded vessels on behalf of James Merriman (Prideaux 1988:118).)

F   In 1875 there were two stations at Mabuiag Island, one owned by Merriman and one by John Bell. Merriman's station was managed by Capt. Tucker. The boats associated with this station were the *Margaret & Jane* (Tucker, 1872; McAuley, 1875), the *Retrieve* (Thompson, 1875, who had been Tucker's mate on the *Margaret & Jane*) and the *Root Hog or Die* (Tucker, 1875). By 1879 the Mabuiag Island station was registered in Tucker's name, and by 1880 Tucker had moved the station to Goode Island. It was reported that Tucker refused medicine to sick employees on the station, and no rations were distributed on Sundays. (Aplin 1875; Chester 1877; Moresby 1872; de Hoghton 1880; Chester 14.11.1881, Col A 326/5118).

G   Delaigny had a station at Campbell Island. He was captain of the *Active* (1869–72), *Fanny* (1872), and *Crishna* (1873). The link between Merriman and the Campbell Island Station consists of the use of the *Crishna* and *Margaret and Jane* both used in the labour trade, the latter belonging to Merriman's Mabuiag station (see F). In 1872 nine Rotumah men deserted from Campbell Island due to the brutality of the mate Thompson (*Margaret and Jane*) 'who was in the habit of compelling them to dive for shell by firing at them with a revolver. They also stated that Thompson sunk a canoe full of Mabuiag men who were making their escape from the schooner' (Chester). Complaints about Thompson's behaviour were also heard from Port Moresby (Lawes, LMS to Aplin, 10.1.1875 in Prideaux 1988:140). In 1873 Delaigny's *Crishna* was placed under arrest for kidnapping. In 1874 the *Margaret and Jane* was impounded for illegally shipping Polynesians to Queensland; Captain McAuley and his mate Delaigny were charged accordingly (Chester 1870, 1872; Prideaux 1988:134).

H   In 1873 Delaigny's Campbell Island station was removed to Darnley Island (Jardine, 12.1.1873).

I   William Walton (*Matilda*, 1872; *Crishna*, 1873; *Lady Denison*, 1875) collaborated with Thompson (*Enchantress*) in manning three boats with

Coconut Islanders. Thompson lived at Coconut Island and was associated with Merriman. The number of boats skippered by Walton within a few years indicates that he was also working for a large company during this period. (Moresby 1872; Jardine 12.2.1873; Aplin 1875; Prideaux 1988:116).

J In 1879 Walton had formed his own company, fishing for bêche-de-mer with six vessels on the GBR, with a station at Bourke Island (Pennefather 1882).

K John Bell and Co. had a station at Mabuiag Island. It was managed by Owen Owens who had a fatal accident in 1875 (Aplin 1875; de Hoghton 1880).

L Joseph Frazer (*John Bell*) managed a bêche-de-mer station at Night Island for John Bell of Sydney (Aplin 1875).

M In 1884 there were two pearling stations on Badu, one of them belonging to Bell. (Beckett 1987:152; Walker in Mackay 1908:206).

N T. G. Chapman was the first captain in charge of a Melbourne vessel to participate in the fishery in 1872. He set up a station on Friday Island but found himself harassed by Jardine's officers. He moved to Mabuiag Island in 1873, and was charged in 1874 for infringements of the Kidnapping Act. His vessels were *Peveril* and *J. S. Lane*. He was still active in 1877, but by 1879 all ten boats registered for Mabuiag were in the name of Bell (Prideaux 1988:113, 123, 134; de Hoghton, 1880).

O In 1871 Douglas Pitt from Jamaica arrived in Torres Strait. He set up a station on Murray Island in partnership with James Doyle and J. S. Bruce. Bruce arrived at Murray in 1886 and later became the government-appointed schoolteacher there. Doyle moved to Mabuiag Island, and in 1903 the DNA received complaints from Mabuiag and Saibai Islanders about the conduct of James Doyle, J.P. at Mabuiag. It was reported that he had policemen in his pay and imprisoned natives without warrants or authority. His recruiting permit was withdrawn in 1904, although a permit to recruit Torres Strait Islanders was not required at that time. Doyle's Mabuiag station was probably taken over from Bell. Doyle had bought the *Alice May*, a former Burns Philp vessel. (Pitt in Mackay 1908:212; Bleakley,1962:278; Parsons 1978:29; Roth and Howard, Annual Reports of the Chief Protector of Aborigines, *QVP* 1904, 1905, 1906.)

P Frank Jardine had a station at Somerset and Nagir Island. It is little known that, at least for a time, he had a share-trading agreement with Towns. Charles Beddome also had five boats registered at Nagir Island in association with Jardine's station (Chapman letter, 9.9.1873 in Prideaux 1988:123; Aplin 1875).

Q   Yankee Ned Mosby from Boston worked on the *Three Brothers* when he arrived in Torres Strait in 1871. From 1873 to 1876 he was in association with Jardine on Nagir Island. He then settled on Yorke Island to establish a bêche-de-mer station with Jack Walker, dealing with Burns Philp & Co. (Mosby in Mackay 1908:215; Pennefather 1882).

R   The *Three Brothers* (a 90-ton schooner) was also used by Scott and Craig for their Endeavour Strait station, on a small island east of Possession Island, from which they ran nine vessels. The schooner was the home of the pearlers. It is unlikely that a small independent station could have afforded such a large ship, but its ownership could not be traced (Aplin 1875; Chester 1877; de Hoghton 1880).

S   In 1880 Scott and Henderson ran four boats from Prince-of-Wales Island (Chester QVP 1880:1158).

T   A. J. Miller was manager of the Australasian Pearl Company at Prince-of-Wales Island. He also had shares in the Queensland Pearl Fishing Company, and used the Wai-Weer station. Captain Miller had previously been employed by the Eastern and Australian Mail Company. He was the first Australian pearl-sheller to recruit directly in Japan in 1883 (Sissons 1979:9, 22; Summers in Mackay 1908:78–80).

U   In 1877 Wai-Weer was occupied by Lamb and Browne, who had a comfortable station and jetty. In 1879 the Wai-Weer station was in the name of Summers, Parbury and Lamb, Moodie, and Munro, who had just amalgamated into one company, the Queensland Pearl Company (QPF), based in Sydney. They also had a station on Possession Island, running 22 vessels altogether (Douglas 1877; de Hoghton 1880; Summers in Mackay 1908:78).

V   In 1879 the Goode Island station was registered for Moodie and Munro, but by 1880 Moodie and Munroe were part of the QPF, and the Goode Island station now appeared in Tucker's name. It is possible that the QPF retained a financial interest in Goode Island. H. Clark, who worked as a tender from 1882 to 1892 said that he was first employed bu Summers on Wai-Weer, and then 'went to Goode Island with Mr Kelly' (de Hoghton, 1880; Clark in Mackay 1908:187).

W   From 1877 to 1880 (and perhaps longer) the Friday Island station was registered by O'Hagan. A few years later it was occupied by James Clark who had been in partnership with Jardine (Chester, *QVP*, 1877, 1879; de Hoghton, 1880, Smith, 1985:77).

Appendix II

Statistics on Productivity

For the years before 1890 no statistics on productivity are available. But from 1890 to 1904 catch per unit effort declined sharply and steadily from an average annual take of 6 to 2 tons per boat, associated with a steady increase in the number of boats employed. Table 4 shows an increase in total take, accompanied by a decrease in average take per boat. The increase in the number of boats was accompanied by an increase in the size of vessels and in the number of crew employed. The 10-ton vessels had been staffed with seven crew, but the larger vessels employed twelve or more. Even without adequate data to calculate catch per unit effort (the Coombs Commission in 1946 faced the same lack of data to make such a calculation) the trend of productivity decline is evident.

TABLE 4   AVERAGE TAKE PER BOAT (1890–1904)

	Boats engaged (pearl-shell boats only)	Average take per boat (rounded)	Total (in tons)
1890	92	6 tons 17 cwt	632
1895	204	4 tons 5 cwt	873
1900	341	3 tons 2 cwt	1060
1904	353	2 tons 4 cwt	777

Sources: Mackay 1908:xlix

Two pearl-shellers in 1897 estimated their profit at around 6 per cent, and two in 1913 stated that they averaged 10 per cent return on investment (Dashwood 1902:10; Bamford 1913:66, 107). A more thorough, but still imperfect profit estimate, shown in Table 5, indicates a rise from 6.8 per cent in 1907 to over 34 per cent in 1911, a period of fairly steady export volume.

TABLE 5   ESTIMATE OF PROFITS (1907–11)

Year	Expenses (£)	Value of shell raised (£)	Profit (£)	Percentage of profit
1907	64 630	69 429	4 799	6.8
1908	50 918	57 960	7 042	12.1
1909	58 688	70 140	11 452	16.3
1910	65 048	82 795	17 747	21.4
1911	53 655	82 140	28 485	34.7

Source: Bamford 1913:192

Productivity (Figures 2 and 3)

To test the productivity of the fishery the data available continuously over many years for Thursday Island are (1) the total production of mother-of-pearl in tons (including trochus shell); (2) the number of men signed on before the shipping master, i.e. divers, swimming divers, and crew, gathering pearl-shell, bêche-de-mer and trochus; and (3) the number of pump-boats licensed, i.e. those vessels which were engaged in dress-diving for pearl-shell.

Neither the number of men engaged in the whole fishery nor the number of pump-boats give an accurate indication of the relationship between effort and yield in fishing for mother-of-pearl. Swimming-diving boats also produced mother-of-pearl, and both kinds of boats also collected bêche-de-mer. It is therefore impossible to judge which of the two sets of data is a more reliable indicator of the intensity of the mother-of-pearl fishing effort. Both indicators need to be read in conjunction to shed light on the relationship between fishing effort and resource stocks, so that the number of men engaged and the number of pump-boats together serve as an indication of mother-of-pearl fishing intensity. Combined with the total annual yields of mother-of-pearl, an average annual mother-of-pearl yield 'per man engaged' and 'per pump-boat' is arrived at. The average annual yields portray relative productivity, that is, output in relation to fishing effort, or catch per unit effort.

A graphical representation of these data from 1890 to 1940 allows a statement to be made about the relative impact of different types of crises. Figure 2 uses the total number of men engaged as an indicator of productivity; Figure 3 uses the number of pump-boats. It is useful to consider these

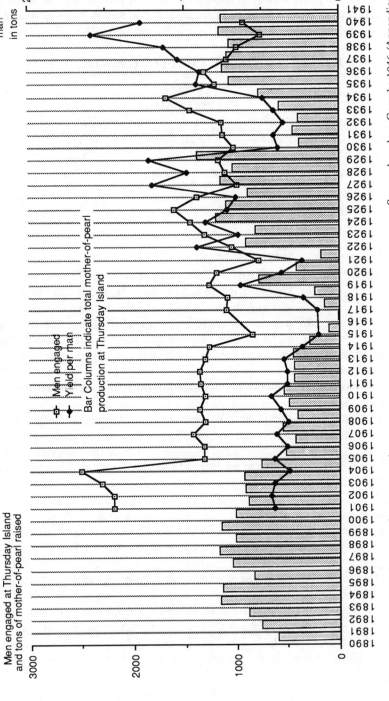

Figure 2 Productivity in terms of men engaged

Source: based on Coombs 1946 (Apperdices)

data from year to year since increasing catch encouraged an increase in the number of employees and boats, and at the same time led to over-use, often resulting in a decreasing catch. The following analysis is a combined reading of five factors: the number of men engaged, the number of pump-boats licensed, the total annual harvests of mother-of-pearl shell, average yield per man, and average yield per boat.

Figure 3 clearly indicates that the first resource crisis began in 1898, when a large increase in boats coincided with a declining yield. Until 1904 the number of boats increased, while mother-of-pearl yield fell off. This is confirmed by Figure 2. From 1902 to 1903, an increase in men did not lead to a corresponding increase in yield, and when the number of men was further raised in 1904 and 1905, the total yield declined.

Thereafter both figures show that the number of boats and men was reduced sharply (when the fleets left for Aru), after which the fishery attained a balance, at a lowered level of fishing effort, and far below its former output, from 1906 to 1913. (The 1905 figures cannot serve to arrive at a catch per unit effort, because a large number of boats departed during the year, and the number of men and boats is taken according to the beginning of the season, whereas the total mother-of-pearl production is arrived at at the end of the season.)

Figure 3 also shows that from 1893 to 1914 the decline in yield per boat is inversely related to the number of boats employed. From 1906 to 1914 the tendency was for the number of boats to decrease and the average yield to increase somewhat, without returning to pre-1900 levels. The number of men engaged and the average yield per man during this period were fairly steady. The link between fishing intensity and resource stocks appears more directly in periods of resource exhaustion (1890–1914) than during stock recovery (1922–29, 1931–39).

A decline in yield in 1913–14 is not matched in magnitude by the slight decline in the number of men, and is accompanied by an increase in the number of boats. The decline in relative productivity, both per man and per boat, signals a resource crisis.

These trends indicate that market conditions (World War I) were not the sole factor in operation in the 1915 crisis. In 1914–15 the industry reacted with a decline in the number of boats and men. (Figures for 1916 are not included in the curves because mother-of-pearl production levels fell to almost zero–6 tons.)

After World War I, total production gradually recovered and exceeded prewar levels with a peak in 1919, but quickly fell back, to below prewar levels, in 1920–21. In 1920 the number of boats increased, while the number of men decreased. This suggests that the industry responded to the excellent 1919 harvest by turning to mother-of-pearl more intensively, but the total output nevertheless decreased. The years 1919 and 1922 were

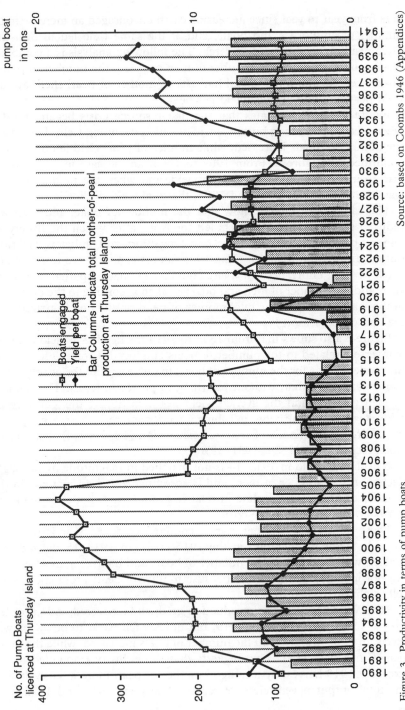

Figure 3   Productivity in terms of pump boats

periods of high output and peak productivity but each peak was immediately followed by a decline in productivity.

Thereafter, the fishery was on an erratic upward trend, during which the the number of men and boats bore almost no relationship to the total production. For example, it is difficult to explain the high mother-of-pearl output of 1924, when a similar increase in the number of men and boats in the previous year had resulted in a reduced tonnage. Again, in 1927 a considerable decline in the number of men and boats coincided with an equally considerable rise in production. These discrepancies may be due to shifts between mother-of-pearl fishing and trochus and bêche-de-mer collection, or natural conditions (such as weather or a particularly successful year-class of shell), neither of which can be reconstructed. In 1929 the total mother-of-pearl production reached an all-time high, while the number of men and boats employed had stabilised at a low plateau. The peak in average yield on both indicators suggests that the high production of that year was due to favourable natural conditions and not to increased fishing intensity.

The declining number of men and boats after this bumper crop suggests that market forces were at least partly responsible for the steep decline in production which followed (1930). (In fact, production was limited by voluntary agreement—see Chapter 6 on federal intervention) However, average yield also declined steeply. The dramatic decline in average yield per boat as well as per man suggests that, in addition, mother-of-pearl was scarce. It had probably been fished out in the previous year's harvest.

From 1935 to 1940 a high level of production is accompanied by a steady decrease in the number of men engaged, and a very slight decrease in the number of pump boats. This may be taken as an indication that mother-of-pearl was abundant. The steep rise in average yield on both indicators from 1932 to 1939 also suggests that it was now harvested at a sustainable level. The number of boats had returned to pre-1890 levels, and the number of men was far below any previously recorded level, save during World War I. (This reading is confirmed by the fact that the industry was in the midst of a deep marketing crisis—see Chapter 6.)

The inverse relationship between fishing intensity and relative productivity is visually represented in Figure 2. In the first phase, to 1904, the gap between effort and success widens, and from 1932 to 1940 there is again a clear inverse trend, this time in the opposite direction—as fishing intensity decreases, the yield per boat improves.

A comparison of the different indicators suggests that the industry suffered three resource crises in the period to 1940, the first occurring in 1898–1905, the second in 1913–14, and the third in 1930–32.

Glossary

agreements	employment contract entered on to ship's articles before the shipping master (Clerk of Court).
apparatus boats	see **pump boats**
bends	divers' bends, manifested as pulmonary barotrauma or air embolism, is caused by the formation of nitrogen bubbles in the blood vessels under pressure changes. Popularly referred to as 'divers' bends' because sufferers double up with pain. Bends are more likely to occur when a diver is exhausted. Bends usually occurs from surfacing too quickly, without **staging**.
bêche-de-mer	*holothurians*, also referred to as trepang, or sea-cucumber. The Creole term biche-la-mar is derived from the Portuguese *bicho do mar*, literally beast of the sea. A sea-slug which was exported to China where it is used as a soup ingredient in traditional Chinese *haute cuisine*. Valued for its aphrodisiac qualities.
black-lip	*Pinctada margaritifera*, an inferior pearl-shell of small size (15–18 cm, weighing 0.45 to 0.79 kg) named after its black edge to distinguish it from gold-lip or silver-lip **pearl-shell**.
blister pearls	semicircular half-pearls attached to the inside

shell, often used to mount on jewellery where a full pearl is not required, e.g. on pendants.

chicken shell   immature pearl-shell, declared as undersized shell under protective legislation

company boats   boats acquired by Torres Strait Islanders under the lugger scheme operated by the Papuan Industries Limited and the Queensland Government's Department of Native Affairs.

crew   the members of a boat crew who performed the tasks classed as unskilled (deckhands, pumphands, cooks, shell-cleaners, swimming-divers, **tenders**) and who were paid wages, as distinct from divers and first tenders who were engaged on a **lay** basis.

dress-diving   diving with the use of breathing equipment, i.e. deep-water diving, as distinct from **swimming-diving**. Pearl-shell divers used hard-helmet equipment to which air was supplied either by a hand-pump or using diesel motors, even when hookah equipment and air tanks became available, because of the length of time spent under water (**staging** sometimes took an hour). The first diving apparatus was supplied by the German firm Siebe & Gorman and consisted of a copper helmet weighing 50 kg and an inflatable suit. An 11 kg lead corselet and 12 kg lead shoes prevented the diver from being buoyant. Walking across the seabed in this outfit was strenuous work, made more difficult by the impossibility of bending over to pick up shells, which would have allowed water to enter the helmet.

dummying   fictitious or nominal ownership to circumvent legal ownership restrictions. Boat-dummying occurred when Japanese were barred from renting or owning boats by legislation introduced in 1898.

floating stations   large fleets with a mother schooner to which the shell was delivered and from which supplies were obtained, so that the fleet could stay at sea for an entire season without coming into port. Floating stations operated in the Queensland pearl-shell fishery from 1890 to 1905.

government teacher
schoolteachers stationed on Torres Strait islands, employed by the Department of Native Affairs, with responsibilities similar to those of reserve superintendents on the mainland.

half-dress
an adaptation of the full diving suit where the sleeves and pants are cut off, invented by Japanese divers to ease the water pressure on the limbs and allow greater mobility on the ocean floor. A further innovation was helmet-and-corselet diving, where only the weights and the helmet of the diving suit were used. This increased the risk of diving accidents, because it became possible to throw off the helmet if the air pipes were fouled. Many panic-stricken inexperienced divers died as a result of throwing off the helmets and surfacing too quickly.

in charge
a special category of licence issued to non-diving skippers, mostly the captains of bêche-de-mer boats.

lay
an incentive system of remuneration whereby the diver was paid according to catch on a sliding scale.

lugger
a general term referring to vessels used in the pearl-shell industry. Specifically, luggers are sailing boats with two masts, lug-rigged with mainsail (or mizzen), foresail and jib, and renowned for their ease of handling. Typically, luggers were from 10 to 12 tons, and 9–10 metres long, i.e. quite small. The characteristic design at Thursday Island was distinguished from the Broome model by its deeper draft and long counter-stern.

mamoose
Torres Strait Islander 'headmen' appointed and regarded as local rulers by the colonial administration. The term derives from the name

Mamus used in Torres Strait and the Cape York Peninsula.

mother-of-pearl the nacreous internal lining of **pearl-shell**, **trochus** shell, greensnail, or sweet water mussels. In this book mother-of-pearl is used to denote the combination of trochus and pearl-shell.

pearl-shell *Pinctada maxima*, a bivalve growing in depths below 13 metres. Its rate of growth depends on regional conditions, but reproductive maturity is reached in about three years, at which time the shell spans 12–15 centimetres. Also referred to as gold-lip or silver-lip. The average pearl-shells harvested were about 1 kg each, but in the early years of the industry, shells weighing from 3 to 4 kg were found. If impurities enter a pearl-shell they are enclosed by nacreous lining and sometimes form a pearl. A smaller type of pearl-shell, *Pinctada margaritifera* or black-lip, is found in shallower waters. It was not extensively collected because the nacre is inferior.

pearl-shell industry this term is used to refer to the commercial collection of pearl-shell, trochus shell and bêche-de-mer, which were all administered under a single legislation. The boats used, the owners, and the staff overlapped to a great degree. The term does not refer to pearling activities which are centred on the artificial cultivation of pearls.

pearl-sheller usually a white owner of several pearling boats. The term master pearler appropriately denoted the social standing and political influence of pearl-shellers at Thursday Island, but this term now has a specific meaning since the introduction of master pearler's licences in 1976.

pump boats boats which were rigged for dress-diving, rather than **swimming-diving**. Also referred to as apparatus boats.

shore stations fleets operated from Thursday Island, not serviced by a mother schooner like floating stations. Typically shore-station fleets were much smaller and less capitalised than floating stations.

sign on   to be signed on to a ship's articles before the shipping master; to be employed on a boat.

skipper   the captain in charge of the boat and crew. On pearl-shelling boats the captains were normally the head diver (also referred to as stern diver, or first diver).

slop chest   a figurative term referring to the supply of merchandise to boat employees while at sea, the cost of which was subtracted from wages. Normally the items supplied through the employer's 'slop chest' carried a high surcharge over retail prices. Typical commodities were tobacco, alcohol, calico and clothing items.

staging   a diver's calculated ascent or descent, resting at different depths prescribed by staging tables to allow the body to adjust to changing water pressures. The depth dived to, the time spent there, and the degree of fatigue (1st, 2nd or 3rd dive) are the variables determining the stages of ascent. Most divers used a rule of thumb for staging rather than the navy's precise staging tables.

swimming-diving   also referred to as naked diving. Shallow-water diving (5–6 fathoms or 9–11 m) with goggles, usually from dinghies. The term diver does not include swimming-divers but refers only to dress-divers. The task was classed as unskilled and carried no particular prestige or responsibility. Trochus boats carried or towed several rowing dinghies to the reefs from where groups of swimming-divers dispersed with the dinghies. At low tide they collected trochus or bêche-de-mer by reef-wading, and picked up the bundles of shell with the dinghies as the tide came in.

tender   the person assisting and dressing the diver. The tender held the lifeline while the diver was down, receiving signals from the diver. By means of pulls and shakes on the line, the diver could direct the drift of the boat, call for shell baskets, ask to be pulled up, regulate the air supply, and signal danger. If there was only one diver on a boat, the tender was in charge of the boat while the diver was submerged.

trepang   see **bêche-de-mer**

trochus   *Trochus niloticus*, a conical shell which bears no pearls, and inhabits the shallow areas of the outer edges of reefs in depths of up to 8 metres, accessible by swimming-diving. This shell was first commercially gathered in Queensland in 1912 and came to replace pearl-shell for the cheaper type of buttons used on shirts. It occurs all along the Great Barrier Reef as far south as Mackay.

try-diver   apprentice diver, a crew member who is being trained in diving.

verandah pearlers   owners of one or more pearl-shelling boats who take no active interest in the business and use boat-ownership merely as an investment. Verandah pearlers were accused of contravening the law by boat-**dummying**.

wages boats   boats owned by pearl-shellers, as distinct from **company boats**.

Notes

Abbreviations

AA	Australian Archives
ACA	Australia. Commonwealth Acts
AGPS	Australian Government Publishing Service
BP	Burns Philp & Co.
CPD	*Commonwealth Parliamentary Debates*
CPP	*Commonwealth Parliamentary Papers*
CSIRO	Commonwealth Scientific and Research Organisation
Col. Sec.	Colonial Secretary
DAIA	Department of Aboriginal and Islander Affairs, Qld (1965–71), Department of Aboriginal and Islander Advancement, Qld (1971–84)
DCS	Department of Community Services, Qld (1984–89)
DNA	Department of Native Affairs, Qld (1922–65)
DPI	Department of Primary Industries, Qld
GBRMPA	Great Barrier Reef Marine Park Authority
IIB	Island Industries Board
LMS	London Missionary Society
PIL	Papuan Industries Limited
PZJA	Torres Strait Protected Zone Joint Authority
QCFO	Queensland Commercial Fishermen's Organization
QFMA	Queensland Fish Management Authority
QFS	Queensland Fisheries Service (within DPI)
QGG	*Queensland Government Gazette*
QPD	*Queensland Parliamentary Debates*
QPP	*Queensland Parliamentary Papers* (from 1901)
QSA	Queensland State Archives
QVP	*Queensland Votes and Proceedings* (to 1900)
TI	Thursday Island

Introduction

[1] Passmore 1974; Bennett 1976; Commoner 1963, 1971; Ehrlich 1968; Cotgrove 1982.
[2] Sabel and Zeitlin 1985:133.

[3] Piore and Sabel 1984:ch. 2.
[4] In case studies dealing with Italy, Japan, Britain and the United States, the state emerges as a central actor (Sabel and Zeitlin 1985).
[5] Weiss 1988:211.
[6] Weiss (1988:162, 211) examines the persistence, and resurgence, of small business in Italy. The Italian small business manufacturing sector employs at least 53 per cent of the national manufacturing workforce, or some 15 per cent of the total national workforce (ibid.:14, 15). See also Mann 1984; Skocpol 1985.
[7] These three structural weaknesses have already been identified by Bach (1956).
[8] Sabel and Zeitlin 1985:161.
[9] See O'Farrell 1979:4–8; Thompson 1978.
[10] Thorpe 1980; Murphy 1976.
[11] J. P. S. Bach, pers. comm., May 1991.

1   A Colonial Birthmark?

[1] The creolised term 'all kind of nation' is often used among indigenous people when referring to the workforce in the pearl-shell industry. See also Chase 1981.
[2] Census of 1890, the first year for which detailed figures are available. Evans 1972: Appendix.
[3] Dalrymple, *QVP* 1875, vol. 2:1412.
[4] *Sydney Gazette*, 3.8.1830.
[5] Shineberg 1967.
[6] Bolton 1981:53.
[7] Gilson 1970:184.
[8] See Macknight 1976:97, Crawford 1969:90; Mulvaney 1966:449–57.
[9] See McInnes 1984:7–9; MacGillivray 1853:308 footnote; Mullins 1987; McInnes 1978–79:47–73; Wilson 1835:95.
[10] Shineberg 1967:194.
[11] Jardine, 1.1.1872, Somerset Letterbook CPS 13/C G1 QSA.
[12] See Shineberg 1967:107.
[13] The outpost was moved to Somerset on Cape York peninsula in March 1863 and its Government Resident, Frank Jardine, concentrated on 'pacifying' mainland Aborigines to establish a cattle station on the tip of the Cape, rather than making an effort towards regulating the shipping traffic. In 1867 the imperial government withdrew from the joint venture, and the Queensland government staffed the outpost with colonial police to replace the imperial marines. In 1876–77, under a new Government Resident (Henry Chester, a former officer of the East India Company), the outpost was moved closer to the shipping lanes, to Thursday Island/Waiben, and became known as Port Kennedy.
[14] See Haddon 1935:190; Jack 1921:340. According to Mullins, Edwards began trepanging in the north-westerly season of 1863–64 at Darnley, in association with Robert Towns.
[15] Singe 1979:33.
[16] Chester to Col. Sec., 20.10.1870, 3425/70 Col/A 151 QSA.
[17] The ornaments were fist described by J. Dumont d'Urville in 1840, and shortly afterwards by O. W. Brierly and John McGillivray of the *Rattlesnake*. Until 1948 Brierly had been a whaler at Boyd's station in Twofold Bay, near Bega in New South Wales. See Pearson 1980; McGillivray 1852; Moore 1979.
[18] See Shineberg 1967; Bolton 1981.
[19] Bain (1982:42) describes him as 'an elderly sea captain who had gathered m.o.p. shell in the South Seas fifty years earlier'.
[20] Shineberg 1967:132.
[21] Jardine to Col. Sec., 1.11.1870. *Bluebell* and *Fanny* had been used by Paddon for

sandalwooding between 1855 and 1860, the *Kate Kearney* and *Melanie* by Towns between 1860 and 1865 (Shineberg 1967:245).

²² See Shineberg 1967:114.

[22] See Shineberg 1967:114.

[23] Johan Cesar Godeffroy und Sohn, Hamburg, had become a household name in the Pacific area (Bain 1983:51, 66). The firm established an ethnographic museum in Hamburg.

[24] Chapman, letter 9.9.1873, in Prideaux 1988:123.

[25] McKinlay and Hardman (5), Hunter Brothers of Brisbane (3), J. Cussen (2), J. Stevens (5), F. Caddell (*sic*) (2). Chester, *QVP* 1877, vol. 3:1124.

[26] Cussen (3), Stevens (4), Cadell (6), Raff (2). Chester, *QVP* 1879, vol. 2:948.

[27] Cousens (*sic*) (4), Stevens (4), Cadell (2), Raff (2) (Hoghton 1880:1163–6).

[28] Perry 1923:349–50; see also Buckley and Klugman 1981:53.

[29] Mullins 1987.

[30] Pennefather 1880.

[31] Chester 1879:948. In 1879 there were three bêche-de-mer stations on Murray and one on Darnley Island, and one in the Great Barrier Reef, employing 4 Europeans, 17 Polynesians, 87 Aborigines and 1 Malay. Until 1879, these islands were outside the territorial limits of Queensland.

[32] Jardine, 1.1.1872, Somerset Letterbook, QSA.

[33] Interview with Jack Kennell (64), Brisbane 8.10.1986.

[34] Normally the introduction of dress-diving in Torres Strait is dated at 1874, but a letter by Chester in 1871 letter already makes reference to diving apparatus. Chester to Col. Sec., 10.10.1871 Col/A 2499/71 QSA.

[35] Evidence by Sinclair, in Mackay 1908:98.

[36] John Bleakley 1961:37.

[37] To give an indication of the mixture of races on Thursday Island, the Government Resident's annual report of 1887 referred to representatives from 25 nationalities having passed through the gaol during the year (Milman 1888).

[38] Evans 1972:114.

[39] H. W. Mountain to P. G. Black, 23.3. 1898, in Buckley and Klugman 1981:121.

[40] Hamilton 1897:xxxvii.

[41] This incident is extensively documented in Prideaux 1988:ch. 22. Reference to Jardine's pearl-shelling activities are also in Aplin 1875 and de Hoghton 1880.

[42] John Foley 1980:48–9. Island stations continued to operate on Prince of Wales Island, Hammond, Goode, Friday and Waiweer Island.

[43] Douglas, in Hamilton 1897:1318.

[44] See Hartwig 1978.

[45] Reynolds 1981; Reece 1987; Beckett 1988; Attwood 1989; Loos 1982.

[46] The letters patent authorising Queensland's annexation of these islands made reference only to the islands themselves, not to the seas in between them and the mainland. The territorial extension of Queensland's jurisdiction therefore does not constitute a proper border. The letters patent were issued on 30.5.1872 and published in *QVP* 1873.

[47] Moresby 1876:14.

[48] Chester 1877:1123. See also Mullins 1987.

[49] Hamilton 1897:1309. 'Binghis' refers to mainland Aborigines. Like most pernicious appellations, the word has quite a respectable etymology. It derives from an address for elder brother, denoting respect (like *bung* or *abang* in Indonesian): *bingay* in the Awabakal language (Sydney to Newcastle area) or *bindhi* in the Dharuk language (Port Jackson).

[50] Petition by Broomfield, Parbury, Lamb and Knox, *QVP* 1879, vol. 2:951. The Bill was passed in 1881.

[51] Chester to Col. Sec., 20.10.1870 Col/A151 QSA; S. McFarlane, in Haddon 1935:186.

[52] Parry-Okeden 1897:13.
[53] Jukes 1874, vol. 1:295–7.
[54] *QGG* 1926.
[55] Costin, in Mackay 1908:60.
[56] Evidence by Bleakley, in Mackay 1908:37.
[57] Evidence by Luff, in Mackay 1908:80.
[58] Meston 1896; Parry-Okeden 1897. Concerning the relative importance of Meston and Parry-Okeden in the drafting of the legislation, see Ganter and Kidd 1993.
[59] Hamilton 1897:1309.
[60] Walter Roth, Annual Report of the Chief Protector of Aborigines, *QPP* 1905.
[61] Aborigines Preservation and Protection Act, and Torres Strait Islanders Act. From 1965 they were administered under a single legislation (Aborigines and Torres Strait Islanders Affairs Act), but from 1971 to 1989 Torres Strait Islanders and Aborigines were again administered under separate legislation.
[62] Hanlon (Health and Home Affairs), *QPD* 174, 1939:452–5, in Johnston 1987:138–43.
[63] Roth 1902; Mackay 1908:269; Bleakley 1916. Presumably the latter figure refers to Torres Strait Islanders as well as mainland Aborigines, but does not include those signed on at Cooktown.
[64] Meston 1896. See also Chris Anderson 1984.
[65] Evidence by Hey in Mackay 1908:217. Fahey to Collector of Customs, 2.3.1882, in Haviland 1980.
[66] Annual Reports of the Department of Harbours and Marine, *QVP* 1884.
[67] Col/A 394 letter 4976/1884, QSA, in Haviland 1980:135.
[68] See Loos 1982:ch. 5.
[69] This was a short-lived effort by Revd F. C. Jagg of the Society for the Propagation of the Gospel in London and William Kennett, a lay schoolteacher, at the invitation of Governor Bowen. The missionaries became a political playball between competing coastal and island communties. The mission was aborted when the naval post, staffed by marines, was abandoned in 1867. The marines were replaced by constables, and Somerset became a civilian rather than a military post (see note 13). See Moore 1979:237ff.; Bayton 1969.
[70] In 1897 there were six mission stations in Queensland funded partly by the government (four of them on Cape York), and fifteen food-distributing stations; 151 stations distributed government blankets.
[71] Roth, Annual Report, 1902.
[72] Evidence by Hey, in Mackay 1908:218.
[73] Roth, Annual Report, 1904.
[74] Aborigines nevertheless engaged in pearl-shelling in order to obtain tobacco, which was not permitted on the reserve. Mapoon was apparently the only instance where the addictive qualities of tobacco were taken seriously, although reference to tobacco addiction was sometimes made. Meston's 1896 report mentioned that 'Introduced among wild tribes it is a potent pacificator [sic] and a valuable social agent', and Chester considered in 1877 that once introduced to tobacco, the natives would not be able to resist the temptation to satisfy their wants. Chester to Col. Sec., 10.10.1871, Col/A 2499/71, QSA.
[75] James Clark had described how he employed old Aboriginal women in Western Australia to collect *Cassidula angulifera*, a pearl-bearing mussel, in return for rations. In four weeks they could collect 10s worth of seed pearls, and keep the mussels as food supplement. Roth, Annual Report, *QVP* 1900.
[76] Ibid.
[77] Roth to Home Department, 4.10.1899, in Loos 1982:142.
[78] Loos 1982:139; Saville-Kent 1890; Douglas 1894, in Loos 1982:ch. 5.
[79] Interview with Dicky Nandy (58), Wujal-Wujal 20.11.1986.

80 *Sydney Daily Herald*, 20.6.1933, in Anderson 1984.
81 The major areas of recruitment on the east coast were (from north to south) Cape Grenville, Lloyd Bay and Night Island at Cape Direction (Iron Range, later Lockhart River mission), Princess Charlotte Bay (including Flinders Island, Cape Melville, Barrow Point and Starcke River), and Cape Tribulation. (See Map 2.)
82 Richard Howard, Annual Report of the Chief Protector of Aborigines, *QPP* 1907, vol. 2.
83 In 1909 sandalwooding was a 'new field of engagement' at Cape York Peninsula, employing 43 natives. Weipa mission started sandalwooding because commercial sandalwooders were encroaching on the reserve. In the following year, Coen Aborigines were engaged in sandalwooding. In 1915 sandalwooding declined and most Europeans returned to the lower Gulf district. Howard and Bleakley, Annual Reports, *QPP* 1910–16.
84 Howard, Annual Report, *QPP* 1912.
85 Ibid. 1913.
86 Bleakley, Annual Report, *QPP* 1917.
87 It was first established at Orchid Point where the recruiting camps were, but moved to more fertile lands at Bane Hill. Within a year its population was 180 and the mission owned a sailing vessel.
88 Howard, Annual Report, *QPP* 1908.
89 Bleakley, Annual Report, *QPP* 1935.
90 Parry-Okeden 1897.
91 Saville-Kent 1892:228.
92 Alick Naiga, in Chase 1981:13. Chase dates this meeting in the 1890s.
93 See Chase 1981; Anderson 1984.
94 Interview with Monty Prior, Palm Island, 1986.
95 Loos, paraphrasing Saville-Kent (1890) 1982:147.
96 *Torres Strait Pilot*, 13.10.1894, in Loos 1982:148.
97 Interview with Dicky Nandy.
98 Lowah 1988.
99 Interview with Jimmie Doctor (61), Lockhart River 4.1.1987. This incident must have taken place around 1940.
100 Interview with Sandy Yiela, Lockhart River 3.1.1987.
101 Interview with Claude Maza (64), Innisfail 28.11.1986.
102 Evidence by Thomson, in Mackay 1908:252.
103 Evidence by Costin, in Mackay 1908:63.
104 Interview with Sandy Yiela, Lockhart River 3.1.1987.
105 Interview with Michael Sandy (71), Lockhart River 4.1.1987.
106 Interview with Fred Deeral, Hopevale 19.11.1986. Interestingly, Hopevale was funded partly by the Red School in Bavaria (Haviland 1980).
107 Interview with Bob Flinders (72), Hopevale 19.11.1986. Flinders is referring to the wartime evacuation of Hopevale mission to Woorabinda reserve in Central Queensland. The Queensland government's Department of Aboriginal and Islander Affairs was so called from 1965 to 1984.
108 Evidence by Hey, in Mackay 1908:220.
109 Evidence by Evanson, in Mackay 1908:236.
110 Evidence by Wells, in Mackay 1908:242; Flamsteed, in Mackay 1908:239; Graham, in Bamford 1913:110.
111 Roth, Annual Report, *QPP* 1902.
112 Interview with Takao Koonosuke (68), Ajiro (Ehime, Japan) 25.10.1987.
113 Interview with Robert and Lorraine Baird, Wujal-Wujal 2.1.1986.
114 Chase 1981:11.
115 Ibid.:13.
116 Ann Curthoys 1973.

[117] Loos 1976:733–4; and 'The Pragmatic Racism of the Frontier', in Evans, Saunders and Cronin 1988 (1975).

[118] Mercer 1978:303–26.

[119] Andrew Markus explains racism as the result of types of contact experiences and distinguishes between two ideal types of race relations (or contact experience). The 'competitive type' is where the subordinate group competes in a free labour market and overlaps in class status with the dominant group. It typically engenders racial hatred, which results in various forms of physical segregation. (Postwar European immigration to Australia might serve as an illustration of this type of race relations.) The 'dominant type' of race relations typically occurs in plantation farming economies where the dominant group is numerically weak but has a monopoly of power, and the subordinate group is restricted to manual labour by the substitution of a free labour market with slavery, indenture or other forms of compulsion, so that role and status are defined along racial lines. This division is ideologically sanctioned and supported by elaborate codes of behaviour. The institutionalisation of racial difference permits close contact between the two groups (Markus 1979:242ff.). The debate surrounding the employment of Japanese divers, presented in Chapters 3 and 4, was in effect the struggle to confine Japanese participation to the second type of race relations, to prevent Japanese from seriously competing with whites, and to assert white dominance.

2 The Eclipse of an Alternative Production Strategy

[1] Wolpe 1975. See also Blauner 1969; Rowley 1971. Other works in this tradition are Hartwig 1978; Beckett 1977. Beckett has expressed misgivings about the concept of 'internal colonialism' in his more recent book *Past and Present*, where he prefers to use the term 'welfare colonialism' to describe an administration which grants special benefits for indigenous populations who are depressed and disenfranchised, as an alternative to full citizenship. This term refers to the state's attempts to deal with the political pressures of a growing indigenous population since the 1960s. It is not so useful in the framework of this study, which takes its narrative only to the 1960s.

[2] Beckett 1987:39.

[3] E.g. Shnukal 1985; Haddon 1935.

[4] This term, referring to an autocracy of religious leaders, is borrowed from Sharp 1980.

[5] Interviews with George Kaddy (49), Mackay 13.8.1986 and Jack Kennell (64), Brisbane 8.10.1986.

[6] Beckett 1987:111.

[7] Evidence by Bruce, in Mackay 1908:210.

[8] Beckett 1987:151; Haddon 1904:265.

[9] Sharp 1980.

[10] In 1908 no Torres Strait Islanders were employed on pump boats, and 181 on swimming-diving boats; thus all Torres Strait Islanders on wages boats were swimming-divers. Sixteen were in charge of wages boats for swimming-diving, whereas in the previous year that number had been 40. Evidence by Costin, in Mackay 1908:60.

[11] Freshwater 1972.

[12] Beckett 1987:50.

[13] Walker to Thompson, 22.6.1898, M98 National Library, in Austin 1972:47.

[14] Austin 1972:49.

[15] Walker to Papuan District Committee of LMS, 24.2.1902, M99 National Library, in ibid.:48.

[16] W. G. Lawes, of the LMS Papuan District Committee, to Thompson, 13.2.1904, M100 National Library, in ibid.:49.

[17] Ibid.:50.

[18] PIL, London, 1912 in ibid.; External Affairs memo A1 05/5434 AA.

[19] *Torres Strait Pilot*, 15.3.1907, in External Affairs file A1 05/5434 AA.

20 Austin 1972:56.
21 *Government Gazette*, 23.12.1905.
22 R. Raven Hart, *The Happy Isles*, Melbourne 1949:61, in Austin 1972:57.
23 Roth, Annual Report, *QPP* 1906.
24 *Evening News*, 17.5.1904.
25 Sir Hubert Murray, in Austin 1972.
26 Evidence by Coco, in Mackay 1908:214.
27 How directly this is related to the boat which Mabuiag purchased with Walker's assistance is unclear. The department received complaints from Mabuiag and Saibai Islanders about the conduct of James Doyle, JP, at Mabuiag Island in 1903. It was later reported that he had policemen in his pay and imprisoned natives without warrants or authority. His recruiting permit was withdrawn in 1904, although a permit to recruit Torres Strait Islanders was not required at that time. Roth and Howard, Annual Reports of the Chief Protector of Aborigines, *QPP* 1904, 1905, 1906.
28 Howard, Annual Reports, *QPP* 1905.
29 Interview with Imasu Waigana (68), Saibai 15.1.1987.
30 Roth, Annual Report, *QPP* 1906.
31 Evidence by Cairns, in Mackay 1908:205.
32 Evidence by Mosby from Yorke Island, in ibid.:216.
33 Guilletmot, teacher at Darnley, in Howard, Annual Report, *QPP* 1911:20.
34 Evidence by Bruce, in Mackay 1908:20.
35 Minniss, in Howard, Annual Report, *QPP* 1911.
36 Costin, in ibid., 1908.
37 Ibid., 1913.
38 Ibid., 1908.
39 Evidence by Walker, in Mackay 1908.
40 Evidence by Costin, in ibid.:60.
41 Howard, Annual Report, *QPP* 1908.
42 Evidence by Costin, in Mackay 1908:60.
43 Evidence by Cairns, in ibid.:204.
44 Milman, in Howard, Annual Report, *QPP* 1908, 1909.
45 Ibid., 1909.
46 Evidence by Walker, in Mackay 1908:208.
47 Evidence by Costin, in ibid.: 61.
48 Ibid.:612.
49 Evidence by Bruce, in ibid.:210.
50 Reg Hockings to Sub-Collector of Customs, 5.4.1927, CRS A1 27/21645 AA.
51 Interview with Jack Kennell (64), Brisbane 8.10.1986.
52 Minniss, in Howard, Annual Report, *QPP* 1912.
53 Bruce, in ibid., 1913.
54 Ibid., 1912.
55 Handley, in Bleakley, Annual Report, *QPP* 1917.
56 Ibid.
57 Lee Bryce, in ibid., 1914. Mabuiag had had a bad experience with the insurance company, who refused to compensate for the loss of the *Mabuiag* because its hull was found after six months somewhere in Papua.
58 Lee Bryce, in Bleakley, Annual Report, *QPP* 1914.
59 Ibid.
60 Ibid.
61 Roth, Annual Report, *QPP* 1905.
62 O'Leary, Annual Report, *QPP* 1949.
63 Lee Bryce, in Bleakley, Annual Report, *QPP* 1915.
64 Interview with Jack Kennell (64), Brisbane 8.10.1986.
65 Foxton, in Bleakley, Annual Report, *QPP* 1919.

[66] O'Leary, in ibid., 1923.

[67] Buxton, in ibid., 1932.

[68] O'Leary, Annual Report, *QPP* 1952.

[69] Interview with Claude Maza (64), Innisfail 28.11.1986.

[70] Bleakley, Annual Report, *QPP* 1934.

[71] Interviews with Saulo Waia (70), Townsville 8.8.1986; Lui Bon, Thursday Island 12.1.1987; Erra Namok (69), Townsville 2.12.1986.

[72] Interview with Richard AhMat (65), Mackay 3.12.1986.

[73] Bleakley, Annual Report, *QPP* 1937.

[74] McLean, in ibid., 1936.

[75] Singe 1979:111.

[76] Sharp 1982:110.

[77] Interview in ibid.:116–17.

[78] Interview with Imasu Waigana (68), Saibai 15.1.1987.

[79] Interview with Mugai Elu (76), Bamaga 6.1.1987.

[80] Interview with Stephen Nona (64), Townsville 1.12.1986.

[81] Sharp 1982:122.

[82] At the request of military authorities, 200 coloured citizens of Thursday Island were moved to Cherbourg mission, 80 Hammond Islanders to Cooyar, the residents of St Paul's mission to Scarborough, and the Cape Bedford Aborigines to Woorabinda reserve.

[83] Interview with Imasu Waigana (68), Saibai 15.1.1987.

[84] O'Leary, Annual Report, *QPP* 1947.

[85] Four hundred and six families were receiving widow's pension or child endowment, 97 received old age and invalid pensions, and 73 Torres Strait Islanders received war pensions. The income from soldiers' wages and dependance allowance had been £180 000. O'Leary, Annual Report, *QPP* 1947.

[86] Interview with Bob Jacob (69), Bamaga 7.1.1987.

[87] O'Leary, Annual Report, *QPP* 1952.

[88] Ibid., 1958.

[89] Ibid., 1953.

[90] Ibid., 1952

[91] Interview with Bob Jacob (69), Bamaga 7.1.1987.

[92] O'Leary, Annual Report, *QPP* 1949.

[93] Ibid., 1950.

[94] Ibid., 1959.

[95] Interviews with Reg Dodd (81), Rockhampton, Palm Island, Brisbane, 1987.

3   A Matter of Convenience

[1] The most voluminous account is by Mary Albertus Bain (1982). J. P. S. Bach (1961) analyses the contribution which their participation made to the decline of the industry, and Lorraine Philipps (1980) examines their participation as an issue in the White Australia policy debate. In an authoritative and well-researched account David Sissons (1979) gives historical detail of the increase in numbers of Japanese, the areas from which they came, and the legislative framework surrounding their participation.

[2] A small-scale trade with China was maintained during the 200-year period of isolation, and the Dutch trading post at Nagasaki was also retained (Edgar 1962:310).

[3] Masuda Sanjiro to Masuda Mankichi, 19 March 1884, *Nihon Gaiko Bunsho* 1884:487, in Sissons 1979:10.

[4] Dives below 36 metres are more dangerous, and staging techniques to readjust the diver to pressure change are more crucial. Using the US navy tables for scuba diving, 1 per cent of divers get bends if diving to less than 36 metres, but 8 per cent of divers get bends if diving deeper than 36 metres. One former diver asserted that 'below 13

fathoms (23 metres) you're in the bends area'. Interview with Ken Corn (64), Cairns 24.11.1986.

[5] Sissons 1979:15. These figures apparently include floating population, i.e. crew engaged on floating stations and island stations who were not domiciled at Thursday Island. The statistics supplied by the Government Resident give a much less spectacular increase.

[6] In 1891 cannons were installed at Green Hill on Thursday Island to ward off an expected Russian invasion (Foley 1980:25).

[7] Quoted in Sissons 1979:15.

[8] Douglas to Col. Sec., 11.11.1893, quoted in Sissons 1979:15.

[9] Douglas 1898:427. This statement aptly illustrates the difference between 'dominant' and 'competitive' race relations referred to by Andrew Markus (see Chapter 1, note 119).

[10] Gaynor Evans writes that the manipulation of law by government officials was part of a syndrome of fear among the white minority which controlled power and wealth at Thursday Island. This view sits well with the 'competitive type' of race relations identified by Markus.

[11] 63 Victoria 3. Similar legislation had been passed in Western Australia in 1886 which prevented indentured Chinese from gaining a financial interest in boats (Bach 1961:110).

[12] Quoted in Sissons 1979:15.

[13] Interview with Wabuka Kiyomi (67), Susami 10.10.1987.

[14] Interview with Horimoto Shinichi (75), Wakayama 20.10.87.

[15] Five such delegates toured America in 1860, described in Miyoshi 1979 and Sayle 1985, and at least one was in Australia in 1893. Sissons (1979) refers extensively to the reports of K. Watanabe, 1894.

[16] Because the type of pearl found in Torres Strait was inferior to that of Western Australian waters—mostly baroque (irregularly shaped)—it had become the custom for the head divers to claim the pearls. The annual value of pearls found in the Torres Strait fishery was estimated at between £4000 and £5000, or enough to pay for all working expenses (the estimate given in 1897 was £20 000 to £25 000) (Hamilton 1897:xxxvii).

[17] Evidence by Hockings, in Mackay 1908:169.

[18] Evidence by Clark, in ibid.:30.

[19] One witness thought that there had been nearly 100 white divers; one had known 40 to 50 but never more than 20 to 25 in any one year. John Bleakley (Clerk for the Chief Protector of Aborigines) thought there had been 34 at one time, but Andrew Sinclair, a former diver, said there had been 10 at most at any one time. According to the reports of the Government Resident at Thursday Island, 13 was the highest number of white divers licensed between 1896 and 1914. However, some were also working out of Cooktown. Evidence in Mackay 1908.

[20] Evidence by Fowles, Secretary of the Queensland Treasury, in Bamford 1913:164; and *West Australian*, 15.9.1913, in Sissons 1979:17.

[21] Edgar 1962:318.

[22] Evidence by Craig, secretary of the Australian Fisheries Association and bêche-de-mer fisher, in Bamford 1913:2. AWU refers to Australian Workers' Union.

[23] Evidence by Hockings, in Bamford 1913:100.

[24] Evidence by Craig, in ibid.:2.

[25] The death rate among divers was 10 per cent in 1910, over 11 per cent in 1911, and 10 per cent in 1913. Moreover, casualties among crew ran high from malaria, dysentery, and beriberi. From 1906 to 1911, 50 divers out of 1031 died from beriberi and 72 in diving accidents. Evidence by Allen, pearl-shell inspector, in Bamford 1913:44; and evidence by Hockings, in ibid.:97–8.

[26] Mackay, supplementary report, unpublished, referred to in evidence by Mackay in ibid.:177.
[27] Bamford, Final Report 1916.
[28] Lockyer 1904, in Bamford 1913:185.
[29] Bach 1956:272.
[30] Philipps 1980:67.
[31] Interview with Tatsuno Matuso (65), Honai 23.10.1987.
[32] Interview with Tada Tomiharu (72), Wakayama, 15.10.87. Japanese refer to both their employers and captains as *oyakata*.
[33] Interview with Seike Ukio (67), Arashi 24.10.1987.
[34] Interview with Takao Koonosuke (68), Ajiro 25.10.1987.
[35] This is the convincing impression gained from interviews with former Japanese divers and crew.
[36] Annual Report of the Department of Harbours and Marine, *QPP*, vol. 2, 1919.
[37] Bach (1956) gives the number of strikers as 500. The archival references are below that figure.
[38] A photo was taken at Thursday Island which shows Japanese marching through the main street. Some respondents identified this march as a celebration, indicated by the fact that all participants were wearing white shirts. Those who had never participated in a strike expressed disbelief that such a thing had ever taken place. However, two who were at Thursday Island at the time explained the photograph as a strike by the crew. They said that divers, who had led the negotiations, had no business taking to the streets, but the crewmen marched to the house of Burns Philp manager Adams to demand higher wages.
[39] Using the neap tides, the luggers might work up to twelve consecutive days if they were able to follow the slack tide, and had five to eight days off during strong tides. Interview with Col Jones, Thursday Island 12.1.1987.
[40] Interview with Miyamoto Sadakichi (87), Wakayama 19.10.87.
[41] Interview with Takao Koonosuke.
[42] Evidence by Cleveland, in Mackay 1908:142.
[43] Interview with Takenaka Yasuichi (80), Miwazaki 18.10.87.
[44] Interview with Tatsuno Matsuo (65), Honai 23.10.87.
[45] Interview with Wabuka Kiyomi (67), Susami 20.10.1987.
[46] Interview with Morishita Kazuo (65), Susami 20.10.1987.
[47] Interview with Takemoto Iwakichi (81), Shionomisaki 17.10.1987.
[48] Interview with Ogawa Taira (74), Tanabe 21.10.1987.
[49] Evidence by F. Hodel, in Bamford 1913:57.
[50] Interview with Ogawa Taira (74), Tanabe 28.10.1987.
[51] K. Watanabe, *Goshu Tanken Hokokusho*, Gaimusho, Tokyo, 1894:195–6, in Sissons 1979:15.
[52] Watanabe 1894:147, in Sissons 1979:12.
[53] Evidence by Hockings, in Bamford 1913:96.
[54] Evidence by Murray, in ibid.:8. Seamen on coastal steamers received £7 10s per month (ibid.:101).
[55] Interview with Ogawa Taira (74), Tanabe 21.10.1987.
[56] Interview with Ogawa Taira, Wakayama, 21.10.87, the author of *Arafura-kai no Shinju (Pearls of Arafura)*, Aiumi, Tokyo, 1976.
[57] Interview with Horimoto Shinichi (75), Susami 20.10.1987.
[58] Interview with Tatsuno Ryuhichi (67), Honai 23.10.1987. Tatami mats are straw mats used as floor covering in Japanese homes.
[59] O'Leary, Annual Report of the Chief Protector of Aborigines, *QPP* 1952.
[60] Thirty-five experienced Japanese divers had already in 1952 been admitted to Broome, where there was no indigenous labour pool, to take up diving.

61 Interviews with Jack Kennell (63), Mackay 8.10.1986 and George Kaddy (49), Mackay 13.8.1986.
62 Interview with Harold Hockings, Innisfail 28.11.1986. The other employers of Okinawans were Bowden (Jack Dunwoodie) and Cape York Pearling Company (Boris Norman).
63 Interview with Kyozo Hirakawa (52), Thursday Island 18.1.1987.
64 Ibid.
65 Interview with Hal Hockings, Innisfail 28.11.1986.

4 Losing Grip

1 Evidence by Graham, in Bamford 1913:104.
2 Evidence by Hockings, in Mackay 1908:167.
3 Bain 1982:114ff.
4 Evidence by Craig, in Bamford 1913:50.
5 How widespread this practice was is not certain. Hodel, Farquhar and Carpenters certainly engaged in it, whereas Hockings (Wanetta Co.) apparently did not.
6 Evidence by Allen, Inspector of Pearl-Shell and Bêche-de-Mer Fisheries, in Bamford 1913:39.
7 Evidence by Bruce, Portmaster at Thursday Island, in ibid.:128.
8 Ibid.:7.
9 The Federal Council of Australasia was established in 1885 by the imperial Parliament as an intercolonial legislative body. It could deal with fisheries outside territorial limits. Its legislation was subject to Royal Assent.
10 See Map 1. The schedule defined Australasian (i.e. extra-territorial) waters as: 'All waters included within a line drawn from Sandy Cape northward to the south-eastern limit of the Great Barrier Reefs, thence following the line of the Great Barrier Reefs to their north-eastern extremity near the latitude of $9\frac{1}{2}$ deg. south; thence in a north-westerly direction, embracing East Anchor and Bramble Cays; thence from Bramble Cays in a line west by south (south 79 deg. west) true, embracing Warrior Reef, Saibai, and Tuan Islands; thence diverging in a north-westerly direction so as to embrace the group known as the Talbot Islands; thence to and embracing the Deliverance Islands, and onwards in a west by south direction (true), to the meridian of 138 deg. of east longitude; and thence by that meridian southerly to the shore of Queensland'. 51 Vic. No. 1, in Bamford 1913:7. This definition followed that of the Queensland Coast Islands Act 1879, which claimed the islands, and a 3-mile zone around them, within that area as Queensland territory.
11 Evidence by Craig, in Bamford 1913:46.
12 Ibid.; and evidence by Murray as defence counsel, in ibid.:7. The question of extra-territorial powers was settled by the Supreme Court in 1938: Captain Haultain of the patrol boat Larrakia confiscated a Japanese vessel near an Aboriginal reserve island. But because the incident took place outside the 3-mile limit, the vessels were returned to their owners, and damages of $20 000 awarded. The Supreme Court found that while extra-territorial powers extended only to British subjects, 'territorial waters' was not defined by any Federal Act of Parliament (Bain 1982:218).
13 Evidence by Clark, in Bamford 1913:168.
14 The South Australian government (which administered the Northern Territory) passed legislation in 1906 to stop Macassan visits. See Macknight 1976.
15 The Mildred was a famous lugger, noted for its size and speed, and its captain, Kono Tesaburo, has become part of the pearling folklore. Interviews with Robert (50) and Lorraine Baird, Wujal-Wujal 2.11.1986, Sandy Yiela (c.85), Lockhart River 3.1.1987.
16 Mitsui Bassan Kaisha of Kobe, and its subsidiary in Palau Taiyo Shinju Kaisha (Bain 1982:208). Seicho Maru is sometimes referred to as Shizo Maru (Australian Secret Intelligence Report 5/36 p. 94, in Bach 1956:316). At the same time Mitsui and

Mitsubishi (Mitsubishi Shoji Kaisha) were attracting the attention of the British MI5 with their fishing activities off Burma as it was suspected that they engaged in espionage (Bach 1956:223).

[17] Barclay 1937:38.

[18] 14.7.1936, in Bach 1956:317.

[19] In 1935, 53 per cent of United States mother-of-pearl imports came from Australia, in 1938 only 23.7 per cent. Japan displaced Australia in its position as major mother-of-pearl exporter in 1937 (Coombs 1946:66 Table 15).

[20] Littler 1982:157.

[21] Department of Commerce, 21.12.1938, in Bain 1982:220.

[22] Evidence by Thomson, in Mackay 1908:251.

[23] Bishop of North Queensland to Secretary of External Affairs, 20.5.1909, CRS A1 09/13685 AA.

[24] External Affairs CRS A1 11/1594 AA. The only survey of pearl-shell beds ever undertaken was that by the DPI in association with CSIRO in 1956–61.

[25] External Affairs CRS A1 11/1594 AA.

[26] External Affairs file CRS A 1838/T184 AA; Bach 1956:309ff (Appendix).

[27] *Courier Mail* 13.2.1936, see Bach 1956:309, 311.

[28] Interview with Claude (73) and Harold White (80), Mackay 14.8.1986.

[29] Interview with Arthur Busuttin (85), Mackay 13.8.86.

[30] Bach 1956:309.

[31] Ibid.:311.

[32] Major E. L. Piesse, Piesse Papers, Series 5, 1–9, MS 882, National Library, in Bain 1982:205 ff.

[33] Bach 1956:235 ff. (see also note 12 above.)

[34] External Affairs minute 'Inter-departmental Committee on Japanese Encroachment in Australian Waters' 4.7.1939, CRS A 981 100 (Japan) AA.

[35] Shepherd 1940:165.

[36] External Affairs minute 'Inter-departmental Committee on Japanese Encroachment in Australian Waters' 4.7.1939, CRS A 981 100 (Japan) AA.

[37] Prime Minister's Department to External Affairs, 26.6.1933, in Bach 1956:226.

[38] Interview with Wabuka Kiyomi (67), Susami 20.10.1987.

[39] Interview with Ogawa Taira (74), Tanabe 21.10.1987.

[40] Dr Evatt, leader of the opposition, made reference to these orders on 25.2.1953. *CPD* 1953, vol. 221:256.

[41] The Japanese were demanding the bonds which had been deposited for them by their employers, and their wages. External Affairs A 1066 IC 45/32/3/1 AA.

[42] 'An Act relating to Pearl Shell, Trochus, Bêche-de-mer and Green Snail Fisheries in certain Australian Waters.' This replaced the Federal Council Acts regulating the pearl-shell fisheries since 1888, the *Queensland Pearl Shell and Bêche-de-mer Fisheries (Extra-Territorial) Act 1888* and the *Western Australian Pearl Shell and Bêche-de-mer Fisheries (Extra-Territorial) Act 1889*. The *Pearl Fisheries Act 1952* was replaced by the *Continental Shelf (Living Natural Resources) Act 1968*, which extended the application of the act to all sedentary resources (so defined by declarations of the Governor-General) on the continental shelf.

[43] External Affairs file CRS A 1838/T 184 AA.

[44] *CPD* 26.2.1953, vol. 221:315.

[45] External Affairs file CRS A 1838/T 184 AA. The Australian continental shelf extends up to 200 miles from the coast. It meets Papua New Guinea, and Indonesia at the Aru Islands. The Australian legislation specified the 100-fathoms line as the boundary of the continental shelf according to the definition used by the International Law Commission. Since 1979 Australian waters are defined as the Australian Fishery Zone, extending 200 nautical miles from the territorial limits. This represents a limited application of the Exclusive Economic Zone principle.

[46] Senator Byrne, Qld, 17.9.1953, *CPD* 1953, vol. 221:104.

[47] At its 1953 convention the International Law Commission recognised that resources other than mineral ones might be included. This recognition was however not formalised until several years later (Goldie 1953).

[48] Income from pearl-shell in 1950–51 was £760 000, overshadowed by whaling at £1.5 million, crayfish, prawn and oyster fishing at £1.6 million, and fin-fishing at £3.7 million. McEwen, Minister for Commerce and Agriculture in *CPD* 1952:565.

[49] *CPD* 1953, vol. 221, passim. The Torres Strait Pearlshellers' Association again reminded the federal government of the strategic value of the pearl-shell industry as 'the lifeblood of Thursday Island and Broome': 'as this industry is the sole reason this strategic northern outpost is populated by white people, the extinction of the industry would undoubtedly cause the evacuation of all whites from the area'. Reginald Hockings to Prime Minister, 11.2.1953, CRS A 1838/T184 3101/10/1/1 AA.

[50] Department of Territories memo, 13.7.1956, CRS A432 56/3159 Pt 1 AA. The Japanese catch was 942 tons in 1953, 940 tons in 1954, and 740 tons in 1955.

5   Resource Use and Management

[1] Technology refers both to the machines and equipment, and to the way in which these are used, or in which production is organised.

[2] This term is borrowed from Bennett 1976.

[3] Chester to Col. Sec., 10.10.1871. Col/A 2499/71 QSA. The industry at this time concentrated on Warrior Reef (Wapa Reef) and the New Guinean coast, and Endeavour Strait—the channel between Badu and Moa and the small islands to the north and south of Badu in the Prince of Wales group.

[4] See e.g. Banfield 1908; Serventy and Raymond 1975; Barrett 1923.

[5] Catch per unit effort is measured—for want of more comprehensive data—as catch per man per year, and/or catch per boat per year.

[6] Chester to Col. Sec., 10.10.1871. Col/A 2499/71 QSA.

[7] Saville-Kent 1890b, vol. 3:703–12.

[8] Evidence by Zarcal, in Mackay 1908:154, also Hockings, in ibid.:173.

[9] Lockyer 1904:187.

[10] Saville-Kent 1890a, in Bach 1956:55, 65.

[11] Hamilton 1897:xxxiii.

[12] Evidence by Hockings, in Mackay 1908:168.

[13] This possibility was pointed out by Noel Haysom, pers. comm.

[14] Evidence by Hodel, in Mackay 1908:65.

[15] Evidence by Clark, in ibid.:32. Clark was referring to the short-lived restriction on the number of boats, introduced by the Philp government (1899–1903).

[16] Evidence by Hayne, in Mackay 1908:119.

[17] Evidence by Hayne, in Bamford 1913:63.

[18] Cited in Bach 1956:260.

[19] 'Red-hot air' pumped through copper pipes produced carbon monoxide. Interview with Ken Corn, Cairns 24.11.1986.

[20] Annual Report of the Marine Department, *QPP* 1901:13. The areas fished were the west coast of Cape York Peninsula, the Warrior Reefs to Daru in New Guinea, Darnley, west of Orman Reef between Mabuiag and New Guinea, and Old Ground. Deliverance Island was tested unsuccessfully, and Red Point was still exhausted after three years of rest.

[21] Hodel to Dashwood, 30.6.1902, in Dashwood 1902:22.

[22] Mackay 1908:xlviii.

[23] Evidence by Noetke, in Dashwood 1902:6.

[24] Clark, in Bamford 1913:169.

[25] Evidence by Hunt, in Mackay 1908:139, referring to a visit to Thursday Island by Mr Batchelor, the Minister for External Affairs.

[26] Mackay 1908:xiviii.

[27] Many of the pearl-shelling companies at Thursday Island remained in the business for a long time. Burns Philp, engaged since the 1880s, had 33 boats registered in 1909. In 1955 only 2 Wyben boats were left. Farquhar commenced in 1893 and had 9 boats in 1935. Cleveland, operating since 1895, had 14 boats in 1900 and 12 in 1935. Hockings started to operate in 1898 and had 15 boats in 1910, but only 4 in 1955. This company became Australasian Pearls in the 1960s. Morey had 13 boats in 1908 and 14 in 1935. After World War II this became part of Bowden. Bowden had 19 boats in 1908 and 11 in 1955; in 1960 it became Pearls Proprietary Ltd. Carpenter, represented with 8 boats in 1908, was still active in 1935 with 1 boat.

[28] G. S. Smith 'The Queensland Oyster Fishery—An Illustrated History', Queensland Department of Primary Industries, Brisbane, 1985.

[29] After selling most of his fleet to a Dutch company, Clark entered into partnership with the leading pastoral company of Peter Tait (now Clark and Tait Solicitors, Brisbane). He died in Brisbane in 1933 and was buried at Toowong cemetery. (Smith 1985:78; Bain 1982:195).

[30] Hardin 1968:1240.

[31] Ibid.

[32] This phenomenon also is well understood by economists, who argue that regulation is inefficient in addressing externalities. (Negative externalities are the unintended effects on firm B caused by the activities of firm A.) Regulation limits the activity which causes externalities, but creates no incentive to address the problem and correct the flow of effects. It gives no inducement to cultivation, reafforestation, etc.

[33] Economists refer to this as the 'polluter pays' principle. Ideally, polluting is made more expensive, through fines, taxes or positive incentives, than preventing pollution.

[34] Quiggins 1986:115–16.

[35] Johannes 1978:349–64. See also Ruddle 1986:3–5.

[36] W. Saville-Kent, 'Investigation into the Beche-de-Mer and Pearl-Shell Fisheries of Northern Queensland', *QVP* 1890, vol. 3:4.

[37] Saville-Kent 1890b:706–7.

[38] Queensland Act 55 Vict. No. 29. Saville-Kent had identified the pearl-shell as *Meleagrina margaritifera*, and the term was adopted into the legislation. Soon afterwards, Saville-Kent realised that this term was applied to three or four distinct species in the conchological literature. In 1913 the legislative nomenclature was repealed.

[39] Saville-Kent 1892:214.

[40] Evidence by Munro (manager for Clark), in Mackay 1908:2.

[41] Bach 1956:55. Information obtained from newspaper cuttings.

[42] Hamilton 1897:xxxiii.

[43] See Regina Ganter and Ros Kidd, 1993. The other commissioners were Queensland parliamentarians W. O'Connell, J. Hoolan, W. Smyth and A. Dawson.

[44] Pearl-shellers requested rewards for discoveries of new beds. They also complained of excessive fees: they requested that harbour fees (imposed in 1893) and pilotage be abolished, that tendering vessels be exempt from licensing, that boat licences be restructured to reduce the expenses of large vessels, that licence fees for floating stations be reduced, and that shipping fees be reduced by 50 per cent. They also pointed out that there was no provision in the licensing requirements by which diving could be learned. As a result, try-divers' licences were introduced.

[45] Noel Haysom, pers. comm.

[46] Annual Report of the Marine Department, *QVP* 1899.

[47] Evidence by Mitchell (BP), in Bamford 1913:83, referring to the floating-station era.

[48] Although the Dutch claim over Western New Guinea was recognised by Britain and Germany in 1880, the Dutch control was not established until 1898 (Edgar 1962:258).

[49] Dashwood 1902:9.

[50] Presumably these areas were also closed because of fatalities (Dashwood 1902, App., map W).

[51] Evidence by Hayne, in Bamford 1913:67.

[52] Both Mackay (head of department) and Bleakley (pearl-shell inspector) made recommendations to that effect. Annual Reports of the Marine Department, *QPP* 1905, 1906.

[53] Evidence by Mackay, in Bamford 1913:178.

[54] Evidence by Clark, in Mackay 1908:42.

[55] Evidence by Mackenzie, in Bamford 1913:47.

[56] Mackay 1908:11.

[57] Captain John Mackay was Portmaster in Brisbane, and therefore head of the Marine Department. In 1912 he received the Imperial Service Order. The other commissioners were G. H. Bennett, Protector of Aborigines, Sub-Collector of Customs, Shipping Master, and Pearl-Shell Inspector at Thursday Island (1897–1904); and H. A. C. Douglas, a former pearl-sheller, who now represented the far northern electorate in the Queensland Parliament. Douglas disagreed with the reinstatement of the 6-inch size limit and the freezing of licences, recommended in the Commission's report.

[58] Mackay 1908:205.

[59] Evidence by Hockings, in Bamford 1913:93.

[60] F. W. Bamford was federal member for Herbert (Qld). The other commissioners were also parliamentarians: H. Mahon, W. E. Johnson, W. Malney, W. J. McWilliams, and Senator Givens.

[61] Annual Reports of the Marine Department, *QPP* 1917. This shortcoming was rectified with a 1931 amendment.

[62] The account of the pearl-fishery in Ceylon is based on an official report by the colonial government's marine biologist and Inspector of Pearl Banks (Hornell 1905).

[63] Since time immemorial, the Parawas, a coastal people of the Tamil Kingdom of Pandya, dived for pearls. When Vijaya conquered Ceylon he included 'rich offerings of pearls among the presents to his father-in-law, the Pandyan King of Madura', according to the *Mahawansa*. The Parawas were wealthy and powerful enough to defend their independence from the rajahs, paying only an annual present rather than the usual heavy taxes. In the sixteenth century the Parawas were subjugated by the Portuguese.

[64] The Moors or Muhammadans who penetrated the Indian subcontinent, known as Lubbais, set up a pearl-fishery in competition with the Parawas, at Kayal on the Tambrapurni River, which Marco Polo (1290–91) described as a 'great and noble city'. For 500 years there were two competing pearl markets on this coast. To the extent that the Muslim pearl centre prospered, and rajahs shifted their alliance to them, the Parawas were politically weakened in their independence, and military rivalry ensued. This political instability coincided with the arrival of the Portuguese, who offered to protect the Parawas if they converted to Christianity. The Hindu rulers of Madura, meanwhile, allied themselves with the Muslim Lubbais at Kayal and continued to test the 'Portuguese protection'. The Portuguese established separate church and secular administrations. When the Dutch East India Company established its stronghold in Ceylon in the early seventeenth century, the Portuguese rule was riddled by internal divisions between priests and military. In 1658 the Dutch ousted the Portuguese from the Tuticorin area to which the Parawa fishery belonged.

[65] Juan Ribeyro, *History of Ceylon*, 1685. In Hornell 1905:9.

[66] Ibid.

[67] Baron van Imhoff, 1740, in Hornell 1905:16–17.

[68] Evidence by Mackenzie, in Mackay 1908:130

[69] This account of the Mergui pearl-shell fishery is based on a government report by two scientists, R. Rudmose Brown and J. Simpson, in 1907. AA CRS CP 661/2 # Bundle 1.

[70] Rudmose Brown and Simpson 1907:3–4.

[71] The Dutch presence in Indonesia commenced in 1602, with the formation of the Vereenigte Oost-Indische Compagnie, the Dutch East India Company. The Dutch state took over the East Indies when the company went bankrupt in 1798. Dutch rule was weakened when Britain took control of Java and Sumatra from 1811 to 1824, instituting several reforms which were in stark contrast to the feudalist and repressive policies of the Dutch. After the withdrawal of the British to the Malay peninsula, the Dutch dominance was weakened by widespread anti-colonial revolts, the last of which was crushed in 1911 in Celebes. As the European colonial scramble for spheres of influence intensified, the Dutch also took possession of western New Guinea, and their rule was recognised by Britain and Germany in 1880 (Edgar 1962:248).

[72] This account is substantially based on the recollections of Mikimoto and his family, rendered by Eunson (1956).

[73] The term village co-operative stems from translated recollections of Mikimoto. It is likely that the organisational structure of the enterprise was more in the nature of an *oyakata* and his *kokata* (band of followers). Cf. Littler 1982:148.

[74] The patenting process was actually subject to intense dispute, as three candidates claimed to have discovered the technique of producing round pearls, at about the same time: Mikimoto, T. Nishikawa, a science graduate of Tokyo University, and T. Mise, a carpenter whose father-in-law had been inspector of pearling boats departing for the Arafura Sea. According to Denis George, Mikimoto's claim to the discovery was not (or at least is not now) taken seriously (George 1987).

6   The Last Thing on their Minds

[1] Evidence by Mitchell, in Mackay 1908:96.

[2] Saville-Kent 1892:207.

[3] See Lockyer 1904, Mackay 1908 App. VIII:269. Attempts to produce buttons in Australia were made in Sydney (1934–38) and Cairns (1952–56); see pp. 219ff.

[4] It could be used as lime, or as a component for paint, cosmetics or ceramic tiles. The hinge or butt of the larger shell was suitable for umbrella and knife handles (Nash 1985:27).

[5] Commonwealth Board of Trade, Memo, 1.2.1917. AA CRS A 457 9.306/6.

[6] Evidence by Munro, in Mackay 1908:19.

[7] Evidence by Farquhar, in Mackay 1908:107.

[8] Commonwealth Board of Trade, Memo, 1.2.1917:18. AA CRS A 457 9.306/6.

[9] Coombs 1946:20.

[10] Ibid.:44–6, Tables 3–6.

[11] Pearl-shell was used for inlay work in powder boxes, opera glasses, for revolver, knife or umbrella handles, for rosary beads, and medallions.

[12] Lockyer 1904, in Bamford 1913:190.

[13] Evidence by Hayne, in Bamford 1913:65.

[14] 26.11.1917. AA CRS A 457 9.306/6.

[15] Evidence by Mitchell, in Bamford 1913:82.

[16] Campbell (London manager for BP), January 1914, in Buckley and Klugman 1981: 209.

[17] Coombs 1946:Table 12B.

[18] Burns to Black, 11.11.1910, in Buckley and Klugman 1981:208.

[19] Interview with Arnold Duffield, Cairns 25.11.1986.

[20] Evidence by Clark, in Bamford 1913:168. Emphasis added.

[21] Ibid.

[22] Interview with Harold Hockings, Innisfail 28.11.1986.
[23] A. K. Mackintosh, Annual Report, February 1927, in Buckley and Klugman 1983:195.
[24] Buckley and Klugman 1983:196.
[25] Evidence by Lockyer, in Bamford 1913:30. There were a few other indicators that all was not well with the marketing of pearl-shell. When the *Torres Straits Pilot* published a programme in 1906 for the rehabilitation of the industry based on cultivation, it also called for concessions for small button manufactures at Thursday Island, or a larger Australia-wide manufacture. It was also suggested that a market may exist in the Far East. This indicates that at least some pearl-shellers at Thursday Island sought an extension of their market. Evidence by J. Clark, in Mackay 1908:42.
[26] Evidence by Lockyer, in Bamford 1913:30.
[27] Commonwealth Board of Trade, Memo, 1.2.1917. AA CRS A 457 9.306/6.
[28] Coombs 1946:25.
[29] Mackay 1908:96. Commonwealth Board of Trade, Memo, 1.2.1917:4. AA CRS A 457 9.306/6.
[30] Bowden, in Mackay 1908:196.
[31] During World War II virtually all of the Australian shell (94–100 per cent) was sold to America, whereas Australia's share of shell contribution to the American market dropped from 58 per cent to 19.5 per cent. By 1949 Australia had rehabilitated itself as the foremost contributor of shell (57 per cent of American shell imports). See Bach 1956:297 Table XVIII.
[32] Gerdau had a lively correspondence with the federal Department of Commerce; see Bach 1956:261. His proposal became the blueprint for the bilateral agreement with Japan in the 1950s (see Chapter 4).
[33] Patrick Killoran pers. comm. Clark mentioned in 1913 that 'the buyers are nearly all Jews in the Old Country', and German Jews apparently continued to dominate shell-buying. Evidence by Clark, in Bamford 1913:168.
[34] Interview with Arnold Duffield, Cairns 25.11.1986.
[35] Nott, member for Herbert, in *CPD* 1927:982.
[36] *Pearl-Shell Overseas Marketing Act* (No. 13 of 1927), Australia. Commonwealth Acts, vol. XXV 1927:23.
[37] This figure excludes the Japanese production. Annual Report of the Inspector of Pearl-Shell and Bêche-de-Mer Fisheries, *QPP* 1938.
[38] Annual Report of the Inspector of Pearl-Shell and Bêche-de-Mer Fisheries, *QPP* 1940.
[39] Dunwoodie came to personify the old-style master pearler with the mannerism of colonial 'aristrocracy'. He became mayor of Thursday Island, and is well remembered for 'holding court' in the Blue Room of the Royal Hotel, and for sporting a pearl-shell number-plate on his car. Interviews with Harold Hockings, Innisfail 28.11.1986 and Blue Bedford, Cairns 26.11.1986.
[40] The division was initially called Division of Fisheries and Oceanography.
[41] This optimism has given way to some gloom as global environmental priorities are increasingly seen to conflict with the aim of building a national economy with clout on the international market.
[42] Coombs 1946:1.
[43] A board was appointed to establish the school consisting of the Bishop of Carpentaria, Rev. Fr Dixon (at Hammond Island), the Director of the IIB, O'Leary, Reg Hockings and J. Duffield from the Pearl-Shellers Association, and Tanu Nona and Frances Sabatino to represent employees. Annual Report of the Inspector of Pearl-Shell and Bêche-de-Mer Fisheries, *QPP* 1953.
[44] Dave Tranter conducted research on the reproductive biology of pearl-shell from 1954 to 1956. His colleague Stan Hynd stayed for several years before and after that date. Tranter, pers. comm.
[45] Coombs 1946:28.

46 Among the businessmen were a solicitor, an engineer and a pharmaceutical chemist. The chemist and engineer also had six trochus boats and a pearl-shell lugger. Interview with Sir Thomas Covacevich, Cairns 27.11.1986.
47 Nash 1985:27.
48 The cutting of blanks for export is successfully conducted in the Solomon Islands and in Indonesia.
49 Interview with Keith Bradford, Cairns 23.11.1986. Trochus shell were measured by the kerosene tin.
50 Interview with Jack Kennell, Mackay 8.10.1986.
51 Interview with Arnold Duffield, Cairns 25.11.1986.
52 The fishery recommenced in 1978 on a small scale, producing under contracts to buyers. Recently the inroads of Indonesian and Taiwanese trochus boats into extra-territorial waters has caused concern.

7   Beyond the 1960s

1 Partners of the Nippo Pearl Co. were Otto Gerdau Co., Brown & Dureau, and Male & Co. The Company commenced pearl-culture in Western Australia in 1956 at Augustus Island, and later moved to Kuri Bay (Brecknock Harbour), and now produces 60 per cent of the world's finest round pearls. Gerdau also partnered Male and Dureau in Pearls Pty Ltd (1968) which had culture farms at Friday and Moa Island. His partners in South Sea Pearling Company (later South Sea Enterprise) were Col Jones and Ryan.
2 'Report of the Grounding of the Oil Tanker Oceanic Grandeur in the Torres Strait on 3rd March, 1970 and the Subsequent Removal of Oil from the Waters', Government Printer, Brisbane, 1970.
3 McGregor 1974:164.
4 Wright 1977:141.
5 Haemen Mendis, pers. comm., 1993. The pearl-culture farms are at Albany Island, Packe Island, Roko Island in Endeavour Strait (near Possession Island), and two in Friday Passage (between Friday Island and Prince-of-Wales Island). Other farms in Queensland are at Arlington Reef, Flinders Island, Turtle Head Island, Trochus Island, Fitzroy Island and Walker Bay. Rob Coles, Northern Fisheries Service, pers. comm.
6 Interview with Harry Drieberg (88), Cairns 16.11.1986. Metric measurements were introduced in that year, so that it is uncertain whether the price referred to imperial tons or metric tonnes. In what follows, the account will oscillate between 'tons' and 'tonnes' according to which measurement was used at the time in question.
7 Inteview with Keith Bradford, Cairns 23.11.1986.
8 All recreational fishing and some commercial fishing is administered by the States. The PZJA administers the fisheries for prawn, spanish mackerel, tropical rock lobster, pearl-shell, dugong and turtle in Torres Strait. *Torres News*, 14.3.1991.
9 Interview with Jack Kennell, Mackay 8.10.1986.
10 Interview with Saulo Waia, Woodstock 2.12.1986.
11 John Kerin, Minister for Primary Industry to John Gayler, Member for Leichhardt, 7.3.1985. Courtesy Keith Bradford.
12 Interview with Keith Bradford, Cairns 23.11.1986.
13 Ibid.
14 *Cairns Post* 13.3.1991.
15 Based on a maximum of 525 tonnes at an estimated $4000 per tonne. In 1985 Nash estimated the maximum annual value of trochus shell at $1 million. Nash 1985:2.
16 Noel Haysom, pers. comm.

8 Explaining Decline

1 In 1872 all islands within 60 miles of the coast were annexed to Queensland by letters patent. The *Queensland Coast Islands Act 1879* extended the boundary to encompass nearly the whole of the Torres Strait. The *Pearl-Shell and Bêche-de-Mer Fisheries Act 1881* enabled Queensland to supervise the industry.

2 Aplin, Brown and Crawshay had sold their assetts to Fred Morey by 1908. James Clark shifted his interests to edible oyster farming in 1917. Burns Philp considered leaving the industry in 1908, and separated the main firm from pearl-shelling with the establishment of Wyben in 1913. In 1925 the company made its last attempt to form a producers' cartel, and thereafter withdrew from pearl-shell marketing. In 1955 only two boats were registered for Wyben.

3 Until 1905 the Chief Protector reported to the Secretary for Public Works, thereafter to the Home Secretary. In 1922 the sub-department of Native Affairs was created within the Department of Health and Home Affairs. The DNA was later called the Department of Aborigines and Torres Strait Islanders Affairs (1965–71), Department of Aborigines and Torres Strait Islanders Advancement (1971–84), Department of Community Services and Ethnic Affairs (1984–89), and now Department of Family Services and Aboriginal and Islander Affairs (1990).

4 The earliest fisheries legislation in Queensland was passed in 1874 (Oyster Act), followed soon after by the *Fisheries Act 1877* and the *Pearl-Shell and Bêche-de-Mer Fishery Act 1881*. The administration of fisheries fell to the Department of Harbours and Marine until 1968, when it became part of the Department of Primary Industries.

5 All Chief Protectors after Roth and Howard had served as local Protectors at Thursday Island, although the position of Chief Protector was later referred to as the Director of DNA: John Bleakley was local protector at Thursday Island from 1902 to 1907, and became director from 1913 to 1942; Cornelius O'Leary was local protector from 1922 to 1930, and returned to Thursday Island in 1937 and 1949; he was director from 1943 to 1963; Patrick Killoran was stationed at Thursday Island from 1947 to 1964, and became director from 1964 to 1986.

6 Haysom, pers. comm.

Bibliography

Primary and archival sources

Anderson, J. C. (1984) The Political and Economic Basis of Kuku-Yalanji Social History, PhD, University of Queensland

Annual Reports of the Chief Protector of Aborigines (1900–38), Annual Reports of the Director of Native Affairs (1939–64), Annual Reports of the Director of Aboriginal and Island Affairs (1968–75)

Annual Reports of the Department of Harbours and Marine (including Reports of the Inspector of Pearl-Shell and Bêche-de-Mer Fishery at Thursday Island), 1894–1968

Aplin, D'Oyly, 'Report on Pearl Fisheries of Torres Strait' 3 March 1875. Somerset Letterbook, CPS 13/C G1 QSA

Bach, J. P. S. (1956) 'The Pearling Industry of Australia. An Account of its Social and Economic Development', Prepared for Department of Commerce and Agriculture, University College, Newcastle

Bamford, F. W. (Chair) (1913) Royal Commission on the Pearl-Shelling Industry. Progress Report. *CPP*

—— (Chair) (1916) Royal Commission on the Pearl-Shelling Industry. Report and Recommendations. *CPP* 1914–17, vol. 5:831–41

Chase, A. (1980) Which Way Now? Tradition, Continuity and Change in a North Queensland Aboriginal Community, PhD, University of Queensland

Chester, H. M., (1870) Account of a Visit to Warrior Island in September and October 1870 with a Description of the Pearl Fishery on the Warrior Reef 3425/70 Col/A 151 QSA

—— (1877) Report on Pearl Shell Fisheries in Torres Straits, *QVP*, vol. 3:1123–4

Chester, H. M. et al. (1879) Report on Pearl Shell Fisheries. *QVP*, vol. 2:943–55

Coombs, H. C. (Chair) (1946) Northern Australia Development Commission, Pearl-Shell, Bêche-de-Mer and Trochus Industry of Northern Australia (MS—North Queensland Collection, James Cook University)

Crawford, I. M. (1969) Late Prehistoric Changes in Aboriginal Cultures in the Kimberleys, West Australia, PhD, University of London

Curthoys, A. (1973) Race and Ethnicity, PhD, Macquarie University, Sydney

Dale, A. (1993) An Assessment of Planning for Government-funded Land Use Development Projects in Australian Aboriginal Communities, PhD, Griffith University, Brisbane

Dashwood, W. (1901–2) Pearl-Shelling Industry in Port Darwin and Northern Territory, CPP vol. 2:21–91

de Hoghton, T. (1880) Lieutenant-Commanding of the HMS Beagle Reporting on the Pearl-Shell Fisheries of Torres Straits, 22 September 1879. QVP, vol. 2:1163–6

Douglas, J. (1894) Report of the Government Resident at Thursday Island, QVP, vol. 1, pp. 501–10

—— (1898) Report of the Government Resident at Thursday Island, QVP, vol. 1, pp. 241–430

Endean, R. (1969) Report on Investigations Made into Aspects of the Current Acanthaster planci (Crown-of-Thorns Starfish) Infestations of Certain Reefs of the Great Barrier Reef, Fisheries Branch, Department of Primary Industries, Brisbane

Evans, G. (1972) Thursday Island, 1878–1911, a Plural Society, BA (Hons), University of Queensland

Frith, P. R. (n.d.) Torch Light of the Torres Strait (MS), North Queensland Collection, James Cook University Library

Ganter, R. (1987) Oral History of Human Use and Experience of Crown of Thorns Starfish on the Great Barrier Reef, report submitted to GBRMPA, Brisbane (Separate Appendix: Resumes of Interviews)

—— (1988) The Japanese Experience of North Queensland's Mother-of-Pearl Industry, report submitted to GBRMPA, Brisbane

Hamilton, J. (Chair) (1897) Departmental Commission on Pearl-Shell and Bêche-de-Mer Fisheries, Report, QVP, vol. 2: 1301–52

Hornell, J. (1905) Report to the Government of Madras on the Indian Pearl Fisheries in the Gulf of Mannar, Government Press, Madras, 1905

Hoskin, G. (1967) Aboriginal Reserves in Queensland 1871–85, BA (Hons), University of Queensland

Jardine, F. Correspondence with Colonial Secretary. Somerset Letterbook CPS 13/C G1 QSA; and 3424 Col/A 151 QSA

Johannes, R. E. (n.d.) Research on Traditional Tropical Fisheries: Some Implications for Torres Strait Islands and Australian Aboriginal Fisheries. MS, courtesy Bob Johannes, CSIRO, Perth

Lockyer, N. C. (1904) A Report by Mr. N. C. Lockyer Respecting the Employment of White Men in the Pearling Industry, unpublished report to the Minister of External Affairs. In Bamford 1913:185–92

Loos, N. A. (1976) Aboriginal–European Relations in North Queensland, 1861–1897, PhD, James Cook University, Townsville

Mackay, J. (Chair) (1908) Report of the Royal Commission appointed to enquire into the working of the Pearl-shell and Bêche-de-Mer Industries, *QVP*, vol. 2, pp. 1–284

Meston, A. (1896) Report on the Aboriginals of Queensland, *QVP*, vol. 2:723–40

Milman, H. M. (1888) Annual Report of the Government Resident at Thursday Island, *QVP*, vol. 3

—— (1886) Visit of Inspection to Various Islands, in the GSS *Albatross QVP*, vol. 2, pp. 1027–31

Moresby, Capt. J. R. N. (1873) Report. 23 February 1872 QGD No.16 QSA

Nash, W. (1985) Aspects of the Biology of *Trochus Niloticus* and Its Fishery in the Great Barrier Reef Region, report submitted to Fisheries Branch (DPI) and GBRMPA

Parry-Okeden, W. E. (1897) 'Report on the North Queensland Aborigines and the Native Police', *QVP*, vol. 2

Pennefather, C. (1880) Report of an Inspection of Torres Strait on HMS *Pearl*, *QVP*, vol. 2

Rayner, K. (1951) The Attitude and Influence of the Churches in Queensland on Matters of Social and Political Importance (1859–1914), BA (Hons), University of Queensland

Report of the Grounding of the Oil Tanker *Oceanic Grandeur* in the Torres Strait on 3rd March, 1970 and the Subsequent Removal of Oil from the Waters, Government Printer, Brisbane, 1970

Roth, W. (1902) Annual Report of the Chief Protector of Aborigines, *QPP*

Rudmose Brown, R. and J. Simpson (1907) Report to the Government of Burma on the Pearl Oyster Fisheries of the Mergui Archipelago and Moskos Islands, Office of the Superintendent, Government Printing, Rangoon

Saville-Kent, W. (1890a) Pearl and Pearl-Shell Fisheries of Northern Queensland, *QVP*, vol. 3:703–12.

Sissons, C. D. S. (1971) Australian–Japanese Relations: The First Phase 1854–91, MS 3092, National Library, Canberra

Thursday Island State High School (1986) 'Pearling in the Torres Strait—A Collection of Historical Articles'

Books and articles

Alexander, M. (1989) 'A Settler Society in a Changing World', in J. Walter (ed.) *Australian Studies—A Survey*, Oxford University Press, Melbourne

Attwood, B. (1989) *The Making of the Aborigines*, Allen & Unwin, Sydney

Austin, T. (1972) 'F. W. Walker and Papuan Industries Ltd.', *Journal of the Papua and New Guinea Society*, 6(1):38–62

Bach, J. P. S. (1961) 'The Political Economy of Pearl-Shelling', *Economic History Review*, 14(1):105–14

Bain, M. A. (1982) *Full Fathom Five*, Artlook Books, Perth

Baker, D. (ed.) (1975) *Politics of Race—Comparative Studies*, Laxan House, Farnborough

Banfield, E. J. (1908) *The Confessions of a Beachcomber*, Unwin, London

Barclay, A. (1937) 'With the Japanese Luggers off North Australia', *Walkabout*, February:38–42

Barnes, J. and R. Endean (1964) 'A Dangerous Starfish *Acanthaster planci* (Linné)', *Medical Journal of Australia*, (1):592

Barrett, C. (1923) 'The Beachcomber and his Tropic Isle', *Australian Museum Magazine*, 1:301–10

Bartlett, N. (1954) *The Pearl Seekers*, Andrew Melrose, London

Bayton, J. (1969) 'Missionaries and Islanders—A Chronicle of Events Associated with the Introduction of the Christian Mission to the People of Torres Strait During the Period 1866–1873', *Queensland Heritage*, 1(10):16–20

Beckett, J. (1977) 'The Torres Strait Islanders and the Pearling Industry: A Case of Internal Colonialism' *Aboriginal History*, 1(1–2):77–104

——— (1987) *The Torres Strait Islanders: Custom and Colonialism*, Cambridge University Press, Sydney

——— (ed.) (1988) *Past and Present: The Construction of Aboriginality*, Aboriginal Studies Press, Canberra

Benedict, R. (1959) *Race: Science and Politics*, Viking Press, New York (1940)

Bennett, J. (1976) *The Ecological Transition: Cultural Anthropology and Human Adaptation*, Pergamon, New York

Blauner, R. (1969) 'Internal Colonialism and Ghetto Revolt', *Social Problems* 16, Spring:393–408

Bleakley, J. W. (1961) *The Aborigines of Australia*, Jacaranda, Brisbane

Bolton, G. (1981) *Spoils and Spoilers*, George Allen & Unwin, Sydney

Buckley, K. and K. Klugman (1981) *The History of Burns Philp: The Australian Company in the South Pacific*, Burns Philp & Co., Sydney

——— (1983) *The Australian Presence in the Pacific—Burns Philp 1914–1946*, George Allen & Unwin, Sydney

Burgmann, V. (1978) 'Capital and Labour', in A. Curthoys and A. Markus, *Who are our Enemies? Racism and the Working Class in Australia*, Hale & Iremonger, Sydney

Chase, A. (1981) ' "All Kind of Nation": Aborigines and Asians in Cape York Peninsula', *Aboriginal History*, 5(1):7–19

Clark, M. (1963) *A Short History of Australia*, Mentor, New York

Colgan, K. (1988) 'What Does the Future Hold for Pearling in Torres Strait?', *Australian Fisheries*, January:12–16

Commoner, B. (1963) *Science and Survival*, Ballantine, New York

——— (1971) *The Closing Circle*, Knopf, New York

Cotgrove, S. (1982) *Catastrophe or Cornucopia: The Environment, Politics and the Future*, Wiley, New York

d'Urville, J. D. (1846) *Voyage au Pole Sud et dans l'Océanie sur les corvettes l'Astrolabe et la Zélée pendant les années 1837–1840*, vol. 9, Atlas Pittoresque, Paris

Edgar, D. (1962) *Australia and Her Northern Neighbours*, Hall's Book Store, Melbourne

Ehrlich, P. (1968) *The Population Bomb*, Ballantine, London

Endean, R. (1974) '*Acanthaster planci* on the Great Barrier Reef', *Proceedings of the 2nd International Coral Reef Symposium*, pp. 563–76

Eunson, R. (1956) *The Pearl King—The Story of the Fabulous Mikimoto*, Angus & Robertson, Sydney

Evans, R. (1975) 'Helpful, Hurtful and Superfluous—Racism and Colonial Queensland', in R. Evans, K. Saunders and K. Cronin (eds), *Exclusion, Exploitation and Extermination—Race Relations in Colonial Queensland*, Australia & New Zealand Book Company, Sydney

Fels, M. H. (1988) *Good Men and True: The Aboriginal Police of the Port Phillip District 1837–1853*, Melbourne University Press, Melbourne

Finch, N. (1977) *The Torres Strait Islanders: Portrait of a Unique Group of Australians*, Jacaranda, Brisbane

Fitzgerald, R. (1984) *From 1915 to the Early 1980s—a History of Queensland*, University of Queensland Press, Brisbane

Foley, J. (1980) *Timeless Isle—An Illustrated History of Thursday Island*, Torres Strait Historical Society, Thursday Island

Frankel, E. (1978) *Bibliography of the Great Barrier Reef Province*, AGPS, Canberra

Freshwater, J. P. (1936) *The Story of the Papuan Industries Limited*, Birmingham

Ganter, R. and R. Kidd (1993) 'The Powers of Protectors: Conflicts Surrounding Queensland's 1897 Aboriginal Legislation', *Australian Historical Studies*, 25(101): 536–54

George, D. (1987) 'Development of Pearl Cultivation in Australia', *Cairns Historical Society Bulletin*, July–September, pp. 322–4

Gilson, R. P. (1970) *Samoa 1830–1900: The Politics of a Multi-Cultural Community*, Oxford University Press, Melbourne

Goldie, L. F. E. (1953) 'Australia's Sovereignty over its Contiguous Continental Shelf', *Australian Institute of International Affairs Monograph*, 5(4) December (Mitchell Library MS)

Graham, D. (1991) 'Misadventures in the Button Trade', *Good Weekend, Sydney Morning Herald Magazine*, 30 March:30–5

Haddon, A. C. (ed.) (1904) *Reports of the Cambridge Anthropological Expedition to Torres Strait*, vol. 5, *Sociology, Magic and Religion of the Western Islanders*, Cambridge University Press, Cambridge

—— (ed.) (1935) *Reports of the Cambridge Anthropological Expedition to Torres Strait*, vol. 1, *General Ethnography*, Cambridge University Press, Cambridge

Hardin, G. (1968) 'The Tragedy of the Commons', *Sciences*, (162):1243–50

Harrison, J. (1988) 'The People of Queensland, 1859–1900: Where Did the Immigrants Come From?', *Journal of the Royal Historical Society of Queensland*, 13(6):189–200

Hartwig, M. (1978) 'Capitalism and Aborigines: The Theory of Internal Colonialism and its Rivals', in T. Wheelwright and K. Buckley, *Essays in the*

Political Economy of Australian Capitalism, vol. 3, Australia & New Zealand Book Co., Sydney

Haviland, J. and L. (1980) ' "How Much Food will there be in Heaven?" Lutherans and Aborigines around Cooktown to 1900', *Aboriginal History*, 4(2):119–49

Jack, R. Logan (1921) *Northmost Australia*, Simpkin, Marshal, Hamilton, Kent & Co., London

Jennison, A. et al. (1946) 'Labour in the Australian Pearl-Fisheries', *Fisheries Newsletter*, 5(3):4–9

Johannes, R. E. (1978) 'Traditional Marine Conservation Methods in Oceania and Their Demise', *Annual Review of Ecologial Systems*, 9:349–64

Johnston, W. R. (1987) *A Documentary History of Queensland*, University of Queensland Press, Brisbane

Jukes, Joseph (1874) *Narrative of the Surveying Voyage of the HMS* Fly, *commanded by Capt. F. P. Blackwood, R.N. (during the years 1842–1846)*, vol. 1, Boone, London

Keim, Fred (1925) *Über Gold- und Perlengründen Australiens*, Mitchell Library, n.p.

Kerr, G. (1985) *Craft and Craftsmen of Australian Fishing 1870–1970. An Illustrated Oral History*, Mains'l Books, Portland, Vic.

Kirwan, Sir J. (1934) *An Empty Land—Pioneers and Pioneering in Australia*, Eyre & Spottiswoode, London

Kuhn, T. (1970) *The Structure of Scientific Revolutions*, University of Chicago Press, Chicago

Kyuhara, S. (1977) 'Remains of Japanese Settlers on the Torres Strait Islands', unpublished MS. Japanese version published as 'Toresu Kiakyo ni Okeru Shinjukai Gyogyo to Nihonjin no Iseki', *Chiri*, 22(5):74–80

Lindblom, C. (1969) 'The Science of Muddling Through', in A. Etzioni (ed.), *Readings on Modern Organisations*, Prentice Hall, Englewood Cliffs

Littler, C. (1982) *The Development of the Labour Process in Capitalist Societies*, Heinemann, London

Loos, N. A. (1982) *Invasion and Resistance—Aboriginal–European Relations on the North Queensland Frontier, 1861–1897*, Australian National University Press, Canberra

——— (1988) 'The Pragmatic Racism of the Frontier', in R. Evans, K. Saunders and K. Cronin, *Race Relations in North Queensland—A History of Exclusion, Exploitation, and Extermination*, University of Queensland Press, Brisbane

Lowah, T. (1988) *Eded Mer—My Life*, Rams Skull Press, Kuranda, Qld

Lumb, R. D. (1961) 'Sovereignty and Jurisdiction in Australian Coastal Waters', *Australian Law Journal*, 43:433–4

McCorquodale, J. (1986) 'The Legal Classification of Race in Australia', *Aboriginal History*, 10(1):7–24

McFarlane, S. (1888) *Among the Cannibals of New Guinea*, LMS, London

MacGillivray, J. (1853) *Narrative of the Voyage of the HMS* Rattlesnake *(1846–1850)*, Boone, London

McGregor, C. (1974) *Das Grosse Barriere Riff: Die Wildnisse der Welt*, Time-Life Books, Amsterdam

McInnes, A. (1978–79) 'Dangers and Difficulties of the Torres Strait and Inner Route', *Historical Papers*, Royal Historical Society of Queensland, 10(4):47–73

—— (1984) 'Our First Industry, Beche-de-Mer', in A. D. Broughton and S. E. Stephens, *Establishment of Trinity Bay—A Collection of Historical Episodes*, Silver Jubilee Publication of the Historical Society of Cairns

Macknight, C. (1976) *A Voyage to Marege: Macassan Trepangers in Northern Australia*, Melbourne University Press, Melbourne

Mcreadie, M. (1988) 'Kerin Speaks out on Fisheries Issues in the Torres Strait', *Australian Fisheries*, November:2–4

Mann, M. (1984) 'The Autonomous Power of the State: its Sources, Mechanisms and Results', *European Journal of Sociology*, 25(2), pp. 185–213

Marglin, S. (1974) 'What Do Bosses Do? The Origins and Functions of Hierarchy in Capitalist Production', *Review of Radical Political Economics*, 6:60–112

Markus, A. (1979) *Fear and Hatred: Purifying Australia and California, 1850–1901*, Hale & Iremonger, Sydney

Mass, O. (1975) *Dangerous Waters*, Rigby, Adelaide

Maxwell, W. G. H. (1972) 'The Great Barrier Reef—Past, Present and Future', *Queensland Naturalist*, 20:65–78

Maykovich, M. (1975) 'Japanese and Chinese in the United States and Canada', in D. Baker (ed.), *Politics of Race—Comparative Studies*, Laxan House, Farnborough

Mercer, P. (1978) 'Racial Attitudes towards Melanesians in Colonial Queensland', in H. Reynolds (ed.), *Race Relations in North Queensland*, James Cook University, Townsville

Miyoshi, M. (1979) *As We Saw Them: The First Japanese Embassy in the United States, 1860*, University of California Press, Berkeley

Moore, C. R. (1979) *Islanders and Aborigines at Cape York*, Australian Institute of Aboriginal Studies, Canberra

—— (1984) 'Queensland's Annexation of New Guinea in 1883', *Royal Historical Society of Queensland Historical Papers*, 12(1):26–55

Moresby, Capt. J. R. N. (1876) *Discoveries and Surveys in New Guinea and the D'Entrecasteaux Islands. A Cruise in Polynesia and Visits to the Pearlshelling Stations in Torres Straits of HMS* Basilisk, John Murray, London

Mullins, S. (1987) 'On the Frontiers of History—Torres Strait 1864–1884', ANZAAS Conference Paper, Townsville

Mulvaney, D. J. (1966) 'Bêche-de-Mer, Aborigines and Australian History', *Proceedings of the Royal Society of of Victoria*, 79:449–57

Murphy, J. (1987) 'The Voice of Memory: History, Autobiography and Oral Memory', *Historical Studies*, 22(87):157–75

Nish, I. H. (1966) *The Anglo-Japanese Alliance*, Athlone, London

O'Farrell, P. (1979) 'Oral History: Facts and Fiction', *Quadrant*, November:4–8

Outridge, A. H. (1899) *The Pearling Disaster 1899: A Memorial*, Outridge, Brisbane

Passmore, J. (1974) *Man's Responsibility for Nature*, Duckworth, London

Pearson, M. (1980) 'Shore-Based Whaling at Twofold Bay—One Hundred Years of Enterprise', *Journal of the Royal Australian Historical Society*, 71(4):3–27

Perry, H. (1923) *Memoirs of the Hon. Sir Robert Philp KCMG 1851–1922*, Watson & Ferguson, Brisbane

Philipps, L. (1980) 'Plenty More Little Brown Man! Pearlshelling and White Australia in Queensland 1901–18', in T. Wheelwright and K. Buckley, *Essays in the Political Economy of Australian Capitalism*, vol. 4, Australia & New Zealand Book Co., Sydney

Pixley, N. (1971–72) 'Pearlers of North Australia—The Romantic Story of the Diving Fleets', *Royal Historical Society of Queensland Journal*, 9(3):9–29

Prideaux, P. (1988) *From Spear to Pearl-Shell: Somerset, Cape York Peninsula, 1864–1877*, Boolarong Publications, Brisbane

Quiggins, J. (1986) 'Common Property, Private Property and Regulation—The Case of Dryland Salinity', *Australian Journal of Agricultural Economics*, 30(2–3):103–17

Raven Hart, R. (1949) *The Happy Isles*, Georgian House, Melbourne

Reece, R. (1987) 'Inventing Aborigines', *Aboriginal History*, 11(1–2):14–23

Rex, J. (1970) 'The Concept of Race in Sociological Theory', in S. Zubaida (ed.), *Race and Racialism*, Tavistock, London

Reynolds, H. (1981) *The Other Side of the Frontier*, Penguin, Melbourne

Rowley, C. D. (1971) *The Remote Aborigines*, Australian National University Press, Canberra

Ruddle, K. (1986) 'Customary Law and Lore of the Sea', *NAGA, The ICLARM Quarterly*, July:3–5

Ryan, L. (1985) 'Aborigines and Torres Strait Islanders', in A. Patience (ed.), *The Bjelke-Petersen Premiership—1968–1983*, Longman Cheshire, Sydney

Sabel, C. and J. Zeitlin (1985) 'Historical Alternatives to Mass Production: Politics, Markets and Technology in Nineteenth Century Industrialization', *Past and Present*, 108:133–76

Saville-Kent, W. (1890b) Presidential Address to Queensland Royal Society, in Bach 1956:55, 65

—— (1892) *The Great Barrier Reef of Australia: Its Products and Potentialities*, Allan, London

—— (1897) *The Naturalist in Australia*, Chapman & Hall, London

Sayle, M. (1985) 'Japan Victorious', *New York Review of Books*, 32(5):33–40

Schedvin, C. B. (1984) 'Environment, Economy and Australian Biology, 1890–1939', *Historical Studies*, 21(82):11–28

Serventy, E. and R. Raymond (1975) 'Beachcomber Banfield', *Australian Wildlife Heritage*, 6(81):2590–2

Sharp, N. (1980) *Torres Strait Islands 1879–1979—Theme for an Overview*, La Trobe Working Papers in Sociology, Melbourne

—— (1981–82) 'Culture Clash in the Torres Strait Islands: The Maritime

Strike of 1936', *Journal of the Royal Historical Society of Queensland*, 11(3):107–26

Shepherd, J. (1940) *Australia's Interests and Policies in the Far East*, AMS Press, New York

Shineberg, D. (1967) *They Came for Sandalwood: A Study of the Sandalwood Trade in the South-West Pacific 1830–1865*, Melbourne University Press, Melbourne

Shnukal, A. (1985) 'The Spread of Torres Strait Creole to the Central Islands of Torres Strait', *Aboriginal History*, 9(2):220–34

Singe, J. (1979) *The Torres Strait—People and History*, University of Queensland Press, Brisbane

Sissons, C. D. S. (1972) 'Immigration in Australian–Japanese Relations, 1871–1971', in J. A. Stockwin (ed.), *Japan and Australia in the Seventies*, Angus & Robertson, Sydney

—— (1979) 'The Japanese in the Australian Pearling Industry', *Queensland Heritage*, 3(10):9–27

Skocpol, T. (1985) 'Bringing the State Back In: Strategies of Analysis in Current Research', in P. Evans, D. Rueschemeyer and T. Skocpol, *Bringing the State Back In*, Cambridge University Press, Cambridge

Smith, G. S. (1985) 'The Queensland Oyster Fishery—An Illustrated History', Queensland Department of Primary Industries, Brisbane

Smith, H. J. and M. T. Tull (1990) 'The Australian Fishing Industry—A Select Historical Bibliography', Department of Economics Research Monograph Series No.1, Murdoch University, WA

Stoddart, D. R. (1975) *The Great Barrier Reef—A Preliminary Bibliography*, Cambridge University Press, Cambridge

Sumner, R. (1981) 'A Noisome Business—the Trepang Trade in Queensland', *Journal of Australian Studies*, November:61–70

Thompson, E. P. (1963) *The Making of the English Working Class*, Penguin, London

—— (1978) *The Voice of the Past: Oral History*, Oxford University Press, London

—— (1980) 'Time, Work-Discipline, and Industrial Capitalism', *Past and Present*, 38, December:56–97

Thorpe, W. (1980) 'Further Verbals in the Oral History Debate', *Quadrant*, July:54–57

Treadgold, M. L. (1974) 'The Economy of the Torres Strait Area: A Social Accounting Study', *The Torres Strait Islanders*, vol. 2, Research School of Pacific Studies (ANU), Canberra

Watanabe, F. (n.d.) *Japan–Australia Relations in Ehime Prefecture—The Pearl-Shell Industry and Immigrants*, Ehime Books

Weiss, L. (1988) *Creating Capitalism: The State and Small Business Since 1945*, Basil Blackwell, Oxford

Wiesner, J. B. and H. F. York (1964) 'National Security and the Nuclear-Test Ban', *Scientific American*, 211(4):27–35

Wilson, T. B. (1835) *Narrative of a Voyage Round the World*, Sherwood Gilbert & Piper, London

Wolpe, H. (1975) 'The Theory of Internal Colonialism—the South African Case', in I. Oxaal, T. Barnett and D. Booth (eds), *Beyond the Sociology of Development: Economy and Society in Latin America and Africa*, Routledge & Kegan Paul, London

Wright, J. (1977) *The Coral Battleground*, Nelson, Melbourne

Yonge, M. (1930) *A Year On the Great Barrier Reef*, Putnam, London

Newspapers

Cairns Post 5 September 1990
Courier Mail 14 January 1936
Evening News 17 May 1904
Herald (Melbourne) 6 June 1953
Sun Magazine 6 July 1986
Sydney Gazette 3 August 1830
Sydney Morning Herald 26 March 1923, 30 March 1991
Torres Strait Pilot 15 March 1907
Torres News 14 March 1991

Interviewees

The identity of some interviewees has been protected at their request by the use of pseudonyms.

AhMat, Richard (65), Mackay 3 December 1986
Ahwang, Rocky (80), Hervey Bay 26 July 1986
Akiba, Nami (62), Saibai 15 January 1987
Babia, Jeremiah (71), Saibai 15 January 1987
Baird, Lorraine (née Doughboy), Wujal-Wujal 2 January 1986
Baird, Robert, Wujal-Wujal 2 January 1986
Baker, Harry (79), Brisbane 8 June 1986
Bedford, Blue, Cairns 26 November 1986
Bon, Lui, Thursday Island 12 January 1987
Bowen, Ted (74), Hopevale 19 November 1986
Bradford, Keith, Cairns 23 November 1986
Bremmer, George (67), Wujal-Wujal 20 November 1986
Brown, Colin, Gladstone 22 August 1986
Bryson, Keith, Magnetic Island 9 August 1986
Buckley, Sam (77), Gladstone 27 August 1986
Busuttin, Arthur (85), Mackay 13 August 1986
Cook, Noel (50), Cooktown 22 January 1986
Corn, Ken (64), Cairns 24 November 1986
Covacevich, Sir Thomas, Cairns 27 November 1986

Cyran, Wendy, Mackay 12 August 1986
Dan, Henry 'Seaman' (48), Thursday Island 13 January 1987
Deeral, Fred, Hopevale 19 November 1986
'Diver', Townsville, 5 August 1986
Doctor, Jimmie (61), Lockhart River 4 January 1987
Dodd, Reg (81), Rockhampton, Palm Island 1 August 1986
Drieberg, Harry (88), Cairns 16 November 1986
Duffield, Arnold, Cairns 25 November 1986
Ellem, Vic (67), Halifax 12 November 1986
Ellis, Frank (82), Townsville 5 August 1986
Elu, Mugai (76), Bamaga 6 January 1987
'Fisherwoman' (53), Gladstone 19 August 1986
Flinders, Bob (72), Hopevale 19 November 1986
Grigg, Lloyd (70), Cairns 25 November 1986
Hall, Bob (88), Townsville 6 August 1986
Hankin, Sam (70), Mackay 14 August 1986
Hansen, Harold (62), Yeppoon 9 November 1986
Hansen, Mick (86), Yeppoon 18 August 1986
Hawke, Sydney (55), Yeppoon 16 August 1986
Hirakawa Kyozo (52), Thursday Island 18 January 1987
Hobson, Dan (63), Lockhart River 4 January 1987
Hockings, Harold, Innisfail 28 November 1986
'Hopevale' (84), Hopevale 19 November 1986
Horimoto Shinichi (75), Susami 20 October 1987
Inoue Ushimatsu (72), Miwazaki 18 October 1987
Isbel, Ron (54), Gladstone 28 July 1986
Jacob, Bob (69), Bamaga 7 January 1987
Jones, Col, Thursday Island 12 January 1987
Jones, Ken (71), Yeppoon 16 August 1986
Kaddy, George (49), Mackay 13 August 1986
Kennell, Jack (64), Brisbane 8 October 1986
Kepa, George (55), Bamaga 7 January 1987
King, Billy (c. 57), Wujal-Wujal 20 November 1986
Kiwat, Jardine (68), Mackay 11 November 1986
Leach, Ian (68), Gladstone 21 August 1986
LeRoy, Claude (75), Cairns 27 November 1986
McGree, John (50), Gladstone 20 August 1986
Mass, Tina, Surfers' Paradise 8 June 1986
Matt, Bill, Bundaberg 27 August 1986
Maza, Claude (64), Innisfail 28 November 1986
Meier, Otto (87), Bundaberg 27 August 1986
Miyamoto Sadakichi (87), Nachi (Ugui) 19 October 1987
Morishita Kazuo (65), Kuchi Wabuka (Susami) 20 October 1987
'Murray Island', Thursday Island 12 January 1987

Nakamura Unosuke (69), Arita (Kushimoto) 15 October 1987
Namok, Erra (69), Townsville 2 December 1986
Nandy, Dicky (58), Wujal-Wujal 20 November 1986
Newitt, Charlie, Brisbane 16 July 1986
Nona, Stephen (64), Townsville 1 December 1986
Ogawa Taira (74), Tanabe 21 October 1987
Oku Saioshi (56), Taiji 15 October 1987
Pitt, Douglas (50), Mackay, 15 August 1986
Playo, Chappy (81), Mackay 13 August 1986
Porteus, Bill (68), Gladstone 20 August 1986
Porteus, Stan (56), Gladstone 19 August 1986
Prior, Monty, Palm Island 1 August 1986
Raynor, Ian (63), Gladstone 19 August 1986
Sailer, Norm (58), Mackay 11 November 1986
Sailor, Jim, Bamaga 7 January 1987
Sandy, Michael (71), Lockhart River 4 January 1987
Saylor, Bill ('Bully Hayes') (59), Cairns 27 November 1986
Seden, Mike (48), Mackay 11 November 1986
SeePoy, Herbert, Innisfail 28 November 1986
Seike Ukio (67), Arashi (Tsushima-cho) 24 October 1987
Sharrock, Roy (71), Yeppoon 18 August 1986
Shiosaki Mantaro (82), Shionomisaki (Kushimoto) 17 October 1987
Singleton, Bernie (Snr.) (63), Yarrabah 17 November 1986
Smith, Mick (59), Hervey Bay 5 November 1986
Smith, Pat (60), Hervey Bay 5 November 1986
Snow, George (64), Cairns 26 November 1986
Stapleton, Jack, Emu Park 18 August 1986
Stevenson, Jack, Emu Park 18 August 1986
Tada Tomiharu (72), Arita (Kushimoto) 15 October 1987
Takao Koonosuke (68), Ajiro (Minamiuwa-gun) 25 October 1987
Takemoto Iwakichi (81), Shionomisaki (Kushimoto) 17 October 1987
Takenaka Yasuichi (80), Miwazaki 18 October 1987
Tapau, Jim (53), Mackay 4 December 1986
Tatsuno Matsuo (65), Honai (Nishiuwa-gun) 23 October 1987
Tatsuno Ryuhichi (67), Honai (Nishiuwa-gun) 23 October 1987
Thorogood, Ed, Brisbane 8 September 1986
Wabuka Kiyomi (67), Kuchi Wabuka (Susami) 20 October 1987
Waia, Saulo (70), Townsville and Woodstock 8 August 1986, 2 December
    1986
Waigana, Imasu (68), Saibai 15 January 1987
Ware, Robbie (64), Cairns 23 November 1986
Watkins, 'Frisco' (50), Cardwell 13 November 1986
White, Claude (73), Mackay 14 August 1986
White, Harold (80), Mackay 14 August 1986

Whittaker, Neil (68), Gordonvale 27 November 1986
Wickham, Lionel, Gladstone 28 August 1986
Williams, Mara (48), Mackay 14 August 1986
Wosoop, 'Snowy', Bamaga 6 January 1987
Yiela, Sandy, Lockhart River 3 January 1987

Index

Compiled by Russell Brooks